Writing CGI Applications with Perl

Kevin Meltzer
Brent Michalski

Addison-Wesley

Boston • San Francisco • New York • Toronto • Montreal
London • Munich • Paris • Madrid
Capetown • Sydney • Tokyo • Singapore • Mexico City

Many of the designations used by manufacturers and sellers to distinguish their products are claimed as trademarks. Where those designations appear in this book, and Addison-Wesley was aware of a trademark claim, the designations have been printed with initial capital letters or in all capitals.

The authors and publisher have taken care in the preparation of this book, but make no expressed or implied warranty of any kind and assume no responsibility for errors or omissions. No liability is assumed for incidental or consequential damages in connection with or arising out of the use of the information or programs contained herein.

The publisher offers discounts on this book when ordered in quantity for special sales. For more information, please contact:

Pearson Education Corporate Sales Division
One Lake Street
Upper Saddle River, NJ 07458
(800) 382-3419
corpsales@pearsontechgroup.com

Visit AW on the Web: www.awl.com/cseng/

Library of Congress Cataloging-in-Publication Data
Meltzer, Kevin.
    Writing CGI applications with Perl / Kevin Meltzer & Brent Michalski.
        p. cm.
    Includes bibliographical references and index.
    ISBN 0-201-71014-5
        1. Perl (Computer program language) 2. CGI (Computer network protocol)
I. Michalski, Brent. II. Title.

QA76.73.P22 M45 2001
005.2'762--dc21   00-066512

ISBN 0-201-71014-5
Text printed on recycled paper
1 2 3 4 5 6 7 8 9 10-MA-0504030201
First printing, February 2001

From Brent:
For Chris, Luc, Rae, and Logan. Let's wrestle!

From Kevin:
For my daughter, Kyla, and my wife, Suzy. You both give me reasons to actually walk away from a computer.

Contents

Chapter 3   Using Your Environment   45

Chapter 4   Introduction to Web Forms   69

Chapter 5   Working with Cookies   105

Chapter 14 Document Management via the Web   369

Chapter 15 Dynamically Manipulating Images   419

Chapter 16 RSS And XML   449

Foreword

When the popularity of the Web exploded in the mid '90s, sweeping away Gopher, WAIS, Hyper-G and other competing technologies, a big part of its phenomenal success was the ease with which developers could attach back-end processing to pretty front-end Web pages. Rather than offering an arcane programmer's interface to a limited number of programming languages, the Web offered the Common Gateway Interface, or CGI.

CGI is the vice grip of the Internet. It is language-independent, platform-neutral, and best of all, easy to learn. You can write a CGI script to generate a dynamic Web page in just a couple of lines of code. With not much more work, you can accept user input from a fill-out form, pass it to a backend program or database for processing, and generate a new Web page to show the results. CGI allows you to take any new or legacy application and wrench it into a form that can be served over the Web.

Almost from the start, CGI was associated with the Perl programming language. In fact, to many people, CGI is synonymous with Perl and vice versa. There are good reasons for this. If CGI is the vice grip of the Internet, then Perl is its duct tape. Perl's interprocess communications abilities coupled with its powerful text parsing facilities create an environment that makes it easy to combine unrelated software components into a seamless whole.

For example, a typical e-commerce site needs to interface to a search engine, display catalog pages using up-to-date price information contained in a database, manage a shopping cart, handle order entry, credit card validation, and order fulfillment. Perl excels at these types of tasks. It can run the search engine and transform its output into a hyperlinked Web page, generate on-the-fly catalog pages from information contained in the stock database, transmit credit card information across the network to a verification service, and enter the user's order into the fulfillment database.

The range of innovative applications that people have built on top of Perl/CGI is nothing short of amazing. Tourism agencies use Perl/CGI to generate interactive maps of cities and towns. Medical schools use Perl/CGI to run interactive simulations of human physiology. The human genome project uses Perl/CGI to share its vast holdings of mapping and sequencing data with the biological research community. Perl/CGI has also been used to glue a vast array of hardware devices to the Web—everything from fish-cams to robotic arms.

The Web has gotten a lot more complicated over the years. It's no longer sufficient just to accept user input from a fill-out form and generate an HTML page in response. Web sites must be prepared to parse XML, generate XHTML and DHTML, manipulate cookies, and interact with increasingly distributed back-end systems. Users also have heightened expectations for the Web site experience. Users expect Web sites to remember them from visit to visit, and to allow them to customize the site to meet their particular needs.

Thankfully, as the Web has evolved, Perl and CGI have grown to meet the challenges. This book demonstrates just how potent and vital the combination of Perl and CGI remains. In these pages you will learn how to glue Web pages to databases, track users' click trails, exchange information with other sites using XML, and generate graphics and animations on the fly. Just as importantly, this book focuses from the outset on three issues that are often ignored in the pell-mell pace of Web development: security, reliability, and scalability.

I know that you'll find the combination of Perl and CGI to be both powerful and enjoyable, as I have over many years.

Lincoln Stein
Stonybrook, NY
December 8, 2000

Preface

Purpose of this Book

Perl's popularity as a CGI scripting language is growing by leaps and bounds. However, there are few books available today that cover this subject in depth including a broad range of concepts. We wanted our book to help people learn to use Perl and convince them that it is the best choice for their Web-based applications. The goal of this book is not to teach the Perl language—although certain tricks and features may be learned—but to show how Perl can accomplish the tasks needed for many of today's online applications. In short, we wanted to provide a resource that not only teaches new uses of Perl but challenges the reader with exercises that use the concepts. Standard Perl documentation is also provided. The book covers a wide range of concepts, and using these, you should be able to write almost any Perl/CGI application with the techniques provided.

This book is different from others about Perl and CGI. It takes a cumulative approach and introduces applications that use concepts learned in previous chapters. Each chapter will cover at least one specific Web-based application and explain the code line by line (or block by block) so you not only learn what the scripts are doing but how they are doing it. And in order to help induce self-learning and application building, each application is working but incomplete. We provide skeleton applications that can stand on their own, but we leave out certain features that can be added (and we suggest adding them in the exercises) using the information in that chapter and in previous chapters. Our goal is not to give you "cut and paste" software but rather to show you how to write the software yourself.

Chapter Summaries

Chapter 1, Perl, CGI, and this Book. This chapter explains what Perl and CGI are. It also supplies more detail about this book and shows how to use the CPAN module.

Chapter 2, What You Should Know. We don't expect the reader to know everything, but we do expect at least a base level of knowledge. This chapter outlines what you should already know and explains a few things that you may not already know but should to get the most out of this book, such as tainting, security concerns, and troubleshooting.

Chapter 3, Using Your Environment. Many times in CGI applications you need information from the client, such as IP address or browser information. This chapter covers how to access the Web server environment variables and what they mean.

Chapter 4, Introduction to Web Forms. There are few online applications where there is not some sort of Web form used to allow an end user to submit information. Chapter 4 explains the HTML elements of creating a Web form, as well as how to obtain the user input.

Chapter 5, Working with Cookies. Using cookies to store data on a Web client can be very useful to record the preferences of and remember things about users. You will learn how to set, get, and use cookies in this chapter.

Chapter 6, Access Counters. Many people want to count how many people come to their Web site. The examples in this chapter show you how to do this.

Chapter 7, Web-Based File Uploading. Here you will learn how to safely allow end users to upload files to a server from their local hard drives.

Chapter 8, Tracking Clicks. It can sometimes be useful to know what links on a Web site are being followed and from where. The examples in this chapter show how to track these clicks.

Chapter 9, Using mod_perl. The popular mod_perl Apache module can be extremely useful when it is appropriate for an application. You will see how to configure mod_perl, as well as how to use and write mod_perl Perl modules.

Chapter 10, Web-Based E-mail. The examples in this chapter demonstrate how to connect to a POP3 server to view e-mail, view attachments, and send e-mail via the Web.

Chapter 11, Introduction to DBI and Databases on the Web. Chapters 1–10 presented basic uses for database connectivity in previous examples. This chapter examines the Perl DBI in more depth.

Chapter 12, Tied Variables. The magic of tying data structures to variables and how to do this when the data structure is a database is explained in this chapter.

Chapter 13, Embedding Perl in HTML with Mason. This popular tool is examined and explained. This chapter shows you how to embed Perl within HTML and use the HTML::Mason module to speed up development and maintenance time.

Chapter 14, Document Management via the Web. By now you will have learned how to upload files to a server. This chapter shows you how to manage your files remotely via the Web.

Chapter 15, Dynamically Manipulating Images. Creating charts, graphs, thumbnails, and galleries, and changing images on the fly are all concepts that can be useful in CGI applications. This chapter shows you how to add these techniques to your software.

Chapter 16, RSS and XML. XML is another tool that is gaining in use and popularity. This chapter shows you how to use both XML and a derivative of it, RSS and RDF, to share information and use in applications.

Appendix A, Server Codes. Learn what the codes returned by a Web server mean.

Appendix B, Environment Variables. This is a list of the most common Web server environment variables.

Appendix C, POSIX::strftime() Formats. This book uses the POSIX module a few times to format date strings. This list shows the formats that the module uses and what the formats do.

Appendix D, General Public License. If you didn't read the copy that came with Perl, you can do so here.

Appendix E, Artistic License. Another license under which Perl is distributed.

Appendix F, Perl Documentation. A list of the documentation that comes with Perl. This list is useful for interactive learning along with this book.

Appendix G, ASCII Codes. A list of ASCII, hex, and decimal codes.

Appendix H, Special HTML Characters. A list of special characters, such as £, ®, and Æ. Although these aren't specific to Perl, you will probably need some of them sooner or later when generating HTML with Perl.

Other Resources

One of the best resources for Perl is the Perl documentation and the documentation included in various Perl modules. Chapter 1 covers how to read this documentation with the *perldoc* command. The Perl homepage at *http://www.perl.com* is extremely useful with articles, tips, documentation, other resource links, and what's new in the world of Perl. The Perl Mongers home-page at *http://www.perl.org* supplies good information on the world of Perl and Perl advocacy. Perl News at *http://news.perl.org* will keep you abreast of the latest happenings, events, and module releases. The use Perl Web site at *http://use.perl.org* is a community page where Perl information is shared and discussed. The Perl Documentation Web site at *http://www.perldoc.com* is a very useful site containing the latest Perl documentation. Finally, the Perl Monks at *http://www.perlmonks.com* is another community where people can ask questions, answer questions, chat, and share knowledge.

Usenet has Perl newsgroups that are also useful: *comp.lang.perl.announce* has Perl announcements; *comp.lang.perl.misc* is a high traffic list for asking Perl-related questions; and *comp.lang.perl.modules* announces and discusses Perl modules. A non-Perl-specific news group that deals with CGI is *comp. infosystems.www.authoring.cgi.* Here you can discuss all topics CGI.

Contacting Us

We would love to hear from you. You can find information on this book and errata at *http://www.perlcgi-book.com* and *http://www.awl.com*

Acknowledgments

From Kevin

Writing a book is quite a process! There were many people who directly, and many more indirectly, helped with this book with their encouragement, technical comments, and answers to questions while I double-checked my facts, idioms, and code. First, I would like to thank my wife, Suzy, for the patience she has shown me over the past year while I worked on this project. Much thanks to my mother and father for all their support and love. I would also like to thank Elaine Ashton, Chris and Dale from OWLS, the EFNet #perl regulars, Scott Farley, the Gladdens, John "Goose" Gosselin, Joseph Hall, the Hartford Perl Mongers, Clinton Pierce, Jim Pryke from Netinstitute.com, Peter Scott, Randal Schwartz, Dennis Taylor, Jim Woodgate, Ed Wright, and Yosseff Mendelssohn. I am grateful to Mariann Kourafas and Mary T. O'Brien from Addison-Wesley for allowing Brent and me the opportunity to do this; Larry Wall, without whom this book would never have been written; and, finally, my daughter, Kyla, to whom I dedicate this book. I look forward to the day when she is also hacking at Perl.

From Brent

I want to start out by thanking my wife, Chris, who supported me throughout the writing of this book. I admire and love her so much. She put up with a lot during the whole process and is still here by my side. Thanks, babe. To my kids, Luc, Rae, and Logan: You are my world and I thank you so much for your patience while I wrote this book. To my parents, thanks for all your support over the years! Without you, I wouldn't be where I am today—literally. A special thanks to Bill Eger. Bill was my captain when I was in the Air Force and was the whole reason I was able to get out of the Air Force when I did and get a "real job." Bill believed in me and helped me pursue my dream. He is the kind of person that makes the military great. The #perl regulars really helped me out during this process, too! They were nice enough to laugh at and heckle me when I asked stupid questions on the channel, but, hey, I kept it lively. I have to thank Larry Wall, the man behind this great language. I am sure he didn't think he would affect as many lives as he did when he designed Perl. Finally, my sincere thanks to Al Gore for inventing the Internet. Okay, guys, we can wrestle now.

Chapter

Perl, CGI, and this Book

1.1 What Is Perl?

In 1986, while working at NASA's Jet Propulsion Lab, Larry Wall had the task of synchronizing data exchanges between computers in Santa Monica, California, and Paoli, Pennsylvania. This project also included the task of creating reports based on the data exchanges. At the time, Larry didn't feel that any of the available tools were a good fit for this job. While working on this project, Larry discovered something about the tools available to him. C had the advantage of being able to manipulate complex things, as well as the ability to get to the guts of various processes, which he called "multiplexity." The shell languages were beneficial because people could quickly write a program in a short amount of time. (Larry called this "whipupitude.") Perl was born from the lack of both multiplexity and whipupitude.

On December 18, 1987, Larry posted version 1.000 of Perl to the comp.sources Usenet newsgroup. This is when the Practical Extraction and Reporting Language was officially introduced to the world. Perl was able to fill a niche that no other available tool could, and because of this, people flocked to Perl. This is an excerpt from the manual for Perl version 1.000, which sums up this new language well.

```
NAME
perl | Practical Extraction and Report Language
SYNOPSIS
    perl [options] filename args
DESCRIPTION
    Perl is an interpreted language optimized for scanning arbi-
    trary text files, extracting information from those text
    files, and printing reports based on that information. It's
    also a good language for many system management tasks. The
    language is intended to be practical (easy to use, effi-
    cient, complete) rather than beautiful (tiny, elegant, mini-
    mal). It combines (in the author's opinion, anyway) some of
    the best features of C, sed, awk, and sh, so people familiar
    with those languages should have little difficulty with it.
    (Language historians will also note some vestiges of csh,
    Pascal, and even BASIC|PLUS.) Expression syntax corresponds
    quite closely to C expression syntax. If you have a problem
    that would ordinarily use sed or awk or sh, but it exceeds
    their capabilities or must run a little faster, and you
    don't want to write the silly thing in C, then perl may be
    for you. There are also translators to turn your sed and awk
    scripts into perl scripts.  OK, enough hype.
(18 December)
```

Perl evolved over the next few years, with version 2.000 being released in June 1988 and version 3.000[1] in October 1989. In March 1991, version 4.000[2] of Perl was released. At that time, and into 1992, Perl was considered very stable and had become a widely used programming language on Unix systems. Now that it was so widespread, some of Perl's limitations were revealing themseves. Perl was excellent when short programs were desirable to solve problems, but it was cumbersome when it came to writing larger applications. To help remedy this, the group led by Larry that was now designing the Perl language began to fix many of the problems with Perl that might cause people to choose other languages. The result was Perl version 5.000, released in late 1994.

With version 5.000, Perl came into a sort of fruition and became more of a general purpose programming language and not something more geared toward system administrators. Version 5.000 introduced things such as objects, POD, perldoc, lexical scoping with "my," the "use" keyword, and other advancements.

Perl was then, and is now, used as a "glue" between various data formats and applications. Perl is affectionately called a "Swiss Army Chain Saw" because it has a multitude of uses and can be helpful in almost any

---

1. First time released under the terms of the GNU Public License.
2. Now with an Artistic License as well as GPL.

situation. When Larry Wall created Perl for himself and his officemates, he combined the best features of various languages, and this legacy lives on for the rest of us.

Perl is now maintained by a group of people called "porters" (called the perl5-porters, or p5p), led by Larry Wall. The perl5-porters create new features, fix bugs, update documentation, and coordinate the new releases of Perl. Everyone can see what is happening in the development of Perl and even provide patches to Perl and the documentation by reading the perl5-porters mailing list.[3] An archive of this list can be found on the Web at *http://www.xray.mpe.mpg.de/mailing-lists/perl5-porters/*.

1.2 What Is CGI?`

The Common Gateway Interface, or CGI, is a standard for allowing external programs to interface with servers such as HTTP servers, database servers, e-mail servers, and so on. When a Web server retrieves an HTML document, it is static. This means that the HTML is in a constant, unchanging state. A CGI program, on the other hand, is executed in real-time so that it can output dynamic information. Being able to create documents in real-time allows information to be retrieved from multiple sources, manipulated, and displayed to the end user.

"Common" refers to the ability to write CGI scripts with many different languages on many different systems. "Gateway" is what the CGI script is— a gateway between different applications, in real-time, to transmit information. "Interface" means that there are ways to interface and use the CGI protocol.

CGI itself is not mysterious or intangible. It is a protocol that allows people to use different languages to speak to different systems in real-time to create dynamic content for the Web. For example, let's assume you have a database of contact information on your database server. Now you want to be able to access and query that information from the Web by accessing your Web server. Obviously, a static HTML document can't do this for you. To accomplish this, you need a CGI script that is accessible from the Web. The CGI script will be run by the Web server and connect to the database engine. The script will then retrieve the desired data and display the results back to the Web client. This script acted as a gateway between the Web server and the database server.

The preceding was a simple example of how to use CGI. There is really no limit to using CGI scripts for interfacing. CGI is used to interface with databases, graphic generators, proprietary software, Open Source Software, operating system functions, and so forth.

---

3. Before doing so, it is helpful, but not obligatory, to read the mailing list archives as well as the perlguts manual pages and the p5p FAQ.

1.2.1 Why Perl Is Good for CGI

There is a growing trend in the world today to take applications and convert them to Web-based applications or to create new applications on the Web rather than creating software that must be installed on any computer that will use it. Being able to have an application on the Web is an easy way to ensure that customers and employees can access the application from anywhere there is an Internet connection and a Web browser. Because of this desire to have application on the Web, CGI is needed. Deciding which language to use to write these CGI applications can sometimes be difficult.

There is a common misconception that Perl *is* CGI. Perl is not CGI, but it is a popular and easy way to write CGI scripts. Perl is by no means the "be all, end all" language for writing CGI scripts, but it is a viable tool to have in your toolbox when CGI scripting is needed. Other languages, such as PHP, ASP, Tcl, and Cold Fusion, also use tools for writing CGI scripts. Perl, however, has advantages over other languages when it comes to using it for CGI, as well as for general use.

First, Perl is supported on multiple platforms. You can use Perl for CGI scripts on Win32, multiple Unix platforms, MacOS, BeOS, VMS, and various other platforms.[4] Because Perl programs are not compiled, it is not necessary to recompile them for every platform you wish to run the software on.

Perl, unlike some other languages, comes with features like an internal debugger, facilities to do database interaction, network functions, and arguably the best regular expression engine. These features and more make Perl a terrific language to develop CGI scripts.

Development time is greatly decreased when using Perl. In some languages it would take dozens of lines of code to do what Perl can do in just a few lines. This means more time for developing new scripts and fewer lines of code to maintain and debug.

Perl is also a good choice when a project is not only dependent on CGI scripts but also on backend programs. Most large-scale projects are this way. Let's suppose a project has the requirement of updating multiple databases on regular intervals, providing the information from the databases on the Web, and creating user-defined reports on the data. Perl can handle all of these tasks. PHP, for example, could only handle the piece where data needs to be displayed to a Web client. This means there would have to be multiple languages to accomplish the project goals. By using one language to handle everything, code can be shared, development time can be faster, and anyone who knows Perl can maintain any piece of the code (well-written code).

There are more reasons why Perl is a good choice for use as CGI and general use, but Perl is only one of many tools. The main objective of a

---

4. Refer to the perlport manual page for a list of platforms and tips for porting applications between them.

project is to get it done with quality and within time or budget constraints. Perl may not always be the right choice for every project, but it is a valuable tool to have in the toolbox. Even if you do not use Perl for all of your projects, it is always a viable option to bring to the table when planning how the project will be done.

1.3 About this Book

This book is meant to show you how Perl can be used for CGI applications. It demonstrates the wide range of uses for Perl as CGI, such as database interaction, form handling, XML, graphics manipulation, file handling, POP and SMTP interaction, mod_perl, and other functions that are needed in a large majority of Web-based applications. The discussions of all these concepts define for the reader the host of different uses that allow you to write almost any CGI application with the tools and techniques shown.

The examples in this book are frameworks of CGI applications written in Perl. Although you can use the code in this book as is, there are features deliberately left out of many of the examples. At the end of each chapter there will be reader exercises suggesting that you add some of these features yourself. We do not give you the "answers" to these exercises because everything you need to complete the exercises is found somewhere in this book and sometimes in the documentation that comes with Perl or a certain module being used. The purpose of this is to create an interactive learning experience among this book, the Perl documentation, module documentation, and valuable resources on the Web. Our goal is not to simply provide fully featured applications for you to cut and paste onto your Web server but rather to assist you in learning how to use Perl for CGI and teach you how the various resources available will help you learn to program better Perl.

As you can see on the cover, there are two authors of this book. Therefore, you may see a few differences in style and technique. Since it is a well-known feature of Perl that There Is More Than One Way to Do It, getting the opportunity to see the distinct methods of the authors; as well as in comparison to your own, should inspire "Oh, I never thought of doing it in *that* way!" discoveries. The code always tries to use currently accepted idioms and to be error free (of course). The code is somewhat Unix-centric and geared toward being run on the Apache Web Server. Changes that should be made in an example to run on a Win32 system are noted, but it is always a good idea to read the perlport manual page that comes with Perl. Because Perl itself will likely be running on your system, the majority of applications should run with Web servers other than Apache. The exceptions to this are examples that use mod_perl as an application server. As long as your Web server is properly configured to run CGI scripts (consult your server documentation for configuration), however, the examples should run fine on your system. All of the examples have been tested on at least FreeBSD 4.0 and Red Hat Linux 6.x operating systems as well as Apache versions 1.2.x and 1.3.x, using Perl versions 5.005 and 5.6 (which is the latest release as of this writing). All of the modules used in this book for the examples were the latest available on CPAN at the time. We strongly encourage you to consult the documentation for these modules to learn about new methods as well as possible different ways to use the methods shown here.

1.3.1 Who Is this Book For?

This book is for those who have not yet started or for those who have just begun to write CGI applications with Perl. Even if you have experience writing CGI applications with Perl, you will find this book helpful because it presents techniques and tools that allow you to get projects done quickly and easily. This book covers a wide range of topics, and there are likely a handful that you may not yet have dealt with. If you have done minimal or no CGI programming with Perl before, this book will teach you many things.

This book is also meant for people who are learning Perl by using it for CGI. It is a fact that with the explosion of the Web and the great need for CGI applications, many people learn Perl by using it for CGI as opposed to learning it by writing system administration applications. This book will not teach you Perl, but it will teach you things about Perl and how useful it is with CGI. This book is also for those of you who wish to learn how easy it is to use Perl for writing CGI applications.

We have already suggested that you consult other forms of documentation. We hope you have Perl documentation on hand as well as module documentation to help you understand all the concepts in this book and the full functionality of the modules used throughout this book. Don't fret. You will not need to have this book in your lap while sitting in front of your computer. We suggest, however, that you mark any pages that deal with topics you would like to delve into more deeply later.

Finally, this book is meant for those who truly wish to learn. It isn't for people who want feature-complete applications to drop on a server and just use. We wrote this book for those readers who really want to be better Perl programmers and want to learn to create idiomatic, secure, quality Web-based applications.

1.3.2 Conventions Used in this Book

There are a few conventions used in this book to help you spot things at a glance. First, all of the example code is numbered and placed in boxes like this.

```
01: my $foo = "bar";
02: my $baz = 2;
```

Following the code there are explanations of each numbered line. For example, after the preceding box, you will see an explanation in this form.

Lines 1 and 2 initialize two variables. **Line 1** sets the variable $foo to the value "bar," and **line 2** stores the value 2 in the scalar $baz.

All method, subroutine, and function names are in *italics*, and followed by parentheses. Here are some examples.

We want to use the *split()* function to get the values . . .

We want to *use()* the Fcntl module to import the constants . . .

The *Foo::bar()* method is extremely useful for . . .

All of the scripts in this book use the strict pragma, as well as warnings. Most of the scripts you will see also use the -T switch to turn on tainting (explained in more detail in Chapter 2). This book was being written in the midst of the release of Perl 5.6, and we realize that many people will be using Perl 5.005 for some time before moving on to Perl 5.6. For this reason, the use of warnings is done with the -w switch and not the warnings pragma distributed with Perl 5.6. We have not included anything in this book that is 5.6 specific except for a few notes on small changes between 5.005 and 5.6 where needed. So if you have Perl 5.005 or 5.6, you can use these scripts.

1.3.3 Using perldoc

As we have already stated, it is a good idea to refer to the documentation that comes with Perl while you read this book. Perl comes with documentation on its functions as well as various FAQs and tutorials. Also, when you install a module (as with the modules installed with Perl itself) its documentation is available for you. One of the easiest ways to access this documentation is with the perldoc program, which comes with Perl. If you are not already familiar with the perldoc program, here is a brief primer.

One good way to get acquainted with the perldoc program is to use it to observe its own documentation. This is done by typing the following on the command line.

```
$ perldoc perldoc
```

Let's say that you come across an unfamiliar Perl function in this book—for example, *map()*. This would be one of the useful times to use perldoc to find out what the Perl documentation says on the subject. To find out what documentation there is on a Perl function, you give perldoc the -f switch (think f for function), followed by the function name. Listing 1-1 displays what you would see if doing this for the *map()* function.

Listing 1-1 **Output of perldoc -f map**

```
# perldoc -f map
=item map BLOCK LIST
=item map EXPR,LIST
Evaluates the BLOCK or EXPR for each element of LIST (locally
setting C<$_> to each element) and returns the list value com-
posed of the results of each such evaluation.  Evaluates BLOCK
or EXPR in a list context, so each element of LIST may produce
zero, one, or more elements in the returned value.
In scalar context, returns the total number of elements so
generated.
    @chars = map(chr, @nums);
translates a list of numbers to the corresponding characters.
And
    %hash = map { getkey($_) => $_ } @array;
is just a funny way to write
    %hash = ();
    foreach $_ (@array) {
        $hash{getkey($_)} = $_;
    }
Note that, because C<$_> is a reference into the list value, it
can be used to modify the elements of the array.  While this is
useful and supported, it can cause bizarre results if the LIST is
not a named array.
Using a regular C<foreach> loop for this purpose would be clearer
in most cases.  See also L</grep> for an array composed of those
items of the original list for which the BLOCK or EXPR evaluates
to true.
```

Next, let's assume that you want to learn more about the **strict** pragma that we will constantly be telling you to use. To see the documentation for any pragma or installed module, simply type the name of the module after the perldoc command, as shown in Listing 1-2.

Listing 1-2 **Output of perldoc strict**

```
# perldoc strict
strict(3)      User Contributed Perl Documentation      strict(3)
NAME
       strict - Perl pragma to restrict unsafe constructs
SYNOPSIS
           use strict;
           use strict "vars";
           use strict "refs";
           use strict "subs";
```

```
        use strict;
        no strict "vars";
DESCRIPTION
        If no import list is supplied, all possible restrictions
        are assumed.  (This is the safest mode to operate in, but
        is sometimes too strict for casual programming.)
        Currently, there are three possible things to be strict
        about:  "subs", "vars", and "refs".
etc...
```

There will also likely be times where you want to see the source code for a module. It would be somewhat of an inconvenience to find the source on your system, then look that. The perldoc program allows you to do this by using the -m switch (think m for module) followed by the name of the module. For example, if you wanted to see how the CGI::Carp module works by inspecting the source code, you could use the following command.

```
$ perldoc -m CGI::Carp
```

NOTE When using -m, if a module uses a separate .pod file, the output may not show you the source code.

There may also be times when you want to learn about a certain concept, not module or Perl function, and see if it is covered in any of the FAQs that come with Perl. For example, say you want to find out what it says in the FAQs about the environment. Using the -q switch (think q for question) followed by a keyword,[5] perldoc will search the questions in the FAQs for a match on your keyword. If a match (or matches) is found, you will be presented with the specific question(s) that matched, what FAQ the match is from, and the answer from FAQ. This is truly a tremendous resource for you to have while learning more about Perl. If "environment" was your keyword, Listing 1-3 shows the results.

Listing 1-3 Output of perldoc -q environment

```
# perldoc -q environment
=head1 Found in /usr/lib/perl5/5.00503/pod/perlfaq8.pod
=head2 I {changed directory, modified my environment} in a perl
script.  How come the change disappeared when I exited the
script?  How do I get my changes to be visible?
=over 4
=item Unix
```

---

5. Actually, the argument is a regular expression. Look at perldoc perldoc for more information.

```
In the strictest sense, it can't be done -- the script executes
as a different process from the shell it was started from.
Changes to a process are not reflected in its parent, only in its
own children created after the change.  There is shell magic that
may allow you to fake it by eval()ing the script's output in your
shell; check out the comp.unix.questions FAQ for details.
=back
```

Perl also comes with other documents such as perlrun, perlfunc, and perlop (shown in Appendix F) that can be extremely useful for learning and problem solving. The perldoc program can be used to read these documents. This is done, as one may expect, by putting the name of the document after the perldoc command.

```
$ perldoc perlre
```

By using the preceding command, you would be presented with the perlre manual page, and by reading this page, you would learn a bit about regular expressions with Perl. The perldoc command has more features than those we've just seen, but these are the most common ways perldoc is used. Appendix F lists the main documentation that comes with Perl.[6]

1.4 Using the CPAN

This book uses many different modules. Some of them, like CGI.pm and various pragmas, are distributed with Perl itself. However, many of the modules used in this book, like Untaint.pm and GD.pm, are not. When you want to obtain a Perl module, the place to go is the CPAN[7] (Comprehensive Perl Archive Network). The CPAN is a repository for Perl modules written for a multitude of uses by fellow Perl hackers all over the world. It is generally the first place to look when you are wondering if there is "something that does X" or "F there is an API into Y."

Choosing how you will use a Web interface to the CPAN is up to you. You can use the directory structure style of the main CPAN mirrors or the more friendly interface on cpan.org. Whichever you choose, it is an incredibly useful tool to familiarize yourself with what is available before you try to reinvent the wheel (so to speak). It is also handy for the times when you need to do something and you think, "Oh, yeah! I saw a module on the CPAN that does that!" Web front ends to the CPAN allow you to download the files as well as view the author's documentation for the

---

6. Perl 5.6.
7. See *http://www.perl.com/CPAN-local/SITES.html* for a list of global mirrors or *http://search.cpan.org* for a friendly search interface.

module. This, again, is a very useful way to learn about what tools are available to you.

Another way to interface with the CPAN is by using the CPAN module, CPAN.pm, which is distributed with Perl. This module, among other things, provides an easy way to install modules from your shell.[8] Let's say you want to install the URI::Escape module. You can, of course, go to the CPAN Web site nearest you and download the module. You would then unpack it and install it with make. Or you can use the CPAN.pm module to do it all for you with one command. By typing the following line, the CPAN module will do the work.

```
$ perl -MCPAN -e 'install URI::Escape'
```

This command line loads the CPAN.pm module with the -M switch, then runs the method *install()*, with the argument that of the module you want to install—in this case, URI::Escape. If this is the first time you have used the CPAN.pm module, you will be asked some questions. The questions are for things like cache size, location of the "tar" program, if a proxy server is needed, and other configuration issues that the module needs to know in order to fetch and install modules. For the most part, the default settings will be okay, but it is good to follow the questions to make sure everything is correct. If you already have configured the module, then by typing this command the URI::Escape module will be fetched from the Internet and installed.

One neat thing you may notice while installing URI::Escape is that it has a dependency, the MIME-Base64 module. What is so neat about that? Well, most of the time when you install a module you find these dependencies during the make process and then have to go back to the Internet to fetch the dependencies, install them, and then install the module you first wanted. When using the CPAN.pm module, it will see that a dependency is needed, fetch it for you, install it for you, and continue. So when installing the URI::Escape module, you will see that the CPAN module will see the dependency for MIME::Base64, check if you have the module (and the proper version), and install it if you do not have it.

One frequent question is "How can I see what modules I have installed?" This task can certainly be done by writing a brief script to traverse the directories in @INC and find files with a .pm extension. However, the CPAN.pm module also provides a way to do this. Using the following command, a file will be created listing all the installed modules as well as their version numbers.[9]

---

8. Win32 users can use CPAN.pm but may prefer the Perl Package Manager (PPM), which is a tool to help Win32 users install various modules.
9. If there is no $VERSION variable in a module, it will show 'undef'.

```
$ perl -MCPAN -e autobundle
```

This will do two things. First, it will display a list of installed modules with their version number of the installed files as well as the latest version available on the CPAN and where on the CPAN to find the module. This data isn't saved to a file by default.[10] What is saved to a file is a snapshot of the currently installed modules and their version numbers. This information is handy when you want to see what you have and what is now available on the CPAN. The snapshot file that is created will not be in your current working directory but saved in your CPAN home directory ($HOME/.cpan by default) in the Bundle subdirectory.

The CPAN module also can be used in shell mode. You can also install modules in shell mode, but a good use of this mode is searching for modules, authors, and bundles. This can be useful when trying to find out information on a module author as well as what modules and bundles are available based on your search criteria. We will look at examples of each of these uses, but first we should show you how to enter the CPAN shell.

```
$ perl -MCPAN -e shell
```

After typing the preceding line, you will enter the shell. Let's begin by looking at how you would search for an author's information. When using the shell, as stated before, you can look for authors, modules, and bundles. What you are searching for is denoted by a keyword (a, m, and b, respectively), followed by your search criteria.

The search criteria can be a regular word or a regular expression. When using a regular word, that word must be found for a match to occur. When using a regular expression, it is treated differently. This is best explained by simply showing output. See Listing 1-4.

Listing 1-4   Searching for an author using a CPAN ID

```
cpan> a KMELTZ
Author id = KMELTZ
    EMAIL       perlguy@perlguy.com
    FULLNAME    Kevin Meltzer
```

As you can see in Listing 1-4, by using a CPAN ID as a keyword, the name and e-mail address of the corresponding author is given. That is good if you happen to know the author's CPAN ID, but what if you don't? You may think that Listing 1-5 would give similar results, but it does not.

---

10. You can do this by redirecting the STDOUT of the command.

Listing 1-5   **Searching for an author using a partial CPAN ID**

```
cpan> a KM
No objects of type Author found for argument KM
```

This obviously wouldn't be much help. So it is time to use a regular expression to find what is being looked for. Listing 1-6 shows the output of this when used as a regular expression.

Listing 1-6   **Searching using a partial CPAN ID as a regular expression**

```
cpan> a /KM/
Author        KMACLEOD (Ken MacLeod)
Author        KMELTZ (Kevin Meltzer)
Author        MARKM (Mark Mielke)
Author        STAS (Stas Bekman)
Author        TKML (The Tk Perl Mailing list)
```

As you can see, Listing 1-6 returned all the author matches where "KM" is in the CPAN ID or the author's name. Now, let's take a look at using this to search for modules. When searching for a module without using a regular expression, you will get information on that specific module, as shown in Listing 1-7.

Listing 1-7   **Searching for module information**

```
cpan> m URI::Escape
Module id = URI::Escape
    DESCRIPTION  General URI escaping/unescaping functions
    CPAN_USERID  GAAS (Gisle Aas <gisle@aas.no>)
    CPAN_VERSION 3.13
    CPAN_FILE    G/GA/GAAS/URI-1.07.tar.gz
    DSLI_STATUS  Rmpf (released,mailing-list,perl,functions)
    MANPAGE      URI::Escape - Escape and unescape unsafe
                 characters
    INST_FILE    /usr/lib/perl5/site_perl/5.005/URI/Escape.pm
    INST_VERSION 3.13
```

You can see that we are now using an "m" to search for modules, as opposed to the "a" used for authors. The results show information on the module including the description, the author, the latest version currently on CPAN, where the file is if it is installed, and the installed version number. This is another handy way to find out if a module you have installed can be updated to a newer version. Now let's assume you want to look for all modules on the CPAN that have a common topic. It could be CGI, Apache, XML, or anything you want to know that may be available to you. Maybe you are doing a project that involves using XSLT and want to see what modules are on the CPAN containing the word XSLT. Listing 1-8 shows how to do this.

Listing 1-8   Searching for all modules containing XSLT

```
cpan> m /XSLT/
Module   Apache::AxKit::Language::NotXSLT (M/MS/MSERGEANT/AxKit-
0.67.tar.gz)
Module   Apache::AxKit::Language::XSLT (M/MS/MSERGEANT/AxKit-
0.95.tar.gz)
Module   XML::EP::Processor::XSLT (J/JW/JWIED/XML-EP-
0.01.tar.gz)
Module   XML::EP::Processor::XSLTParser (J/JW/JWIED/XML-EP-
0.01.tar.gz)
Module   XML::XSLT         (B/BR/BRONG/XML-XSLT-0.24.tar.gz)
Module   XSLT              (J/JO/JOSTEN/XML-XSLT-0.20.tar.gz)
Module   XSLTParser        (J/JO/JOSTEN/xslt-parser-0.13.tar.gz)
```

You are now presented with a listing of available CPAN modules that can be used to handle XSLT. The final way to search is by bundle. A bundle is a group of modules distributed together. For example, there are many modules that deal with LDAP, and there are bundles of these modules available. If you needed to use Perl to interface with LDAP, you may want to see what bundles are available, which is shown in Listing 1-9.

Listing 1-9   Searching for a bundle for LDAP

```
cpan> b /ldap/
Bundle   Bundle::Net::LDAP (G/GB/GBARR/perl-ldap-0.19.tar.gz)
Bundle   Bundle::Wizard::LDAP (J/JW/JWIED/Wizard-LDAP-
0.1008.tar.gz)
```

We felt that it was important to show you some of the uses of the CPAN.pm module and the CPAN itself early in this book. It is an incredibly useful resource, and it can make it easier to install modules that are used in the examples in this book.

Chapter

What You Should Know

2.1 Prerequisites

We, the authors, have a few expectations of the readers. These assumptions and expectations are not outlandish or unreasonable, but they cover many basic issues and information only touched upon briefly. This book shows you how to write viable and efficient CGI applications with Perl, using both your current skills and new ones you will learn here. Unlike some other books, our goal is not to show you fully featured, cut and paste CGI applications and simply explain how to use them. Instead, this book presents working frameworks of applications that are usable, secure, and illustrate good programming practices. (TIMTOWTDI—There Is More Than One Way To Do It.)

Although you do not have to be a Perl guru or even know a lot of Perl to use this book, you should already have some Perl knowledge. In fact, you do not need to know a lot of Perl to use Perl. This book touches on some advanced Perl programming, but it is not geared completely toward the advanced Perl programmer. It does not explain basic Perl concepts like data structures, data types, printing output, or opening a file. However, it will explain things like *map()*, DBI, *system()*, and other information that some programmers may not yet have used. Therefore, it is assumed that the reader has a basic understanding of the Perl language or at least simple programming constructs.

You must also have a Web server to work on. All of the scripts and applications in this book were written and tested on Apache Web server. However, most operations work the same on a variety of Web servers, such as IIS and Netscape FastTrack.[1] Throughout this book we will point out differences between core Perl and Win32 Perl. The most up-to-date information on differences can be seen in the *perlport* manual page and the Perl distributions release notes. The main difference to keep in mind is those between system calls. For example, to get a directory listing on UNIX, you may use 'ls', but on a Win32 system, you would use 'dir'. When appropriate, we will note the changes in the examples that should be made to account for these Operating System differences, as well as differences for portability.

It is expected that you have Perl installed, preferably on the same machine as your Web server. If you are using a UNIX-like machine, it is likely that Perl is already installed. If you are using Windows 9x/NT/2000, you must install it yourself. To see if your system already has Perl, at the shell prompt, type this.

```
perl -v
```

If Perl is installed on the system, it should give you an output similar to Listing 2-1.

Listing 2-1   Output of Perl version

```
This is perl, version 5.005_04 built for i386-freebsd
Copyright 1987-1999, Larry Wall
Perl may be copied only under the terms of either the Artistic
License or the GNU General Public License, which may be found
in the Perl 5.0 source kit. Complete documentation for Perl,
including FAQ lists, should be found on this system using 'man
perl' or 'perldoc perl'. If you have access to the Internet,
point your browser at http://www.perl.com/, the Perl Home
Page.
```

If you do not receive a similar message, you may have to install Perl yourself. All scripts in this book were written and tested using at least Perl version 5.005_03. If you have an older version of Perl on your system, you may want to update your Perl. The latest versions of Perl can be obtained from *http://www.perl.com* or *http://www.activestate.com* for standard Perl or Perl for Win32, respectively. If you need or want to update your version of Perl, obtain the latest distribution for your type of operating system and

---

1. Netscape Servers can be found on *http://www.netscape.com*, and Microsoft Web Servers can be found at *http://www.microsoft.com*. The Apache Web Server is available for Win32 and UNIX systems at *http://www.apache.org*.

follow the install instructions. We have chosen not to include instructions to install Perl because there are various options from which to choose for the installation, and it is best that you read the documentation and install Perl exactly as, where, and how you wish.

You should also have an FTP program that you are familiar with if you are not writing your CGI on the Web server itself. If you are using an FTP program, know how to run the 'chmod' command (if using a UNIX-like server) so you can properly change the permissions on your CGI scripts. You also want to make sure that your mode is set to ASCII, not binary, when uploading Perl scripts to your server. Uploading them as binary will cause errors when you attempt to run them.

This book is written with the assumption that you have read a fair portion of the Perl documentation and the documentation for the Web server you are using. If you have not, don't fret! It is not necessary to immediately drop this book and go read all of the Perl and Web server documentation. You should, however, know where they are so you can consult them if and when you need to. For example, if you do not have a CGI-enabled directory for your Web server, you should consult the documentation of your Web server to learn how to make a directory CGI enabled. With Apache, the cgi-bin directory off the server's root directory is CGI enabled by default. Other directories can be CGI enabled by adding this line in the appropriate spot in the httpd.conf file.

```
Options +ExecCGI
```

To have a directory that is enabled to use the examples in this book, you can create a directory with the name 'cgibook' off the root directory of your Web server and add Listing 2-2 to your httpd.conf file.

Listing 2-2   httpd.conf example to enable CGI

```
<Directory "/usr/local/apache/htdocs/cgibook">
    Options Indexes FollowSymLinks ExecCGI Includes
    AllowOverride All
    Order allow,deny
    Allow from all
</Directory>
```

The configuration entry shown in Listing 2-2 will allow the cgibook directory to execute CGI scripts and Server Side Includes. It will also show directory listing and allow for the following of symbolic links. You will want to change the path to the directory shown in Listing 2-2 if you have your server root as something other than /usr/local/apache/htdocs/cgibook. You will also want to make sure that the configuration of the server root directory allows overrides. By default, the Apache configuration is most restrictive, and you should see the following in httpd.conf.

```
AllowOverrides None
```

This tells the server that subdirectories may not override the configuration of options that are set in the root directory. If the root directory does not allow for subdirectories to use the needed options (which it does not do by default), this directive will need to be changed to look like the following.

```
AllowOverride All
```

After making these changes to the httpd.conf file, the server will need to be restarted for them to take effect. This can also be placed in a .htaccess file in the cgibook directory.

2.2 Editors

For the most part, you can use your favorite text editor (no, Word™ is *not* a text editor). On UNIX-like systems a few popular editors are vi, vim, emacs, pico, and ed. On Win32 systems, WordPad does the job well. WordPad will work with files that have come from UNIX systems and contain UNIX line separators. Many people use NotePad, but that editor doesn't read the UNIX line separators, and it displays them as black boxes. When working in a multiplatform environment, it is wise to use an editor that can read line separators from other operating systems. There are also other Win32 editors that are ports of UNIX text editors, such as vim and emacs, as well as various Perl IDEs. Use whichever text editor you feel comfortable with, and even try out one or two new ones!

2.3 File Permissions

On Win32 systems, file permissions needed for CGI scripts can be set up to be executable, and the best way to find out how your Win32-based Web server does this is to refer to its documentation. However, on UNIX-like systems it is more important that you know about UNIX file permissions. The standard file permissions used for CGI scripts are 755. This means that the file is readable and executable by all, as well as read/write permissions granted to the owner. In case you are unfamiliar with UNIX file permissions, here is a quick overview.

There are three permission bits that can be set for a file: read, write, and execute. There are also three types of people for whom permissions are set: owner, group, and world. You may see something like the following when giving a directory listing with a Perl/CGI script in said directory. The first three permission bits are set for the owner permissions, the second three for the group, and the last for the world.

```
-    rwxr-xr-x 1 kevin users 1736 Oct 29 10:29 my.cgi
```

Here you can see that the file permissions for my.cgi is 755. How do you know that rwxr-wr-w is 755? Each of the three permission bits have a numerical equivalent. Listing 2-3 shows these equivalents.

Listing 2-3   **UNIX file permissions**

r	4
w	2
x	1

You can now see that rwx, which is the first set of permissions, totals 7; the second, r-w, totals 5; and the third, r-w, also totals 5. File permissions are not only important on the CGI script itself but on any files to which a CGI script may be writing. A common example would be a text file to which a CGI script writes. Assuming that a CGI script will want to read and write from that file, the permissions should be –rw-rw-rw-, or 666. Sometimes you may see people allowing CGI scripts to write to files, which have the permissions 777, thinking that it is safe to do so because there should be nothing to execute in the file. This is a misconception that can be danger-ous. If that file happens to be in a directory in which the Web servers allow executable script to be run, then someone could run that file. In most cases there would be no harm in executing a file that is full of arbitrary data. However, if someone was to somehow write a shell executable script to that file, there could be trouble. The moral of this is to be mindful of the file per-missions you are using and to always assign the minimum amount of per-missions needed. Those are the basics of UNIX file permissions and how they relate to using CGI. To find out more about file permissions and the chmod command, consult the UNIX chmod manual page.

2.4 Basic Security Concerns

There are various security concerns relating to CGI. Some of these con-cerns are not so much CGI related as related to Web server or network security (such as passwords, permissions, firewalls, and so forth). Few of them are related to CGI scripts. In reality, if a competent system adminis-trator is maintaining the server, there is little to fear from CGI scripts. One of the main issues to be concerned with from a programmer's perspective is using untrusted data in a harmful manner (for example, putting it into a file with permissions of 777). What is untrusted data? Untrusted data is simply any data that comes from outside of your program. This could be arguments coming from a command line, arguments being passed from other scripts, and, what we are most concerned about, data being passed to the script by a user, such as via a Web form. When data is passed to a CGI script from an unknown or untrusted source, it is considered "tainted," and a user is always an untrusted source. For the most part, unless you specifically assign a value to a variable in your script and the value assigned to that variable whose value originates from within the script, the data is considered tainted. This is a very good thing because it alerts you to what may be dangerous to use in certain ways. However, information on what is tainted and what is safe is not given to you by default.

2.5 Using -T

The -T switch instructs the Perl interpreter to perform "taint checks" on data by turning on the taint mode. Normally, this is done by default with scripts running setuid or setgid. Otherwise Perl must be specifically told to use -T. When the -T switch is used, the Perl interpreter will make sure that your script is not trying to use data received from an external source to affect something else that is outside the script. For example, it will make sure that your script does not take a value submitted by a user through a Web form and run a system command with it, unless you have untainted the data. All data received by command line arguments, file input, various system calls, and environment variables are considered to be tainted. This tainted data cannot be used with commands to modify files, directories, processes, and sub-shell commands. One exception is that when you pass a list of arguments to the functions *exec()* or *system()*, the elements of that list are not taint checked individually. If one element in the list is tainted, the entire list is tainted—guilt by association, so to speak. Also, a variable will be considered tainted if you set its value to that of another tainted value. Let's look at a few examples of tainted data in Listing 2-4.

Listing 2-4   Examples of tainted data

`$foo = $ARGV[0];`	`$foo is tainted.`
`$bar = $foo;`	`$bar is tainted because it is set to the value of $foo, which is tainted.`
`$file = <FOO>;`	`Tainted. Anything obtained via the diamond operator (<>), <STDIN>, <FILEHANDLE>, etc....) is considered to be tainted.`

$foo = "Hello";	$foo is no longer tainted.
$path = $ENV{'PATH'};	$path is tainted.
$ENV{'PATH'} = '/bin:/usr/bin'; $path = $ENV{'PATH'};	$path is not tainted because you set the environment variable PATH from within the script.
$param = param('Name');	$param is tainted. All data returned from the CGI.pm method param() will be considered tainted.

Considering the example variables in Listing 2-4, $foo, $file, and $param would still be tainted. If you were to try to use these tainted variables in a dangerous manner, you would get an error such as "Insecure dependency" or "Insecure $ENV{PATH}." Let's take a look at a few examples of how you could safely use this tainted data and try to use it in a way that will throw an error when using the -T command line switch.

Listing 2-5 **Examples if using tainted data**

unlink $foo;	Insecure and cannot be done.
open(FOO, "$foo");	This is okay, since it is a read-only open.
open(FOO,">>$foo");	This is considered insecure because you are opening for writing.
exec "cat $foo";	This would be insecure because it uses a sub-shell.
exec "cat", $foo;	This would be considered secure because it does not use the shell.

Let's look at Listing 2-5, specifically the final two variables. Why is one secure and the other considered insecure? After all, they are both calls to *exec()*! When *exec()* and *system()* are called, they look at the number of arguments being passed to them. If there is a singular scalar argument or an array with only one element passed to it (as in exec "cat $foo";, which is a single scalar argument), it passes the command to the systems shell to be parsed. This would usually be /bin/sh on a UNIX system. When no shell metacharacters are passed to the function, it is split into words and run somewhat literally. Perl's *system()* function acts the same way, as it should, being that it does the same as *exec()* except that it returns control back to your script.

Data must be untainted, or laundered, before using it in what would normally be considered an unsafe manner. By using Perl in taint check mode, you have no choice but to do so, and you should get into this habit, especially when doing CGI. Throughout this book all examples will be using taint checking whether it is really needed or not. Our hope is that by looking at and using these scripts, you will get into this good habit yourself and habitually write safe and secure Perl/CGI scripts.

2.6 Checking for Taintedness and Laundering Data

If you wanted to, you could get the Taint.pm module, by Tom Phoenix, off your favorite CPAN site to use for checking taintedness, but it is easy to do it yourself. Take the method in Listing 2-6, which will return 1 (true) if any of the arguments passed to it are tainted.

Listing 2-6   The is_tainted() subroutine

```
01: sub is_tainted {
02:     my $check = shift;
03:     return !eval { $check++, kill 0; 1; };
04: }
```

Line 1 begins the is_tainted subroutine.

Line 2 is pulling the argument passed to the routine and assigning it to the scalar $check. As you just learned, when you assign tainted data to a new variable, that variable is then tainted. So when a tainted scalar is passed as an argument to the subroutine, $check will also be tainted.

Line 3 returns the negated value of an *eval()*. An *eval()* is being used because this way the script will not die when something tainted tries to do something naughty. Instead, we can use the return value of it and continue on appropriately with the script. This line is somewhat tricky to test if data is tainted but not really doing anything harmful with it. If the increment of $check was on its own line, it would be harmless, even with tainted data. However, when you couple it with the *kill()* command, it would then throw an error because the tainted data shares a line with it. Why the increment of the tainted variable? We do this because you need to perform an operation on the tainted variable for Perl to consider it as being used unsafely. In this case, the increment is considered dangerous because it is being coupled with that *kill()* statement. There are a few operating systems that may have a **PID** of 0 (most Linux and BSD systems do not), but using "kill 0" is an idiom, and does not trigger the system kill(). Also, there should never be a process with the **PID** of 0, so actually running a kill 0 would be harmless because it would kill[2] no processes. If there is no tainted data, the *eval()* would return a 1, which is then negated to a 0. If the *eval()* fails, the 0 returned would be negated to a 1. Then this could be used as in Listing 2-7.

---

2.   Some operating systems may not have a kill command.

Listing 2-7   **Example checking for tainted data**

```
01: #!/usr/bin/perl -wT
02: use strict;
03: use CGI qw(:standard);
04: print header();
05: my $param = param('Name');
06: print "$param is tainted" if is_tainted($param);
07: sub is_tainted {
08:     my @check = @_;
09:     return !eval { join('',@check), kill 0; 1; };
10: }
```

Listing 2-7 is a somewhat trivial example, since we know that $param will be tainted because it is being passed via form data, but it is still a good way to see it work. Now we know how to catch tainted data before we attempt to run an unsafe operation with it. But how do we untaint, or launder, the data so it is safe to use? There is only one way to launder data, and that is by setting the value of the tainted variable to a substring from a regular expression. This means setting its value to $1, $2, $3, and so on from a pattern match run against the variable. You do not want to simply untaint the variable without doing some sort of valid match. Let's say we are expecting some form input for a person's telephone number. There would be no letters in it, and it may have dashes in it. So we want to be able to validate that the input looks like one of these three examples.

Example 1   555-555-5555
Example 2   5555555555
Example 3   555 555-5555

It is recommended that when you have something such as a telephone number on a Web-based form that you try to have one way for it to be input, such as 555-555-5555. This could help you by making sure you can expect the data to be received in a consistent manner for later use. But we want this to be a general example, so we will allow all of them. To help illustrate the process of checking for taintedness and attempting to launder the tainted variable, we will use a command line script for now. You will see this later in practice in CGI scripts.

```
01: #!/usr/bin/perl -wT
```

Line 1 is the path to Perl. You will notice we are turning on warnings as well as taint checking. Of course, if we did not turn on taint checking, this example would have little use!

```
02: use strict;
```

Line 2 adds some more compile time restrictions by using the strict module. It is always a good habit to do this.

```
03: my $foo = join('',@ARGV);
```

Line 3 gets the command line arguments. Because this is a command line program, the arguments will be passed in @ARGV. We take these arguments, which will be parts of the phone number in this case, and join them together to make a string.

```
04: if (is_tainted($foo)) {
```

Line 4 starts an if block by seeing if the *is_tainted()* subroutine returns true.

```
05:            print "\$foo is tainted. Attempting to launder\n";
```

Line 5 prints a message saying that the variable is indeed tainted.

```
06:            my $pattern = qr(^\d{3}(-|\s+)?\d{3}(-|\s+)?\d{4}$);
```

Line 6 is the pattern where we want the data to match in order to be laundered successfully. The pattern is being created with the *qr()* operator. This is the **quote-as-a-regular-expression** operator and is new in Perl version 5.005. One of the advantages of using *qr()* is that it gives a bit of optimization because it will be compiled once when the *qr()* assignment occurs. This regular expression looks for a string, which matches one of the phone number formats given previously.

```
07:            $foo = untaint($foo, $pattern);
```

Line 7 makes a call to the *untaint()* subroutine, passing along the tainted variable as well as the pattern that it needs to match in order to be laundered. This subroutine is very useful because it allows you to pass a pattern to it, making it extremely reusable. The value returned by *untaint()* will be assigned to the variable $foo. If the laundering is successful, the new value of $foo will be clean and untainted. If it fails, the new value will still be tainted.

```
08: }else{
09:            print "\$foo is not tainted!!\n";
10: }
```

Lines 8, 9, and 10 begin the other end of the conditional if the original data is not tainted. **Line 9** prints out a message of success if the variable is not tainted.

```
11: sub is_tainted {
12:         my $check = shift;
13:         return  !eval { $check++, kill 0;1;};
14: }
```

Lines 11–14 are the *is_tainted()* subroutine. This is the same as described in the previous example.

```
15: sub untaint {
```

Line 15 begins the *untaint()* subroutine.

```
16:         my ($foo, $pattern) = @_;
```

Line 16 assigns the incoming arguments of the tainted data and pattern to match to the variables $foo and $pattern, respectively.

```
17:         if ($foo =~ /($pattern)/) {
```

Line 17 is the regular expression using the pattern we passed it. By passing the pattern that you want a specific variable to match to *untaint()*, it makes this subroutine more useful because it is reusable. If you later wanted to match data that would be all letters, like a first name, you could simply pass a pattern of ^\w+$ to this routine. This is a good example of dynamic programming. Notice that we added the parentheses around the pattern. This is to make sure that if it matches, the value of the matched pattern will be assigned to $1, which, as explained earlier, is needed to launder a variable.

```
18:             $foo = $1;
```

Line 18 handles the reassignment of the variable if the regular expression from line 17 is matched. This line will reassign the value of $foo to the substring matched and saved in $1. The data is now laundered!

```
19:             print "\$foo has been laundered!!\n";
```

Line 19 prints out the success!

```
20:                        return $foo;
```

Line 20 returns $foo, which is now untainted.

```
21:          }else{
22:                  print "Unable to launder \$foo\n";
23:                  return $foo;
24:          }
25: }
```

Lines 21–25 is reached if a launder attempt fails. If the data does not match the pattern and cannot be laundered, this else block will print out this fact, and return the data still tainted.

Next we want to test this! Name this script taint_ex.pl, and try running it with and without the correct arguments. You should see results like those in Listing 2-8.

Listing 2-8   **Examples of using taint_ex.pl**

```
% ./taint_ex.pl 5555555555
$foo is tainted. Attempting to launder
$foo has been laundered!!
% ./taint_ex.pl 555-555-5555
$foo is tainted. Attempting to launder
$foo has been laundered!!
% ./taint_ex.pl I am not a phone number
$foo is tainted. Attempting to launder
Unable to launder $foo
% ./taint_ex.pl 555 KL5-5555
$foo is tainted. Attempting to launder
Unable to launder $foo
% ./taint_ex.pl 555 555-5555
$foo is tainted. Attempting to launder
$foo has been laundered!!
```

As you can see, the telephone number formats we were allowing for are sent through the laundromat and successfully made into safe variables. You can also see that those arguments, which do not match our pattern, are not laundered and remain tainted. You may be wondering if you will always have to launder incoming data. Well, yes and no. The data will always be tainted, but you need to launder only the variable when it will be used in a way that affects the system. We listed these ways earlier, but it is important to remember them, so to recap: Tainted data cannot be used with commands to modify files, directories, processes, or sub-shell commands. The exception is when you pass a list of arguments to the functions *exec()* or *system()*; the elements of that list are not taint checked. When taint checking is turned on, it also has a few other side effects. One is that it tells Perl to ignore PERL5OPT and PERL5LIB. Because of this, this current working directory (known as ".") is not in @INC when the script runs. This does not mean that you will not be able to *use()* or *require()* modules that are installed under the directories contained in @INC. What it does mean is that if you have any modules that you keep under the directory tree of your current work-ing directory, you will have to modify @INC. Throughout this book, the way modifying @INC is done by using the "lib." compile-time pragma. You will also see @INC being modified within BEGIN blocks to remind you TIMTOWTDI (There Is More Than One Way To Do It)! All CGI scripts in this book use taint checking even if there seems to be no reason to. This is because it is good to see it used and good practice to use it.

A side note for the C and XS programmers out there: You have to explicitly set tainting on variables on XS stubs. The -T switch will not do it for you in XS. Keep this in mind when writing XS stubs to use with your CGI scripts.

2.7 Your PATH and -T

There may be times when you see an error that says "Insecure $ENV{'PATH'}" while in taint mode. This will occur when you are trying to do something with data, even nontainted data, which involves the shell. Let's revisit the taint_ex.pl script for a moment. Insert this line between lines 10 and 11.

```
system("echo $foo");
```

Now try running the script again with arguments that you know will be laundered successfully. You will see something like Listing 2-9.

Listing 2-9   **Example of taint_ex.pl laundering data**

```
%./taint_ex.pl 5555555555
$foo is tainted. Attempting to launder
$foo has been laundered!!
Insecure $ENV{PATH} while running with -T switch at ./taint_ex.pl
line 15.
```

What happened? The data was laundered before using it with *system()*! What is wrong with $foo? The answer is nothing. The variable $foo is not the problem in this case; it is $ENV{PATH}. When called in this manner, the

Perl function *system()*, if you remember from before, uses the sub-shell. When using the sub-shell it needs to know your PATH—in this case, to find the "echo" command. Because the sub-shell is getting the value of $ENV{PATH} from the user environment, it is external to the script, and the taint mode will not trust it. The resolution is to set $ENV{PATH} to something known and trusted. Before we fix this problem, let's look at something that you may think will fix this without setting $ENV{PATH} yourself. It seems like a reasonable solution to change the call to use the fully qualified path to the command, which would change the preceding line to something like this.

```
system("/bin/echo $foo");
```

If you try this, you will see that the same error is thrown. Why? Perl doesn't know if this command will call another command that is dependent on your PATH. So it doesn't allow you to inadvertently call a command that may call another that may try to do something naughty. Therefore, Perl makes you set the $ENV{PATH} environment variable in the script to make sure that you have concisely set this to something known and trusted. Now back to the example. To remedy the problem, you can change the new line to the following.

```
system "/bin/echo", $foo;
```

Now it will echo these arguments.

```
%./taint_ex.pl 5555555555
$foo is tainted. Attempting to launder
$foo has been laundered!!
5555555555
```

We'll bet you are saying to yourself right now, "Why did you tell me all that about $ENV{PATH} and then not use it to remedy the problem?" There are two reasons. First, this way shows you the safe way to use *system()*. It is always safer to pass a list of arguments to a system function like *system()* and *exec()* rather than a scalar. Second, setting $ENV{PATH} will solve the original error we saw a moment ago, but it will not produce the desired, and possibly expected, results. Take a moment and add this line before the original *system()* call that caused the error.

```
$ENV{PATH} = '/bin:/usr/bin';
```

Note that if the "echo" program does not live in /bin or /usr/bin on your system, you will want to change that accordingly. Chances are you received another error about $ENV{ENV} or some other environment variable. This is because when Perl is starting a subprocess, it checks other environment variables such as IFS, CDPATH, ENV, and BASH_ENV from the shell to see if they are empty or tainted. Not all shells use these variables. You can solve this problem by adding this line to the top of your CGI scripts.

```
delete @ENV{qw(IFS CDPATH ENV BASH_ENV)};
```

This is an option but not always a reasonable one. Try getting a team of programmers to always add this to every program they write! The more canonical way is to call *system()* and *exec()* in such a way that it will not give the shell a chance to expand characters. The best way to do that is to avoid the shell altogether. Again, passing a list of arguments to these functions instead of a string does this.

Always try to be as safe as possible when writing scripts. Think of yourself as the script, and don't trust anything given to you or how others may try to use you. To make things a little easier with laundering variables, we will use the Perl module Untaint.pm throughout this book. The Untaint.pm module is available online at *http://search.cpan.org/ search?mode=module&query=Untaint*.

2.8 Installing a Script

Now that we have covered the basics of what you need to know for the rest of the book, let's walk through a full uploading of a CGI script. First, we need a CGI script to use. Since it hasn't yet been introduced, we will now use the obligatory "Hello World" example. A "Hello World" example is in all respects a good example to use. It is quick, and easy, and it illustrates the basics of a CGI script written in Perl. Look at Listing 2-10.

Listing 2-10   **Hello World example**

```
01: #!/usr/bin/perl -wT
02: print "Content-type: text/html\n\n";
03: print "<CENTER><H2>Hello World</H2></CENTER>";
```

Line 1, the "shebang" line, will look familiar to you if you have written Perl before (or Python, shell, and so forth). One difference between non-CGI Perl scripts and CGI is that the shebang line must be present. This is so the shell knows which interpreter to use. There is no "perl script.pl" syntax with CGI as there is with the shell.

Line 2 prints out the Content-type header to the client. In this case (and more likely than not, most cases), we are sending the MIME type text/html, denoting that what is coming is HTML. The browser needs to know what type of document is being sent to it to know how to handle the incoming data.

Line 3 prints the text, Hello World, to the client browser.

Now we have our simple example script. The next step is to get our script up to the server. You may be working right on the Web server and in the HTML directory tree and do not need to transfer the file. But you may be doing it remotely, so walking through the process will be valuable. In this book, all FTPing is from the command line, the good, old-fashioned, non-GUI way. Why? Because we don't know what FTP client you are using. You will have to check your client's documentation on how to use the "site" command and make sure you upload your files in ASCII format. To reiterate, *make sure you upload your files in ASCII format*. If you upload in binary format or some other odd format that the Perl interpreter cannot understand, you will get some strange errors when you try to run the script.

```
01: % ftp 127.0.0.1
02: Connected to 127.0.0.1.
03: 220 phish FTP server (Version 6.00) ready.
04: Name (127.0.0.1:kevin):
05: 331 Password required for kevin.
06: Password:
07: 230 User kevin logged in.
08: Remote system type is UNIX.
09: Using binary mode to transfer files.
```

Lines 1–9 are the login process.

```
10: ftp> ascii
11: 200 Type set to A.
```

Lines 10 and 11 set the transfer mode to ASCII (A) so we know that the file will be properly uploaded.

```
12: ftp> cd /usr/local/apache/htdocs/book/c2
13: 250 CWD command successful.
```

Lines 12 and 13 change directories to where the CGI script will live.

```
14: ftp> put hello.pl
15: local: hello.pl remote: hello.pl
16: 200 PORT command successful.
17: 150 Opening ASCII mode data connection for 'hello.pl'.
18: 100%       81         --:-- ETA
19: 226 Transfer complete.
20: 81 bytes sent in 0.00 seconds (42.97 KB/s)
```

Lines 14–20 use the FTP put command to transfer the file to the server.

```
21: ftp> ls
22: 200 PORT command successful.
23: 150 Opening ASCII mode data connection for '/bin/ls'.
24: total 1
25: -rw-r--r--  1 kevin  wheel  78 Dec 27 16:52 hello.pl
26: 226 Transfer complete.
```

Lines 21–26 do a directory listing to show that the transfer worked as well as what the permissions of the file are (for example, purposes).

```
27: ftp> site chmod 755 hello.pl
28: 200 CHMOD command successful.
```

Lines 27 and 28 change the permissions of the file from 644 to 755 with the chmod via the FTP site command.

```
29: ftp> ls
30: 200 PORT command successful.
31: 150 Opening ASCII mode data connection for '/bin/ls'.
32: total 1
33: -rwxr-xr-x  1 kevin  wheel  78 Dec 27 16:52 hello.pl
34: 226 Transfer complete.
```

Lines 29–34 do another directory listing to verify that the chmod took place.

```
35: ftp> bye
36: 221 Goodbye.
```

Lines 35 and 36 quit the session.

Next, we . . . oh, wait! That's all! So next we look at it from our Web browser (see Figure 2-1).

Figure 2-1   **Screenshot of the Hello World example**

2.9 Troubleshooting

It's a fact of a programmer's life: When you develop, you make a few errors along the way. When debugging Perl scripts that are run from the command line, you get instant gratification. If your script has an error, you see it on your console right away. However, when you have an error generated from a Perl/CGI script being run via a HTTP request, you don't, by default, get an extremely useful error message in the client. Plus there are really two levels of errors that can occur. There are errors that could have occurred from the Perl script or from the Web server.

When doing CGI (and Perl in general), one huge rule of thumb to program by is to run Perl with warnings turned on (with -w switch). This way the errors will be sent to the Web server's error log. For example, let us revisit the simple Hello World example we saw in Listing 2-10 and slightly change it so it contains a small syntax error.

Listing 2-11   **Hello World with a syntax error**

```
01: #!/usr/bin/perl -wT
02: print "Content-type: text/html\n\n";
03: print "<CENTER><H2>Hello World</H2></CENTER>;
```

As you can see in Listing 2-11, we removed the final quote from the third line. This type of syntax error in a CGI script will display the error (on Apache) shown in Figure 2-2. This error is quite vague and not very helpful in debugging. What exactly is an Internal Server Error? Is there a misconfiguration in the server, as the message would lead you to believe, or did something fail in the Perl script? The only place to look is the error log for the Web server. Listing 2-12 shows the relevant entry in the server error log.

Figure 2-2   **Screenshot of vague server error**

Listing 2-12   **Hello World syntax error in error log**

```
01: Can't find string terminator '"' anywhere before EOF at /usr/
    local/apache/htdocs/cgi-bin/hello_world.pl line 4.
02: [Wed Feb 16 22:07:08 2000] [error] [client 127.0.0.1]
    Premature end of script headers: /usr/local/apache/htdocs/
    cgi-bin/hello_world.pl
```

The error in the error log may look a little more informative. This is a run-of-the-mill syntax error and will appear in the error log regardless of whether you have warnings turned on or not. As you can see, **line 1** shows what the syntax error is, which is an error generated by Perl. **Line 2** is the error generated from the Web server. When there is a Perl error in the error log (which always precedes the server error), then the Perl script is what needs to be fixed, as opposed to looking for a server misconfiguration.

Viewing the error log is helpful, but it would be nice to be able to see the error in the browser rather than always having to view the error log. Viewing the error log for each and every error can become somewhat cumbersome, especially when doing some extensive debugging. But there is a way to display fatal errors directly to the browser. This can be accomplished by using the CGI::Carp module (installed when CGI.pm is installed) by Lincoln Stein. This module has a method, *fatalsToBrowser()*, that when imported will echo all fatal errors to the browser as well as to the Web server log.

Now let's take a look at the Hello World example again, this time using CGI::Carp (see Listing 2-13). By doing this, it can become much easier to do debugging because you can get some of that instant gratification a programmer so desperately wants! Figure 2-3 shows the error displayed to the browser when the new Hello World example is now run.

Listing 2-13 **Hello World, with syntax error and CGI::Carp.**

```
01: #!/usr/bin/perl -wT
02: use CGI::Carp qw(fatalsToBrowser);
03: print "Content-type: text/html\n\n";
04: print "<CENTER><H2>Hello World</H2></CENTER>;
```

Figure 2-3 **Screenshot of CGI::Carp error**

Now that's a little more like it! You can immediately see the error without having to look at the error log. If you *were* to look at the error log, you would see something missing. You would not see an error generated by the

Web server. This is because *fatalsToBrowser()* sends a minimal amount of HTTP headers to the browser so the server will not stop the process on an error. It also needs to do this in order to somewhat override the server error that would normally be generated. But, remember, this method does exactly what its name implies. It only sends fatal errors to the browser, although it will still help you to know what may be causing the error as far as it being a Perl error or a Web server error. We use CGI::Carp throughout this book because it can be a terrific way to debug and display somewhat useful error messages when needed. Although CGI::Carp is great for debugging, it can reveal a lot more information than the world needs to know. Because of this, you may want to disable it in a production environment.

One question repeatedly seen on CGI mailing lists is "I get a server error when I run my CGI, but it runs fine from the command line! What gives?" It does occasionally happen that a script runs from the command line but not as a CGI. It is important to remember that when Perl is being run as a CGI, it is running in a different environment from when it is being run from the command line with the environment of a normal user account. However, the environment is not the problem—at least in the majority of cases we have seen. Instead, it is from the improper displaying of HTTP headers. Let's revisit the Hello World script again. Listing 2-14 shows hello_world.pl with a small error. The error is not a Perl syntax error and not an error in the usage of a Perl function. In fact, it isn't a Perl error at all! However, it is something, that causes a server error. First, take a look at Listing 2-13.

Listing 2-14 **Hello World, with server error**

```
01: #!/usr/bin/perl -wT
02: use CGI::Carp qw(fatalsToBrowser);
03: print "Content-type: text/html\n";
04: print "<CENTER><H2>Hello World</H2></CENTER>";
```

Did you spot the error in Listing 2-14? In **line 3** there is only one \n. This would cause the server error, but it would run fine from the command line. Whenever you are displaying HTML to the browser, you need to show the Content-type (which is the MIME type), followed by two (2) new line (\n) characters. This is needed as explained in RFC2616, the HTTP/1.1 RFC.

One way to troubleshoot CGI scripts is by trying to run them from the command line. This seems almost natural to do if you have been programming Perl for some time. Debugging this way is very practical, but it may not always be the best option. Depending on what your CGI script is doing, you may not retrieve the results you are expecting. This is mostly true if you are using anything from the Web server's environment (see Chapter 4) that doesn't exist in your own. Environment variables will be discussed at length in Chapter 4.

Throughout this book we use the CGI.pm module for doing things like getting input from Web forms. You will learn more about using CGI.pm, as well as using forms, in Chapter 5, but for the upcoming illustration, it would be helpful for you to know that the CGI.pm method param() handles getting form input for you.

Listing 2-15   **Hello World, with form input**

```
01: #!/usr/bin/perl -wT
02: use CGI qw(:cgi);
03: use CGI::Carp qw(fatalsToBrowser);
04: my $input = param('input');
05: print "Content-type: text/html\n\n";
06: print "<CENTER><H2>$input</H2></CENTER>";
```

Listing 2-15 is another altered version of our once simple Hello World example. In this case, it is expecting to receive form input, namely a form field named "input." If you were to run this from the command line to test or debug, CGI.pm would put you in "offline mode," meaning that you are not running this script as CGI. When you do this, you will see something like Listing 2-16.

Listing 2-16   **Running a CGI script with CGI.pm in offline mode**

```
% ./hello_world.pl
(offline mode: enter name=value pairs on standard input)
input=hello
<EOF>
Content-type: text/html
```

To enter the name value pairs, you would then type them as "name=value", hit Enter, and then use the appropriate EOF (End Of File) for your platform. This is ^D (Cntrl-D) on UNIX systems and ^Z (Cntrl-Z) on Win32 systems. Listing 2-17 shows this with the Hello World script shown in Listing 2-15.

Listing 2-17   **Full example of Hello World example using CGI.pm in offline mode**

```
% ./hello_world.pl
Content-type: text/html
(offline mode: enter name=value pairs on standard input)
input="Hello World"
^D
<H2><CENTER>Hello World</H2></CENTER>
```

One last thing you will want to keep in mind when testing CGI scripts from the command line is that you do not want to use any runtime interpreter switches but rather just run the script itself. This is because, being CGI, you have given the interpreter switches in the shebang line. Actually, you can give interpreter switches, but if you are turning on taint checking in the shebang line (which you should be) and you do not invoke the interpreter from the command line with -T as well, you will get an error. This is because when you run a Perl script from the command line in this fashion

```
% perl -<some switch> script.pl
```

the Perl interpreter will examine the #! line of the script and use any switches it sees that you meant to use.

So if your #! line looks like this.

```
#!/usr/bin/perl -w
```

And you run Perl like this.

```
% perl script.p
```

It will run the script with warnings because it sees that you want it to from the #! line. But if your #! line looks like this.

```
#!/usr/bin/perl -wT
```

And you run Perl like this.

```
% perl script.pl
```

The Perl interpreter will see that you wanted to run the script in taint mode. But because you did not, it feels it is too late to safely provide taint mode, and it aborts. One thing about -T is that it is really designed to protect setuid programs, not CGI. Because of this, there is a lot of protection that makes more sense in the context of a setuid program.

Another good way to test your CGI scripts (well, all Perl scripts really) from the command line is by using the -c switch when invoking Perl. This switch will check the syntax for your script without actually executing it. This can help you see if a script has a syntax error and what that error may be. Keep in mind that if your script has BEGIN or END blocks, they will be executed because Perl considers these to be outside the execution of the script. This is true for versions of Perl before 5.6, but as of version 5.6, only the BEGIN block will be executed when using the -c switch. Here is example output from a script that has good syntax. If you did this with a script with bad syntax, it would display the syntax error.

```
% perl -cwT script.cgi
script.cgi syntax OK
```

A final suggestion is to use the *diagnostics* pragma to see more verbose warning messages, especially if you are somewhat new to Perl. By default, this pragma will enable -w and display verbose messages based on warnings that -w throws. The text it uses is from the perldiag manpage. Here is an example output when debugging the following simple script from the command line using the *diagnostics* pragma.

```
#!/usr/bin/perl -wT
print "hello
```

Assuming the preceding script is called script.cgi, here is the output.

```
% perl -Mdiagnostics -T script.cgi
Can't find string terminator '"' anywhere before EOF at
script.cgi line 3 (#1)
    (F) Perl strings can stretch over multiple lines.  This
message means that the closing delimiter was omitted.  Because
bracketed quotes count nesting levels, the following is missing
its final parenthesis:
        print q(The character '(' starts a side comment.);
    If you're getting this error from a here-document, you may
    have included unseen whitespace before or after your closing
    tag. A good programmer's editor will have a way to help you
    find these characters.
Uncaught exception from user code:
Can't find string terminator '"' anywhere before EOF at
script.cgi line 3.
```

2.10 Caching

Web caching is a way to help reduce network traffic over the Web as well as help people browsing the Web to retrieve some documents in a more timely manner. With so many people on the Internet today, there is only a certain amount of network bandwidth available for everyone to use. This can be especially true on internal networks that also connect to the Internet via a proxy server. With so many people trying to get requests out and their information back in limited bandwidth, things can really slow down. This is when you hear people saying things like "The Internet is slow!" Caching is a way to help curve this problem. A cache, whether it is a browser cache or a server cache, will "save" a copy of documents that were requested from the Internet. By doing this, the document can later be served by showing the end user a local cached copy rather than going out to the network to retrieve the entire document again and again. In this section we will discuss both browser cache and server cache and how to make sure that your documents are not cached.

This is all important when writing CGI applications because there may be some times when a page is reloaded and the information didn't change as you expected it would. For example, in Chapter 7 you will learn different ways to count hit to Web pages. There may be a time when you reload a page, expecting to have seen the counter increment, but it doesn't. Don't worry, it isn't broken! This could be because the page is being displayed to you from a cache, and it wasn't actually re-requested from the Web server. At the end of this section we will show you how to ensure that the results of CGI scripts are not cached. First, it is important that we discuss the differences between browser cache and server cache.

Browser caching is when the Web browser itself caches what an end user is viewing on the Internet. All of the major Web browsers use both disk and memory caching and give an end user a way to allocate resources for each type of caching. Disk cache is when the browser saves the files (text and image) in a directory on the hard drive. Memory cache is when it uses RAM to store the information, as opposed to writing it to disk. Browser caching is very useful to the end user. For example, if you visit a site several times during the day—let's say a Web site that gives you news—it would be a waste of time and bandwidth if the browser had to retrieve data from that site each and every time the page is refreshed (if the data hasn't expired)[3]. With caching, the browser knows when it should retrieve updated information from the remote Web server only if the data is stale.[4]

Server caching works on the same principles as browser caching, except that it is meant to be used by multiple browsers instead of just one. Many times companies set up caching on their Internet proxy servers. By doing this, the server keeps a cache of what users are requesting and can send back the data to the end user in the same fashion that the browser cache does. This greatly helps in reducing network traffic and latency. Proxy caches are shared caches because all the users going through that proxy are using the cache. The best place to look to configure caching on your Web browser or Web proxy is by looking at their included documentation.

Now that you have a general idea of what caching is, let's take a look at how to make sure that you know how to stop proxies and browsers from caching documents you don't want them to. Why would you want this to

---

3. Expired data is considered "stale," and nonexpired data is considered "fresh."
4. Check your Web browser for various settings on when it should look for updated information or to not cache at all.

happen? If you have a page (or pages) that change frequently, you want to ensure that visitors will always see the latest updates. Or if you change images on your Web page frequently, you may want to be sure that these images are loaded whenever the end user wants to view your page.[5] One way many people consider effective for not having a page cached is by using an HTML META tag such as "Pragma: no-cache." This is not an effective way to make sure that pages aren't cached because proxy caches will not see this HTML. A proxy does not read HTML, so your efforts will be subverted. However, the browser cache is likely to not cache the document because it does read the HTML. One out of two isn't good enough. If you want your documents not to be cached, you want to make sure that both proxies and browsers obey. The best way to do this is by using HTTP headers. There are two important things you can set in a HTTP header: Expires and Cache-Control.[6]

Before we look at those, we just want to mention what happens with caching and Secure (SSL) and protected documents. Secure documents (using SSL) are neither cached nor decrypted by proxy caches. Web pages that are accessed through HTTP Authentication are generally marked as private and therefore not cached by shared caches (proxy cache). There is, however, a way via the Cache-Control header to allow for secure documents to be cached, which will be covered in a moment. To recap this issue, SSL documents will not be decrypted or cached, and secure documents are not cached by default, but they can be.

2.10.1 The Expires HTTP Header

The **Expires** HTTP header is used to tell a cache when a document is to be considered stale. This way the browser knows that it needs to check back to the origin server to see if the document has been changed. The Expires part of a header takes a date as a value. When you want to ensure that your document is not going to be cached, you want to set a past date. This way, when the browser or proxy looks at the header, it will see that the document isn't fresh, and it will not cache it. A valid Expired entry would look like the following.

```
Expires: Fri, 31 Dec 1990 23:59:59 GMT
```

As you may notice, this time is in Greenwich Mean Time (GMT), not your local time. If you wanted to make sure that your document is cached until a certain date, you could set a future date. This is a very useful way to either avoid or ensure that your documents are cached.

---

5. Check the documentation of your Web server on how to set up caching of individual objects, such as images and text.
6. If you do not have control of your Web server and those who do have not given you a way to set HTTP headers, you may want to encourage them to allow this.

2.10.2 Cache-Control HTTP Header

With the introduction of HTTP 1.1, a new header was brought into the mix: Cache-Control. This useful header gives developers a better way to not only tell a cache whether to cache a document but how to handle the document.[7] Because this is discussed in great detail in the HTTP 1.1 Specification, we will cover only a few of the relevant Cache-Control directives.

```
max-age=[seconds]
s-maxage=[seconds]
```

The *max-age* directive sets the number of seconds for which this document is to stay fresh from the time it was originally requested. This is somewhat similar to the Expires header, except that it is done in seconds and it is from the time of the request, not a certain date. The *s-maxage* directive is the same except it only applies to shared caches.

```
no-cache
```

This directive tells the cache not to cache this document, and the request must be validated *every* time from the origin server. We haven't discussed validation yet. A Web cache validates a document by (currently) checking the Last-Modified time of the document and by using an If-Modified-Since request to see if the document on the origin server is fresher than the one in the cache. If it is not, it shows you what is in cache; if it is, then the fresher version is retrieved. So using this will ensure that visitors to your site always see the latest you have to offer. Keep in mind that the document is still physically being cached, but the cache must first look to the origin server for a fresher document before releasing the one from cache.

```
public
```

This tells a cache that it may cache the document even though it normally wouldn't, such as if it were a secure document. By using this directive in conjunction with *no-cache*, you can allow your secure documents to be caches but force the client to reauthenticate itself by having to check the If-Last-Modified on the origin server each time. By doing this, the authentication challenge/response will happen and the cached document will not be shown to an unauthenticated client.

Now that you know what needs to be in the header of a document in order to have it not cache (or in order to make sure it caches, for that matter) let us take a look at a sample HTTP header. See Listing 2-18.

---

7. The Cache-Control directive is discussed in great detail in the HTTP 1.1 Specifications in RFC2626, section 14.9.

Listing 2-18 Example HTTP Header

```
HTTP/1.1 200 OK
Date: Fri, 31 Dec 1999 23:59:59 GMT
Server: Apache/1.3.11 (Unix)
Cache-Control: no-cache, public
Expires: Wed, 31 Dec 1980 23:59:59 GMT
Last-Modified: Fri, 31 Dec 1999 23:59:59 GMT
Content-Length: 1040
Content-Type: text/html
```

In the header shown in Listing 10-18, you will notice we are sending an HTML document and do not want it cached. In Listing 2-10 you saw how to print out part of a header. You can take what you learned thus far to print out a header, or you will learn later in the book how to use CGI.pm to do much of this for you.

2.11 Listings

Listing 2-19 Command line laundering example. taint_ex.pl

```
01: #!/usr/bin/perl -wT
02: use strict;
03: my $foo = join('',@ARGV);
04: if (is_tainted($foo)) {
05:        print "\$foo is tainted. Attempting to launder\n";
06:        my $pattern = qr(^\d{3}(-|\s+)?\d{3}(-|\s+)?\d{4}$)
07:        $foo = untaint($foo, $pattern);
08: }else{
09:        print "\$foo is not tainted!!\n";
10: }
11: sub is_tainted {
12:        my $check = shift;
13:        return  !eval { $check++, kill 0;1;};
14: }
15: sub untaint {
16:        my ($foo, $pattern) = @_;
17:        if ($foo =~ /($pattern)/) {
18:                $foo = $1;
19:                print "\$foo has been laundered!!\n";
20:                return $foo;
21:        }else{
```

(continued)

```
22:                    print "Unable to launder \$foo\n";
23:                    return $foo;
24:            }
25: }
```

Listing 2-20 **Example FTP session**

```
01: % ftp 127.0.0.1
02: Connected to 127.0.0.1.
03: 220 phish FTP server (Version 6.00) ready.
04: Name (127.0.0.1:kevin):
05: 331 Password required for kevin.
06: Password:
07: 230 User kevin logged in.
08: Remote system type is UNIX.
09: Using binary mode to transfer files.
10: ftp> ascii
11: 200 Type set to A.
12: ftp> cd /usr/local/apache/htdocs/book/c2
13: 250 CWD command successful.
14: ftp> put hello.pl
15: local: hello.pl remote: hello.pl
16: 200 PORT command successful.
17: 150 Opening ASCII mode data connection for 'hello.pl'.
18: 100%        81        --:-- ETA
19: 226 Transfer complete.
20: 81 bytes sent in 0.00 seconds (42.97 KB/s)
21: ftp> ls
22: 200 PORT command successful.
23: 150 Opening ASCII mode data connection for '/bin/ls'.
24: total 1
25: -rw-r--r--  1 kevin  wheel  78 Dec 27 16:52 hello.pl
26: 226 Transfer complete.
27: ftp> site chmod 755 hello.pl
28: 200 CHMOD command successful.
29: ftp> ls
30: 200 PORT command successful.
31: 150 Opening ASCII mode data connection for '/bin/ls'.
32: total 1
33: -rwxr-xr-x  1 kevin  wheel  78 Dec 27 16:52 hello.pl
34: 226 Transfer complete.
35: ftp> bye
36: 221 Goodbye.
```

3

Chapter

Using Your Environment

3.1 Introduction to %ENV

Environment variables are hidden values that the Web server makes available to CGI scripts. When the Web server is started, it runs in its own environment, which includes, and creates, these variables. This means that the Web server has information about the running process that it uses to serve requests. A partial list of server environment variables is in Appendix B, but it is recommended that you also read your Web server documentation to see what default environment variables it may provide. The Web client also provides some data to the Web server, which is then stored as environment variables on the server. Exactly what the server does with any of these environment variables is not within the scope of this book. Rather, this book explains how you can retrieve, use, and set these variables from your CGI scripts. You can utilize all these environment variables in your scripts to use information about the visitor (Web client), the request that has been made, and the Web server itself.

What exactly is an "environment"? You may be familiar with environments from your shell that hold information such as your PATH, HOME, EDITOR, and so forth and create the environment in which you work. To make another, less technical analogy, think of your workspace as your environment. My "shell" at work is like my cubicle. In the "process" of work, I have various things that make up my environment, such as my telephone number, mail stop, desk, lighting, computer, chair, and supplies. You can consider all these things that make up my environment as my environment variables. Some of these variables will not change, such as my telephone number, computer, mail stop, and desk. Others may change when needed, such as the supplies I use, the lighting, or my chair. This is just like the Web server environment and its environment variables. It has a known set of environment variables that may (lighting) or may not (telephone number) change. Some are used more than others (I use my computer more than my pen), and some are used almost all the time (like my chair).

Some information in the environment is determined when the Web server starts, such as SERVER_NAME, and will not change while the Web server is running. Some environment variables are determined by the Web server itself, such as the server's name and software. A few of the variables are determined from the user under which the server process runs (usually as user *nobody*), such as PATH. Other variables are determined from information passed from the Web client to the server—for example, the user agent and remote IP. Environment variables created by data passed to the Web server by the client are always information about the client itself. Keep in mind that Web clients can be dishonest about the information they are sending you. They may not do this deliberately, but people create their own custom clients to modify this information. This is not necessarily an issue for the run-of-the-mill Web site, but it is good to remember that this information *can* be faked. No matter how environment variables are set, it is available to you to use and modify. The environment is also available for you to add new variables when needed, just like your shell does.

What good are the environment variables if you do not know what they are? Well, not a whole lot of good, so let's write a script that will display the Web server's environment variables to the browser. Something new in this script will be the %ENV hash. This is the hash that Perl uses to store all of the environment variables it has available. The keys of %ENV are names of the environment variables, and the corresponding values are the current value of that key. Note that %ENV always contains the current values. We use the term "current" because you may change these values for the life of your script. If you do make any changes to %ENV, those changes will be made available to any child processes created as part of their respective environments, but changes in the child environment will not affect the parent. If you are familiar with programming Perl in the shell, you should already be familiar with %ENV to some extent. To view your user's environment variables, type the following at the command prompt.

```
% perl -e 'print qq($_ - $ENV{$_}\n) foreach sort keys %ENV'
```

Now, let's CGIify the above one-liner. The example in Listing 3-1 displays the environment variables of the Web server to the Web client.

Listing 3-1   CGI script to display environment variables

```
01: #!/usr/bin/perl -wT
02: $|=1;
03: print "Content-type: text/html\n\n";
04: print <<HTML;
05: <HTML>
06: <HEAD>
07: <TITLE>Server Environment</TITLE>
08: </HEAD>
09: <CENETR><H2>Server Environment</H2></CENTER>
10: <BODY>
11: HTML
12: print qq($_ - $ENV{$_}<BR>) for sort keys %ENV;
13: print qq(
14: </BODY>
15: </HTML>
16: );
```

Line 1 is our ever-present shebang line to tell the program where it will find Perl. We also have warnings turned on with the -w switch. Although the -w switch may not be needed for this simple script, it is just a good habit to use it. Habit is the same reason that the -T, taint checking, switch is on. It is a much better, and safer, practice to have too much security and warnings at the beginning and then, after testing, relax security where appropriate. Generally, it is better practice to use as much security persuasions as you can when using CGI.

Line 2 will autoflush the buffer so we can see the results as they occur.

Line 3 prints the header's Content Type information to the Web client. This will tell the client to expect a file whose content is composed of text in HTML format.

Line 4 starts a here document with "HTML" as the delimiter.

Lines 5–10 are lines of HTML being printed from within the here document.

Line 11 is the here document terminator. Remember that this must appear on a line by itself and at the beginning of the line.

Line 12 is what does the work. It prints all of the key/value pairs in %ENV. We are listing the pairs in sorted order for easier reading.

Lines 13–16 are a *print()* statement that closes out the HTML <BODY> and <HTML> tags.

When you point your browser to this CGI script, you will see something similar to Figure 3-1.

Figure 3-1   Screenshot of environment variables

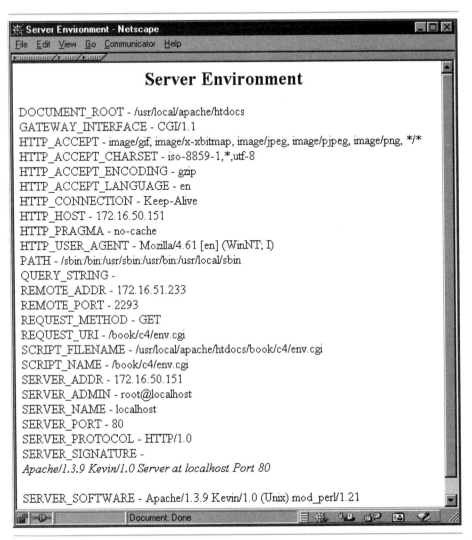

```
Server Environment - Netscape

File  Edit  View  Go  Communicator  Help

                    Server Environment

DOCUMENT_ROOT - /usr/local/apache/htdocs
GATEWAY_INTERFACE - CGI/1.1
HTTP_ACCEPT - image/gif, image/x-xbitmap, image/jpeg, image/pjpeg, image/png, */*
HTTP_ACCEPT_CHARSET - iso-8859-1,*,utf-8
HTTP_ACCEPT_ENCODING - gzip
HTTP_ACCEPT_LANGUAGE - en
HTTP_CONNECTION - Keep-Alive
HTTP_HOST - 172.16.50.151
HTTP_PRAGMA - no-cache
HTTP_USER_AGENT - Mozilla/4.61 [en] (WinNT; I)
PATH - /sbin:/bin:/usr/sbin:/usr/bin:/usr/local/sbin
QUERY_STRING -
REMOTE_ADDR - 172.16.51.233
REMOTE_PORT - 2293
REQUEST_METHOD - GET
REQUEST_URI - /book/c4/env.cgi
SCRIPT_FILENAME - /usr/local/apache/htdocs/book/c4/env.cgi
SCRIPT_NAME - /book/c4/env.cgi
SERVER_ADDR - 172.16.50.151
SERVER_ADMIN - root@localhost
SERVER_NAME - localhost
SERVER_PORT - 80
SERVER_PROTOCOL - HTTP/1.0
SERVER_SIGNATURE -
Apache/1.3.9 Kevin/1.0 Server at localhost Port 80

SERVER_SOFTWARE - Apache/1.3.9 Kevin/1.0 (Unix) mod_perl/1.21

Document: Done
```

3.2 Adding to %ENV

There may be times that you want to add something to your environment
or create your own environment variables. For the most part, this would be
most useful when there is information that should be shared with multiple
scripts or every script. There are two ways to do this easily. The first way is
by creating an environment variable from your Web server's configuration
file. With Apache this can be in the httpd.conf file with SetENV directive.

From your favorite text editor, you would open the httpd.conf file and add the directive with this syntax.

```
SetENV variable value
```

After adding this, you will want to restart your Web server for the new environment to take effect. Keep this in mind because whenever you make changes to your Apache configuration files, you will need to restart the server for them to take effect.

A real-life example of using a predefined environment variable in this manner may be when you have a database that is used by many of your scripts or there are multiple databases used. Let's assume there is a team of programmers, and you do not want them to be concerned about the names and locations of certain databases while writing their scripts. Or maybe you are the only developer and do not want to concern yourself with this static information. To be able to ignore this information, it is much easier to have an environment variable predefined from within the Web server configuration. Many times you will come across the situation where there is a database used to keep management information or "Server A" and another database for another department like sales located on "Server B." The sales database may be named *sales_info*, which resides on the remote server *sales-server*, and the management database is named *manager_info*, which resides on the remote server *manager-server*. Knowing this information, we can create environment variables that hold this information like the following.

```
SetENV SALESDB sales_info@sales-server
SetENV MANDB manager_info@manager-server
```

After restarting the server, %ENV will contain these two new name-value pairs for use in CGI scripts. To continue with the preceding example, we will assume that these databases are MySQL databases and that the DBI.pm module is being used to connect to them. In order to help make a programmer's life easier, this is the perfect time to create a module that will contain the code that does the connections to the database using DBI. The focus of this chapter isn't DBI, but it is important that you see how to use the environment in a real world way. Using the Perl DBI is covered in more detail later in this book.

```
01: package MyConnect;
```

Line 1 declares the package name for the module—in this case, MyConnect. The file's name is therefore going to be MyPackage.pm. When declaring a package name like this, the name of the file is always the main class's name with the .pm file extension.

```
02: use DBI;
03: use strict;
```

Lines 2 and 3 use the strict pragma to turn on compiler restrictions as well
as use the DBI module, which is going to handle the handshaking and dirty
work between the Perl script and database.

```
04: sub salesDB {
```

Line 4 begins the salesDB method.

```
05:    my ($sales_dbname, $sales_dbhost) = split(/\@/
          ,$ENV{'SALESDB'});
```

Line 5 creates two variables, $sales_dbname and $sales_dbhost, which will
house the names of the database name and host server, respectively. This is
also where the new environment variable comes into play. Because the new
%ENV value called SALESDB was created, this value may now be obtained
the same way as any other hash value. This value is being split on the @
character, which was used to separate the database name and host name.

```
06:    my $sales_dsn = "DBI:mysql:database=
              $sales_dbname;host=$sales_dbhost";
```

Line 6 is creating a data source name (DSN), whose format is defined by
the DBI module and stored in the variable $sales_dsn. The makeup of a
DSN is the following:

DBI:<Driver Name>:database=<Database Name>;host=<Host of Database>

This information is used by the DBI module to know what machine the
database is on, what the name of that database is, and what type of database it is. But it isn't just saying what type of database it is but which driver
to use to connect to it—in our case, the driver for MySQL. There are drivers
for most RDMS written in Perl (these drivers can be found on CPAN under
the DBD namespace). DBI is a very useful module because it basically
allows you to install a driver and simply name that driver in the DSN definition. Everything else is transparent to the programmer. For example, we
are using MySQL, but you may use Oracle or possibly Informix. You could
simply install the DBD::Oracle driver (which itself is a Perl module), change
the DSN to point to the Oracle or Informix driver instead of the MySQL
driver, and be on your merry way. The DBI module is invaluable when it
comes to database interaction using Perl. The module itself has extensive
documentation, which we suggest you take the time to read, as some of its
functionality will not be used in this book but you may find helpful.

```
07:    my $sales_dbh=DBI->connect($sales_dsn, "username",
                                    "password");
```

Line 7 makes the connection to the database, and the database handle (DBH) is stored in the $sales_dbh scalar. This DBH is a pointer, or cursor, to the open connection to the database. Think of the *connect()* method opening as a doorway into the database. The $sales_dbh variable is a way to get in and out of that doorway.

```
08: if (!defined($sales_dbh)) {
09:    print "\nerror: There is a problem connecting to the MySQL
           database:\n";
10:    print DBI->errstr;
11:    print "-" x 25 . "\n";
12:    return;
13: }
```

Lines 8–13 do a little error checking. The DBI::connect method returns undef if it fails. **Line 8** checks to see if the connection failed, and if it did, there will be a message displayed stating what the connection error is.

```
14:    return $sales_dbh;
```

Line 14 returns the variable "holding" the database connection. This will allow the external script calling the *SalesDB()* method to assign a variable the value of the returned DBH, $sales_dbh in this case.

```
15: }
```

Line 15 closes the *SalesDB()* method.

```
16: 1;
```

Line 16 returns a true value to any script that use()'s it. This is necessary, and an error would be given if the script did not return a true value.

Here is how to use this module and the database connection it created from another script, sales.cgi, shown in Listing 3-2.

Listing 3-2   Example of using module to make database connection

```
01: #!/usr/bin/perl -wT
02: # sales.cgi
```

```
03: $|=1;
04: use strict;
05: use lib qw(.);
06: use MyConnect;
07: my $sales_dbh = MyConnect->salesDB;
08: my $sales_sth = $sales_dbh->prepare("SELECT * FROM table where
                                        ID='5' ORDER BY date");
09: $sales_sth->execute;
10: etc...
```

Line 1 is the ever-present shebang line to tell the program where it will find Perl. We also have warnings turned on with the -w switch and are in taint check mode. Although the -w switch may not be needed for this simple script, it is just a good habit to use it until your move into the production environment.

Line 2 is the name of this script.

Line 3 autoflushes the buffer so we can see the results as they occur.

Line 4 turns on compiler restrictions with the strict pragma.

Line 5 does something very important. When taint checking is turned on, as explained in Chapter 2, one of the effects is that it removes the current working directory (.) from @INC, the array that contains the include directories. lib.pm is a compile time pragma, much like strict.pm. When it is use()'d it accepts a list of directories and adds those directories to @INC. This is needed because MyConnect.pm is currently located in the current working directory, and there must be a way of making sure that Perl will see it. Using lib to modify @INC in this script is considered idiomatic and is recommended when using taint checking in CGI.

Line 6 use()s the MyConnect module that we just created. Now we will be able to use our connection method.

Line 7 calls the method, *salesDB()*, we created in MyConnect.pm and assigns the returned value to the variable $sales_dbh. Now we will be able to use that connection in the main script because the module returned, or passed back, the DBH.

Line 8 is an example prepare() of a query, which is stored in a new variable $sales_sth, commonly used for denoting a statement handle (STH). The prepare() method readies a query for execution.

Line 9 executes the query on *sales_info* on the server sales-server.

Line 10–??? is where the rest of your code would go.

We will leave it as an exercise for you, the reader, to create a second method in the MyConnect module that connects to the manager database.

3.3 Form Input Primer

In the next chapter you will learn in detail how to process forms with CGI, sending them to the browser and manipulating the information they return. However, learning about environment variables wouldn't be complete if one of the most common uses for them wasn't shown. This is getting form input using the QUERY_STRING environment variable. This variable contains the query that is being sent to the CGI. For example, consider the following form in Listing 3-3.

Listing 3-3   HTML Form

```
<FORM ACTION="/cgi-bin/query_string.cgi" METHOD="GET">
    First Name: <INPUT TYPE="text" NAME="fname" SIZE=20><P>
    Last Name: <INPUT TYPE="text" NAME="lname" SIZE=20><P>
    <INPUT TYPE="submit" VALUE="Submit">
</FORM>
```

When this form is submitted, it will go to the URL.

```
http://your.domain.com/cgi-bin/query_string.cgi?fname=
                        Joseph&lname=Hall
```

Of course, it would have the values you submitted, not necessarily Joseph and Hall. When this is submitted, the server takes the query part, everything after the ?, of the URL, and puts it into $ENV{'QUERY_STRING'}. This value would look like the following.

```
fname=Joseph&lname=Hall
```

The methods GET and POST will be explained in the next chapter, since they do not work the same way or both use QUERY_STRING. But, for the time being you can create some forms to see how the data submitted via the GET method is read and displayed. This example script illustrates how to parse the QUERY_STRING into their appropriate name/value pairs. Listing 3-4 is query_string.cgi to go along with the preceding HTML form.

Listing 3-4   Example of parsing QUERY_STRING by hand

```
01: #!/usr/bin/perl -wT
02: use strict;
03: print "Content-type:text/html\n\n";
04: my %FORM;
```

```
05: my @pairs = split(/&/, $ENV{'QUERY_STRING'});
06: foreach  (@pairs) {
07:    my ($name, $value) = split(/=/, $_);
08:    $value =~ tr/+/ /;
09:    $value =~ s/%([a-fA-F0-9][a-fA-F0-9])/pack("C", hex($1))/eg;
10:    $FORM{$name} = $value;
11: }
12: print <<HTML;
13: <HTML>
14:    <HEAD><TITLE>Form Output</TITLE></HEAD>
15: <BODY BGCOLOR="#ffffff">
16: <CENTER><H3>Form Output</H3></CENTER>
17: <P>
18: HTML
19: foreach  (keys %FORM) {
20:    print "$_ = $FORM{$_}<BR>";
21: }
22: print <<HTML;
23:    </BODY>
24:    </HTML>
25: HTML
```

Most of what is in Listing 3-4 should look familiar except for lines 5 through 10, so we will concentrate on those.

Line 5 performs a split on QUERY_STRING, which, again, looks like name=val&name2=val2&name3=val3 and so on. This split statement splits this line into name/value pairs by splitting on the & and adding each pair as an element in the @pairs array. Each element in the array will look like name=val.

Line 6 starts a loop to process each of the name/value pairs in @pairs.

Line 7 splits the elements by the =, and two variables are created with the pairs name and value, respectively.

Line 8 handles the URI decoding. When information is sent via forms, in the background they will be URI-encoded. This topic will be covered in more detail in the next chapter, but in a nutshell, this means that certain characters will be turned into their hexadecimal counterpart that the Web server sends to the CGI script. A list of these characters is in Appendix D. Here all + signs are being transliterated into spaces.

Line 9 is also doing URI-decoding but with a slightly more involved regular expression. This line takes all of the hex values (%HH) and translates them back to their ASCII value using *pack()*, which returns the string in a binary structure. When this is done, the $value variable will be in the exact form that the user submitted.

Line 10 adds the name/value pair to the hash %FORM. You could do whatever you wanted to with the pair (for example, put them into an array or other data structure), but adding it to a hash like this makes it easy to retrieve values later on.

Line 11 is where the loop ends.

The preceding example demonstrates how to parse incoming form data "by hand." Of course, in Perl There Is More Than One Way To Do It (TIMTOWTDI), and another way, using CGI.pm, will be shown in more detail in the coming chapters. However, here we can see the differences between the preceding example and Listing 3-5 using CGI.pm, which does the same task.

Listing 3-5   **Example getting form input with CGI.pm**

```
01: #!/usr/bin/perl -wT
02: use strict;
03: use CGI qw(:standard);
04: my $first_name = param('fname');
05: my $last_name  = param('lname');
06: print header,
07:     start_html('Form Output'),
08:     h3({-align=>'center'}, 'Form Output'),
09:     p;
10: print $_ . " = ". param($_) . br foreach param;
11: print end_html;
```

What a difference! You may be asking yourself why anyone would want to parse QUERY_STRING by hand and not just let CGI.pm do it. If there *are* any reasons, there are no valid ones that should convince you to do it by hand. In fact, it is best to just let the magic behind Lincoln Steins CGI.pm module do it for you. So why show an example of how to do it in the first place? We feel it is important to see how it is done and not just accept the fact that a module does this in the background for you. Another reason is that this is an environment variable and this is a chapter on environment variables! As this book progresses you will see more and more uses if CGI.pm and more in-depth explanations of what it does and how you can use it.

3.4 Example Script: Visitor Log

It is extremely common to use CGI for creating a custom logging system for a Web site. Of course, there are quite a few Web server access log-reporting applications, but you may find it useful to have this information in your own custom database. Imagine the scenario where you need to produce reports on your Web site visitor's information. The information needed for these reports are visitor's domain names, Web client, referring page, and date information. These few, but important, pieces of data could allow you to produce many different types of reports. For example, reports could show a breakdown of what Web clients are used to view your site, the times of day when there is more activity, how people are getting to the site, and who is coming to the site.

This example uses all of what you learned in this chapter. It involves creating new environment variables in the Web server configuration file, using a library file to do the database connection, and using some default environment variables that hold information about the visitor.

The first thing that would need to be done is to create the database. We are storing six pieces of information in the database, so we can create a table with six columns. The table will be called "access_info" on a database named "visitors" on "mysqlhost." The SQL query in Listing 3-6 would create the needed table.

Listing 3-6   SQL create statement

```
create table access_log (
    IP CHAR(15),
    DOMAIN CHAR(255),
    CLIENT CHAR (75),
    PAGE_TO CHAR(255),
    PAGE_FROM CHAR(255),
    TIME_STAMP CHAR(20)
)
```

NOTE The documentation of the database being used should be checked for limits to length of CHAR and VARCHAR types. Depending on what reports are generated and what queries are most often done, it would be a good idea to put the appropriate indexes on the table. Next the custom environment variable will be added in the httpd.conf file. The only environment variable that we will create is the location of the database in case any future scripts also need this information.

```
SetENV VISLOGDB visitors@mysqlhost
```

Next we will create a small module that will be used to create the database connection. It is good practice to create reusable code by wrapping up methods for tasks that will be needed by multiple scripts. In a previous example, we showed how to do this by making a 'library' script to make the connection. This is another, and likely a better, way to do it. We wanted to illustrate both ways to help you gain the widest amount of knowledge.

Since connecting to the visitors log database will likely be something done by multiple scripts and applications, creating this module, Listing 3-7, will save some time in the future.

Listing 3-7   LogConnect module to make connection to database

```
01: package LogConnect;
02: use DBI;
03: use strict;
04: sub connect {
05:    my ($log_dbname, $log_dbhost) = split(/\@/,$ENV{'VISLOGDB'});
06:    my $log_dsn = "DBI:mysql:database=$log_dbname;host=
                   $log_dbhost";
07:    my $log_dbh=DBI->connect($log_dsn, "user", "password");
08:    if (!defined($log_dbh)) {
09:       print "\nerror: There is a problem connecting to the MySQL
              database:\n";
10:       print DBI->errstr;
11:       print "-" x 25 "\n";
12:       return;
13:    }
14:    return $log_dbh;
15: }
16: 1;
```

Line 1 begins the module by stating the package name of the module we are creating. This can be anything you would like it to be as long as it is the same name as the file itself (without the .pm).

Line 2 *use()*s the DBI module, since that is what we will use to handle the actual connection to the database.

Line 3 turn on compiler restrictions with the handy strict pragma.

Line 4 begins the creation of a *connect()* method. Usually you would see a *new()* method here. However, we aren't really creating a new class or an OO-based module. The goal here is to have a collocation of routines that can be used over and over.

Line 5 creates two variables, $log_dbname and $log_dbhost, which will house the names of the database name and host server, respectively. As shown earlier, this line takes the environment variable created in the Web server configuration file, splits it, and creates these two variables.

Line 6 creates a DSN, as defined by the DBI module, and it is assigned to the variable $log_dsn.

Line 7 makes a connection to the database, and the database handle is stored in the $log_dbh variable.

Lines 8–13 do error checking to make sure the *connect()* method returned a value. If it did not, we want to display a message with the error returned from the DBI module. It is good practice to do some sort of error checking whenever making a connection.

Line 14 returns the value of $log_dbh, which is the DBH itself, to the calling script. Now that calling script has the open database connection to use at will!

Lines 15 and 16 end the method and return a true value.

Now that the MySQL table has been created, our custom environment has been created, and we are able to connect to the database. The rest is left as the script that does the logging, vislog.cgi.

```
01: #!/usr/bin/perl -wT
02: # vislog.cgi
```

Line 1 is again the shebang line. Notice that warnings are turned on, as well as taint checking. Although no user-generated input is passed to this script, it is still a CGI script, and it is a good practice to have this turned on.

```
03: use strict;
```

Line 3 turns on compiler restriction to restrict unsafe constructs with the strict pragma.

```
04: use POSIX:
```

Line 4 pulls the POSIX module into the mix. The POSIX module gives access to almost all POSIX1003.1 identifiers. This module is being used in this example in order to nicely format the time to a string with *strftime()*. You should consult your databases documentation to see if it provides a built-in field to store time and date stamps. For example's sake, however, we have made our own.

```
05: use Socket;
```

Line 5 pulls in the Socket.pm module. The Socket module is being used for one specific purpose: To retrieve the value of AF_INET. AF_INET is a constant that is set in socket.h and used by the operating system in socket processes dealing with TCP, UDP, and the like. Many times you will see the value of "2" in place of where AF_INET would go because that is the most common value for it in socket.h, but that is very bad practice. Although that may be the most common setting, the value may be different on another machine and the script would not work well and not be very portable. The Socket.pm module will set the value of its exported AF_INET constant to the value set on your operating system.

```
06: use lib qw(.);
```

Line 6 should now look familiar from a preceding example. To reiterate, because taint mode removes the current working directory from @INC, we need to add it back because our module is living there.

```
07: use LogConnect;
```

Line 7 *use()*s the LogConnect module we just created. Now we will be able to use its method to connect to the database.

```
08: my $dbh = LogConnect->connect;
```

Line 8 calls the *connect()* method from our LogConnect module and sets the value of the returned DBI database handle to the variable $dbh.

```
09: my $ip = $ENV{'REMOTE_ADDR'};
```

Line 9 looks at the REMOTE_ADDR environment variable, which holds the IP address of the visitor. This value is then assigned to the scalar variable $ip.

```
10: my $browser = $ENV{'HTTP_USER_AGENT'};
```

Line 10 now looks at the HTTP_USER_AGENT environment variable, which contains the visitor's Web client information. This value is saved in $browser.

```
11: my $referer = $ENV{'HTTP_REFERER'};
```

Line 11 is getting the HTTP_REFERER, which is the URL of the Web page from which the visitor got to this site. If there is no HTTP_REFERER value, then the user came directly to the site.

```
12: my $here = $ENV{'REQUEST_URI'};
```

Line 12 fetches the REQUEST_URI environment variable. This variable holds the value of the URI of the page being requested. This value is saved to $here. The URI is the path to the script on your server without the domain. For example, if the URL to the script is *http://www.you.com/cgi-bin/script.pl*, the URI would be */cgi-bin/script.pl*, which is the URL minus the domain information.

```
13: my @digits = split (/\./, $ip);
```

Line 13 creates the array @digits, splitting the octets of the visitor's IP address. We do this because we need to pass this information to the *pack()* function without the dots.

```
14: my $address = pack ("C4", @digits);
```

Line 14 *pack()*s the integer in @digits as a four-byte unsigned character. This creates a binary structure whose value is stored in $address.

```
15: my $host = gethostbyaddr ($address, AF_INET);
```

Line 15 assigns the value of the variable $host, which receives its value from what is returned from the *gethostbyaddr()* function. This function translates the raw IP address given to it into a domain name, such as me.myself.com. Here is where the AF_INET is used. The *gethostbyaddr()* function uses this to determine what type of address it is finding. Because it is being passed AF_INET, the function will know that it is finding a UDP, TCP, and so forth type of address.

```
16: my $time = strftime("%Y-%m-%d %H:%M:%S",gmtime);
```

Line 16, the $time variable, is obtaining its value by using the *strftime()* (string format time) function imported by the POSIX module. It uses the Perl *gmtime()* function to get the current time. This will return a string of the time based on the Greenwich time zone. This may not be extremely useful for you, so you can substitute *gmtime()* for *localtime()* to retrieve the string based on your own time zone. In this example, the output format will be in YYYY-MM-DD HH:MM:SS, which is represented by %Y-%m-%d %H:%M:%S.

```
17: my $query = qq(insert into access_log values
                  ('$ip','$host','$browser','$here','$referer',
                   '$time'));
```

Line 17 sets up the query to insert the data into the database. This SQL query is saved in the $query variable.

```
18: my $sth = $dbh->prepare($query);
```

Line 18 creates the variable that will hold the STH, $sth. The value of this is the return value of the prepared query from the DBI *prepare()* method. The SQL query is now ready to be made.

```
19: $sth->execute;
```

Line 19 executes the SQL query, and the information is saved in the database.

```
20: $dbh->disconnect;
```

Line 20 closes the open connection to the database.

The preceding script is longer than it could be in order to illustrate what is happening every step of the way. A shorter way of writing it is shown in Listing 3-8.

Listing 3-8   Example of another way to do the logging

```
01: #!/usr/bin/perl -wT
02: use strict;
03: use Socket;
04: use POSIX;
05: use lib qw(.);
06: use LogConnect;
07: my $dbh = LogConnect->connect;
08: (my $digits = $ENV{'REMOTE_ADDR'}) =~ s/\.//g;
09: my $address = pack("C4", $digits);
10: my $host = gethostbyaddr($address, AF_INET);
11: my $time = strftime("%Y-%m-%d %H:%M:%S",gmtime);
12: my $sth = $dbh->prepare(qq{insert into access_log values
            ('$ENV{REMOTE_ADDR}','$host', '$ENV{HTTP_USER_AGENT}',
            '$ENV{DOCUMENT_URI}', '$ENV{HTTP_REFERER}', '$time')});
13: $sth->execute;
14: $dbh->disconnect;
```

The differences in the two scripts should be apparent. This SSI script can be called from any of your Web pages that have the ability to run SSI. It would be invoked with the following command.

```
<!--#exec cgi="/cgi-bin/vislog.cgi"-->
```

3.5 Example Script: Basic Report

Now that you have all this great information saved in a database, it would be good to use it. As stated earlier, this type of data can be useful for creating reports. One of these reports could be Web client statistics that provide a breakdown of which Web clients are being used to view your site. This can help Web developers figure out exactly what they are designing for. If it was found that more Netscape clients are visiting, the use of more IE specific technologies such as VBscript and JScript may be undesirable. It could also show that more text-only clients, such as Lynx, are being used, and the text-only capabilities could be beefed up.

This example script will connect to the **vislog** database and use the information in the **access_log** table to create a dynamic Web page to display the statistics of the visitor's Web clients. Much of this should now be very familiar to you. We will call this script viewlog.cgi.

```
01: #!/usr/bin/perl -wT
02: # viewlog.cgi
03: $|=1;
04: use strict;
```

Lines 1–4 do something that should look very familiar to you by now: the shebang line. We again turn on warnings and taint checking. Although there is no user input given to the script, we keep taint checking on as a matter of good form and practice.

The Perl variable $| is a special variable that programmers can use to tell Perl to autoflush the output buffer. By setting this special variable to a non-zero value, Perl will send output to the Web client after each write, as opposed to waiting for the buffer to be filled before flushing. One caveat of using "$|=1" with Web pages that contain tables is that some Web clients will only display a table when the table is complete and the </TABLE> tag has been displayed. So it may seem, at times, like this is not doing what it should. This is not an error in Perl but just how Web clients work. Finally, we again use the strict module to turn on compiler warnings.

```
05: use lib qw(.);
06: use LogConnect;
```

Lines 5 and 6 again use lib.pm to make sure the current working directory is in @INC, and then we are able to *use()* the LogConnect module.

```
07: my $dbh = LogConnect->connect;
```

Line 7 makes the connection to the database via *LogAccess::connect()*, and the returned DBH is stored in the $dbh variable. You have likely figured out by now that it is good practice to name the variables holding your DBH with the letters "dbh" in the variable name. Good, and common, naming conventions for variables are a good thing.

```
08: print "Content-type: text/html\n\n";
```

Line 8 prints out our header telling the client to expect to receive and interpret the upcoming information as HTML.

```
09: my $query = qq(select CLIENT from access_log);
```

Line 9 defines the query to get the needed information from the database. This query will retrieve all of the CLIENT columns in the database.

```
10: my $sth = $dbh->prepare($query);
```

Line 10 prepares the query and readies it to be executed with the DBI *prepare()* method.

```
11: $sth->execute;
```

Line 11 executes the query.

```
12: my %clients;
```

Line 12 declares a hash called %clients. This will be used to store the types of clients in the log, as well as a count of each.

```
13: while ($_ = $sth->fetchrow) {
14:     $clients{$_}++;
15: }
```

Lines 13–15 are a block of code that loops through the data being returned from the SQL query to the database. When an entry for a Web client is seen for the first time, the name of the client is stored as a hash key, and the value is set to 1. For each subsequent instance of that client, the value of that key is incriminated.

```
16: $dbh->disconnect;
```

Line 16 disconnects from the database.

```
17: my @clients = sort {$clients{$b} <=> $clients{$a}} keys
                       %clients;
```

Line 17 handles the last thing needed before the information can be shown to the client. We will display the Web client data based on the number of the clients from highest to lowest. This will be accomplished by creating an array—in this case, @clients—whose elements are the Web clients in order from highest to lowest occurrences. This is done by sorting the keys of %clients based on the values.

```
18: print <<HTML;
19: <HTML>
20: <HEAD>
21:     <TITLE>Simple Report</TITLE>
22: </HEAD>
23: <BODY BGCOLOR="#ffffff">
24: <CENTER><H1>Simple Report</H1></CENTER>
25: <CENTER><H3>Web Client Breakdown</H3></CENTER>
26: <HR NOSHADE>
27: <CENTER>
28: <TABLE BORDER=1 CELLPADDING=3 CELLSPACING=3>
29: HTML
```

Lines 18–29 are the start of the Web page, which is printed out using a here document. Note that the start of the table is also printed in here.

```
30: foreach (@clients) {
31:     print qq(<TD ALIGN=center>$_</TD><TD ALIGN=center>
        $clients{$_}</TD><TR>);
32: }
```

Lines 30, 31, and 32 comprise a foreach loop that loops through the @clients array and prints out two cells per element. The left cell will print the Web client information from the $_ variable that holds the latest value of the foreach iteration. The right cell prints the value of that client from %clients.

```
33: print <<HTML;
34: </TABLE>
35: </CENTER>
36: </BODY>
37: </HTML>
38: HTML
```

Lines 33–38 are a here document displaying the closing HTML tags that finish up the display to the user. When this is done, the results should look like those in Figure 3-2.

Figure 3-2 **Screenshot of client breakdown example**

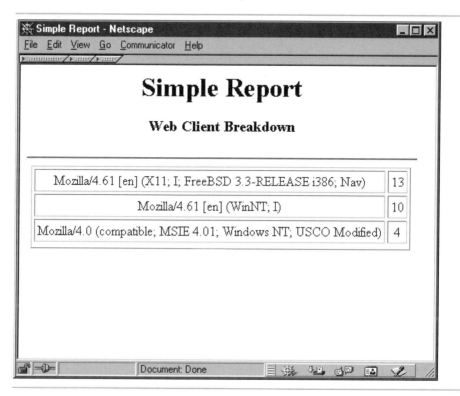

3.6 Reader Exercise

As with the other scripts in this book, you now have a Web application that is production ready but will likely need to be customized for your own needs. Also, some of the concepts shown may not be the shortest or most idiomatic way to do things because they are meant to help you learn, but they are effective and efficient. We would like to leave it as an exercise to the reader to play with this code and possibly cut out steps and add your own personalized features.

One exercise that should help you better understand the concepts taught in this chapter is to create a report that gives more information based on the same data being requested from the database. For example, the CLIENT field actually holds a few bits of useful information such as

Web client version and operating system. Use some matching and regular expressions to get that data from the strings returned by the **CLIENT** field and change this report to include a better breakdown including total visitors, totals of each Web client, a breakdown of Web client versions, and what OS visitors are using.

Doing this customizing should create a script with output similar to that in Figure 3-3.

Figure 3-3 Screenshot of detailed report

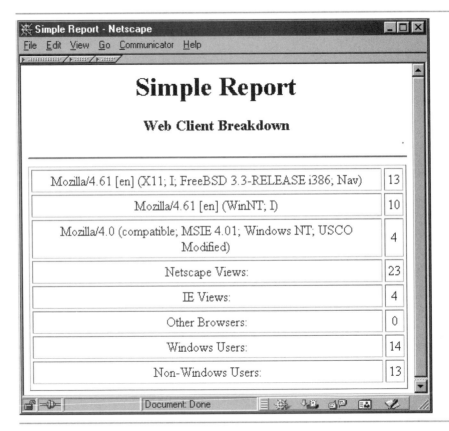

3.7 What Have We Learned?

- What %ENV is and what it contains.

- How to add to the Apache Web server environment using SetENV.

- The *gethostbyaddr()* function was introduced.

- How to parse a QUERY_STRING "by hand."

3.8 Listings

Listing 3-9   **MyConnect.pm**

```
01: package MyConnect;
02: use DBI;
03: use strict;
04: sub salesDB {
05:    my ($sales_dbname, $sales_dbhost) = split(/\@/,$ENV
                                             {'SALESDB'});
06:    my $sales_dsn = "DBI:mysql:database=$sales_dbname;
                        host=$sales_dbhost";
07:    my $sales_dbh=DBI->connect($sales_dsn,"username","password");
08:  if (!defined($sales_dbh)) {
09:    print "\nerror: There is a problem connecting to the
              MySQL database:\n";
10:    print DBI->errstr;
11:    print "-" x 25 . "\n";
12:    return;
13:  }
14:    return $sales_dbh;
15: }
16: 1;
```

Listing 3-10   **vislog.cgi**

```
01: #!/usr/bin/perl -wT
02: # vislog.cgi
03: use strict;
04: use POSIX:
05: use Socket;
06: use lib qw(.);
07: use LogConnect;
08: my $dbh = LogConnect->connect;
09: my $ip = $ENV{'REMOTE_ADDR'};
10: my $browser = $ENV{'HTTP_USER_AGENT'};
11: my $referer = $ENV{'HTTP_REFERER'};
12: my $here = $ENV{'REQUEST_URI'};
13: my @digits = split (/\./, $ip);
14: my $address = pack ("C4", @digits);
15: my $host = gethostbyaddr ($address, AF_INET);
16: my $time = strftime("%Y-%m-%d %H:%M:%S",gmtime);
17: my $query = qq(insert into access_log values('$ip','$host',
                   '$browser','$here','$referer', $time));
```

```
18: my $sth = $dbh->prepare($query);
19: $sth->execute;
20: $dbh->disconnect;
```

Listing 3-11   viewlog.cgi

```
01: #!/usr/bin/perl -wT
02: # viewlog.cgi
03: $|=1;
04: use strict;
05: use lib qw(.);
06: use LogConnect;
07: my $dbh = LogConnect->connect;
08: print "Content-type: text/html\n\n";
09: my $query = qq(select CLIENT from access_log);
10: my $sth = $dbh->prepare($query);
11: $sth->execute;
12: my %clients;
13: while ($_ = $sth->fetchrow) {
14:     $clients{$_}++;
15: }
16: $dbh->disconnect;
17: my @clients = sort {$clients{$b} <=> $clients{$a}} keys %clients;
18: print <<HTML;
19: <HTML>
20: <HEAD>
21:    <TITLE>Simple Report</TITLE>
22: </HEAD>
23: <BODY BGCOLOR="#ffffff">
24: <CENTER><H1>Simple Report</H1></CENTER>
25: <CENTER><H3>Web Client Breakdown</H3></CENTER>
26: <HT NOSHADE>
27: <CENTER>
28: <TABLE BORDER=1 CELLPADDING=3 CELLSPACING=3>
29: HTML
30: foreach (@clients) {
31:    print qq(<TD ALIGN=center>$_</TD><TD ALIGN=center>$clients{$_}
               </TD><TR>);
32: }
33: print <<HTML;
34: </TABLE>
35: </CENTER>
36: </BODY>
37: </HTML>
38: HTML
```

Chapter

Introduction to Web Forms

4.1 Introduction

If you do any information gathering via the Web, you are going to encounter HTML forms. HTML forms allow you to create Web pages with data entry fields on them. In a vast majority of CGI applications, an HTML form is involved somewhere in the process. An HTML form is really just a user-interface, or a GUI, for Web applications.

Without forms, nearly all of the data on the Web would be static because there would be no way to enter any data! Forms move the Web from a static medium to a dynamic one with the ability to pass information *back* to the Web server. Getting the *user's* input back to the server gives the Web great power. Now not only can information be served but forms can gather information about a user and serve them with information tailored specifically for *them*.

There are currently just a handful of HTML form tags, so learning how to use them should not be *too* difficult. The Web specifications are in a state of constant change. We are beginning to see newer technologies such as XML and XHTML so do not be surprised if HTML forms become even more powerful in the near future. No, HTML is not going anywhere, so don't worry. HTML is just going to get more powerful, possibly with features such as spreadsheet-like table entries, sliders, and/or multiple-page form layouts.

We will be covering most of the HTML form tags, but we will not go too in-depth on the explanations. This chapter is meant to be an introduction. If you need a comprehensive document with *all* of the possibilities explained, please go to *http://www.w3.org* and view the documents on the current HTML specification (currently XHTML 1.01), specifically the section on HTML forms.

<FORM>

All forms must begin and end with the <FORM> tag. When we talk about forms, we are referring to a *logical* form on a Web page (the stuff between the opening <FORM> tag and the closing </FORM> tag). A Web page can have multiple forms on it, so don't confuse a Web page itself with a form *on* the Web page.

Forms may not be nested. You cannot have a form inside of another form. That would cause unexpected results because Web browsers are not prepared to handle forms inside forms.

The <FORM> tag also has ACTION, NAME, METHOD, and ENCTYPE attributes that are optional. See the example in Listing 4-1.

Listing 4-1   **Fully loaded form tag**

```
<FORM ACTION="/cgi-bin/myprogram.cgi" METHOD="POST" NAME="form1"
 ENCTYPE="multipart/form-data">
```

ACTION tells the HTML form what CGI script to call when the form is submitted. The CGI script does not have to be on the same server as the HTML form. If the CGI script is on a different server, a full URL must be used in the ACTION argument. If the CGI script is on the same server as the HTML form, the server information can be left off as it is in Listing 4-1.

NAME is the name of the FORM. This attribute is omitted most of the time, but if you will be manipulating the form with JavaScript, have multiple forms on the same HTML form, or if you are writing CGI that perform different tasks based on which form was submitted, you will need to know the name of the form that was submitted.

METHOD tells the browser what type of submit to perform. The available choices are **GET** and **POST**. We'll talk a bit more about GET and POST soon, but for now you need to know that the default is GET.

ENCTYPE tells the browser how to encode the data for transmission. When left off, the default ENCTYPE is application/x-www-form-urlencoded. The other ENCTYPE is multipart/form-data. multipart/form-data is the newer ENCTYPE and is more efficient for passing large amounts of data and binary data, and it is required for file uploads. For newer browsers, version 4.x and above, you could simply use the multipart/form-data ENCTYPE all the time, but because it is incompatible with older browsers, it is typically only used when uploading files.

Listing 4-2   Fully loaded form tag

```
<FORM ACTION="/cgi-bin/myprogram.cgi" METHOD="POST" NAME="form1"
 ENCTYPE="multipart/form-data">
```

In Listing 4-2, we used all of the possible <FORM> attributes. The AC-TION attribute says that the CGI program to be run is called myprogram.cgi. The METHOD attribute says we are going to use the POST method, so the data will be sent via STDIN rather than on the URL. The NAME of this form is form1. And the ENCTYPE we are using is multipart/form-data.

Listing 4-3   Compact form tag

```
<FORM ACTION="/cgi-bin/newprogram.cgi">
```

In Listing 4-3, we passed only the ACTION attribute. In this case, we are calling a CGI program called newprogram.cgi. Since we didn't pass the METHOD or ENCTYPE, they will be the default values of GET and application/x-www-form-urlencoded, respectively. The NAME attribute is not required and has no default value, so it is simply not set.

Listing 4-4   Minimal form tag

```
<FORM>
```

In Listing 4-4, we only used the <FORM> tag! In this case, all of the default values will be used. The server knows which CGI application to execute because if an ACTION value is not passed, the form defaults to the current script, and therefore, it will run itself. This may sound a bit weird, but it is actually very useful when using CGI scripts that have many different functions. For example, a simple CGI that is called with no parameters will print out an HTML form, but when it is submitted with data, the program will perform an action on the data. This is sometimes done because it can be easier to maintain a single program rather than the program and the associated HTML file.

If you forget to begin an HTML form with the <FORM> tag, Netscape won't show any form elements, but some versions of Internet Explorer will still show the elements. If you forget to close a form tag with a </FORM> tag, you will get varying results depending on the browser.

GET vs. POST

GET and POST are different in how they pass data back to the sever. GET passes all of the data to the server on the URL and can be accessed via the QUERY_STRING environment variable. POST passes the data back to the server in STDIN. Both methods have their advantages and disadvantages.

With the GET method, all of the data is easily seen on the URL. A programmer can create "canned" queries by creating links that pass data in the URL.

Listing 4-5   HTTP get example

```
http://www.google.com/search?q=brent+michalski&sa=Google+Search
```

Notice in Listing 4-5 that in the search for "brent michalski," it was passed in via the q= variable. The sa= value of "Google Search" came from the submit button. The +, &, and = are encodings used so that there is no whitespace on the URL. If the space had been left between my first and last name, the search would have actually only seen the first part, "brent," or return an error. Different browsers handle spaces differently according to the specification documents. There should be no spaces in a URL.

The GET method works just fine in most situations, but it can be a disadvantage. The GET method has a limit on the amount of data that can be sent, the actual amount depends on the Web server. Also, when you don't want the users to see what is being passed, the GET method won't work for you because it displays *all* passed data on the URL. For example, if you had some sensitive or private data being passed in from the form, your users would probably appreciate it if the data did not display for others to see. Password fields are another reason GET can be a disadvantage. Look at Figures 4-1, 4-2, and Listing 4-6 for an illustration of password fields being passed using the GET method.

Listing 4-6   Password example

```
<HTML>
<FORM ACTION="/cgi-bin/book/pwd.cgi">
  Enter Secret Word:
  <INPUT TYPE=PASSWORD NAME="SECRET"><P>
  <INPUT TYPE="SUBMIT">
</FORM>
</HTML>
```

Figure 4-1   Password text box

Enter Secret Word: ***********

Submit Query

Figure 4-2   **GET method query string**

Notice in Listing 4-6 that the data that *was* masked with the <INPUT TYPE="PASSWORD"> is no longer masked but is just plain text! The *privatedata* you see on the URL is what was entered in the password box.

With the POST method, the data being passed back to the CGI program is not seen by the user. The drawback with the POST method is that you, the programmer, cannot see what is being passed. The POST method has no limit on the amount of data that can be sent to the server, although the Web server may have a limit. When you are writing and debugging your CGI applications, it is sometimes helpful to use the GET method to see exactly what is happening and then change to the POST method when you move the script to the production environment.

One last note: It is perfectly legal to use the POST method for your forms but to also pass data on the URL. This can be useful in situations where you want to pass configuration information or other data that you want to be able to readily change from the URL instead of having to go back to the form each time. The example in Listing 4-7 shows how configuration information can be passed on the URL.

Listing 4-7   **Passing a configuration file**

```
http://www.myscripts.com/cgi-bin/myscript.cgi?config=test.cfg
```

You can manually decode the data that was sent back in your CGI program, but be very careful if you do this. The CGI.pm module has been doing this for years, and it has gone through many revisions to make it easy to use and secure. Writing your own decoding routines should only be done in limited situations, such as to learn more about CGIs and how they work or, if you know everything about how CGIs work, to write a streamlined routine that handles the data better than CGI.pm. The CGI.pm module decodes the values, and it does it very well. You can even use the POST method *and* pass data on the URL a la the GET method! CGI.pm just chugs along when you do things like that. It would be hard to try to handle all of these possibilities on your own.

4.2 Form Tags

Now that you know how to begin and end an HTML form, we can move on to the other tags that you will most likely encounter when creating HTML forms. We will cover the most commonly used/encountered form elements and attributes. Covering all of the different possibilities is beyond the scope of our discussions here, but you can get all of the most current and up-to-date information you could ever want at *http://www.w3.org*.

<INPUT>

The <INPUT> tag is by far the tag you will use most often. <INPUT> has many different attributes that you will use, and you should become very familiar with them. <INPUT> has no closing tag. <INPUT> tags must contain a NAME attribute because the name is what is used to access the data elements in the CGI program. Each different field on a form usually, but not always, has a unique name.

If there are multiple elements with the same name, CGI.pm will handle the data two different ways. It will retrieve all of the values if you read them into an array or just the first value if you read them into a scalar.

Figure 4-3   Text input fields form

In Figure 4-3, we have a simple HTML form. Assuming that each of the <INPUT> fields are named "kids," <INPUT TYPE="text" NAME="kids">, we can see the different ways that CGI.pm parses the data based on what type of variable you store the data in.

Listing 4-8 **Reading data with param**

```
my @data = param('kids');
my $data = param('kids');
```

In the first example in Listing 4-8, all of the items from an HTML form with the name "kids" are stored in the @data array. In the second example, only the data in the first input field named "kids" was stored in the $data scalar variable.

TYPE

TYPE tells what kind of <INPUT> field it is. Each different type of <INPUT> box is displayed and/or acts differently on the HTML form. The possible values for the TYPE attribute are TEXT, RADIO, CHECKBOX, HIDDEN, PASSWORD, FILE, SUBMIT, RESET, and IMAGE.

<INPUT TYPE="TEXT">

The TEXT attribute is used most often. TEXT is used for gathering one line of typed input from the user, just like a text input box in a Windows application. When using the TEXT attribute, you can also use the MAX-LENGTH and SIZE attributes. SIZE tells the browser how wide, in characters, to display the input field on the HTML form; the default is 20. MAXLENGTH is used to limit how many characters a user can enter. Once the number of characters exceeds the MAXLENGTH value, the field will stop accepting input.

Listing 4-9 **Limiting amount of text input**

```
<INPUT TYPE="TEXT" NAME="state" MAXLENGTH="2" SIZE="3">
```

In Listing 4-9, we have a text <INPUT> field named **state**. It is **3** characters wide (SIZE) and has a maximum length (MAXLENGTH) of **2** characters. It is a good idea to make the field size a little larger than the maximum length to allow for differences in browsers and fonts. If MAXLENGTH is not set, the default is to allow an unlimited amount of text to be entered into the <INPUT> box.

<INPUT TYPE="PASSWORD">

PASSWORD is another type of <INPUT> field (see Listing 4-10). Fields using the PASSWORD attribute behave the same way as fields using the TEXT attribute, except the PASSWORD field will display asterisks (*) instead of the actual characters typed. It is very important to realize that *absolutely no* encryption or hiding is done when the text is sent to the CGI program. In fact, if you have a password field and use the GET method for the form, the user will see the password in plain text on the URL! Look back at Figure 4-2 for an example of this. If you need any sort of real security, use server-side authentication with basic authentication and the .htaccess file or some other method.

Listing 4-10   Using the password input type

```
<INPUT TYPE="PASSWORD" NAME="secret" MAXLENGTH="20" SIZE="10">
```

<INPUT TYPE="HIDDEN">

With the HIDDEN attribute, the data is not modifiable by the user because no <INPUT> field is displayed on the Web page. HIDDEN fields are often used to maintain data between forms that have multiple screens. By using HIDDEN fields, the script can look like it "remembered" the previous values. In reality, the data is passed back to the Web server each time.

Like the PASSWORD attribute, the HIDDEN attribute does not do any sort of encryption. HIDDEN fields, too, are passed on the URL when the GET method is used and can therefore easily be changed by a user by simply modifying the data on the URL and resubmitting the form. Also, hidden fields are not really hidden because if a user views the source of the Web page, he or she will see all of the hidden fields and the data they contain in the HTML source. Because of this, don't put important things, like item prices, in hidden fields. A naughty user could easily save the HTML of the page to his or her computer, edit the prices in the hidden fields, and then use the page to submit an order. This would be like handing out pricing guns to customers as they enter a store—not a good idea.

Listing 4-11   Using the hidden input type

```
<INPUT TYPE="HIDDEN" NAME="widget" VALUE="This is a test.">
```

VALUE

With all of the HTML form tags described so far, you can also use the VALUE attribute to set a default value. We used the VALUE attribute in

Listing 4-11 for the HIDDEN example, but we could have also used it in the TEXT and PASSWORD examples just as easily. When you use the VALUE attribute, the value will be displayed when the form is first loaded (asterisks in the case of TYPE="PASSWORD"). Also, if there is a RESET button on the form and the user hits it, all of the default values get restored, so this can be a great way to set up your HTML forms with initial values.

<INPUT TYPE="CHECKBOX"> and <INPUT TYPE="RADIO">

The CHECKBOX attribute is used to present the user with a group of items to choose from. With the CHECKBOX attribute, more than one item can be selected at a time.

The "cousin" to the CHECKBOX attribute is the RADIO attribute. RADIO is also used to present the user with a group of items to choose from. The big difference is that with the RADIO items only one can be selected at a time. When the user selects one item, any other that was checked is automatically unchecked.

The CHECKBOX and RADIO items are grouped by using the same NAME attribute for each item in the group. It is perfectly legal to have a "group" of only one item, but if you do and use the RADIO attribute, once the item is selected, the user cannot unselect it. Listing 4-12 shows an example. It is easier to understand when you see it.

Listing 4-12   **Checkboxes and radio buttons**

```
<INPUT TYPE="CHECKBOX" NAME="sports"> Hockey><BR>
<INPUT TYPE="CHECKBOX" NAME="sports"> Football<BR>
<INPUT TYPE="CHECKBOX" NAME="sports"> Soccer<BR>
<P>
<INPUT TYPE="RADIO" NAME="favorite"> Scooby Doo<BR>
<INPUT TYPE="RADIO" NAME="favorite"> Shaggy<BR>
<INPUT TYPE="RADIO" NAME="favorite"> Velma<BR>
<INPUT TYPE="RADIO" NAME="favorite"> Scrappy Doo<BR>
<P>
<INPUT TYPE="CHECKBOX" NAME="os"> BeOS<BR>
<INPUT TYPE="CHECKBOX" NAME="os" CHECKED> BSD<BR>
<INPUT TYPE="CHECKBOX" NAME="os" CHECKED> Linux<BR>
<INPUT TYPE="CHECKBOX" NAME="os"> Windows<BR>
```

Listing 4-12 would look like Figure 4-4.

Figure 4-4 **Checkbox and radio buttons form**

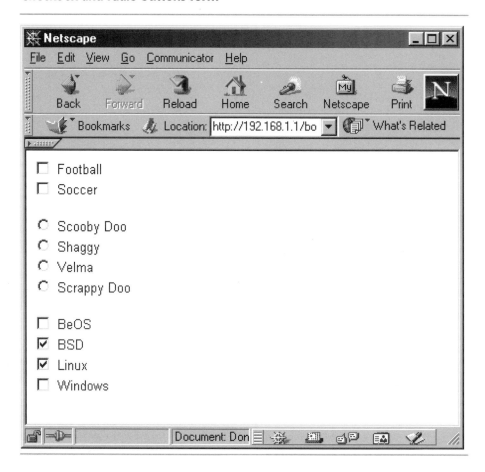

Notice that the Linux and BSD options are already checked. With the RADIO and CHECKBOX <INPUT> types, you use the CHECKED attribute to make an item selected by default. With the RADIO attribute, only one item can be checked at a time, so you can only use one CHECKED attribute. With the CHECKBOX attribute, more than one item can be CHECKED by default, as you can see in Figure 4-4.

<INPUT TYPE="FILE">

Another type of <INPUT> box we have to choose from is the FILE type. The FILE type is used for file uploading. It creates a text input box with a button next to it that says **Browse...** (see Figure 4-5). When the user clicks on the "Browse" button, a file select dialog box is opened (Figure 4-6) so the user can pick a file to upload from their system. For security reasons, this type of input field cannot have a default value. Chapter 8 covers file uploading in detail.

Listing 4-13 **File upload input type**

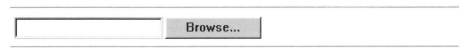

```
<INPUT TYPE="FILE" NAME="upload1">
```

Listing 4-13 produces an input area that looks like Figure 4-5.

Figure 4-5 **File input/browse box**

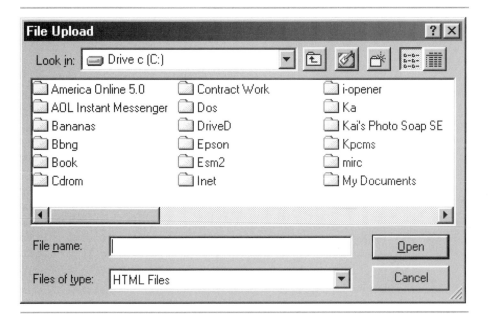

Figure 4-6 shows the window displayed when the user clicks the "Browse..." button.

Figure 4-6 **File browsing display**

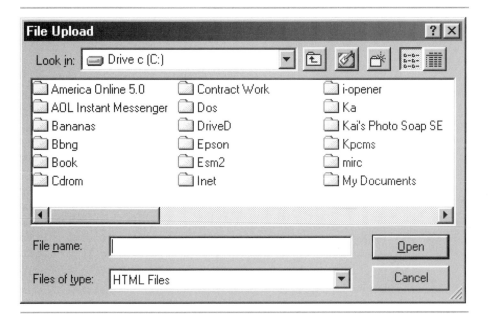

<INPUT TYPE="SUBMIT"> and <INPUT TYPE="RESET">

These two <INPUT> types create buttons on the HTML form. The <INPUT TYPE="SUBMIT"> is used to submit the data and run the CGI program to which the current HTML form points. The default text for a submit button is, oddly enough, **Submit Data**. By using the VALUE attribute, you can change the text that the button displays.

Neat trick: By using spaces in the VALUE attribute, you have a little control over the width of the button. For example, Listing 4-14 displays the buttons in Figure 4-7. Notice the width difference in the second button. Five spaces on each side of the word *Test* were used to do this. Also, like any other <INPUT> field, the text that is in the VALUE attribute is sent back to the CGI, so you can have multiple SUBMIT buttons with different values and know which one the user pressed. If you are using spaces to make the button wider, remember in your CGI program that "test" and " test " are different. Don't forget to make the appropriate code changes to handle spaces.

Listing 4-14   Submit input type

```
<INPUT TYPE="SUBMIT" VALUE="Test">
<BR>
<INPUT TYPE="SUBMIT" VALUE="    Test    ">
```

Figure 4-7   Submit buttons

The <INPUT TYPE="RESET"> is displayed the exact same way as the SUBMIT type shown except with "Reset" displayed on the button. When the RESET button is pushed, it resets all the values on the HTML form to their default. If the form elements do not have a default value, they are cleared.

<INPUT TYPE="IMAGE">

The <INPUT TYPE="IMAGE"> is used to make images act as a SUBMIT button. When an IMAGE attribute is sent back to the CGI program, the *name.x* and *name.y* are both sent back. The *x* and *y* are the coordinates on the image where the user clicked, and *name* is the name of the button itself.

Listing 4-15   Image input type

```
<INPUT TYPE="IMAGE" SRC="camel.jpg" NAME="mybutton" BORDER=0>
```

Listing 4-15 will display the camel.jpg image without a border. If you leave the border attribute off, the default is a border of 1, which normally is not what is desired around an image. If a user clicked on this image at the *x,y* coordinates of 10,23, *mybutton.x=10* and *mybutton.y=23* would be sent back to the CGI program. The CGI program can then take this information and act accordingly.

<SELECT> and <OPTION>

<SELECT> and <OPTION> do not go inside an INPUT tag like all of the previous examples. Instead, <SELECT> and <OPTION> are separate HTML tags that you use to form a block that makes up a drop-down list or a list of items that can be chosen by the user. The <OPTION> tags are nested within a <SELECT> block to make up a coherent list of choices. Listing 4-16 shows an example.

Listing 4-16   Allowing multiple selections from a list

```
<SELECT NAME="list1" MULTIPLE>
 <OPTION>Linux</OPTION>
 <OPTION>FreeBSD</OPTION>
 <OPTION>MacOS</OPTION>
 <OPTION>OS/2</OPTION>
 <OPTION>BeOS</OPTION>
 <OPTION>AIX</OPTION>
 <OPTION>Windows</OPTION>
</SELECT>
<SELECT NAME="list2">
 <OPTION>Linux</OPTION>
 <OPTION>FreeBSD</OPTION>
 <OPTION>MacOS</OPTION>
 <OPTION>OS/2</OPTION>
 <OPTION>BeOS</OPTION>
 <OPTION>AIX</OPTION>
 <OPTION>Windows</OPTION>
</SELECT>
```

Listing 4-16 would look like Figure 4-8 on the HTML form.

Figure 4-8   Two select inputs

And, once you choose items, Listing 4-16 looks like Figure 4-9.

Figure 4-9   Selects with chosen items

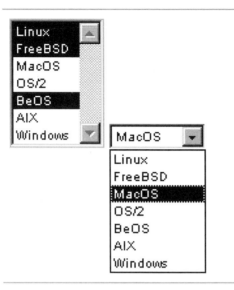

The list on the right in Figure 4-9 would not normally be dropped down, but it was left that way to show you what happens when you click to choose an item. The list on the left can have multiple items selected, whereas the list on the right cannot. To select multiple items, the user can hold down the *shift key* or the *control key* while clicking the items with the mouse. To make data preselected when the form is loaded, use the **SELECTED** tag inside of the opening OPTION tag, as seen in Listing 4-17.

Listing 4-17   Preselecting an option

```
<OPTION>Linux</OPTION>
<OPTION SELECTED>FreeBSD</OPTION>
<OPTION>MacOS</OPTION>
```

<TEXTAREA>

Finally, we come to the <TEXTAREA> tag. The <TEXTAREA> tag is used to input large blocks of text, such as comments or Web-based e-mail. <TEXTAREA> requires a closing </TEXTAREA> tag. <TEXTAREA> requires that you use the ROWS and COLS attributes to tell the browser how many rows and columns to display.

There is also a WRAP attribute that is not in the HTML specifications, but it works with both Netscape and Internet Explorer. The options for the WRAP attribute are PHYSICAL and VIRTUAL. PHYSICAL is supposed to actually insert linefeeds at the end of each line, while VIRTUAL is just supposed to word-wrap the text but not insert linefeeds. *Supposed to* is used here because since the attribute is not in the standards document, there is no set way for the browsers to implement it. The WRAP attribute should be used in most situations because without it as the user types, the text just keeps going and going (like the Energizer bunny) until the user hits the *enter* key. By adding the WRAP attribute, the text will automatically wrap when it reaches the edge of the text box. Let's take a look at a couple of examples to illustrate this.

Listing 4-18   Textarea input type

```
<TEXTAREA ROWS="4" COLS="40">
</TEXTAREA>
```

Figure 4-10   Textarea

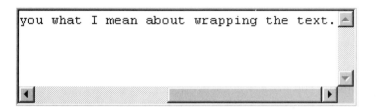

Listing 4-19   Automatic text wrapping of a textarea

```
<TEXTAREA ROWS="4" COLS="40" WRAP="PHYSICAL">
</TEXTAREA>
```

Figure 4-11   Wrapped textarea

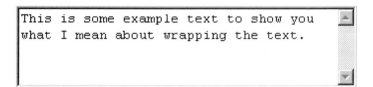

In Listing 4-18 and Figure 4-10, there is both a horizontal and a vertical scrollbar. Also, notice that you cannot see all of the text even though the same text was entered in both examples. In Listing 4-19 and Figure 4-11, the horizontal scrollbar is gone, so the text box takes up less room, and you can see all the text that was entered because it automatically wrapped when it reached the right-hand edge of the text input box.

If you were to want to have some default text, all you need to do is enter it between the opening and closing tags, as in Listing 4-20.

Listing 4-20   **Default text in a textarea**

```
<TEXTAREA ROWS="4" COLS="40" WRAP="PHYSICAL">
This is some default text.
</TEXTAREA>
```

There are still some form tags and attributes that we have not covered. They are not used very frequently, and the ones we covered here will probably be used more than 98 percent of the time when you are designing HTML forms. If you want to learn the rest or learn all of these tags and attributes much more intimately, feel free to check out the expansive documentation at *http://www.w3.org*.

Well-thought-out and well-designed forms can make a big difference in user satisfaction. Happy users tend to come back *and* tell others about sites they like.

Try to keep your forms simple but useful, and make sure that you are able to gather all the information that you need from the user. Creating user-friendly interfaces is not as easy as simply creating a page with some input boxes on it. Make sure that you start slowly, plan out the user interface, and take your time.

4.3 Reading Form Input with CGI.pm

CGI.pm is like the Holy Grail for Perl/CGI programmers. Lincoln Stein has done the Perl community a great favor by writing and perfecting this module for us all. CGI.pm takes the hard work out of parsing the information that comes from HTML forms and makes it as simple as a call to the *param()* function. Remember back in Chapter 4 when we talked about how to read in HTML form input? That showed a very primitive way to fetch and parse the data from an HTML form, and that is okay for a learning environment. However, since we are programmers, and, as Larry Wall says, the three traits of a programmer are laziness, impatience, and hubris, let's stick to those traits and be lazy. CGI.pm does all the hard work for us so we can deal with the more important parts of our programs.

Listing 4-21 shows an example of just how easy CGI.pm makes handling forms.

Listing 4-21   Simple HTML form

```
<HTML><HEAD>
 <TITLE>Form Example</TITLE>
</HEAD>
<BODY>
<FORM NAME="form_example" ACTION="/cgi-bin/book/form1.cgi"
METHOD="POST">
First Name: <INPUT TYPE="TEXT" NAME="f_name"><BR>
Last Name: <INPUT TYPE="TEXT" NAME="l_name"><BR>
<BR>
Favorite Color:<BR>
  <INPUT TYPE="RADIO" NAME="color" VALUE="red">Red<BR>
  <INPUT TYPE="RADIO" NAME="color" VALUE="blue">Blue<BR>
  <INPUT TYPE="RADIO" NAME="color" VALUE="green">Green<BR>
  <INPUT TYPE="RADIO" NAME="color" VALUE="yellow">Yellow<BR>
<BR>
Favorite Sport(s):<BR>
  <INPUT TYPE="CHECKBOX" NAME="sports" VALUE="hockey"
CHECKED>Hockey<BR>
  <INPUT TYPE="CHECKBOX" NAME="sports" VALUE="football">Foot-
ball<BR>
  <INPUT TYPE="CHECKBOX" NAME="sports" VALUE="baseball">Base-
ball<BR>
  <INPUT TYPE="CHECKBOX" NAME="sports" VALUE="basketball">Bas-
ketball<BR>
  <INPUT TYPE="CHECKBOX" NAME="sports" VALUE="golf">Golf<BR>
<BR>
<INPUT TYPE="SUBMIT" NAME="doit" VALUE="Send Info">
</FORM>
</BODY>
</HTML>
```

The HTML in Listing 4-21 creates a simple form with some form input fields on it, as shown in Figure 4-12. The form won't look exactly like this because some information has already been entered into it and we are ready to click the "Send Info" button. Now, using the CGI.pm module, let's take a look at how easy it is to see exactly what was submitted.

Figure 4-12   **A complete form**

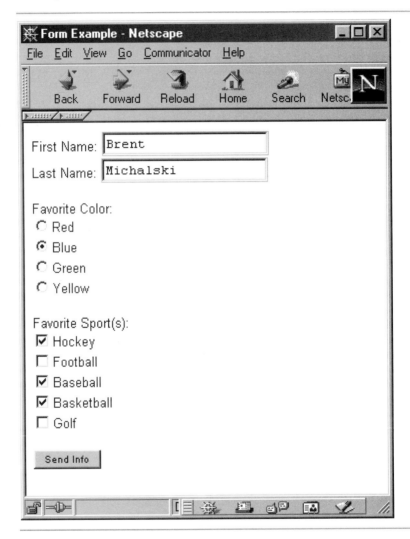

Figure 4-13   Output of CGi.pm's dump()

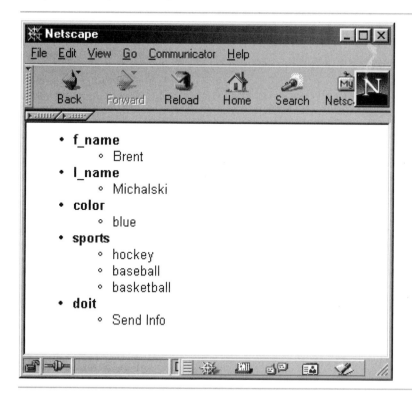

The output of the CGI program, shown in Figure 4-13, is simply the field names in **bold** followed by a list of the values that were entered. If more than one form element had the same NAME attribute, then there are multiple items listed below the field name. Take a look at Listing 4-22. It is the *complete* CGI program that was used to parse the form and produce the output in Figure 4-13!

Listing 4-22   Dumping the passed form data

```
1: #!/usr/bin/perl -wT
2: use strict;
3: use CGI qw(:standard);
4: use CGI::Carp qw(fatalsToBrowser);
5: print header;
6: print dump();
```

We were able to produce real output from an HTML form with just six lines of Perl! Actually, the use strict and the CGI::Carp lines could be removed and the program would still function just as well, so we would be down to four lines of code! This example shows how CGI.pm takes the hard work out of writing CGI applications and allows you to worry about the other details of your application rather than wasting time on parsing the form data properly.

The preceding example uses CGI.pm's *dump()* function to display all the values that were submitted with the form. While *dump()* is a good debugging tool, it doesn't help you out when you are writing real CGI applications that other users will be seeing. The "crème de la crème" of useful functions for CGI applications is the *param()* function.

param() is simply used to get the data that was sent from the HTML form and read it in to the CGI program. Let's take a look at the example we just saw, but instead of using the *dump()* function, we will use the *param()* function and produce a much friendlier output page.

Figure 4-14   **Singular dynamic output**

Do you see the difference between Figures 4-14 and 4-15? In Figure 4-14 we had only one favorite sport, so we kept the phrase in a singular context. In Figure 4-15, we had more than one favorite sport, so we made the phrase plural. It is attention to little details like this that make your applications stand out. If you don't, it may appear to the user that you, the programmer, didn't bother to take the time to do it right. It took a little more work to do this, but it's worth it. Let's walk through the code needed to produce the output like we have in Figures 4-14 and 4-15.

Figure 4-15   Plural dynamic output

```
01: #!/usr/bin/perl -wT
02: use strict;
03: use CGI qw(:standard);
04: use CGI::Carp qw(fatalsToBrowser);
```

Lines 1–4 are going to be in just about every CGI program in this book and for good reason.

Line 1 tells the system where to find Perl and turns on warnings **-w** and taint checking T. Taint checking is a safety feature that keeps the programmer from running commands with unsafe data that was passed from the user. With warnings turned on, **-w**, you will get more messages about possible program errors from the interpreter. Having warnings turned on is a good idea because the more verbose the interpreter when you are developing a program, the better. It also keeps you from making silly programming mistakes.

Line 2 turns on strict for us. This will add even more protection against common mistakes, such as giving the same names to two variables or using unquoted text (barewords).

Line 3 loads the CGI.pm module and imports the standard set of functions.

Line 4 loads the CGI::Carp module and imports the method *fatalsToBrowser()* so that most programming errors are echoed to the browser rather than a 500 Server Error.

```
05: my $first_name  = param('f_name');
06: my $last_name   = param('l_name');
07: my $fav_color   = param('color');
```

Lines 5–7 create some my variables and use the *param()* function from CGI.pm to read the data that was passed from the HTML form. The name that is entered as the function argument is the name of the form element for which you want to get the data. These form element names are case-sensitive, so make sure your spelling and capitalization are correct.

The *param()* function is an extremely flexible and powerful little function. There are four different ways to use the *param()* function!

■ `$scalar = param('element_name');`

If you read the return values into a scalar, like in lines 4–7, param will return a single value and that is what gets stored in the scalar variable. If there is more than one item with the same name, the *param()* function will return the first, and only the first, value.

■ `@array = param('element_name');`

If you read the return values into an array instead of a scalar, the *param()* function will return all values and store them in the array. If it was a checkbox or multiple select list, all elements selected will be returned to the array.

■ `$scalar = param();`

If you leave the argument off and just call an empty *param()* function, then the *param()* function will store the number of named form elements in the scalar variable.

■ `@array = param();`

If you call an empty *param()* function and read the return value into an array, the array will be populated with the *names* of all form elements.

```
08: my @fav_sports  = param('sports');
```

Line 8 reads all the items that were checked in the "Favorite Sport(s)" checkboxes on the HTML form.

```
09: my $sport_count = @fav_sports;
10: my $sport_text;
```

Line 9 stores the number of elements in the @fav_sports array in the variable $sport_count.

Line 10 simply declares a variable called $sport_text. Since the program uses the strict pragma, all variables must be declared before they can be used.

```
11: print header;
12: print start_html('Form Example');
```

Line 11 uses the *header()* function from CGI.pm. The CGI.pm module is used for just about any CGI programming task, not just for getting values from the HTML forms. The *header()* function returns the HTTP header, "Content-type: text/html\n\n" in this case. So **line 11** simply prints out the header information that was returned.

Line 12 uses the *start_html()* function from CGI.pm. *start_html()* will return the text needed to begin an HTML page. In **line 12**, what actually gets printed out is shown in Listing 4-23.

Listing 4-23   **Basic HTML page header**

```
<!DOCTYPE HTML PUBLIC "-//IETF//DTD HTML//EN">
<HTML><HEAD><TITLE>Form Example</TITLE>
</HEAD><BODY>
```

It is much easier to remember what was typed in **line 12** instead of all the text from Listing 4-23.

```
13: print qq(Hello $first_name $last_name<P>);
14: print qq(Your favorite color is: $fav_color<BR>);
```

Lines 13–14 simply print out some text that is displayed on the resulting page. By putting the text in *qq()*, it acts like the text is double-quoted, but you do not have to escape quotes inside the text strings. Since HTML typically has a lot of quotes, using *qq()* is very useful.

```
15: if($sport_count > 1){
16:     $sport_text = "sports are";
17: }
18:  else{
19:     $sport_text = "sport is";
20: }
```

Lines 15–20 are an if . . . else statement.

Line 15 checks to see if the variable $sport_count is greater than 1. If it is, then the block of code is entered.

Line 16 is where we get to if **line 15** is true. It sets the $sports_text variable to the text string "sports are."

Line 17 closes the if block.

Line 18 is the else statement that begins the block that is reached if the preceding if failed.

Line 19 sets the $sports_text variable to "sport is."

Line 20 closes the whole if . . . else block. All **lines 15–20** really do is set the text to either singular or plural so that when the page is displayed, it looks like the programmer took the time to do it right.

```
21: print qq(And your favorite $sport_text:<BR>);
```

Line 21 prints out the sentence that heads the favorite sports that were chosen by the user.

```
22: foreach(@fav_sports){
23:     print qq(- $_<BR>);
24: }
```

Lines 22–24 loop through the @fav_sports array and print out each element of the array. The foreach loop will iterate through each element in an array, and set the current value to $_.

Line 23 prints the current value.

Line 24 closes the foreach block.

```
25: print end_html();
```

Line 25 is the last line of the program and it uses another function from CGI.pm. The *end_html()* function simply returns </BODY></HTML>. It is not that it is hard to remember how to type but, it is sometimes just easier to remember this alternate method. You as the programmer are free to choose how you print and format your output, so remember that there is always more than one way to do it.

4.4 Making Your Users Happy

When users visit your site, you want them to have a pleasant experience, just like they expect when they go to a regular store. When you go to a store and the employees treat you courteously, chances are that you will remember the experience as a good one and will probably return. The same goes for Web sites: You want your users to enjoy themselves. A thank you page goes a long way, so make sure that you give the users some positive feedback whenever they submit a form. Let them know that their form submission was successful, address them by their first name, and show them what they submitted. If the user leaves your site happy, there is a good chance he or she will be a return customer.

4.5 Final Example

We have covered a lot of ground in this chapter, but we need one last example to give you some more experience before turning you loose on the CGI programming world. In this example, we will gather a user's name, address, and other information. Then we will allow the user to verify the data while using hidden fields to maintain the data that was entered. Once satisfied, the user can click a button to "send" the information. The form won't actually do anything with the data (that will come in later chapters), but it will show you a simple example of using a form to gather information and then let the user verify the data before doing anything with it.

```
01: #!/usr/bin/perl -Tw
02: # form3.cgi
03: use strict;
04: use CGI qw(:standard);
05: use CGI::Carp qw(fatalsToBrowser);
```

Line 1 tells the system where to find Perl and turn on taint checking and warnings.

Line 2 is a comment with the program name.

Lines 3 tells Perl to use the strict pragma.

Line 4 brings in the CGI module with the standard functions.

Line 5 loads the CGI::Carp module.

Lines 3–5 will be in nearly every program we write.

```
06: print header;
```

Line 6 uses the *header()* function from CGI.pm to print out the standard HTTP header.

```
07: my ($F_Name, $L_Name, $review, $Address,
08:      $Eye_Group, $Eye_Color, $City, $State,
09:      $Zip, $Page_Title, $Buttons, $Butt_Val,
10:      $Hidden);
```

Lines 7–10 are actually one Perl "line" that declares several global my variables. When using the strict pragma, all variables must be declared before they can be used.

```
11: Initialize_Values();
12: Print_Form();
```

Line 11 calls the *Initialize_Values()* subroutine. *Initialize_Values()* handles getting the data from the HTML form and all other tasks that need to be performed before the page is printed.

Line 12 calls the *Print_Form()* subroutine to handle printing the HTML page.

```
13: sub Initialize_Values{
```

Line 13 begins the *Initialize_Values()* subroutine.

```
14:    $Butt_Val  = param('sendit');
15:    $review    = param('review');
16:    $F_Name    = param('f_name');
17:    $L_Name    = param('l_name');
18:    $Address   = param('address');
19:    $City      = param('city');
20:    $State     = param('state');
21:    $Zip       = param('zip');
22:    $Eye_Color = param('eyecolor');
```

Lines 14–22 use the *param()* function from CGI.pm to get the data that was passed in from the Web page. The data is then stored in the scalar variables.

```
23:    if($Butt_Val =~ /Edit Data/){ $review = ""; }
24:    if(($Butt_Val =~ /Submit Data/) && ($review > 0)){
25:      Print_Thanks();
26:    }
```

Line 23 checks to see if $Butt_Val contains the string "Edit Data." If it does, then the user clicked the "Edit Data" button and we need to set the $review variable to nothing.

Line 24 checks to see if $Butt_Val contains the string "Submit Data" *and* if $review is greater than 0.

Line 25 is called if **line 24** is true. It calls the *Print_Thanks()* subroutine to print a thank you message to the user.

Line 26 closes the if block that began on **line 24**.

```
27:    $F_Name    = Text_Field("f_name",   20, 20, $F_Name);
28:    $L_Name    = Text_Field("l_name",   20, 20, $L_Name);
29:    $Address   = Text_Field("address",  20, 20, $Address);
30:    $City      = Text_Field("city",     20, 20, $City);
31:    $State     = Text_Field("state",     2,  3, $State);
32:    $Zip       = Text_Field("zip",      10, 12, $Zip);
```

Lines 27–32 use the *Text_Field()* function to construct the type of field that is going to be displayed. If this is the first time the program is called, or if the user wishes to update his or her information, then the text fields will be input boxes. If the user is just reviewing their data, then the fields are non-editable. We pass the *name, maxwidth, size,* and *default* to the *Text_Field()* function, and it returns the text that makes up what is displayed.

```
33:    if(!$review){
```

Line 33 begins an if . . . else block. Here we are checking to see if we don't want to review (if *not* $review). What this means is we are checking to see if $review contains data. If it does, we drop down to the else block on **line 44**. Otherwise we continue and enter the block of code.

```
34:    $Eye_Group  = radio_group( -name    => 'eyecolor',
35:                               -default => $Eye_Color,
36:                               -values  => ['blue','green',
37:                                            'brown','grey','red'],
38:                             );
```

Lines 34–38 are a single Perl statement that call the *radio_group()* function from CGI.pm and generate a group of radio buttons for the user to choose from. The default is obtained from the data that was sent from the calling HTML page. The values we pass are the values that are both displayed to the user and what get put into the VALUE= field on the form.

```
39:      $Buttons = submit( -name  => "sendit",
40:                          -value => "Submit My Data");
```

Lines 39–40 use the *submit()* function from CGI.pm to generate the HTML for a submit button. The value returned is then stored in $Buttons.

```
41:      $Hidden     = ""; # Clear $Hidden
42:      $Page_Title = "Enter Your Data";
43:   }
```

Line 41 clears any data that was in the $Hidden variable.

Line 42 sets the page title.

Line 43 closes this portion of the if . . . else block.

```
44:   else{
```

Line 44 begins the else portion of the if . . . else block.

```
46:      $Hidden    .= hidden(-name  =>"eyecolor",
47:                            -value =>$Eye_Color);
```

Lines 46–47 append onto the $Hidden variable. **Line 46** begins the call to the *hidden()* function, which generates the HTML for a hidden form variable, and stores the eye color in it.

```
48:      $Buttons    = submit(-name  => "sendit",
49:                            -value => "Edit Data");
50:      $Buttons   .= submit( -name  => "sendit",
51:                            -value => "Submit Data");
```

Lines 48–51 create the two buttons needed on the "Review Data" page. These lines use the same *submit()* function that was called on **line 39**.

```
52:      $Page_Title = "Edit Data or press 'Submit Data'";
53:   }
54: }
```

Line 52 creates the page title.

Lines 53–54 close the if . . . else block and the subroutine respectively.

```
55: sub Print_Thanks{
56:    print<<HTML;
```

Line 55 begins the *Print_Thanks()* subroutine. This subroutine is used to print a simple "thank you" page so that the user knows that their form submission worked.

Line 56 begins a here document that is used to print out the "Thank You" page.

```
57:    <HTML><HEAD><TITLE>Thanks!</TITLE></HEAD>
58:    <BODY>
59:    <CENTER><B>Thank you $F_Name!!!<P>
60:     Your data is very important to us!
61:    </B></CENTER>
62:    </BODY></HTML>
```

Lines 57–62 are simply the HTML that makes up the "thank you" page. Notice on **line 59** we print out the user's first name ($F_Name) to give the page a more "personal" touch.

```
63: HTML
```

Line 63 ends the here document that began on **line 56**.

```
64:    exit;
65: }
```

Line 64 exits the program. If we got to this subroutine, we want to simply print out the page and then quit the program. We have to exit the program here because if we did not, the program could continue printing more data, which would cause some confusion.

Line 65 closes the subroutine.

```
66: sub Print_Form{
67:    print<<HTML;
```

Line 66 begins the *Print_Form()* subroutine.

Line 67 begins a here document that will be used to print out the HTML page.

```
68:    <HTML><HEAD>
69:     <TITLE>$Page_Title</TITLE>
70:    </HEAD>
```

Lines 68–70 handle starting the HTML and printing out a page title. Notice here that the *start_html()* function was not used. It could have been used but in Perl there is always . . . well, you know.

```
71:    <BODY>
72:    <FORM NAME="form_example" METHOD="POST">
73:    <INPUT TYPE="HIDDEN" NAME="review" VALUE="1">
74:    $Hidden
```

Lines 71–74 print out some more HTML for the resulting page. On **line 74** we are putting all of the "hidden" HTML variables into our program to keep track of the data between submissions.

```
75:    <TABLE BORDER=1 CELLSPACING=0>
76:     <TR>
77:      <TD COLSPAN=2 ALIGN=CENTER>
78:        <B>$Page_Title</B>
79:      </TD>
80:     </TR>
81:     <TR>
82:      <TD>First Name:</TD><TD>$F_Name</TD>
83:     </TR>
84:     <TR>
85:      <TD>Last Name:</TD><TD>$L_Name</TD>
86:     </TR>
87:     <TR>
88:      <TD>Address:</TD><TD>$Address</TD>
89:     </TR>
90:     <TR>
91:      <TD>City:</TD><TD>$City</TD>
92:     </TR>
93:     <TR>
94:      <TD>State/Zip:</TD><TD>$State $Zip</TD>
95:     </TR>
96:     <TR>
97:      <TD>Eye Color:</TD><TD>$Eye_Group</TD>
98:     </TR>
99:     <TR>
100:      <TD COLSPAN="2" ALIGN="CENTER">
101:       $Buttons
```

```
102:      </TD>
103:      </TR>
104:    </TABLE>
105:    <BR>
106:    </FORM></BODY></HTML>
```

Lines 75–106 are the HTML that print out the table with the data or form fields in it.

```
107: HTML
108: }
```

Line 107 ends the here document that was used for printing the page.

Line 108 closes the subroutine.

```
109: sub Text_Field{
110:    my($name, $max, $size, $value) = @_;
111:    my $field;
```

Line 109 begins the *Text_Field()* subroutine. This subroutine is used to generate the HTML or text that is needed display the text fields on the HTML form.

Line 110 reads in all the data that was passed to the subroutine and stores the data in some new variables.

Line 111 declares a scalar variable.

```
112:    $Hidden .= hidden( -name=>$name, -value=>$value );
```

Line 112 appends onto the $Hidden variable. Since we send all text fields through this subroutine, having the code that generates the hidden fields for use saves a lot of typing.

```
113:    if(!$review){
114:      $field = textfield( -name       => $name,
115:                          -maxlength => $max,
116:                          -size      => $size,
117:                          -value     => $value);
118:    }
```

Line 113 checks to see if *not* $reviewed—does it *not* have any data? If $review did not have any data stored in it, we enter the if portion of this if . . . else loop.

Lines 114–117 use the textfield from CGI.pm to generate the text needed.

Line 118 closes the if . . . else block.

```
119:    else{
120:      $field = $value;
121:    }
```

Lines 119–121 are the else block from the if . . . else block that began on **line 113**. If $review *did* have data in it, we don't want to display an input field yet, so we just set $field to $value.

```
122:    return($field);
123: }
```

Line 122 returns the $field scalar back to the function.

Line 123 closes the subroutine.

That's it for the final example! It should help give you a head start on writing CGI applications that provide feedback to your users as well as let them review their data before actually doing something with the data. The review process is an important one for business applications. If you can cut down on entry errors, even by a few percent, your business will save money because they will have to correct less data.

When designing your HTML forms, try to remember to keep them simple but effective in gathering the information you need. The best way to do this is to plan ahead. The more thought out and well planned your user interface screens are, the better they will be. Remember to provide the user with feedback! Users like that warm, fuzzy feeling they get when they've accomplished something.

4.6 User Exercises

- Make an HTML form with a text box, a text area, a radio group, a checkbox group, a drop-down list, a hidden field, and a password field. Then write a CGI application to read and display all the information that was entered.
- Write a CGI application that will accept numbers and print out their sum.
- (For fun) write a "Mad Lib" program. Mad Libs are fill-in-the-blanks with hints such as "a noun," "a verb," or "a color." Then when the results are displayed, the words entered are inserted into a story. The results can be pretty funny.

4.7 Program Listings

Listing 4-24   **Reading and presenting form data**

```
01: #!/usr/bin/perl -Tw
02: # form3.cgi
03: use strict;
04: use CGI qw(:standard);
05: use CGI::Carp qw(fatalsToBrowser);
06: print header;
07: my ($F_Name, $L_Name, $review, $Address,
08:     $Eye_Group, $Eye_Color, $City, $State,
09:     $Zip, $Page_Title, $Buttons, $Butt_Val,
10:     $Hidden);
11: Initialize_Values();
12: Print_Form();
13: sub Initialize_Values{
14:    $Butt_Val  = param('sendit');
15:    $review    = param('review');
16:    $F_Name    = param('f_name');
17:    $L_Name    = param('l_name');
18:    $Address   = param('address');
19:    $City      = param('city');
20:    $State     = param('state');
21:    $Zip       = param('zip');
22:    $Eye_Color = param('eyecolor');
23:    if($Butt_Val =~ /Edit Data/){ $review = ""; }
24:    if(($Butt_Val =~ /Submit Data/) && ($review > 0)){
25:      &Print_Thanks;
26:    }
27:    $F_Name   = Text_Field("f_name",  20, 20, $F_Name);
28:    $L_Name   = Text_Field("l_name",  20, 20, $L_Name);
29:    $Address  = Text_Field("address", 20, 20, $Address);
30:    $City     = Text_Field("city",    20, 20, $City);
31:    $State    = Text_Field("state",    2,  3, $State);
32:    $Zip      = Text_Field("zip",     10, 12, $Zip);
33:    if(!$review){
34:      $Eye_Group  = radio_group( -name    => 'eyecolor',
35:                                 -default => $Eye_Color,
36:                                 -values  => ['blue','green',
37:                                              'brown','grey','red'],
38:                               );
```

(continued)

```
39:      $Buttons = submit( -name  => "sendit",
40:                         -value => "Submit My Data");
41:      $Hidden    = ""; # Clear $Hidden
42:      $Page_Title = "Enter Your Data";
43:    }
44:    else{
45:      $Eye_Group = $Eye_Color;
46:      $Hidden    .= hidden(-name  =>"eyecolor",
47:                           -value=>$Eye_Color);
48:      $Buttons   = submit(-name  => "sendit",
49:                          -value => "Edit Data");
50:      $Buttons   .= submit( -name  => "sendit",
51:                            -value => "Submit Data");
52:      $Page_Title = "Edit Data or press 'Submit Data'";
53:    }
54: }
55: sub Print_Thanks{
56:   print<<HTML;
57:     <HTML><HEAD><TITLE>Thanks!</TITLE></HEAD>
58:     <BODY>
59:     <CENTER><B>Thank you $F_Name!!!<P>
60:      Your data is very important to us!
61:     </B></CENTER>
62:     </BODY></HTML>
63: HTML
64:   exit;
65: }
66: sub Print_Form{
67:   print<<HTML;
68:   <HTML><HEAD>
69:    <TITLE>$Page_Title</TITLE>
70:   </HEAD>
71:   <BODY>
72:   <FORM NAME="form_example" METHOD="POST">
73:   <INPUT TYPE="HIDDEN" NAME="review" VALUE="1">
74:   $Hidden
75:   <TABLE BORDER=1 CELLSPACING=0>
76:    <TR>
77:     <TD COLSPAN=2 ALIGN=CENTER>
78:       <B>$Page_Title</B>
79:     </TD>
80:    </TR>
```

(continued)

```
81:    <TR>
82:     <TD>First Name:</TD><TD>$F_Name</TD>
83:    </TR>
84:    <TR>
85:     <TD>Last Name:</TD><TD>$L_Name</TD>
86:    </TR>
87:    <TR>
88:     <TD>Address:</TD><TD>$Address</TD>
89:    </TR>
90:    <TR>
91:     <TD>City:</TD><TD>$City</TD>
92:    </TR>
93:    <TR>
94:     <TD>State/Zip:</TD><TD>$State $Zip</TD>
95:    </TR>
96:    <TR>
97:     <TD>Eye Color:</TD><TD>$Eye_Group</TD>
98:    </TR>
99:    <TR>
100:      <TD COLSPAN="2" ALIGN="CENTER">
101:        $Buttons
102:      </TD>
103:    </TR>
104:    </TABLE>
105:    <BR>
106:    </FORM></BODY></HTML>
107: HTML
108: }
109: sub Text_Field{
110:    my($name, $max, $size, $value) = @_;
111:    my $field;
112:    $Hidden .= hidden( -name=>$name, -value=>$value );
113:    if(!$review){
114:      $field = textfield( -name      => $name,
115:                          -maxlength => $max,
116:                          -size      => $size,
117:                          -value     => $value);
118:    }
119:    else{
120:      $field = $value;
121:    }
122:    return($field);
123: }
```

Chapter

Working with Cookies

5.1 Introduction

The kind of cookies we'll be talking about are not Mrs. Field's kind. They are small pieces of data that are passed in the HTTP header and used to store information about you. Cookies have been present in browsers for a long time. Netscape introduced them way back when Netscape was a 1.x version browser.

If they store information, why are they called something like "cookies"? The name *cookie* was explained by Lou Montulli, who was the protocols manager in Netscape's client product division. According to Montulli, "A cookie is a well-known computer science term that is used when describing an opaque piece of data held by an intermediary. The term fits the usage precisely; it's just not a well-known term outside of the computer science circles." So this is how the name *cookies* was chosen.

Since the Web is a "stateless" environment, each time a user visits a site is considered a first visit. The browser connects, gets the requested information, displays the information, and then disconnects. There is no connection between the browser and server. If the browser and server don't maintain a connection, how is it possible for some sites to *remember* information about the user when they return to the site? The answer is simple: cookies!

Cookies are a very useful tool that a Web programmer can use to do things like store items in an e-commerce shopping cart, remember a user's name, maintain user preferences, or even to keep user login information. Incidentally, storing login information in cookies is a bad idea because they are not encrypted in any way and are not a secure storage method. Even so, many sites use cookies to store login and password information so the user does not have to login each time.

5.2 Security

Just because cookies are not good for storing login information, they are still a very simple and effective way to store other user information. It is not possible to pass a virus in a cookie because a cookie is simply a text file that is not, and cannot be, executed. Also, cookies are only available to the server or domain in which they were set, so this provides even more security by preventing unauthorized sites to view the cookie information set by other sites.

5.3 Limitations

The cookie specification provides minimum limits. All Web browsers that support cookies provide at *least* this much support. Web browsers are allowed to support more than this, but they should support at least these limits so the programmer has a baseline when designing an application that uses cookies. The programmer must keep in mind that the user may have cookies turned off or that the Web browser is not accepting cookies for some other reason.

- 300 total cookies
- 4 kilobytes per cookie
- 20 cookies per server or domain

When one of these is exceeded, such as the total cookies, the oldest cookie is purged and the new data is placed into the cookie file. If the cookie length is exceeded—more than 4kb—then the cookie may be truncated until it is less than 4kb.

Cookies are loaded into memory when the browser starts and written to disk when the browser exits if the cookie is still valid. You may have noticed that if a new cookie is set on your system and your browser crashes, you lose the value of the new cookie that was set. This is because the browser did not exit gracefully and therefore did not get a chance to write the new cookie to disk.

5.4 Cookie Pieces

Cookies are made up of six different parts, but the parts are *not* called crumbs!

- *Name* of cookie
- *Value* for this cookie
- *Expiration* date
- *Path* information
- *Domain* that cookie is valid for
- *Secure* (is server using SSL?)

Name

The cookie name is the only required element of a cookie. The name and value typically go together, but when clearing the contents of a cookie, the value element is normally left blank.

Value

The value is the second half of the name/value pair of a cookie. The value is the text that is stored for the cookie. In fact, the name/value pair for a cookie is very similar to the name/value pair for a hash in Perl. It is recommended that the text be URL encoded so that whitespace becomes its *%xx* equivalent, but it is not required.

Expiration Date

The expiration date is when the cookie expires. If no expiration date is given, the cookie will go away once the browser is shut down. The data format looks like this.

```
Weekday, DD-MMM-YYYY HH:MM:SS GMT
```

This date format must be followed. If the date is not set correctly, the browser will either ignore it and expire the cookie when the browser is shut down, or the cookie may not be set at all because of the date format error. We'll learn a few tricks later that will make setting the expiration date a piece of cake (or cookie). *Hint:* CGI.pm.

Domain

The domain is used by the browser to check if the current page being fetched should have a cookie sent to it. When setting a cookie, if the domain is left off, the hostname of the server that generated the cookie response is set as the default. A server can only set cookies for the domain that they are in.

One very important thing to note is that *at least* two dots are required when specifying a domain. Why this limitation? Because allowing a cookie to be set with a domain of **.com** would be bad because the cookie would then be globally accessible to *any* .com address.

Acceptable: domain=.perlguy.net
Not Acceptable: domain=perlguy.net   # only has one dot!

Path

The path is used to further restrict which pages should see the cookie. Setting the path to something like /foo would not send the cookie unless the page being served is under the /foo hierarchy. This means that if the user was requesting a page in the root domain or a domain such as /blech, the cookie would not be served.

One interesting note is that the match that is performed is not an "exact" match, but more of a pattern match, or regular expression without anchor tags. For example, if you set a cookie with a path of /foo, the cookie would get sent not only to requests in the /foo hierarchy but to the /foobar and /foowhatever hierarchies as well! Keep this in mind when using cookies on your site.

Secure

If a cookie is marked as secure, it will only be transmitted if it is over a secure method, such as SSL. If secure is not specified, the default value is for the cookie to be transmitted over nonsecure methods.

5.5 Working with Cookies the Manual Way

Since working with cookies manually can be rather tricky, and there are better methods, we will only cover a quick, simple example and then move on to the easier way. The scripts in this section are small enough so we'll list the entire script and then talk about what it is doing (see Listing 5-1).

Listing 5-1   Manually Setting a Cookie

```
01: #!/usr/bin/perl -wT
02: # Example 5-1
03: use strict;
04: print qq(Content-type: text/html\n);
05: print qq(Set-Cookie: username=Fred Flintstone; );
06: print qq(expires=Mon, 01-Jan-2001 00:00:00 GMT; );
07: print qq(path=/\n\n);
08: print qq(A cookie has been set in your browser...<P>);
09: print qq(<A HREF="example_5-2.cgi">);
10: print qq(Click to view the cookie</A>);
```

Line 1 is like all the other first lines in our example programs. It tells the system where to find Perl and turns on warnings and taint checking.

Line 2 is simply a comment so that we can easily tell which program this is.

Line 3 turns strict on. Although we are not using any functions or variables in this program and strict is not really needed, programming with strict turned on is a good habit to get into. Therefore, we include it in all programs whether they need it or not.

Line 4 prints out the HTTP header type. The document that we are generating is of type text/html. Notice, however, that instead of placing two linefeeds at the end of this line, there is only one. This is because the next line is the cookie that is also part of the header. We cannot pass two linefeeds (a blank line) until we have generated the entire header. If we forgot this and sent two linefeeds on the end of **line 4** instead of **line 5** setting a cookie, it will simply be printed to the browser. Try it out and see what happens.

Lines 5–7 set the cookie. These are normally sent on one line, but to make it fit properly on the page, it was broken up into three separate lines. On **line 7**, since we are now done with the header, we send two linefeeds. This tells the browser that the header is finished and to get ready for some content.

Line 8 simply prints out some text to the user so they know that something actually did happen.

Lines 9–10 print out a link that points to our next program that reads the cookie so that the user can make sure that it was indeed set. The output of the program is shown in Figure 5-1.

Figure 5-1   **Manual cookie-setting program output**

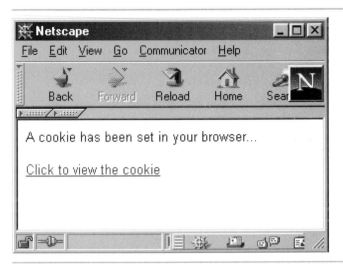

When you run this program, set your Web browser to warn you when cookies are set. Cookie warnings are a great tool to see what cookies are being sent back and forth between the server and Web browser. Also, cookie warnings can aid you when debugging your scripts.

We've manually set a cookie. Now we need to write a small script so that we can see the cookie and make sure that it worked the way we expected it to. This small application in Listing 5-2 will read the cookie and print out what it contains (see Figure 5-2).

Listing 5-2 **Manually getting a cookie**

```
01: #!/usr/bin/perl -wT
02: # Example 5-2
03: use strict;
04: my ($key, $value) = split(/=/, $ENV{HTTP_COOKIE});
05: print qq(Content-type: text/html\n\n);
06: print qq(The cookie <B>$key</B> contained <B>$value</B>);
```

Lines 1–3 are the same as the previous example.

Line 4 uses the *split()* function to split the cookie at the equal sign (=). The cookie is passed back from the server to the browser in the HTTP_COOKIE environment variable. So we pass $ENV{'HTTP_COOKIE'} as an argument to the *split()* function to get the cookie.

Line 5 prints out the standard HTTP header.

Line 6 prints out the key and value of the cookie so that the we can see that it worked.

Figure 5-2 **Manual cookie-setting output**

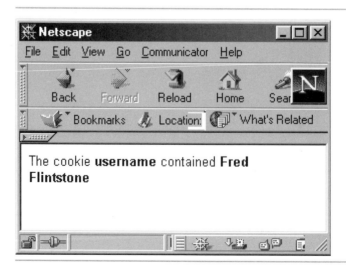

These two examples were pretty simple, but they are good starting points. Things get much more complex when you want to set a cookie so that it expires in one month and you want to set it to the values stored in a hash or array. Can you imagine what that code would look like! Thankfully, Lincoln Stein comes through for us again with the CGI.pm. The rest of this chapter will focus on how to use the functions in the CGI module, since it makes things much, much easier.

5.6 Baking Cookies with CGI.pm

Using CGI.pm to handle cookies makes the programmer's task much easier. Just as CGI.pm makes handling HTML forms much easier, it takes much of the hassle out of using cookies.

With CGI.pm you still pass the same parameters to the *cookie()* function, but you have more options with CGI.pm. For example, say you want to make a cookie expire in three months. If you choose the manual method, you would need to come up with some way of determining what the date and day of the week will be three months from now. With CGI.pm you simply pass "+3M" in the *expires* argument. The CGI module handles all the details about the date format. Features like this make working with cookies much easier!

We'll begin with an example that mimics the manual method we did earlier. Then we'll move on to more powerful examples. Again, since this program is so short—12 lines—we'll just list the whole thing out and then talk about it (see Listing 5-3).

Listing 5-3   Setting cookies with CGI.pm

```
01: #!/usr/bin/perl -wT
02: # Example 5-3
03: use strict;
04: use CGI qw(:standard);
05: my $cookie1 = cookie( -name    => 'username2',
06:                       -value   => 'Barney Rubble',
07:                       -expires => '+1y',
08:                     );
09: print header( -cookie => $cookie1 );
10: print qq(Another cookie has been set in your browser...<P>);
11: print qq(<A HREF="example_5-4.cgi">);
12: print qq(Click to view the cookie</A>);
```

Lines 1–3 are identical to the earlier examples. On **line 4** we bring in the CGI module.

Lines 5–8 set the cookie, using the *cookie()* function. Notice that we still have the same names for the cookie items. The difference is that we are using a hash to pass the data instead of the item name/item value pair that we used for the manual method. In this example, we set the cookie to expire in one year with the "+1y."

Line 9 prints the standard HTTP header, using the CGI module's *header()* function. We pass the cookie as an argument to the *header()* function to set the cookie on the user's browser. Passing multiple cookies is also allowed (we'll be passing multiple cookies in later examples).

Lines 10–12 print out some information so the user knows that the program worked. It also prints out a link to another program that allows you to check and make sure that the cookie was properly set.

Figure 5-3   **Setting cookie using CGI.pm program output**

The output from this example, shown in Figure 5-3, is just as exciting as the first example. However, we now have two cookies set because each cookie has its own name.

This program was very similar to the first example that we covered in this chapter. There are actually more lines in this example than in the manual cookie example! But just because the program is longer does not mean that the program is more difficult. When we get to programs that set multiple cookies or pass arrays of hashes as data, then you'll see the real power of using the CGI module for cookies. Let's move on to reading the cookie that we just set. Then we can get into some of the more challenging examples (see Listing 5-4).

Listing 5-4   **Reading cookies with CGI.pm**

```
01: #!/usr/bin/perl -wT
02: # Example 5-4
03: use strict;
```

```
04: use CGI qw(:standard);
05: my $old_value = cookie('username');
06: my $new_value = cookie('username2');
07: print header;
08: print qq(The new cookie <B>username2</B> );
09: print qq(contains <B>$new_value</B><P>);
10: print qq(The old cookie <B>username</B> );
11: print qq(contains <B>$old_value</B>);
```

Lines 1–3 are, again, identical to the previous examples.

Line 4 brings in the CGI module and the standard functions, just like in Listing 5-3.

Lines 5–6 create the my variables $old_value and $new_value. These are used to store the contents of the cookies. They are set immediately with the contents of the cookies, using the *cookie()* function from the CGI module. Once the cookies are stored in the variables, we move on. The *cookie()* function is another great part of CGI.pm. In Listing 5-3 we used the *cookie()* function to create our cookies the easy way. Now we are using the *cookie()* function to get the cookies from the browser simply by calling the function with the cookie name. The return value is the contents of the cookie, if it existed.

Line 7 prints out the standard HTTP header. We are not setting a cookie here so we don't pass any cookie information to the *header()* function.

Lines 8–11 print out the information that was sent back from the cookies so that the user can see that the program worked.

Figure 5-4   Reading cookies with CGI.pm

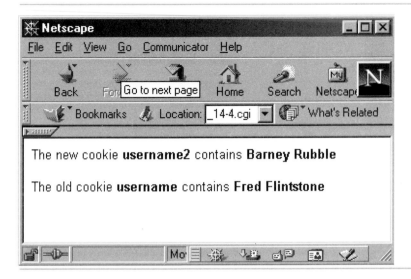

In Figure 5-4 from Listing 5-4, we can see that we had two different cookies set. One was called *username2* and the other was called *username*. We set one of these cookies manually and the other using the interface provided by the CGI module. As you can see, it does not matter *how* you set a cookie, once a cookie is set it can be read using whatever method you prefer.

5.7 Controlling User Preferences with Cookies

Now we'll move on to a more practical example of cookies. In this example, the page title, page color, text color, and name will be controlled by cookies. This example will also show you how to set multiple cookies so that you can see that it is almost as simple as setting a single cookie. Since this program is longer, it will be broken up for its description.

```
01: #!/usr/bin/perl -wT
02: # Example 5-5
03: use strict;
04: use CGI qw(:standard);
05: use CGI::Carp qw(fatalsToBrowser);
```

Lines 1– 5 are again pretty standard for all of the programs we have written so far. **Line 1** tells the system where to find Perl and turns on warnings and taint checking. **Line 2** is a comment, **line 3** loads strict, **line 4** loads the CGI module, and **line 5** loads the CGI::Carp module.

```
06: my ($Page_Cookie1, $Page_Cookie2);
07: my $Flag    = 0;
```

Line 6 creates the my variables where the cookies will be stored.

Line 7 creates a my variable called $Flag and sets it to an initial value of 0. $Flag will be set to 1 if we detect that any cookies need to be changed.

```
08: my %Values = cookie('page_values');
09: my $Title  = cookie('page_title');
```

Line 8 creates a my variable that is a hash named %Values and gets the values from the cookie named *page_values* via the CGI module's *cookie()* function.

Line 9 creates a my variable called $Title and gets the values from the *page_title* cookie. Notice that the cookie function returned a hash on **line 8** but a scalar on **line 9**. The *cookie()* function will return whatever was passed to it (hash, array, scalar).

```
10: foreach(param()){
11:   next unless param($_);
12:     $Values{$_} = param($_);
13:     $Flag      = 1;
14: }
```

Lines 10–14 loop through each of the parameters that were sent from the HTML form. On **line 10** the *param()* inside of the *foreach()* is perfectly legal because the *param()* function will return a list of all parameters if nothing is passed to it. The *foreach()* will loop through the list returned by the *param()* function.

Line 11 uses the *next()* function to exit this iteration of the loop if the current parameter contains no data.

It works like this: next exits the current iteration of the loop that it is in when it is called. *unless()* is the same as *if not (false)*. So we are checking to see if the *param($_)* function call was false (contained no data). The next will only get executed if there was no data returned by the *param()* function.

In English we are saying, "Exit the iteration of the loop we are in unless the *param()* function call returned some data."

Line 12 sets the %Values hash with a key of $_ (the current value from the *foreach()* and sets its *value* to whatever was returned when we passed $_ to the *param()* function. Since we are only setting one value at a time, we access the *Values* hash with a $ instead of a %.

Line 13 sets the value of $Flag to 1. This is so the program knows if changes were made. We don't want to bother setting a new cookie if nothing has changed.

Line 14 closes the foreach loop.

```
15: $Values{Textcolor} = "#000000" unless($Values{Textcolor});
16: $Values{Bgcolor}   = "#FFFFFF" unless($Values{Bgcolor});
17: $Values{Name}      = "NoName"  unless($Values{Name});
```

Lines 15–17 are used to set the default values to use if any of our values are still empty. We need to make sure that there is at least *some* value to use for our page attributes, so we set a default value if needed. These lines simply use the *unless()* function to see if the hash elements are empty or not. If a hash element is empty, it gets set to the default value.

```
18: $Title = "Cookie Example" if($Title eq "");
```

Line 18 sets the default page title if $Title contains no data.

```
19: if(param('Title')){
20:     $Title = param('Title');
21:     $Flag  = 1;
22: }
```

Lines 19–22 check to see if the Title HTML form field contained any data. If it does, then the if block is entered.

Line 20 sets the $Title variable to whatever was passed from the HTML form.

Line 21 sets the $Flag variable to 1 so that a new cookie will be set.

Line 22 closes the if block.

```
23: if($Flag){
```

Line 23 begins an if . . . else block that is used to see if the $Flag variable has been set.

```
24:     $Page_Cookie1 = cookie(-name    => 'page_values',
25:                             -expires => '+2m',
26:                             -value   => \%Values );
```

Lines 24–26 create the first cookie that we are going to set. **Line 24** calls the *cookie()* function, which is part of the CGI module. The -name, -expires, and -value are all part of the arguments to the cookie function. **Lines 25 and 26** are also arguments passed to the *cookie()* function. On **line 26** we are actually passing a reference to a hash!

The *cookie()* function can take six different parameters. The only required element is name.

- **name** is the name of the cookie being set. It is the only required parameter.
- **expires** is the length of time the cookie is valid. We are setting this cookie to expire in two minutes (+2m) to allow you to verify that it does indeed expire. Possible forms for this argument are **s** for seconds, **m** for minutes, **h** for hours, **d** for days, **now**, **M** for months, and **y** for years, or you can pass the actual date/time string as in the manual cookie method. You can also pass negative values, such as –1d, if you want a cookie to expire immediately.

■ **value** is the actual value of the cookie. Using the CGI module, you can easily pass references to hashes or arrays. If you tried to do this manually, you would find yourself writing a lot more code because the hashes and arrays would need to be expanded into a string before they can be made into a cookie string. Then when the cookie is read, the array or hash would need to be reassembled into its proper structure. The CGI module does all of this for you automatically.

■ **domain** is the range of domains that the browser will send this cookie. The default is that the cookie will only be sent to the server that created it.

■ **path** can be used to set the partial path for which the cookie is valid. If you have several cookies from a server, this could be set to something like /shoppingcart. Then the cookie would only be sent if the page came from the /shoppingcart directory or one of the subdirectories underneath the /shoppingcart directory.

■ **secure** can be set to true, 1, or false, 0. With it set to true, the cookie will only be sent if a secure connection is being used. The default value is false, so this argument usually is not used.

```
27:     $Page_Cookie2 = cookie(-name     => 'page_title',
28:                            -expires => '+2m',
29:                            -value   => $Title );
```

Lines 27–29 set another cookie in the same manner as the preceding **lines 24–26**. This cookie is for the page title.

Instead of creating two cookies, we could have easily set only a single cookie with multiple values. However, if we chose to do this, you would not see an example of multiple cookies being set! You can set several cookies at the same time. Just remember that there are limits to the number of cookies and the size of the cookies that you can send.

```
30:     print header(-cookie => [$Page_Cookie1, $Page_Cookie2]);
31: }
```

Line 30 sends an HTTP header and sets the cookies. Cookies are sent in the HTTP header so any cookies that need to be set are passed as parameters in the *header()* function. If you are passing a single cookie, you can omit the square brackets [], but if you are passing multiple cookies they are required.

Line 31 simply closes the if portion of the if . . . else structure.

```
32: else{
33:     print header();
34: }
```

Line 32 begins the else portion of the if . . . else structure. We get here if there are no cookies to be set. If that is the case, on **line 33** we simply use the *header()* function without any arguments.

Line 34 closes out the if . . . else structure.

```
35: print <<HTML;
36: <HTML><HEAD><TITLE>$Title</TITLE></HEAD>
37:  <BODY BGCOLOR="$Values{Bgcolor}"
38:   TEXT="$Values{Textcolor}">
39:   <FORM>
40:   <H2>Welcome $Values{Name}!!!</H2>
41:   <TABLE>
42:    <TR>
43:     <TD>Name:</TD>
44:     <TD><INPUT TYPE="text" NAME="Name"></TD>
45:    </TR>
46:    <TR>
47:     <TD>Title:</TD>
48:     <TD><INPUT TYPE="text" NAME="Title"></TD>
49:    </TR>
50:    <TR>
51:     <TD>Background Color:</TD>
52:     <TD><INPUT TYPE="text" NAME="Bgcolor"></TD>
53:    </TR>
54:    <TR>
55:     <TD>Text Color:</TD>
56:     <TD><INPUT TYPE="text" NAME="Textcolor"></TD>
57:    </TR>
58:   </TABLE>
59:   <P>
60:   <INPUT TYPE="submit">
61:   </FORM>
62:  </BODY>
63: </HTML>
64: HTML
```

Lines 35–64 are a here document that print out the resulting page. On **lines 36, 37, 38, and 40** there are values that we were working with at the beginning of this program. They are either from the cookie or the HTML form, or they are the default values.

Figure 5-5   Setting user preferences

The first time the preceding example is run, the screen will look like the one in Figure 5-5. It is nothing special, since there are no user preferences to brighten up the page yet. Enter some data in the fields and click the "Submit Query" button to set the cookies, and the appearance of the page will change. Once the user enters some data and presses the submit button, the page will reload with the new settings in place, as shown in Figure 5-6.

Figure 5-6 **Custom settings output**

Remember that the cookies in this example only last for two minutes, so if you wait any longer than that, the colors will revert back to the defaults, like in the preceding example. Granted, two minutes is not very practical for something like user preferences, but it shows you how to set an expire time for the cookie, and it allows you to easily ensure that the cookies do indeed expire.

Having a cookie that expires in a short time, such as 15 minutes, actually does have some very practical applications. Take an online banking application, for example. You probably wouldn't want to stay logged on indefinitely if for some reason you had to leave your keyboard. What many systems do is set a cookie with an expire time of around 15 minutes. Each time the user does something in the application, the cookie is checked to see if it is still valid. If the cookie is still valid, the expire time will get updated, and the task the user is attempting will be performed. If the cookie has expired, the program will not perform the requested task; instead it will ask you to authenticate again. This should prevent someone else from walking up to another user's computer while they have stepped away and perform tasks that the original user would not want them to, such as transferring money.

Although cookies are simply small pieces of data that can't do anything but get set or be read, they are an extremely powerful part of Web application programming. The reason they are so powerful is that they can be used to maintain session timeouts, maintain user preferences, store small but important pieces of data, or even remember how many times a user has visited a page.

5.8 User Exercises

- Create a page that increments a cookie and tells the user how many times he or she has visited the page.
- Create a page that stores a user id as a cookie and uses the cookie to look up user information in a database table.

Chapter

Access Counters

6.1 Introduction

Since the beginning of the mainstream popularity of the Web, there have been Web site maintainers who want to know how many people are visiting their site and be able to report this information to others. These days you see all types and sizes of hit counters on Web sites. Because of the popularity of this type of application, we consider it a necessity to show you how to make your own hit counters.

Hit counters have become so popular that there are even many "free" counter services available on the Web. Many allow you to link to their counter script, which keeps track of hits on your site. Why use someone else's service to remotely keep your count when you can do it for yourself or for your clients? If you use any of these services now, you will not need to by the end of this chapter because you will learn how to create your own CGI script for this application.

There are different ways to use and display counters. One way is as a Server Side Include (SSI) to display the count as either text or an image. Another way is by using the HTML <IMG> tag in a script to display the count as an image. This chapter we will show you how to use both methods. You will also learn how to create an image counter that doesn't use any images. We will also add a little twist to an access counter so it displays how many people have *not* been to your Web site!

The examples in this chapter will use a simple text file to keep the counts. Using a text file is easy, fast, and portable. You could very easily use a simple table in a database for this application, but we chose to use a text file to illustrate how to safely manipulate one and for the reasons noted earlier. One caveat is that access counters do not take into account unique visitors and are actual "hit," or page impression, counters. For the most part, the majority of counters available and used today work like this and record each and every instance a page is served from the Web server. We emphasize *every instance a page is served* because the counter would not be updated if the Web surfer is viewing the page from a cache. Refer back to Chapter 2 to read about caching.

The examples in this chapter are also meant to be shared applications. This means that one counter script can be used to handle multiple pages or multiple Web sites. We will add this functionality by having each script take an argument that is the name and location of the counter file. The scripts will then get the desired count because it will know the location of the proper counter file. Another assumption is that the counters data file is kept in the same directory as the script. Therefore, you will want to change the paths appropriately for your system.

These are the modules and pragmas used in this chapter.

- lib
- strict
- CGI
- Fcntl
- GD
- Image::Size
- LWP::UserAgent
- Untaint

6.2 Example Script: SSI Text Counter

Using SSI to display access counts is very common. SSIs are flexible because they can display images, text, or a combination of both. A counter that displays only text has some advantages, such as not needing any image files. This is a nice way to display a count because there is no overhead for handling the displaying and requesting of images. An image counter may not seem like much of a speed penalty in serving your pages, but if you have a lot of images on your site, why load even more images if you don't have to? Another thing to consider if you have a high traffic Web site is that loading multiple images on many pages will take up bandwidth and possibly cause speed penalties for the loading of your pages (of course, image size and placement are also factors).

The following example, count.pl, is displaying a textual count using an SSI. Make sure that you have SSIs enabled[1] for the directories from which you are using this. To call this script, include this SSI in the Web page text.

```
<!--#include virtual="../cgi-bin/count.pl text_counter.dat"-->
```

This is the code for *count.pl*.

```
01: #!/usr/bin/perl -wT
02: # count.pl
03: use strict;
04: use Fcntl qw(:flock);
05: use Untaint;
```

Lines 1–5 are using all needed modules and pragmas. **Line 4** uses the Fcntl module. This loads in the fcntl.h constants that give you control over your descriptors. We are using this module to import the constants related to file locking, *flock()* (flock(2)).

```
06: my $counter = untaint(qr(.*\.dat$), $ARGV[0]);
```

Line 6 initiates the $counter variable. This variable will be assigned the untainted value of the first argument passed to the script that is the name and location of the counter file. The value will only be untainted if it ends in a .dat file extension because of the pattern we are passing the *untaint()* method. This means you can use this same script for multiple counter files because the script can handle using whatever counter file it is passed!

```
07: my $silent = 0;
```

Line 7 defines the $silent variable. This counter example allows for the count to just be recorded and not shown to the client *or* record the count and display it to the client. If $silent is defined at 0, the count will be displayed. If it is set to 1, it will not.

```
08: my $link = 1;
```

Line 8 defines the $link variable, which is another variable used for configuration. As you will see, this script can display the count as a hyperlink. Defining $link as 1 will make this happen, and 0 will make it simply display as text.

---

1. Make sure that your Web server supports SSI. Most do, but some, such as Personal Web Server from Microsoft, may not.

```
09: my $link_URL = "http://www.perl.org/";
```

Line 9 defines $link_URL, which is the URL to which the counter will be linked if you defined $link to 1.

```
10: my $SEMAPHORE = $counter . ".lck";
```

Line 10 initializes a variable that will be using a semaphore file. This file will be used to ensure that a race condition does not occur. Having a race condition in a Perl script when using a text file is an all too common mishap by many Perl programmers, so let's take a few minutes to discuss them. Much of the time people program a series of events similar to what is shown in Listing 6-1.

Listing 6-1   **Events that lead to a race condition**

```
01: Open file for reading.
02: Lock file.
03: Read File.
04: Close file.
05: Re-open file for writing.
06: Lock file.
07: Write to file.
08: Close file.
```

Can you see where the problem is? There is a race condition here because one program may open the file for reading while another opens it for writing and because the file may be unlocked before the data is completely written to disk. This can cause corruption of data because two programs may be trying to operate on the file in two different ways at the same time. This is a common mistake, and to work around it we will lock a file that is completely separate from the file on which we will be working. When we lock this semaphore file, we can safely operate on the data file because we know that if another instance of this program is run simultaneously, one will have to wait for the semaphore file to be unlocked before beginning to operate on the data file. Listing 6-2 shows the proper order of events that should occur.

Listing 6-2   **Events to prevent a race condition**

```
01: Open semaphore file for writing.
02: Obtain exclusive lock on semaphore file.
03: Open data file.
04: Work on the data file.
05: Close the data file.
06: Close the semaphore file.
```

As you can see in Listing 6-2, the data file will not be worked on unless the semaphore has been exclusively locked. Because of this, there is no way in which one instance of the script (or another script) will be operating on the data file at one time. One of the important things to remember about using *flock()* and locking files is that *flock()* doesn't actually block all other processes on the system from altering the file. Instead Perl's *flock()*, just like the Unix flock(2), issues an advisory lock; it doesn't physically lock the file from all other processes. This means that when another process uses *flock()* to attempt to lock a file, the *flock()* that has the lock says, "Hey! I am operating on this file. Wait until I am finished." The process attempting to lock will wait. If another program tries to operate on the data file and does not use *flock()* to try to lock the appropriate semaphore file, then it will operate on the data file at will. When developing CGI applications you will always need to keep this in mind and use a good, consistent locking process.

In order to help demonstrate what will happen when two instances of a script try to access a data file opened using the technique outlined in Listing 6-2, run the script shown in Listing 6-3 in two (or more) different console windows, side by side, at the same time. In fact, when one instance ends, restart it! You will witness what happens when one file waits to gain an exclusive lock on a file. Also, you will see that it is only possible for one of the instances to operate on the data file at a time.

Listing 6-3   **Command line script to demonstrate *flock()***

```
01: #!/usr/bin/perl -wT
02: use Fcntl qw(:flock);
03: my $file = 'test_lock.txt';
04: my $SEMAPHORE = $file . '.lck';
05: open(S, ">>$SEMAPHORE") or die "$SEMAPHORE: $!";
06: flock(S, LOCK_EX) or die "flock() failed for $SEMAPHORE: $!";
07: open (FH, ">>$file") or die "Can't open $file: $!";
08: print "About to write\n";
09: print FH "I have written ($$)\n";
10: print "Written\n";
11: close FH;
12: print "Going to sleep...\n";
13: sleep 10;
14: print "Woken up...\n";
15: close S;
```

```
11: open(S,">>$SEMAPHORE") || die "Can't open Semaphore file
                                  ($SEMAPHORE): $!";
12: flock (S, LOCK_EX);
```

Lines 11 and 12 open the semaphore file for writing and then attempt to put an exclusive lock in it. If *flock()* detects that the file is already locked, it will wait until it can obtain an exclusive lock. We want to open the semaphore file in write mode because sometimes an exclusive lock will not be granted on a filehandle opened for only reading.

```
13: if (-e $counter) {
14:     open (FILE, $counter) || die "Can't read counter. $!";
15:     my $visits = <FILE>;
16:     close (FILE);
17: }
```

Lines 13–17 open and read our counter file. The value, our count, is stored in the $visits variable, and **line 15** closes the file. This happens only if the counter file exists because **line 14** will die if the read fails, and this would continue to happen if the file hasn't been created by hand.

```
18: open (FILE, ">$counter") || die "Cant write to counter. $!";
19: print FILE ++$visits;
20: close (FILE);
```

Line 18 will handle the creation of the initial counter file. **Lines 18, 19, and 20** now reopen the data file for writing and write the new count to it by auto-incrementing the $visits variable.

```
21: close S;
```

Line 21 closes the semaphore file. We do not need to unlock the file because it is automatically unlocked when the file is closed. Also, because it can create a race condition if you unlock a file, then close it. This is because another process may try to open the file before yours is finished updating and closing it.

```
22: if (!$silent) {
23:     if ($link) {
24:         print qq(<A HREF="$link_URL">$visits</A>);
25:     }else{
26:         print $visits;
27:     }
28: }
```

Lines 22–28 display the count to the client. **Line 22** is checked first to see if the counter is in "silent" mode. If it is, the script has nothing more to do, since the counter file has already been updated with the latest count. If it is not in silent mode, the script then checks **line 23** to see, if we want to display the count as a hyperlink. If so, it prints that hyperlink, and it is done. If not, it simply displays the count as text. That's all! Figure 6-1 shows a screenshot of this text counter.

Figure 6-1   Screenshot of SSI text counter

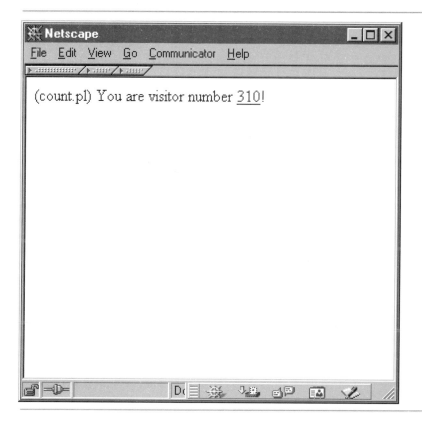

This example was extremely simple and basic, but, it is really all you need to have a counter for your Web site. One thing about counters these days is they do not really need to be images. Using big and fancy images of numbers has almost become a cliché from the mid 1990s. But you or your clients may still want to use images. Using images certainly has its place on the Web, and the following example will show you how to use your own images to create an image counter once again using SSI.

6.3 Example Script: SSI Image Counter

The following counter script, count2.pl, is another that can be used as a shared script. This script will take two arguments, the first being the name of the counter file, just as shown in the previous example. The second argument will be the "style" of the images. This allows multiple users to use the same script as well as choose their own style of images or for one site to use different styles on various pages to keep things interesting. What we mean by "style" is images of different size, color, shape, font, anything!

If you were to set up this script to be used in a shared environment, you would likely have the script itself live in the common cgi-bin, and the counter files and image directories would live outside that. So, for example, you could have the directory structure shown in Listing 6-4.

Listing 6-4   **Example directory structure for shared use**

```
/usr/local/apache/cgi-bin
                    contains count2.pl
/usr/local/apache/htdocs/counters
/usr/local/apache/htdocs/counter/data
                              contains the data files
/usr/local/apache/htdocs/counter/images/*.png
/usr/local/apache/htdocs/counter/images/plain/*.png
/usr/local/apache/htdocs/counter/images/fancy/*.png
/usr/local/apache/htdocs/counter/images/funny/*.png
etc...
```

The example of a directory structure shown in Listing 6-4 would be a good way to use this script in a shared environment. Adding new image styles would be easy because all that would be needed is a new image style directory with the appropriate image files. There should be 10 images for each image style directory, one for each digit from 0 to 9 with the naming convention <number>.png. Simple, scalable, and flexible! Now, let's get on with the script, count2.pl, itself.

```
01: #!/usr/bin/perl -wT
02: # count2.pl
03: use strict;
04: use Fcntl qw(:flock);
05: use Untaint;
06: use Image::Size qw(html_imgsize);
```

Lines 1–6 are similar to the previous example, except for **line 6**. **Line 6** pulls in the Image::Size module as well as imports its *html_imgsize()* method. The Image::Size module is used for finding the size of images. The *html_imgsize()*

method will not only get the size of an image but also return a string usable for the <IMG> tag. More about that in **line 21**.

```
07: my $counter = untaint(qr(.*\.dat$), $ARGV[0]);
08: my $style = untaint(qr(^(\.{0,2}/)*?[\w-/]+$), $ARGV[1]);
```

Lines 7 and 8 launder the arguments. Again, the counter file, saved to $counter, will make sure that the input is a .dat file. **Line 8** launders the argument for the style. The style is expected to be a directory name, and here we are checking for alphanumeric characters or a dash. It also checks to see if it is a relative path or full directory path. This will allow you to put the image directories somewhere other than the current working directory.

```
09: my $SEMAPHORE = $counter . ".lck";
10: open(S,">>$SEMAPHORE") || die "Can't open Semaphore file
                         ($SEMAPHORE): $!";
11: flock (S, LOCK_EX);
12: open (FILE, $counter) || die "Can't read counter. $!";
13: my $visits = <FILE>;
14: close (FILE);
15: open (FILE, ">$counter") || die "Cant write to counter. $!";
16: print FILE $visits++;
17: close (FILE);
18: close S;
```

Lines 9–18 go through the locking of the semaphore file, and reading/writing of the count data to the counter file to avoid a race condition.

```
19: exit unless -d $style;
```

Line 19 checks to see if the directory passed as the directory for the style exists. If it does not exist, the script *exit()*s. This will help avoid trying to open images that do not exist and displaying those ugly broken image icons.

```
20: my @digits = split(//,$visits);
```

Line 20 creates an array, @digits, with each number making up the count ($visits) as an element. This array will be used in the coming lines to display the appropriate images.

```
21: foreach (@digits) {
22:     my $size = html_imgsize("$style/$_.png");
23:     print qq(<img src="$style/$_.png">);
24: }
```

Lines 21–24 loops through the array elements. Recall that each element is a single digit. On line 22 we pass the image path (the style directory, a slash, $_ which holds the current digit being worked with, and the .png extension.) to the *html_imgsize()* method. This method is very handy, and it returns a string all ready to be used in your HTML image tag. For example, if the image being sent to it is 10x10, it will return the string "WIDTH=10 HEIGHT=10." In this case, we save this string into $size. Line 23 then prints the HTML image tag to the client. It will obviously print out one for each image needed. That's it—another easy way to add a counter to your Web site! Figure 6-2 shows a screenshot of this action. The following is the SSI needed to call this script.

```
<!--#exec cmd="../cgi-bin/count2.pl img_counter.dat myStyle"-->
```

Figure 6-2   Screenshot of output for count2.pl

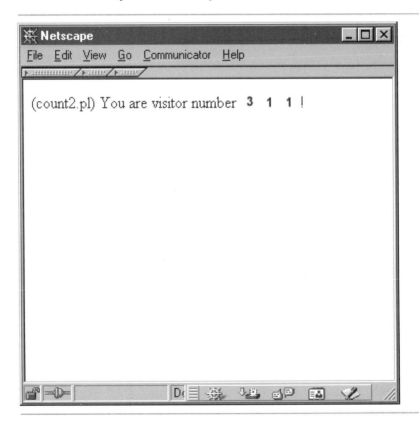

6.4 Example Script: SSI Text Counter, with a Twist

So far we have seen how to use SSI to create a text and image counter to show visitors how many impressions your Web page has received. That is good, but let's make it a little more fun and show how many possible visitors have *not* been to your Web page! This example is a text count, but it takes the hit count and then subtracts that from the U.S. Census Bureau's world population estimate.[2] Based on their estimates and your hit counter, this script (population.pl) will display an *estimated* number of people in the world who have not yet seen your Web page. When completed, you would use the following SSI on your Web page.

```
<!--#include virtual=" ../cgi-bin/population.pl img_counter.dat"-->
```

And the code for population.pl begins with the following.

```
01: #!/usr/bin/perl -wT
02: # population.pl
03: use strict;
04: use Untaint;
05: use LWP::UserAgent;
```

Lines 1–5 only introduce one new module, LWP::UserAgent. The LWP modules handle the task, among others, of fetching a remote URL and in our case from the U.S. Census Bureau so we can get their estimated world population.

```
06: my $counter = untaint(qr(.*\.dat$), $ARGV[0]);
```

Line 6 launders the incoming argument, which is the same as in the previous examples.

```
07: my $ua = new LWP::UserAgent;
```

Line 7 created a new LWP::UserAgent object. We will use this object to literally act as a Web user agent (UA), or client.

```
08: $ua->agent("GetCount/0.1");
```

Line 8 sets the product information for our client. This is what will be sent in the User-Agent portion of the request header to the remote Web server.

---

2. You can find out more about the U.S. Census Bureau's world population estimates on their Web site located at *http://www.census.gov/ipc/www/popwnote.html*.

For our example, we have named our "product" GetCount, with a version of 0.1. This is what will show in the Web server logs on the remote server.

```
09: my $req = new HTTP::Request GET =>
              'http://www.census.gov/cgi-bin/ipc/popclockw';
```

Line 9 creates a HTTP::Request object. We are telling this object that the request will be a GET and the URL that we want to GET. We do not have to *use()* the HTTP::Request module in our script because LWP::UserAgent has done that for us.

```
10: $req->header(Accept => "text/html");
```

Line 10 sets the "Accept" value of our HTTP request header. We are saying we will accept documents with the MIME type of text/html.

```
11: my $res = $ua->request($req);
```

Line 11 uses the *request()* method of LWP::UserAgent via our UA object. In the background the Web page is fetched and returns an object with all of the response data. In our case, the new object is $res.

```
12: if ($res->is_success) {
```

Line 12 uses the *is_success()* method to see if the request was a success. If it is, a true value is returned; if it failed, a false value is returned.

```
13:     my $html = $res->content;
```

Line 13 retrieves the content, or HTML, from the response object by calling the *content()* method. The content of the Web page is then stored as a string in $html.

```
14:     (my $num = $html) =~ s!^.*<h1>(.*?)</h1>.*$!$1!si;
```

Line 14 does a regular expression to pull out the number (world population) from the HTML string in $html. The U.S. Census Bureau Web page from which this information is retrieved has this number between the first set of H1 tags, but be aware that this may change in the future and this line would need to be edited. This regular expression discards everything else in the string and ultimately stores the value of this in $num.

```
15:        open(LOG, $counter) || die "Can't read counter. $!";
16:        my $log = <LOG>;
17:        close LOG;
```

Lines 15, 16, and 17 open our counter file, like the other examples, and store its value in the variable $log.

```
18:        $num =~ s!,!!g;
```

Line 18 removes all commas from $num. The number retrieved and stored in $num will contain commas (if it didn't, then the world population would be less than 1,000 people!), and because we need to do a mathematical operation with this number, they need to be removed (or turned into underscores, _).

```
19:        $num = $num-$log;
```

Line 19 subtracts the number of hits in the counter from the world population. We now know how many people have yet to visit!

```
20:        1 while $num =~ s!^(\d+)(\d{3})!$1,$2!;
```

Line 20 is a simple regular expression that, while going through this little loop, "commify" the number. This line works by maintaining a true value as long as the substitution returns a true value (is successful). The final result will be the number in $num (which had the commas removed earlier) being properly formatted with commas in the appropriate places.

```
21:        print $num;
```

Line 21 prints the number to the client!

```
22: } else {
23:        print "[trouble calculating]";
24: }
```

Lines 22–24 complete the script by displaying a string to the client if the return object wasn't successful. Figure 6-3 shows the screenshot for this example.

Figure 6-3   **Screenshot of world population hit counter**

6.5 Example Script: An Imageless Image Counter

How is it possible to have an imageless image counter? This can be done by displaying an image when no physical image file exists, of course! The following example will do just this—display an image to the client by creating it on the fly. By using the **GD** module, we can create an image on the fly based on the hit count. The following example will display an extremely basic looking counter, but after playing around with GD, you will be able to fancy it up. This script is not an SSI, as in the previous examples, but this script will be called from the HTML <IMG> tag. This is very useful if you do not want to have every page using a counter act as an SSI or do not have SSIs available.[3]

---

3. If you do not have SSIs available, you are likely not in control of the Web server. In this case, we suggest contacting your system administrator to ask them to enable SSIs for you.

How can you run a Perl script from an HTML <IMG> tag? When you use the <IMG> tag, a request is sent to the server for an image or whatever is noted in the "src" parameter. A separate request is sent to the Web server to retrieve the data. For example, if your Web page has 10 images on it, then 11 requests are sent to the Web server—1 for the page itself and 10 more for the images. So we can use the <IMG> tag to send a request to a Perl script, which then returns an image. Beware that if the script does not return the proper MIME header for an image, as well as a valid image, then you will end up seeing that ugly broken image icon. Now, on with the script (gd_count.pl)!

```
01: #!/usr/bin/perl -wT
02: # gd_count.pl
03: use strict;
04: use Untaint;
05: use GD;
06: use CGI qw(param header);
```

Lines 1–6 must look pretty familiar by now. **Line 5** pulls in the GD module, which will be used to create our image. **Line 6** is importing two CGI.pm methods, *param()* and *header()*.

```
07: print header("image/png");
```

Line 7 prints out the Content-Type header. We tell it that we will be sending content with the MIME type of **image/png**, since we will be creating and displaying a PNG image.[4]

```
08: my $counter = untaint(qr(.*\.dat$), param('counter'));
09: open(LOG, $counter) || die "Can't read counter. $!";
10: my $log = <LOG>;
11: close LOG;
```

Lines 8–11 should need no explanation by now!

```
12: my $im = new GD::Image((length($log)*9),20);
```

---

4. Because of patents Unisys holds on the LZW compression algorithm that creates GIF images, GD.pm now only creates PNG images. Not all browsers currently support the newer PNG format. There are tools to convert PNG files to other formats. Look at *http://www.png.org* for current information.

Line 12 creates a new GD::Image. We pass to the *new()* method the length and height that we want our new image to be so GD will create an image with the proper dimensions. In this case, we want the length (the first argument) to be the length of $log, which holds the value of the hit count multiplied by 9. This will give each number 9 pixels of space, which is just enough for the font we will be using. The second argument instructs GD to make the image 20 pixels high, which will also look good with the font we will be using.

```
13: my $black = $im->colorAllocate(0,0,0);
14: my $white = $im->colorAllocate(255,255,255);
```

Lines 13 and 14 allocate two colors, black and white. GD uses the first color that is allocated as the background color for the image, so we allocate black first. We then allocate white for the color of our text. The *colorAllocate()* method takes three arguments, the red, green, and blue color values. A partial list of RGB codes is shown in Appendix E.

```
15: $im->string(gdLargeFont,2,2,$log,$white);
```

Line 15 creates the text string on the image. We pass the *GD::Image string()* method five arguments. The first one, gdLargeFont, is the type of font we want to use for the text. The second and third arguments are the X and Y coordinates where we want the text to be aligned on the image. The fourth argument, $log, is the text itself. And finally, the fifth argument is the color we want the text to be, which is white.

```
16: binmode(STDOUT);
17: print $im->png;
```

Line 16 helps with portability to Win32 systems by setting STDOUT to binary mode so the Win32 system will properly display the binary image data. **Line 17** converts the image to PNG format and prints it to the client. Figure 6-4 shows the screenshot.

Figure 6-4   Screenshot of GD-generated count

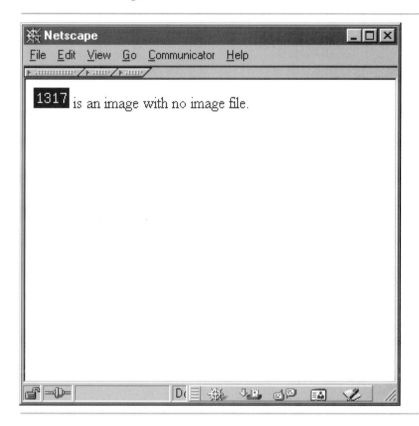

6.6 Counter Conclusion

In this chapter you learned how to create flexible, shared counters for your Web page or Web site. Each method has its own merits and possible drawbacks. For example, the text counter may not be flashy enough, the population counter fetches information from a remote site (but is still a neat, unique way to display a hit counter), the image counter needs to display images (which may be unwanted overhead), and the imageless counter needs to have GD and its related packages installed. The best thing is to experiment with each type and use the one or ones that suit your or your clients' needs the best.

6.7 Reader Exercises

- You may have noticed the last few exercises only read from a counter file. The first exercise is to add the functionality to those scripts to have them also update the count.

- Modify the functionality of one of the counters to block someone from upping your hit count by reloading a page many times. A simple solution for this is to use an environment variable (see Chapter 4) that is unique to a client and log the last five or so IP addresses that have accessed the site. If the incoming IP address matches one of those, you would not up the count on your counter.

- Although using a text file can be fast and efficient for this type of application, you may want to use a database to hold your count instead. For this exercise, create a table in a database and have the count stored and retrieved from it using DBI.

6.8 Listings

Listing 6-5   Full listing of count.pl

```
01: #!/usr/bin/perl -wT
02: # count.pl
03: use strict;
04: use Fcntl qw(:flock);
05: use Untaint;
06: my $counter = untaint(qr(.*\.dat$), $ARGV[0]);
07: my $silent = 0;
08: my $link = 1;
09: my $link_URL = "http://www.perl.org";
10: my $SEMAPHORE = $counter . ".lck";
11: open(S,">>$SEMAPHORE") || die "Can't open Semaphore file
                                 ($SEMAPHORE): $!";
12: flock (S, LOCK_EX);
13: if (-e $counter) {
14:    open (FILE, $counter) || die "Can't read counter. $!";
15:    my $visits = <FILE>;
16:    close (FILE);
17: }
18: open (FILE, ">$counter") || die "Cant write to counter. $!";
19: print FILE ++$visits;
20: close (FILE);
21: close (S);
22: if (!$silent) {
23:    if ($link) {
```

```
24:          print qq(<A HREF="$link_URL">$visits</A>);
25:      else{
26:          print $visits;
27:      }
28: }
```

Listing 6-6   Full listing for count2.pl

```
01: #!/usr/bin/perl -wT
02: # count2.pl
03: use strict;
04: use Fcntl qw(:flock);
05: use Untaint;
06: use Image::Size qw(html_imgsize);
07: my $counter = untaint(qr(.*\.dat$), $ARGV[0]);
08: my $style = untaint(qr(^(\.{0,2}/)*?[\w-/]+$), $ARGV[1]);
09: my $SEMAPHORE = $counter . ".lck";
10: open(S,">>$SEMAPHORE") || die "Can't open Semaphore file
                                  ($SEMAPHORE): $!";
11: flock (S, LOCK_EX);
12: open (FILE, $counter) || die "Can't read counter. $!";
13: my $visits = <FILE>;
14: close (FILE);
15: open (FILE, ">$counter") || die "Cant write to counter. $!";
16: print FILE $visits++;
17: close (FILE);
18: close S;
19: exit unless -d $style;
20: my @digits = split(//,$visits);
21: foreach (@digits) {
22:      my $size = html_imgsize("$style/$_.png");
23:      print qq(<img src="$style/$_.png">);
24: }
```

Listing 6-7   Full listing for population.pl

```
01: #!/usr/bin/perl -wT
02: # population.pl
03: use strict;
04: use Untaint;
05: use LWP::UserAgent;
06: my $counter = untaint(qr(.*\.dat$), $ARGV[0]);
07: my  $ua = new LWP::UserAgent;
```

(continued)

```
08: $ua->agent("GetCount/0.1");
09: my $req = new HTTP::Request GET => 'http://www.census.gov/
                                        cgi-bin/ipc/popclockw';
10: $req->header(Accept => "text/html");
11: my $res = $ua->request($req);
12: if ($res->is_success) {
13:     my $html = $res->content;
14:     (my $num = $html) =~ s!^.*<h1>(.*?)</h1>.*$!$1!si;
15:     open(LOG, $counter) || die "Can't read counter. $!";
16:     my $log = <LOG>;
17:     close LOG;
18:     ($num = $num) =~ s!,!!g;
19:     $num = $num-$log;
20:     1 while $num =~ s!^(\d+)(\d{3})!$1,$2!;
21:     print $num;
22: } else {
23:         print "[trouble calculating]";
24: }
```

Listing 6-8   Full listing for gd_count.pl

```
01: #!/usr/bin/perl -wT
02: # gd_count.pl
03: use strict;
04: use Untaint;
05: use GD;
06: use CGI qw(param header);
07: print header("image/png");
08: my $counter = untaint(qr(.*\.dat$), param('counter'));
09: open(LOG, $counter) || die "Can't read counter. $!";
10: my $log = <LOG>;
11: close LOG;
12: my $im = new GD::Image((length($log)*9),20);
13: my $black = $im->colorAllocate(0,0,0);
14: my $white = $im->colorAllocate(255,255,255);
15: $im->string(gdLargeFont,2,2,$log,$white);
16: binmode(STDOUT);
17: print $im->png;
```

Chapter 7

Web-Based
File Uploading

7.1 Introduction

File uploading is a powerful, yet surprisingly seldom discussed Web tool. While doing research on file uploading, I discovered that there was actually very little information currently available. File uploading is too useful a feature to overlook. We won't be overlooking it, and we intend to help you understand it.

File Uploading Uses

CGI file uploading is a powerful feature that expands your options when you start creating your own CGI programs. File uploading allows you to upload files to the Web server. It is a very simple way for your CGI program users to send data to your Web site.

File uploading, unless you put some thought into it, seems pretty bland, but, in fact, you can do quite a bit with it. You can allow your users to upload graphics, MP3s, configuration files, HTML documents, office suite documents, or anything else you want. You could easily start a file repository for a subject that interests you. Think of all the possibilities!

Brent used CGI file uploading to create an entire document management system (DMS). The DMS that he created was not huge; it had about 250 users and around 2500 documents in the system. The DMS featured versioning of document changes, e-mail reminders for people who had their documents checked out too long, and file check-in/out abilities based on the current user's rights in the system. Also, if a document was checked out, the DMS would display the name, phone, and e-mail address of the person who had it checked out, and much more. The DMS was entirely permissions driven. If a user did not have permission to access a directory or file, he or she simply would not see that item. The DMS system replaced a "commercial" DMS solution that cost several *hundred* thousand dollars and required its own dedicated server and system administrator. The replacement Web-based DMS ran on an existing file-server and did not require a dedicated database administrator to keep it running.

7.2 File Uploading Basics

We have talked about what file uploading can do, but we haven't seen any examples yet. Our first example will be kind of small, but we need a starting point to build on. Figure 7-1 shows what the user interface (UI) for Listing 7-1 looks like.

Figure 7-1   **Upload input example**

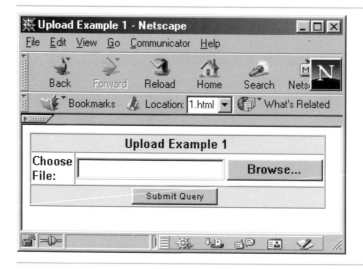

It may not look very useful, but don't worry. Although the user interface will remain pretty simple throughout this chapter, the CGI portions will get more and more difficult. This is a CGI book, not an HTML or user interface design book, so many of the user interfaces will be very basic. Remember that you can use your HTML skills to make your input pages as fancy as you want them to be. Here is the HTML for this first example page.

Listing 7-1   File upload input page

```
<HTML>
 <HEAD><TITLE>Upload Example 1</TITLE></HEAD>
 <BODY BGCOLOR="#FFFFFF">
 <FORM NAME="upload" METHOD=POST ACTION="/cgi-bin/upload1.cgi"
  ENCTYPE="multipart/form-data">
 <CENTER>
  <TABLE BORDER=1 CELLSPACING=0>
   <TR BGCOLOR="#E0E0E0">
    <TD COLSPAN=2>
     <CENTER><B>Upload Example 1</B></CENTER>
    </TD>
   </TR>
   <TR>
    <TD>
     <B>Choose File:</B>
    </TD>
    <TD>
     <INPUT TYPE="FILE" NAME="filename">
    </TD>
   </TR>
   <TR BGCOLOR="#E0E0E0">
    <TD COLSPAN=2><CENTER>
     <INPUT TYPE="SUBMIT" NAME="submit">
    </CENTER></TD>
   </TR>
  </TABLE>
 </CENTER>
 </FORM>
</BODY></HTML>
```

There is something very important in this HTML file that needs mentioning. This looks pretty much like any other HTML form tag, except for that last bit, the ENCTYPE="multipart/form-data." The default content type for HTML forms, *application/x-www-form-urlencoded*, is inefficient for sending large quantities of binary data or text containing non-ASCII characters. The content type *multipart/form-data* is actually the "new" way to make HTML forms. The reason it is not used for every HTML form is to maintain backward compatibility with older Web browsers. For more information on HTML forms, take a look at *http://www.w3.org/TR/REC-html40/interact/forms.html*

```
<FORM NAME="upload" METHOD=POST ACTION="/cgi-bin/upload1.cgi"
 ENCTYPE="multipart/form-data">
```

Without the multipart/form-data enctype, file uploading will *not* work. So don't forget it! Now let's walk through the code and see just how things work.

```
01: #!/usr/bin/perl -Tw
02: # upload1.cgi
03: use strict;
04: use CGI qw (:standard);
05: use CGI::Carp qw(fatalsToBrowser);
```

Lines 1–5 we've seen in many of the examples in this book. They simply tell the system where to find Perl, turn on warnings and taint checking, and load a few modules that we need.

```
06: $CGI::POST_MAX = 1024 * 250;    # Limit to 250kb posts...
```

Line 6 is a setting in CGI.pm that limits the size of files that can be uploaded to the server. The file upload will begin even if the file is larger than this limit, but a server error will be generated as soon as this maximum value is reached. This limit helps prevent denial of service attacks, and it warns users who simply don't realize that they may be uploading very large files. In this case, a denial of service attack would be a malicious user uploading very large files in an attempt to crash your server or cause other problems, such as filling up the server's hard drive. This upload limit is the *total* value of all data uploaded. This means that not only is the data from the file counted but all text that was sent via the form counts as well.

```
07: my $File_Name = param('filename');
```

Line 7 declares a global variable called $File_Name and stores the value that was passed from the calling Web page via CGI.pm's *param()* function.

The term *global* is used rather loosely here. All variables are globally available by default in Perl. But since we are using strict, we need to be more aware of how variables are declared and the scope of the variables. All my variables declared outside any subroutines are global to the program. Any my variables that are declared inside a subroutine, or code block, are only available inside that subroutine or block. To make variable scope easier to recognize, we will be capitalizing the name of globally scoped variables, while variables that are not global will be all lowercase.

```
08: my $Mime     = uploadInfo($File_Name)->{Content-Type};
```

Line 8 declares a global variable called $Mime and uses the CGI.pm function *uploadInfo()* to get the MIME type of the file that was uploaded.

```
09: Print_Results();
```

Line 9 calls the *Print_Results()* subroutine.

```
10: sub Print_Results{
11:    print header;
12:    print start_html('File Upload Example 1');
```

Line 10 begins the *Print_Results()* subroutine.

Line 11 calls the *header()* function from CGI.pm to print out the HTTP header.

Line 12 calls the *start_html()* function to begin the HTML on the resulting page.

```
13:    print qq(<PRE><B>File Name:</B> $File_Name\n);
14:    print qq(<B>Mime:</B> $Mime\n);
15:    print qq(<B>File Contents:</B>\n);
```

Lines 13–15 print some information about the file that was uploaded.

```
16:    while(<$File_Name>) { print; }
```

Line 16 loops through $File_Name and prints the contents out one line at a time. When you do not specify *what* to print after a *print()* statement, Perl defaults to printing whatever is currently in the $_ variable. Perl's power is amazing—this simple line of Perl prints the entire contents of a file!

Wait a minute! Isn't $File_Name a string? How can you loop though it like a filehandle? Well, Lincoln Stein, the genius behind CGI.pm, made things really nice for us. When you get the variable from the calling Web page, like we did on **line 7**, if it is treated like a string, it will be a string with the name of the file and, depending on the browser, the path to the file. If you treat it like a filehandle, it will act just like a filehandle, and you can traverse through the data just like a regular file. Thanks, Lincoln!

```
17:    print qq(</PRE>);
18:    print end_html;
19: }
```

Line 17 prints out the closing PRE tag.

Line 18 prints the closing HTML tags (with the *end_html()* function from CGI.pm).

Line 19 ends the subroutine.

Wow, that was short—only 19 lines of code! Figure 7-2 shows what the output of the program would look like.

Figure 7-2   **Uploaded text file result**

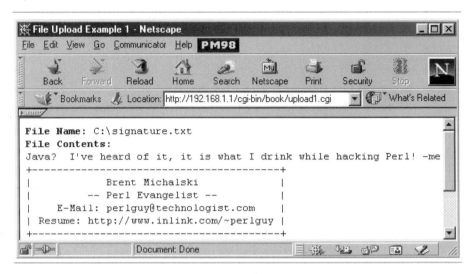

The file uploaded was an old "signature" file. The CGI program prints out the file name and file contents. In this example we didn't even bother to save the file anywhere on the server. We simply printed out the data from the file directly from the temporary file that CGI.pm creates. Now let's upload a graphic file and see what happens (see Figure 7-3).

Figure 7-3   **Results from graphic file upload**

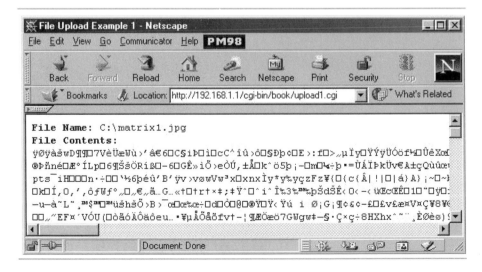

Oops! What happened here? For binary files, we need to do just a little bit more work. When we used the "print header" on **line 11** above, we told the server that the output will be text/html since that is the default for the header function if nothing is passed. When you tell the server this and try to send it a binary file (such as a graphic), you get a whole bunch of funny-looking characters because the server is looking for text but it is getting binary data.

Fortunately, it is easy to fix this problem, and that is exactly what we are going to do.

```
01: #!/usr/bin/perl -Tw
02: # upload2.cgi
03: use strict;
04: use CGI qw(:standard);
05: use CGI::Carp qw(fatalsToBrowser);
06: $CGI::POST_MAX = 1024 * 250;    # Limit to 250kb posts...
```

Lines 1–6 should be familiar by now.

```
07: my $File_Name = param('filename');
08: my $Mime      = uploadInfo($File_Name)->{Content-Type};
```

Line 7 declares a global variable called $File_Name and stores the value that was passed from the calling Web page via the *param()* function.

Line 8 creates a global variable called $Mime and use CGI.pm's *uploadInfo()* subroutine to get the MIME type of the file that was uploaded. Browsers that support file uploading are *supposed* to pass the MIME type of the file that is being uploaded. The *uploadInfo()* subroutine provides an easy way to get at the MIME information.

```
09: print header(-type=>$Mime);
10: Print_Results();
```

Line 9 tells the server what type of data is being sent. The default for the *header()* subroutine is text/html, but by passing -type=>$Mime as an argument, the default is overridden.

Line 10 calls the *Print_Results()* subroutine.

```
11: sub Print_Results{
12:    my $data;
```

Line 11 begins the *Print_Results()* subroutine.

Line 12 declares a variable called $data that is available only in the subroutine because it was declared inside of the subroutine.

```
13:    if($Mime !~ /text/){
14:        binmode($File_Name);
15:        while(read($File_Name, $data, 1024)) { print $data; }
```

Line 13 checks to see that the value stored in $mime does not contain the word *text*. If this evaluates true (not text), then we enter this portion of the if . . . else block.

Line 14 uses the *binmode()* function on the $File_Name filehandle to tell Perl that this is binary data. *binmode()* is not required on Unix machines because they handle linefeeds properly, but it is required on Windows machines. If you do not set it and you are on a Windows machine, any file uploads that have binary data may be corrupted.

Line 15 prints out the data. Since this file is a binary file, it really can't be printed out line-by-line because there is no concept of "lines" in a binary file. Instead, we use the *read()* function to print out binary files. By placing *read()* in a *while()* loop, it will keep reading data until there is no more data to read. Then it will fall through the *while()* loop and continue with the program.

We pass *read()* three arguments: $File_Name is the filehandle that was created on line 7. $data is the temporary storage variable in which we are going to store the current *chunk* of data. Finally, 1024 is the number of bytes that are read each time through the loop. So the *while()* loop will read 1024 bytes, print out the chunk of data, and then do it all over again until it runs out of data to print.

```
16:    } else {
17:        print start_html('File Upload Example 2');
18:        print qq(<PRE>);
19:        print qq(<B>File Name:</B> $File_Name\n);
20:        print qq(<B>File Contents:</B>\n);
```

Lines 16–20 are what happens if the file uploaded *was* a text MIME type. If so, we handle the data exactly as we did in the previous example. In fact, **lines 17–20** are exactly like the code used in the previous example.

```
21:        while(<$File_Name>) { print; }
```

Line 21 prints out the text data. This is also exactly like the code from the previous example.

```
22:        print qq(</PRE>);
23:        print end_html;
24:  }
25:  }
```

Line 22 prints out the closing PRE tag.

Line 23 prints out the closing HTML tags.

Lines 24–25 close the if . . . else block and close the subroutine.

We just created a program that allows the user to upload either text or binary data and have it displayed back to them. What if you want to store the files that were uploaded and saved onto the server? Let's add a feature that will allow the users to upload files and have the files **saved** onto the Web server, then allow the user a method for retrieving the files whenever they want. While we are at it, let's allow them to add a description for the file as well! Figure 7-4 shows what our new user interface will look like.

Figure 7-4   File upload input screen

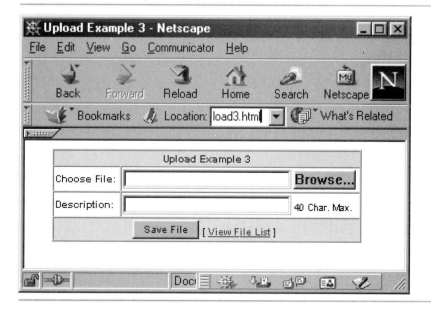

Notice that it looks very similar to the last two examples. The difference here is that we've added a **Description** field and a link called **View File List**. The view file list link is actually a separate CGI program, called view-files.cgi, that simply displays the files along with their descriptions. Listing 7-2 is the HTML for this new user interface.

Listing 7-2   File uploading with description

```
<HTML>
 <HEAD><TITLE>Upload Example 3</TITLE></HEAD>
 <BODY BGCOLOR="#FFFFFF">
 <FORM NAME="upload" METHOD=POST ACTION="/cgi-bin/book/
                                        upload3.cgi"
  ENCTYPE="multipart/form-data">
 <CENTER>
  <TABLE BORDER=1 CELLSPACING=0>
   <TR BGCOLOR="#E0E0E0">
    <TD COLSPAN=2><FONT FACE=ARIAL SIZE=2>
     <CENTER><B>Upload Example 3</B></CENTER>
    </FONT></TD>
   </TR>
   <TR>
    <TD><FONT FACE=ARIAL SIZE=2>
     <B>Choose File:</B>
    </FONT></TD>
    <TD><FONT FACE=ARIAL SIZE=2>
     <INPUT TYPE="FILE" NAME="filename">
    </FONT></TD>
   </TR>
   <TR>
    <TD><FONT FACE=ARIAL SIZE=2>
     <B>Description:</B>
    </FONT></TD>
    <TD><FONT FACE=ARIAL SIZE=2>
     <INPUT TYPE="text" NAME="description" MAXLENGTH=40>
     <FONT FACE="ARIAL" SIZE=1>40 Char. Max.</FONT>
    </FONT></TD>
   </TR>
   <TR BGCOLOR="#E0E0E0">
    <TD COLSPAN=2><CENTER>
     <INPUT TYPE="SUBMIT" NAME="submit" VALUE="Save File">
     <FONT FACE=ARIAL SIZE=2>
     [ <A HREF="/cgi-bin/book/viewfiles.cgi">View File List
     </A> ]</FONT>
    </CENTER></TD>
   </TR>
  </TABLE>
 </CENTER>
 </FORM>
</BODY></HTML>
```

The program that we create for this user interface is a little more complex, but we still keep it relatively short. At under 70 lines, this program is actually a powerful file-uploading program. When we run the program, we should get output that looks something like Figure 7-5.

Figure 7-5   Upload 3 results

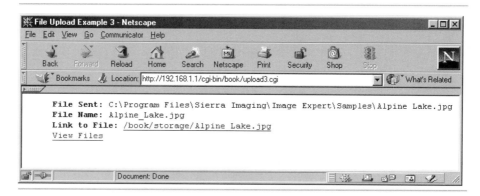

This does not tell us too much, and would most likely not be in an area of the program that your users would see. This page is more of an informational screen for your benefit. For a production system, you would want to present the data in a more user-friendly way. When you click the *View Files* link, you get a screen like Figure 7-6. This shows you a table that contains all the files in the upload directory as well as the descriptions for each file.

Figure 7-6   File viewer screen

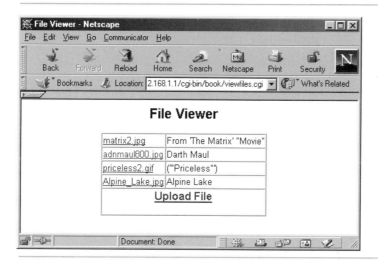

Let's first take a look at the new file upload code, and then we can cover the viewfiles.cgi program.

```
01: #!/usr/bin/perl -Tw
02: # upload3.cgi
03: use strict;
04: use DBI;
05: use File::Basename;
06: use CGI qw(:standard);
07: use CGI::Carp qw(fatalsToBrowser);
```

Lines 1–7 should be very familiar by now. The exception here is **lines 4 and 5** where we introduce new modules. The DBI module is used for database connectivity. DBI stands for DataBase Interface.

DBI is also sometimes called DataBase Independent because the DBI module is needed for all database connectivity, and another module is needed that is database specific. The File::Basename module is used to extract filenames from full paths—for example, if it would extract myfile.cgi from /usr/local/bin/myfile.cgi.

```
08: my $Directory    = "/usr/www/html/book/storage";
09: my $Url_Path     = "/book/storage";
```

Lines 8–9 set some global variables that are used to store some path locations. Creating variables like this is not something you absolutely must do. However, by placing them near the top of the program you help people easily identify where things are happening, cut down on typographical errors, and make your program look cleaner and less cluttered.

```
10: my $File_Name    = param('filename');
11: my $Description = param('description');
12: my $File         = Get_File_Name($File_Name);
```

Lines 10–11 call the *param()* function from CGI.pm to get the filename and description from the calling Web page.

Line 12 calls the *Get_File_Name()* function and passes it $File_Name. It then stores the return value in a new variable named $File.

```
13: $CGI::POST_MAX = 1024 * 250;   # Limit to 250kb posts . . .
```

Line 13 is used to limit the data being sent to the program. This line makes it so that only posts of 250kb or less are allowed.

```
14: Store_Results();
15: Store_Description();
16: Print_Results();
```

Lines 14–16 make function calls that handle storing the results and description, then print the results out. So, simply put, these lines call the functions that do all of the work for this program.

```
17: sub Store_Description{
18:     my $DBH = DBI->connect("DBI:mysql:book","book","addison");
```

Line 17 begins the *Store_Description()* function.

Line 18 creates a my variable called $DBH and sets it to the value returned from the *DBI->connect()* method. If you look at the values that were passed to the *connect()* method, they are the database driver and name (DBI:mysql:book), the username (book), and the password (addison). The variable that holds the return value from this function call is typically called $DBH. DBH stands for DataBase Handle, and the value it is storing is a handle to the database connection.

```
19:     my $sth_insert =
20:        $DBH->prepare( qq{INSERT INTO files (Description,FileName)
           VALUES (?,?)} )   # Line 20 continued.
21:        or die $DBH->errstr;
```

Lines 19–21 are actually one long Perl statement that creates another handle. We named this handle $sth_insert, meaning *StatemenT Handle for insert*.

TIP It is a good idea to name your statement handles $sth, followed by whatever the statement does. You can have several statement handles in a program, each one doing different things, so name them something that will have meaning. ($sth_insert, $sth_update, $sth_delete, and so forth would be good choices.)

The prepare stores the SQL statement passed to it in a compiled form so that it will run faster when executed. In MySQL and mSQL, it is not truly compiled but simply stored because these database servers do not implement *preparing* SQL statements. We used the qq{} operator to quote the text for us. Sometimes in SQL you will need to use quotes, and by using qq, you don't have to worry about escaping quotes inside of quotes.

At the end of line 20 we have *VALUES (?,?)*. The question marks are called *placeholders* and are a good thing to use because when you are ready to execute the SQL statement, you call the *execute()* function and pass a value for each question mark. It is the values that were passed that get substituted into the SQL statement.

Finally, on **line 21** we have an "or die" statement. This is for error checking. If a false value was returned by the *prepare()* function, something must have gone wrong, so we stop the program right here with an error.

```
22:     $sth_insert->execute($Description,$File);
23:     $DBH->disconnect;
24: }
```

Line 22 calls the execute function using the $sth_insert handle. The two fields that are passed in are the two items that are to be inserted into the database.

Line 23 disconnects us from the database.

Line 24 closes the *Store_Description()* subroutine.

```
25: sub Get_File_Name{
```

Line 25 begins the *Get_File_Name()* subroutine.

```
26:     if($ENV{HTTP_USER_AGENT} =~ /win/i){
27:       fileparse_set_fstype("MSDOS");
28:     }
```

Line 26 begins an if . . . elsif block. This line checks to see if the value passed in from the **HTTP_USER_AGENT** environment variable contained the text *win*. If it did, then the code inside the block gets executed.

Line 27 uses the *fileparse_set_fstype()* function from the File::Basename module to set the file parse type to MSDOS. This will cause the program to parse the directories and files with the backslash.

Line 28 closes this portion of the if . . . elsif block.

```
29:     elsif($ENV{HTTP_USER_AGENT} =~ /mac/i) {
30:       fileparse_set_fstype("MacOS");
31:     }
```

Line 29 gets evaluated if **line 26** is false. It checks to see if the **HTTP_USER_AGENT** contains the text *mac*. If so, then we execute **line 30** and set the file parse type to MacOS for MacIntosh systems.

Line 31 closes out the if . . . elsif block. There is no else condition here. If neither condition was true, we simply do not set the file parse type, so it stays with the default, Unix.

```
32:    my $full_name = shift;
33:    $full_name    = basename($full_name);
34:    $full_name    =~ s!\s!\_!g;
```

Line 32 uses the shift function to get the value that was passed in to the subroutine and stores it in the scalar called $full_name.

Line 33 calls the *basename()* function from the File::Basename module and passes it $full_name.

Line 34 uses a regular expression to get rid of any spaces and replaces them with the underscore character. We do this so that we don't have to deal with filenames that have spaces in them. This is a nice, simple, lazy way to deal with spaces. In the regular expression, ! was used as the delimiter because the characters that we were looking for required slashes to escape them. s!\s!_!g looks better than s/\s/_/g. This has the *leaning toothpick* syndrome (it looks like a bunch of toothpicks holding each other up).

```
35:    return($full_name);
36: }
```

Line 35 returns the value stored in $full_name from the subroutine.

Line 36 closes the *Get_File_Name()* subroutine.

```
37: sub Store_Results{
38:    my $data;
39:    my $mime = uploadInfo($File_Name)->{'Content-Type'};
```

Line 37 begins the *Store_Results()* subroutine.

Line 38 creates a my variable called $data, which is used in this subroutine to store data temporarily.

Line 39 uses the *uploadInfo()* function from the CGI module to get the content type of the file that the user uploaded and stores the results in a scalar called $mime.

```
40:    open (STORAGE, ">$Directory/$File")
41:        or die "Error: $Directory/$File: $!\n";
```

Lines 40–41 are again a single Perl statement that spans two lines. On **line 40** we open a new file and give it a filehandle named STORAGE. On **line 41**, we call *die()* and print out an error message if there was a problem opening the file.

So if $Directory contained "/home/brent" and $File contained "address.txt," then the file that is opened/created is "/home/brent/address.txt". The filehandle for this file was called STORAGE.

```
42:     if($mime !~ /text/){
43:         binmode ($File_Name);
44:         binmode (STORAGE);
45:     }
```

Lines 42–45 call the *binmode()* function on the two filehandles if the value stored in $mime does not contain the string *text*. We are using this as a very simple way to check whether the file that was uploaded is text or binary. If the file is indeed binary, you must use the *binmode()* function on the filehandle for non-Unix servers. If your program will always be run in a Unix environment, you can actually omit these lines because Unix handles binary and text data properly.

```
46:     while( read($File_Name, $data, 1024) ){
47:         print STORAGE $data;
48:     }
```

Lines 46–48 take care of writing the file to disk.

Line 46 begins a *while()* loop that will remain true and keep looping as long as there is data left in the file being read. The *read()* function inside of the while condition is used to read in chunks of data. Since the file that was uploaded could be binary, we can't simply print out the file line by line because binary files don't contain line breaks like text files do. The *read()* function is passed three arguments: the *filehandle* of the file being read, the *name* of a variable that will store the current chunk of data, and finally, the *number of bytes* to read each time.

Line 47 then copies the current chunk of data stored in $data into the filehandle STORAGE.

Line 48 closes the *while()* loop.

```
49:   close STORAGE;
50: }
```

Line 49 closes the STORAGE filehandle.

Line 50 ends the *Store_Results()* subroutine.

```
51: sub Print_Results{
52:    my $link = "$Url_Path/$File";
```

Line 51 begins the *Print_Results()* subroutine.

Line 52 creates a variable called $link that contains the URL path and file-name. The URL path is different from the actual directory path on the server because URLs are mapped to their location in the Web server config-uration and do not actually represent the true path on the server. They are more of a virtual path that the Web server uses to find the file.

```
53:    print header;
54:    print start_html('File Upload Example 3');
```

Line 53 prints out a standard HTTP header using the *header()* function from the CGI module.

Line 54 uses CGI.pm's *start_html()* function to begin the HTML for the page that is being created and passes it a string that will become the page title.

```
55:    print<<HTML;
56:      <PRE>
57:       <B>File Sent:</B> $File_Name
58:       <B>File Name:</B> $File
59:       <B>Link to File:</B> <A HREF="$link">$link</A>
60:       <A HREF="/cgi-bin/book/viewfiles.cgi">View Files</A>
61:      </PRE>
62: HTML
```

Lines 55–62 are a here document that prints out the HTML displayed on the page being created. Inside the here document we have several variables that will be interpolated with their values displayed to the user.

```
63:    print end_html;
64: }
```

Line 63 uses the *end_html()* function from the CGI module to end the HTML for the page that was just created.

Line 64 ends the *Print_Results()* subroutine.

7.3 Viewing Files

Remember that we had a program called viewfiles.cgi that was used to dynamically create a page that displayed all the files and their descriptions. Let's take a look at the viewfiles.cgi program to see how it works. It is pretty short and not too complicated.

```
01: #!/usr/bin/perl -wT
02: # viewfiles.cgi
03: use strict;
04: use DBI;
05: use CGI qw(:standard);
06: use CGI::Carp qw(fatalsToBrowser);
```

Lines 1–6 have remained almost identical throughout these applications. Even for this script, they are nearly the same. The only thing different here is that we don't need the File::Basename module.

```
07: my $Web_Directory  = "/book/storage";
```

Line 7 creates a variable that stores the location of the files.

```
08: Print_Html_Top();
09: Get_Descriptions();
10: Print_Html_Bottom();
```

Lines 8–10 call the three functions that make up this program.

```
11: sub Print_Row{
```

Line 11 begins the *Print_Row()* subroutine. This subroutine will print out one row of data or one filename and description pair.

```
12:     my $rec   = shift;
13:     my $fname = $rec->{FileName};
14:     my $desc  = $rec->{Description};
```

Line 12 shifts the value that was passed to the subroutine and stores it in the my variable $rec. Remember that when a value is shifted in a subroutine and there is no argument after the shift command, the value that gets shifted is the next value that was passed into the subroutine.

Lines 13–14 create a couple of variables and use the arrow operator to get the FileName and Description of the current record.

```
15:      print qq(<TR><TD>);
16:      print qq(<A HREF="$Web_Directory/$fname">$fname</A>);
17:      print qq(</TD><TD>$desc</TD></TR>);
18: }
```

Lines 15–17 simply print out the HTML for a row of data in the table that we are creating.

Line 16 creates a link to the file that was uploaded.

Line 18 closes the *Print_Row()* subroutine.

```
19: sub Get_Descriptions{
20:      my $DBH = DBI->connect("DBI:mysql:book", "book", "addison");
```

Line 19 begins the *Get_Descriptions()* subroutine.

Line 20 creates a database connection and stores the database handle in the variable $DBH.

```
21:      my $sth_fetch =
22:        $DBH->prepare( qq(SELECT * FROM files) ) or die $DBH->errstr;
```

Lines 21–22 are a single statement. They create a new statement handle called $sth_fetch that is a prepared SQL statement that selects all the records from the files database table. If there is an error preparing the statement, then the die function is called and the program will terminate.

```
23:      $sth_fetch->execute();
```

Line 23 is the *execute()* statement that actually performs the SQL statement in the database using the statement handle with which it is called.

```
24:      while( my $ptr = $sth_fetch->fetchrow_hashref ){
25:          Print_Row($ptr);
26:      }
27: }
```

Line 24 begins a while loop. In the loops argument we have "my $ptr = $sth_fetch->fetchrow_hashref." This statement creates a my variable called $ptr, which is used as a pointer. This pointer gets filled with the return value from the *fetchrow_hashref()* function.

So what this loop does is fetch a row of data from the database until it runs out of data to fetch. Each time through the loop a reference to the data is stored in $ptr.

Line 25 calls the *Print_Row()* function to handle the printing of the data that was just pulled from the database.

Line 26 ends the *while()* loop.

Line 27 ends the *Get_Descriptions()* subroutine.

```
28: sub Print_Html_Top{
29:     print header;
```

Line 28 begins the *Print_Html_Top()* subroutine. This subroutine is used to print out the top of the HTML page that we are generating.

Line 29 prints the standard HTTP header.

```
30:     print<<EOT;
31:     <HTML><HEAD><TITLE>File Viewer</TITLE></HEAD>
32:     <BODY BGCOLOR="#FFFFFF">
33:     <CENTER><H2>File Viewer</H2><P>
34:     <TABLE BORDER=1 CELLSPACING=0>
35: EOT
36: }
```

Lines 30–36 finish off this subroutine by simply using a here document to print out the beginning HTML and starting a table.

```
37: sub Print_Html_Bottom{
38:     print<<EOT;
39:     <TR><TD COLSPAN=2><A HREF="/book/upload3.html">
40:     <CENTER><H3><B>Upload File</B></H3></CENTER></A>
41:     </TD></TR></TABLE>
42:     <P></CENTER>
43:     </BODY></HTML>
44: EOT
45: }
```

Lines 37–45 make up the *Print_Html_Bottom()* subroutine and are just as simple as the *Print_Html_Top()* function. These lines make up a subroutine that simply uses a here document to print out the HTML that is needed to finish off the page that we are generating.

7.4 Uploading Multiple Files

We now have a file upload program that allows users to upload binary or text files and store descriptions along with each file. We can also display, dynamically, a list of files and their descriptions. This Web application is becoming more and more useful all the time! But what if the user has many files to upload? Uploading files one at a time would be very time consuming, and your users would probably not be very satisfied with the application. In our next example, we will build on our existing code and add the ability to upload several files at the same time.

Figure 7-7 shows what the user interface looks like for example 4. Here the user is allowed to upload as many as five files. The number of files a user can upload is completely up to the user developing the program, but we are using five for this example.

Once the user has uploaded the files, he or she will see a message like this that informs them that everything worked. This should look pretty

Figure 7-7   Multiple file upload screen

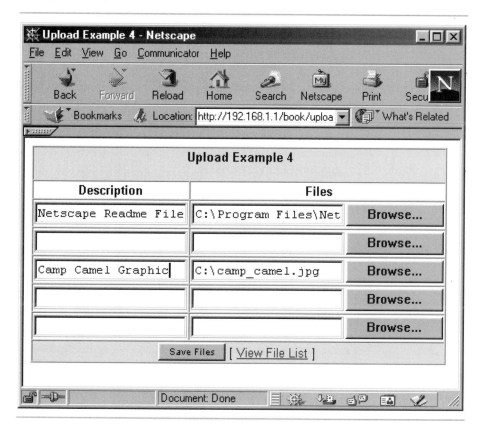

straightforward by now. The only thing we are doing differently here is the multiple file uploading. It will take a little more work for us to get the multiple files and descriptions into the database, mainly because we have to do some looping to make sure we gather all the information. Overall we finish the program at under 100 lines of code—not bad for a program this useful. This final uploading example could easily be built on to make a full-featured program for an Internet or intranet site.

Figure 7-8   Multiple file upload results

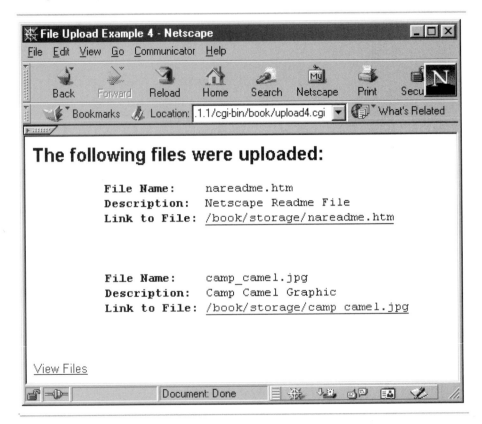

```
01: #!/usr/bin/perl -Tw
02: # upload4.cgi
03: use strict;
04: use DBI;
05: use File::Basename;
06: use CGI qw(:standard);
07: use CGI::Carp qw(fatalsToBrowser);
```

Lines 1–7 are the same as the previous example. You have probably noticed by now that many of the programs we use, and that you will be developing someday, are built on other programs. Reuse as much code as you can to save yourself time when developing.

```
08: my $Directory    = "/usr/www/html/book/storage";
09: my $Url_Path      = "/book/storage";
10: my @File_Names     = param('file_name');
11: my @Descriptions = param('file_desc');
12: my @File_Array    = ();
```

Lines 8–12 create and initialize several variables that will be used throughout the program.

Line 8 creates a *global* variable called $Directory and sets it to the full path to the subdirectory where we will be storing the files.

Line 9 creates a *global* variable called $Url_Path and sets it to the URL path of where we are storing the files. This is the path that the Web server needs to access the files. It must be set up beforehand in the Web server itself.

Line 10 creates a global array called @File_Name and sets it to the values that were passed in the filename fields of the calling HTML form. Each of the file upload fields on the HTML form is called "file_name."

If there are multiple fields on an HTML form with the same name, as in this case, the CGI module passes back an array with all the values that were stored in those fields. This makes parsing forms a breeze. Even forms that have multiple items with the same name are easy to handle!

Line 11 creates a *global* array called @Description and sets it to the values that were passed in the description fields of the calling HTML form.

Line 12 creates a *global* array called @File_Array.

In all the preceding cases we are again using the term *global* rather loosely. A my variable will have a scope of the block in which it is created. In these cases, we are creating my variables that are not enclosed in any blocks. So effectively, they have a scope of the entire program. Therefore, they are (loosely) global variables.

```
13: $CGI::POST_MAX = 1024 * 1500;   # Limit to 1500kb posts . . .
```

Line 13 tells the CGI module that we only want to allow up to 1500kb posts. This will prevent people from trying to upload huge files. The value is increased in this example because this is the size of *all* files that are uploaded. In this example, the user can upload as many as five files, so we increased the POST_MAX value. This is something that the programmer needs to determine for each particular case because sometimes large files may be the norm in their environment.

```
14: Get_Names();
15: Store_Descriptions();
16: Print_Results();
```

Lines 14–16 call the three subroutines that do most of the work in the program. Once we get past line 16, the rest of the program is the code for the subroutines.

```
17: sub Get_Names{
18:     my $counter = 0;
19:     my $full_name;
20:     my $file_name;
```

Lines 17–20 begin the *Get_Names()* subroutine, then create some my variables that only have scope inside of the subroutine. This subroutine is used to get all of the filenames that were passed from the HTML form and store them in the database.

```
21:     foreach $full_name (@File_Names){
22:         my $rec = {};
```

Line 21 begins a *foreach()* loop that goes through all of the values in the @File_Name array and stores the current value in the $full_name variable.

Line 22 creates a pointer to a hash called $rec and clears any contents that it may contain. Since it is a my variable, it will only have scope inside of the *foreach()* block.

```
23:         if($full_name ne ""){
24:             $file_name          = Get_File_Name($full_name);
```

Line 23 checks to see if the value in $full_name is *not* empty. So if it contains text, the program continues on into the *if()* block.

Line 24 stores the value returned from the *Get_File_Name()* subroutine into the $file_name variable. This strips off all of the path information and leaves us with just the filename.

```
25:             $rec->{file_name}   = $file_name;
26:             $rec->{full_name}   = $full_name;
27:             $rec->{description} = $Descriptions[$counter];
```

Line 25 stores the value of $file_name into the file_name key of the anonymous hash pointed to by $rec. Using an anonymous hash like this may seem a little strange, but it is an excellent way to store items that are like records. Doing this is very much like using a structure in C.

Line 26 stores the value of $full_name into the full_name key of the anonymous hash.

Line 27 stores the value of the $counter element of the $Description array into the description key of the anonymous hash.

At this point, we have a "record" containing the filename, fullname, and description of the file. Now we need to store it into an array to make it easier to handle later on in the program.

```
28:            push @File_Array, $rec;
29:            Store_File($full_name, $file_name);
30:        }
```

Line 28 pushes a reference to the anonymous hash, stored in $rec, into the next element in the @File_Array.

Line 29 calls the *Store_File()* subroutine and passes it $full_name and $file_name. This will handle storing the information to the database.

Line 30 closes the if block.

```
31:            $counter++;
32:        }
33: }
```

Line 31 increments the $counter variable. We increment it *outside* of the if block because we still need to increment the counter if the value of $full_name was empty.

The fields on the HTML form do not have to be filled in consecutively, so someone could put data in the first and third lines and leave the second line empty. By going through each element of the array, we make sure that we get all of the data that the user passed to us.

Line 32 closes the *foreach()* loop.

Line 33 ends the *Get_Names()* subroutine.

```
34: sub Store_Descriptions{
35:     my $temp;
36:     my $DBH = DBI->connect( "DBI:mysql:book", "book", "addison" );
```

Line 34 begins the *Store_Description()* subroutine.

Line 35 declares a variable called $temp. This will be used to store the reference to the hash that is stored in the @File_Array variable.

Line 36 connects us to the book database.

```
37:     my $sth_insert =
38:        $DBH->prepare( qq{INSERT INTO files (Description, FileName)
           VALUES (?,?)} )
39:        or die $DBH->errstr;
```

Line 37 creates a scalar that holds a handle to the SQL statement that is created in **line 38**.

Line 39 is the die statement that gets executed if there was a problem preparing the SQL statement. The whole purpose of these three lines is to get the SQL statement that is needed to insert data into the database prepared so that when we are ready to pass it some data, all we need to do is call the *execute()* function to do the database insert.

```
40:        foreach $temp (@File_Array){
41:           $sth_insert->execute( $temp->{description},
              $temp->{file_name} );
42:        }
```

Line 40 begins a *foreach()* loop that goes through each element of the @File_Array array and stores the current value in the $temp variable.

Line 41 calls the *execute()* function and performs it on the $sth_insert handle we created on **line 37**. We pass the description and filename to the *execute()* function using the arrow operator. We use the arrow operator because the value in $temp is a reference to the hash that was created in **lines 25–27**. The arrow operator allows us to point to the key of the value that we wish to get.

Line 42 ends the *foreach()* loop.

```
43:        $DBH->disconnect;
44: }
```

Line 43 disconnects us from the database.

Line 44 closes the *Store_Description()* subroutine.

```
45: sub Get_File_Name{
```

Line 45 begins the *Get_File_Name()* subroutine.

```
46:        if( $ENV{HTTP_USER_AGENT} =~ /win/i ){
47:           fileparse_set_fstype("MSDOS");
48:        }
```

Line 46 checks the environment variable called HTTP_USER_AGENT to see if it contains the text "win." If it does, the file most likely came from a Windows system, so we enter the if block.

Line 47 sets the "filesystem" type to "MSDOS."

Line 48 closes this portion of the if . . . elsif block.

```
49:      elsif( $ENV{HTTP_USER_AGENT} =~ /mac/i ) {
50:          fileparse_set_fstype("MacOS");
51:      }
```

Line 49 this line executes if **line 46** failed. Now we check to see if the user is on a MacIntosh.

Line 50 sets the "filesystem" type to "MacOS."

Line 51 closes the if . . . elsif block.

```
52:      my $full_name =  shift;
53:      $full_name    =  basename($full_name);
54:      $full_name    =~ s!\s!\_!g;
```

Line 52 uses the *shift()* function to get the value that was passed into the subroutine and stores it in the scalar called $full_name.

Line 53 calls the basename function from the File::Basename module and passes it $full_name.

Line 54 uses a regular expression to get rid of any spaces and replaces them with the underscore character. We do this so that we don't have to deal with filenames that have spaces in them. This is a nice, simple, lazy way to deal with them.

```
55:      return($full_name);
56: }
```

Line 55 returns the variable $full_name.

Line 56 closes the *Get_File_Name()* subroutine.

```
57: sub Store_File{
58:      my $file_handle = shift;
59:      my $file_name   = shift;
60:      my $data;
```

Line 57 begins the *Store_File()* subroutine.

Lines 58–59 declare variables and read in, via the *shift()*, the values passed into the subroutine.

Line 60 declares another variable that will be used for temporary data storage.

```
61:     my $mime = uploadInfo($file_handle)->{Content-Type};
```

Line 61 declares a variable called $mime and uses the *uploadInfo()* subroutine from CGI.pm to get the content type of the file that was uploaded.

```
62:     open (STORAGE, ">$Directory/$file_name")
63:        or die "Error: $!\n";
```

Lines 62–63 are a single Perl statement that spans 2 lines. On **line 62** we open a new file and give it a filehandle called STORAGE. Then on **line 63** we call *die()* and print out an error message if there was a problem opening the file.

So if $Directory contained "/home/brent" and $File contained "address.txt," then the file that is opened/created is "/home/brent/address.txt." The filehandle for this file was called STORAGE.

```
64:     if($mime !~ /text/){
65:         binmode ($File_Name);
66:         binmode (STORAGE);
67:     }
```

Lines 64–67 call the *binmode()* function on the two filehandles if the value stored in $mime does not contain the string *text*. We are using this as a very simple way to check whether the file that was uploaded is text or binary. If the file is indeed binary, you must use the *binmode()* function on the filehandle for non-Unix servers. If your program will always be run in a Unix environment, you can actually omit these lines because Unix handles binary and text data properly.

```
68:     while( read($File_Name, $data, 1024) ){
69:         print STORAGE $data;
70:     }
```

Lines 68–70 take care of writing the file to disk.

Line 68 begins a *while()* loop that will remain true and keep looping as long as there is data left in the file being read. The *read()* function inside the while condition is used to read in chunks of data. Since the file that was uploaded could be binary, we can't simply print out the file line by line because binary files don't contain line breaks like text files do. The *read()* function is passed three arguments: the filehandle of the file being read, the name of a variable that will store the current chunk of data, and finally, the number of bytes to read each time.

Line 69 then copies the current chunk of data stored in $data into the filehandle STORAGE.

Line 70 closes the *while()* loop.

```
71:    close STORAGE;
72: }
```

Line 71 closes the STORAGE filehandle.

Line 72 ends the *Store_Results()* subroutine.

```
73: sub Print_Results{
74:    my $temp;
```

Line 73 begins the *Print_Results()* subroutine.

Line 74 declares a variable named $temp.

```
75:    print header;
76:    print start_html("File Upload Example 4");
77:    print h2("The following files were uploaded:");
```

Line 75 uses the header function of CGI.pm to print out the standard HTTP header.

Line 76 uses the *start_html()* function from CGI.pm to print out the beginning HTML for the page. The string that is passed becomes the title for the resulting page.

Line 77 uses the h2 function from CGI.pm to print out a page header. The h2 function wraps the string it was passed inside of <H2> tags.

```
78:    foreach $temp (@File_Array){
79:        my $link = "$Url_Path/$temp->{file_name}";
```

Line 78 begins a *foreach()* loop that goes through each element in @File_Array and stores the current value into the $temp_hash variable. This loop is used to print out each file and its details on the generated HTML page.

Line 79 creates a variable called $link and stores the current URL path and filename into it. This will be used to create the link to the file.

```
80:          print<<HTML;
81:           <PRE>
82:            <B>File Name:</B>     $temp->{file_name}
83:            <B>Description:</B>   $temp->{description}
84:            <B>Link to File:</B> <A HREF="$link">$link</A><P>
85:           </PRE>
86: HTML
87:       }
```

Line 80 begins a "here" document that will be used to print out some HTML. We used HTML here as the ending tag for the "here" document.

Lines 81–85 are simply the HTML that gets printed out on the page that we are creating.

Line 86 ends the "here" document, and **line 87** ends the *foreach()* loop.

Lines 82 and 83 used the arrow operator to get the value stored in the file_name and description key and prints it out. Since we used an anonymous hash and stored references to it, we needed the arrow operator to dereference, and access, the data.

```
88:    print qq(\n<A HREF="/cgi-bin/book/viewfiles.cgi">View Files</A>);
89:    print end_html;
90: }
```

Line 88 prints out a link to the "View Files" program.

Line 89 uses the *end_html()* function of CGI.pm to print out the closing HTML.

Line 90 ends the *Print_Results()* subroutine.

That is all there is to the final file uploading example, which is built on what we covered in the previous three examples. It does not yet contain all the features you could possibly want, but it should be a great kick start to get you on your way to creating a new application that includes file uploading. Use your newfound knowledge and build on these examples to make them even more powerful and to hone your Perl programming skills.

7.5 Reader Exercises

- Design a cleaner user interface and make a file upload program for your site.

■ Incorporate the file uploading capabilities to add attachments to the e-mail program from Chapter 11.

■ Create a program for uploading and storing information about your favorite MP3 files.

7.6 File Listings

Listing 7-3   upload1.cgi

```perl
 1: #!/usr/bin/perl -Tw
 2: # upload1.cgi
 3: use strict;
 4: use CGI qw (:standard);
 5: use CGI::Carp qw(fatalsToBrowser);
 6: my $File_Name = param('filename');
 7: my $Mime      = uploadInfo($File_Name)->{'Content-Type'};
 8: $CGI::POST_MAX = 1024 * 250;   # Limit to 250kb posts...
 9: Print_Results();
10: sub Print_Results{
11:     print header;
12:     print start_html('File Upload Example 1');
13:     print qq(<PRE><B>File Name:</B> $File_Name\n);
14:     print qq(<B>Mime:</B> $Mime\n);
15:     print qq(<B>File Contents:</B><XMP>\n\n);
16:     while(<$File_Name>) { print; }
17:     print qq(</XMP></PRE>);
18:     print end_html;
19: }
```

Listing 7-4   upload2.cgi

```perl
 1: #!/usr/bin/perl -Tw
 2: # upload2.cgi
 3: use strict;
 4: use CGI qw(:standard);
 5: use CGI::Carp qw(fatalsToBrowser);
 6: $CGI::POST_MAX = 1024 * 250;   # Limit to 250kb posts...
 7: my $File_Name = param('filename');
 8: my $Mime      = uploadInfo($File_Name)->{'Content-Type'};
 9: print header(-type=>$Mime);
```

(continued)

```
10:   Print_Results();
11:   sub Print_Results{
12:     my $data;
13:     if($Mime !~ /text/){
14:       binmode($File_Name);
15:       while(read($File_Name, $data, 1024)) { print $data; }
16:     } else {
17:       print start_html('File Upload Example 2');
18:       print qq(<PRE>);
19:       print qq(<B>File Name:</B> $File_Name\n);
20:       print qq(<B>File Contents:</B>\n);
21:       while(<$File_Name>) { print; }
22:       print qq(</PRE>);
23:       print end_html;
24:     }
25:   }
```

Listing 7-5   **upload3.cgi**

```
1:  #!/usr/bin/perl -Tw
2:  # upload3.cgi
3:  use strict;
4:  use DBI;
5:  use File::Basename;
6:  use CGI qw(:standard);
7:  use CGI::Carp qw(fatalsToBrowser);
8:  my $Directory   = "/usr/www/html/book/storage";
9:  my $Url_Path    = "/book/storage";
10: my $File_Name   = param('filename');
11: my $Description = param('description');
12: my $File        = Get_File_Name($File_Name);
13: $CGI::POST_MAX = 1024 * 250;   # Limit to 250kb posts...
14: Store_Results();
15: Store_Description();
16: Print_Results();
17: sub Store_Description{
18:     my $DBH = DBI->connect("DBI:mysql:book","book","addison");
19:     my $sth_insert =
20:       $DBH->prepare( qq{INSERT INTO files (Description, FileName)
                                             VALUES (?,?)} )
21:        or die $DBH->errstr;
22:     $sth_insert->execute($Description, $File);
23:     $DBH->disconnect;
```

(continued)

```perl
24: }
25: sub Get_File_Name{
26:     if($ENV{HTTP_USER_AGENT} =~ /win/i){
27:         fileparse_set_fstype("MSDOS");
28:     }
29:     elsif($ENV{HTTP_USER_AGENT} =~ /mac/i) {
30:         fileparse_set_fstype("MacOS");
31:     }
32:     my $full_name =  shift;
33:     $full_name    = basename($full_name);
34:     $full_name   =~ s!\s!\_!g;          # Replace whitespace with _
35:     return($full_name);
36: }
37: sub Store_Results{
38:     my $data;
39:     my $mime = uploadInfo($File_Name)->{'Content-Type'};
40:     open (STORAGE, ">$Directory/$File")
41:       or die "Error: $Directory/$File: $!\n";
42:     if($mime !~ /text/){
43:         binmode ($File_Name);
44:         binmode (STORAGE);
45:     }
46:     while( read($File_Name, $data, 1024) ){
47:         print STORAGE $data;
48:     }
49:     close STORAGE;
50: }
51: sub Print_Results{
52:     my $link = "$Url_Path/$File";
53:     print header;
54:     print start_html("File Upload Example 3");
55:     print<<HTML;
56:     <PRE>
57:      <B>File Sent:</B> $File_Name
58:      <B>File Name:</B> $File
59:      <B>Link to File:</B> <A HREF="$link">$link</A>
60:      <A HREF="/cgi-bin/book/viewfiles.cgi">View Files</A>
61:     </PRE>
62: HTML
63:     print end_html;
64: }
```

Listing 7-6 **viewfiles.cgi**

```perl
 1: #!/usr/bin/perl -wT
 2: # viewfiles.cgi
 3: use strict;
 4: use DBI;
 5: use CGI qw(:standard);
 6: use CGI::Carp qw(fatalsToBrowser);
 7: my $Web_Directory  = "/book/storage";
 8: Print_Html_Top();
 9: Get_Descriptions();
10: Print_Html_Bottom();
11: sub Print_Row{
12:     my $rec   = shift;
13:     my $fname = $rec->{FileName};
14:     my $desc  = $rec->{Description};
15:     print qq(<TR><TD>);
16:     print qq(<A HREF="$Web_Directory/$fname">$fname</A>);
17:     print qq(</TD><TD>$desc</TD></TR>);
18: }
19: sub Get_Descriptions{
20:     my $DBH = DBI->connect("DBI:mysql:book", "book", "addison");
21:     my $sth_fetch =
22:       $DBH->prepare( qq(SELECT * FROM files) ) or die $DBH->errstr;
23:     $sth_fetch->execute();
24:     while( my $ptr = $sth_fetch->fetchrow_hashref ){
25:         Print_Row($ptr);
26:     }
27: }
28: sub Print_Html_Top{
29:     print header;
30:     print<<EOT;
31:     <HTML><HEAD><TITLE>File Viewer</TITLE></HEAD>
32:     <BODY BGCOLOR="#FFFFFF">
33:     <CENTER><H2>File Viewer</H2><P>
34:     <TABLE BORDER=1 CELLSPACING=0>
35: EOT
36: }
37: sub Print_Html_Bottom{
38:     print<<EOT;
39:     <TR><TD COLSPAN=2><A HREF="/book/upload3.html">
40:     <CENTER><H3><B>Upload File</B></H3></CENTER></A>
```

(continued)

```
41:        </TD></TR></TABLE>
42:        <P></CENTER>
43:        </BODY></HTML>
44: EOT
45: }
```

Listing 7-7   upload4.cgi

```
 1: #!/usr/bin/perl -Tw
 2: # upload4.cgi
 3: use strict;
 4: use DBI;
 5: use File::Basename;
 6: use CGI qw(:standard);
 7: use CGI::Carp qw(fatalsToBrowser);
 8: my $Directory    = "/usr/www/html/book/storage";
 9: my $Url_Path     = "/book/storage";
10: my @File_Names   = param('file_name');
11: my @Descriptions = param('file_desc');
12: my @File_Array   = ();
13: $CGI::POST_MAX = 1024 * 1500;   # Limit to 1500kb posts...
14: Get_Names();
15: Store_Descriptions();
16: Print_Results();
17: sub Get_Names{
18:     my $counter = 0;
19:     my $full_name;
20:     my $file_name;
21:     foreach $full_name (@File_Names){
22:         my $rec = {};
23:         if($full_name ne ""){
24:             $file_name            = Get_File_Name($full_name);
25:             $rec->{file_name}     = $file_name;
26:             $rec->{full_name}     = $full_name;
27:             $rec->{description}   = $Descriptions[$counter];
28:             push @File_Array, $rec;
29:             Store_File($full_name, $file_name);
30:         }
31:         $counter++;
32:     }
33: }
```

(continued)

```
34: sub Store_Descriptions{
35:     my $temp;
36:     my $DBH = DBI->connect( "DBI:mysql:book", "book", "addison" );
37:     my $sth_insert =
38:       $DBH->prepare( qq{INSERT INTO files (Description, FileName)
                                                VALUES (?,?)} )
39:        or die $DBH->errstr;
40:     foreach $temp (@File_Array){
41:         $sth_insert->execute( $temp->{description},
                                  $temp->{file_name} );
42:     }
43:     $DBH->disconnect;
44: }
45: sub Get_File_Name{
46:     if( $ENV{HTTP_USER_AGENT} =~ /win/i ){
47:         fileparse_set_fstype("MSDOS");
48:     }
49:     elsif( $ENV{HTTP_USER_AGENT} =~ /mac/i ) {
50:         fileparse_set_fstype("MacOS");
51:     }
52:     my $full_name =  shift;
53:     $full_name     = basename($full_name);
54:     $full_name     =~ s!\s!\_!g;
55:     return($full_name);
56: }
57: sub Store_File{
58:     my $file_handle = shift;
59:     my $file_name    = shift;
60:     my $data;
61:     my $mime = uploadInfo($file_handle)->{Content-Type};
62:     open (STORAGE, ">$Directory/$file_name")
63:       or die "Error: $!\n";
64:     if( $mime !~ /text/ ){
65:         binmode ($file_handle);
66:         binmode (STORAGE);
67:     }
68:     while( read($file_handle, $data, 1024) ){
69:         print STORAGE $data;
70:     }
71:     close (STORAGE);
72: }
73: sub Print_Results{
74:     my $temp;
75:     print header;
```

(continued)

```
76:        print start_html("File Upload Example 4");
77:        print h2("The following files were uploaded:");
78:        foreach $temp (@File_Array){
79:            my $link = "$Url_Path/$temp->{file_name}";
80:           print<<HTML;
81:            <PRE>
82:             <B>File Name:</B>      $temp->{file_name}
83:             <B>Description:</B>  $temp->{description}
84:             <B>Link to File:</B> <A HREF="$link">$link</A><P>
85:            </PRE>
86: HTML
87:        }
88:        print qq(\n<A HREF="/cgi-bin/book/viewfiles.cgi">View
                   Files</A>);
89:        print end_html;
90: }
```

Listing 7-8   upload4.html file

```html
<HTML>
 <HEAD><TITLE>Upload Example 4</TITLE></HEAD>
 <BODY BGCOLOR="#FFFFFF">
 <FORM NAME="upload" METHOD=POST ACTION="/cgi-bin/book/
                                          upload4.cgi"
  ENCTYPE="multipart/form-data">
 <CENTER>
  <TABLE BORDER=1 CELLSPACING=0>
   <TR BGCOLOR="#E0E0E0"><TD COLSPAN=2>
     <CENTER><B>Upload Example 4</H2></CENTER>
   </TD></TR>
   <TR><TD>
     <CENTER><B>Description</B></CENTER>
   </TD><TD>
     <CENTER><B>Files</B></CENTER>
   </TD></TR>
   <TR><TD>
     <INPUT TYPE="text" NAME="file_desc" MAXLENGTH=40>
   </TD><TD>
     <INPUT TYPE="file" NAME="file_name" MAXLENGTH=40>
   </TD></TR>
```

(continued)

```
<TR><TD>
  <INPUT TYPE="text" NAME="file_desc" MAXLENGTH=40>
</TD><TD>
  <INPUT TYPE="file" NAME="file_name" MAXLENGTH=40>
</TD></TR>
<TR><TD>
  <INPUT TYPE="text" NAME="file_desc" MAXLENGTH=40>
</TD><TD>
  <INPUT TYPE="file" NAME="file_name" MAXLENGTH=40>
</TD></TR>
<TR><TD>
  <INPUT TYPE="text" NAME="file_desc" MAXLENGTH=40>
</TD><TD>
  <INPUT TYPE="file" NAME="file_name" MAXLENGTH=40>
</TD></TR>
<TR><TD>
  <INPUT TYPE="text" NAME="file_desc" MAXLENGTH=40>
</TD><TD>
  <INPUT TYPE="file" NAME="file_name" MAXLENGTH=40>
</TD></TR>
<TR BGCOLOR="#E0E0E0"><TD COLSPAN=2><CENTER>
  <INPUT TYPE="SUBMIT" NAME="submit" VALUE="Save Files">
  [ <A HREF="/cgi-bin/book/viewfiles.cgi">View File List</A> ]
</CENTER></TD></TR>
</TABLE></CENTER></FORM>
</BODY></HTML>
```

Chapter

Tracking Clicks

8.1 Introduction

Tracking click through counts can provide useful information about what visitors are doing on a Web site. A *click through* is a term used for when someone on your Web page clicks on a hyperlink and follows through to the linked Web page. What does tracking click through mean for you? Say you have a set of pages that offer software (hopefully Open-Source Software) and want to specifically track the number of times people download each piece of software. This task can easily be handled by a CGI script that is, in essence, a go-between from the hyperlink and the ultimate destination. From the standpoint of a software developer, you simply want to see what links people are following from your Web pages. It can be extremely useful to know what software people are most interested in and where you may want to concentrate your efforts for support and updates. This chapter will cover scripts that have just that type of functionality.

The first example in this chapter will show you how to do exactly that: track the click through on links. The example shows you how to pass a URL to a CGI script, create or update a record in a database for that URL, and keep a count of click through to that URL. The other two examples work together to extend this functionality to teach you how to create a rotating banner ad application. There will be two scripts for that application, one that will randomly choose and display an image from a database and one that will keep track of the click through for it.

The following pragmas and modules are used in this chapter.

- strict
- DBI
- CGI
- POSIX
- Image::Size

8.2 Example Script: A Simple Click Tracker

The following example is a simple application that is meant to be used to track when people click on a hyperlink on a Web page, or a click through. We will use the scenario of providing software to people on a Web site to help illustrate a real-life twist to this application.

For this scenario we will assume that you are providing a Web page with links to various software distributions. Some of these may be offered by you, and some will be distributions offered on remote Web sites. The goal of this application is to track the number of times visitors to this page click through to download these software distributions. Keep in mind this is just one scenario, and this script can be used to track any link on your Web site. This application will use one script and one simple database table.

First, let's look at the database table we will use. Listing 8-1 shows the create statement for the table. The table name is click_tracker.

Listing 8-1   **Create statement for click_tracker table**

```
CREATE TABLE click_tracker (
  PAGE varchar(255) NOT NULL,
  COUNT int(11) NOT NULL,
  LAST_ACCESS datetime
);
CREATE UNIQUE INDEX page_index on click_tracker (PAGE);
```

This is a simple table with only three fields. The first field **PAGE** will be used to store the entry for each page being tracked. The pages will be dynamically added to the table when a hyperlink containing the URL is clicked. We have made this field *NOT NULL* to try to ensure that no one will attempt to add invalid fields and in turn insert NULL records. For example, the normal way this example script, track.cgi, will be called is like this.

```
http://www.you.com/cgi-bin/track.cgi?url=downloads/file
```

However, some wisenheimer may try the following in an attempt to force an insert failure or insert NULL values:

```
http://www.you.com/cgi-bin/track.cgi?url=dow'nload's/file
```

This may inadvertently cause a NULL value for PAGE to be inserted into the database, but this will not happen because we have the PAGE field set to *NOT NULL* to ensure that the record isn't created without data in this field. The result will be no insertion into the database and the user redirected to a page that does not exist.

The second field is COUNT, which is an integer field that will hold the number of times a URL has been clicked. We also have this field as *NOT NULL* to make sure we always have data for this field. The third and final field is LAST_ACCESS, of field type *datetime*, that will be used to store the value of the last time this hyperlink was clicked.

Finally, we create a *unique index* on the PAGE field to ensure we don't somehow insert a duplicate row for a URL. The script should prevent this by the way it is set up, but it never hurts to also have the database take measures to ensure data integrity.

```
01: #!/usr/bin/perl -wT
02: # track.cgi
03: use strict;
04: use DBI;
05: use CGI qw(:standard);
06: use POSIX;
```

Lines 1–6 provide the path to Perl while turning on warning and taint mode, as well as pulls in all the modules we will be using for this script.

```
07: my $dbname = 'book';
08: my $dbhost = 'localhost';
```

Lines 7 and 8 define the name of the database we will be using, as well as the host where the database resides.

```
09: my $dsn = "DBI:mysql:database=$dbname;host=$dbhost";
10: my $dbh=DBI->connect($dsn,"user","password");
```

Lines 9 and 10 connect to the database. **Line 9** defines the datasource name for the database—in this case, a MySQL database named book residing on the localhost. **Line 10** uses the DBI *connect()* method to attempt to make a connection to the database. The result of the attempted connection is stored to the $dbh variable.

```
11: if (!defined($dbh)) {
12:   print header;
13:   print "\nerror: There is a problem connecting to the MySQL
            database:\n";
14:   print DBI->errmsg;
15:   print "-" x 25;
16:   exit;
17: }
```

Lines 11–17 do a little error checking. If the connection failed, the *connect()* method will return *undef,* and **line 11** checks to see if $dbh is *not* defined. If it is not defined, then we know that the connection failed.

Lines 12–15 display an error message that the connection failed, redirect to the wanted URL, and exit the script. Notice that **line 12** is printing the header information. Since we do not print any headers before this block of code, we need to make sure we do here so the error message is properly displayed to the browser. In a production environment you may not want to have this error printed to the browser and exit the script. Instead, you would rather have the error logged and the browser redirected to the desired URL. We will leave it as an exercise for the reader to modify the script to handle both situations.

```
18: my $url = param('url');
```

Line 18 gets the value of the *url* parameter. Where did this parameter come from? In order for this script to track the clicks to certain URLs, we will execute the script from a hyperlink by passing it the URL, or page name, of what we want to track. For example, if we are tracking software downloads, and the name of one of the software distributions is *my_program.tar.gz,* the proper hyperlink would be like the following.

```
<A HREF="/cgi-bin/track.pl?url=my_program.tar.gz">
My Program v0.1</A>
```

Now you can see where the *url* parameter comes from! The value of this parameter, *my_program.tar.gz,* is then stored in $url. After the explanation of this example is complete, you will see an example of how to track local URLs and remote URLs.

```
19: my $time = strftime("%Y-%m-%d %I:%M:%S", localtime);
```

Line 19 uses the POSIX *strftime()* method to get a nicely formatted time string to insert into the database. The format will be as *YYYY-MM-DD HH:MM:SS*. Most databases, including MySQL, nicely handle POSIX-style date/time strings for *datetime* fields.

```
20: my $query = qq(update click_tracker set COUNT=COUNT+1,
                   LAST_ACCESS='$time' where PAGE='$url');
```

Line 20 initializes the $query variable with the SQL query we want to perform for the update to the database. The update will increment the COUNT field by 1, as well as update the LAST_ACCESS field with the time, based on the *PAGE* field being equal to the url parameter passed to the script.

```
21: my $sth = $dbh->prepare($query);
```

Line 21 *prepare()*s the SQL query and initializes the statement handle variable, $sth.

```
22: if ($sth->execute < 1) {
23:     $query = qq(insert into click_tracker (PAGE, COUNT,
                    LAST_ACCESS) Values ('$url', 1, '$time'));
24:     $sth = $dbh->prepare($query);
25:     $sth->execute;
26: }
```

Lines 22–26 handle the failure of the execution of the update query. If the update fails that means that the value in $url does not have a record already in the database. This is when we need to dynamically add the new $url to the database. This feature will allow you to add new URLs whose clicks you want tracked without also updating the database by hand to know about that URL. If the query failed, we then redefine $query to be an insert statement to insert a new record into the database for the new URL with the initial count of 1. This new query is then *prepare()*d and *execute()*d.

```
27: $dbh->disconnect;
28: print redirect($url);
```

Lines 26 and 27 finish the script by closing the connection to the database, on **line 26**, and redirecting the browser to the desired URL.

Now you can track individual clicks on hyperlinks. Let's take a look at this in use. Figure 8-1 shows a screenshot of a simple Web page linking to six URLs for software. Three of these links are on local pages, and the remaining three are on remote servers.

Figure 8-1   **Screenshot of Web page**

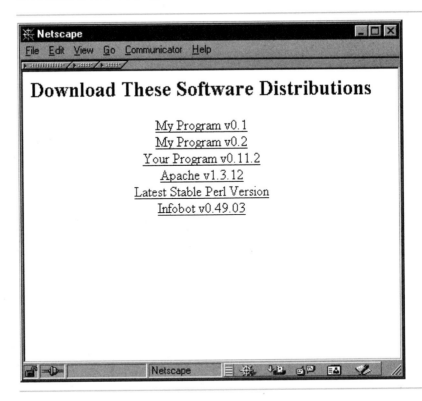

Listing 8-2 shows the relevant HTML associated with the hyperlinks.

Listing 8-2   **Relevant HTML from Figure 8-1**

```
<A HREF="/cgi-bin/track.cgi?url=software/my_prog-0.1.tar.gz">My
Program v0.1</A>
<BR>
<A HREF="/cgi-bin/track.cgi?url=software/my_prog-0.2.tar.gz">My
Program v0.2</A>
<BR>
<A HREF="/cgi-bin/track.cgi?url=software/your_prog.tar.gz">Your
Program v0.11.2</A>
<BR>
<A HREF="/cgi-bin/track.cgi?url=http://www.apache.org/dist/
apache_1.3.12">Apache v1.3.12</A>
<BR>
<A HREF="/cgi-bin/track.cgi?url=http://www.perl.com/CPAN/src/
stable.tar.gz">Latest Stable Perl Version</A>
<BR>
```

```
<A HREF="/cgi-bin/track.cgi?url=http://www.infobot.org/src/dev/
Infobot-0.49.03.tar.gz">Infobot v0.49.03</A>
```

After using this page to connect to the URLs and tracking the clicks on these hyperlinks, you would see something as in Listing 8-3.

Listing 8-3   **Display of contents of click_tracker table**

```
mysql> select * from click_tracker
    -> \g
+--------------------------------------+-------+-----------------+
| PAGE                                 | COUNT |   LAST_ACCESS   |
+--------------------------------------+-------+-----------------+
| software/my_prog-0.1.tar.gz          |   16  |2000-02-22
09:34:27|
| software/my_prog-0.2.tar.gz          |   55  |2000-02-22
09:34:27|
| http://www.you.com/your_prog.tar.gz  |   65  |2000-02-22
09:49:49|
| http://www.perl.com/CPAN/src/stable.tar.gz|116  |2000-02-23
09:08:08|
| http://www.apache.org/dist/apache_1.3.12.tar.gz|39|2000-02-24
10:34:39 |
| http://www.infobot.org/src/dev/Infobot-0.49.03.tar.gz | 97 | 2000-
02-25 10:05:13 |
+--------------------------------------+------+-----------------+
6 rows in set (0.00 sec)
```

8.3 Example Script: Random Images

Another application that is found all over the Web is random rotating images. This type of application can be used for an obvious entrepreneurial function: banner ads. The next example in this chapter will show one way to display random images to a Web page. Then we will take this a step further and track the number of impressions (times viewed) for each image, the number of times the image hyperlink was clicked on, as well as the last time the image was both displayed and clicked on. This is a basic framework for a rotating banner ad application. Of course, you could extend it to use for link exchange applications or for displaying and tracking your own images.

First, let's look at the schema for the backend database we will be using for this application in Listing 8-4.

Listing 8-4   **Schema for rotating banner application database**

```
CREATE TABLE image_tracker (
 ID int(11) NOT NULL auto_increment,
 IMAGE varchar(255) NOT NULL,
 URL varchar(255) NOT NULL,
 ALT varchar(255) NOT NULL,
 CLICKS int(11),
 IMPRESSIONS int(11),
 LAST_IMPRESSION datetime,
 LAST_CLICK datetime,
 PRIMARY KEY (ID)
);
```

In this create statement we define how we want the image_tracker table to look. The first field, **ID**, is an auto_increment that we will use as a unique primary key. You will see how this field is used later in the chapter. The next three fields, IMAGE, URL, and ALT, are used to contain the information we will need for each image. The IMAGE field will hold paths to image, URL will hold the URL to which a hyperlink is created, and ALT is the image's description that will be shown in the ALT attribute of the HTML <IMG> tag. All three of these fields may not have NULL data. This is because all these fields should contain data that is necessary for the application to work smoothly. For example, you would not want to try displaying an image that is just a NULL value or linking to a NULL URL. Although we know we should always put this information into the database for this application, it is good to use the database to help keep the data integrity.

The next two fields, CLICKS and IMPRESSIONS, will be used to keep track of the number of times the image has been clicked on and the number of times it has been displayed to a Web page. When doing this type of application when the goal is to display banner ads, you would certainly want to know both of these pieces of information. A "click" is when someone follows the hyperlink associated with the banner or image. An "impression" corresponds with the image actually being displayed on a Web page. Being able to see that banner A is clicked on %10 of the times it is displayed but banner B is clicked %75 of the time can provide useful marketing information, or even just the information that people simply do not like banner A!

Next, there are two *datetime* fields that will be used to keep track of the last time the image was displayed (LAST_IMPRESSION) and the last time it was clicked on (LAST_CLICK). Say, for example, you were using this application to track impressions and clicks for a client or associate. They may complain that their banner is not being displayed because they aren't getting business from your site. This information is then handy because the LAST_IMPRESSION field will immediately let you know whether their banner is being displayed.

The final field is creating the ID field as a primary key. We need this because we want to ensure that it is a unique value. As you will see, this field is the crux of the application for displaying images randomly. Now that we have the database ready for our application we can create the scripts to handle the displaying and tracking of the images. We will begin with the script that displays the images randomly. This script is being called show_banner.cgi and is being used as a Server Side Include. If you have an application where you do not need, or want, the images to be hyperlinks, this script could be modified to not display any HTML and only display an image. This would allow it to be used from the HTML <IMG> tag. However, we want the hyperlinks because what good is an ad if it doesn't take you to the location being advertised? The SSI would be initiated in this manner.

```
<!--#include virtual="../cgi-bin/show_banner.cgi"-->
```

Of course, you would need to change this to the appropriate paths for your system.

```
01: #!/usr/bin/perl -wT
02: # show_banner.cgi
03: use strict;
04: use DBI;
05: use CGI qw(:standard);
06: use POSIX;
07: use Image::Size qw(html_imgsize);
```

Lines 1–7 give the path to Perl and pull in the needed modules.

```
08: my $dbname = 'book';
09: my $dbhost = 'localhost';
```

Lines 8 and 9 initialize $dbname and $dbhost with the database name and location, respectively.

```
10: my $dsn = "DBI:mysql:database=$dbname;host=$dbhost";
11: my $dbh=DBI->connect($dsn,"user","password");
12: if (!defined($dbh)) {
13:    print header;
14:    print "\nerror: There is a problem connecting to the MySQL
               database:\n";
15:    print DBI->errmsg;
16:    print "-" x 25;
17:    exit;
18: }
```

Lines 10–18 attempt to connect to the database and display an error message on failure.

```
19: my $time = strftime("%Y-%m-%d %I:%M:%S", localtime);
```

Line 19 initializes the $time variable with a POSIX style time-date string. This will be used for updating the time when the image last had an impression. The resulting format of this will be *YYYY-MM-DD HH:MM:SS*.

```
20: my $query = qq(select ID from image_tracker);
```

Line 20 initializes $query with our first query. The first bit of information we will be needing from the database are the IDs of the images in the database. The IDs are really the only unique thing about the records we can count on, so we want to use them to choose the image to display. When designing this script, my first impulse was to use max(ID) to get the highest ID value or count(*) to get the total number of records and use that number to generate a random number between 0 and itself (we will still be generating a random number on **line 27**). One caveat to that is when you delete a record, the ID field doesn't automatically update itself to ensure that all IDs are in consecutive numerical order, starting at 1. This, as you will see, would make it difficult to make sure that a random number generated has a record associated with it. To work around this problem, I decided to get all the IDs and put them into an array, from which I will then choose a random element.

```
21: my $sth = $dbh->prepare($query);
22: $sth->execute;
```

Lines 21 and 22 prepare the query and execute it. The variable $sth is created as the statement handle.

```
23: my @num;
```

Line 23 declared the @num array, into which we are about to put the return values, IDs, of the query.

```
24: while (my $val = $sth->fetchrow_array) {
25:     push(@num, $val);
26: }
```

Lines 24–26 push the IDs into the @num array while the statement handle is returning the data from the query.

```
27: my $rand = int(rand(@num));
```

Line 27 generates our random number and assigns that value to $rand. The random number is generated by finding a random number between 0 and the number of elements in @num. @num is being used in scalar context here, which, as opposed to $#num, will return the actual number of elements in the array. $#num would return the number of elements but starting with 0. It is considered more idiomatic to use an array in scalar context like this rather than adding 1 to the number of the arrays indices, like $#num + 1.

```
28: $query = "select IMAGE, URL, ALT from image_tracker
                where ID=" . $num[$rand];
29: $sth = $dbh->prepare($query);
30: $sth->execute;
```

Lines 28–30 handle the query that will get the image information for the image we want to display. In the query defined in **line 27** we will fetch the IMAGE, URL, and ALT fields where the ID is equal to the value of the random array element, $num[$rand]. This query is then prepared and executed.

```
31: my ($image, $url, $alt) = $sth->fetchrow_array;
```

Line 31 fetches the returned values in array context and assigns those values to $image, $url, and $alt.

```
32: $query = qq(update image_tracker set IMPRESSIONS=IMPRESSIONS+1,
                LAST_IMPRESSION='$time' where IMAGE='$image');
33: $sth = $dbh->prepare($query);
34: $sth->execute;
35: $dbh->disconnect;
```

Lines 32–35 begin by defining the final query to be made. This query on **line 32** is to update the IMPRESSIONS field by adding 1 to the current value and update the LAST_IMPRESSION field with the current date and time, which was stored in $time on line 19. This query is then prepared and executed. Finally, **line 35** closes the connection to the database.

```
36: my $size = html_imgsize($image);
37: print qq(<A HREF="track_banner.cgi?url=$url&img=$image">
            <IMG SRC="$image" $size ALT="$alt"></A>);
```

Lines 36 and 37 complete the script. First, **line 36** uses the Image::Size's method *html_imagesize()* to retrieve the height and width of the image (whose value is in $image) passed to it. This method will return a string suitable for printing in the HTML <IMG> tag, and that string is stored in $size. **Line 37** then finishes it all off by printing the image to the browser. You will notice that the hyperlink is linking to track_banner.cgi, which is the next script you will see in this chapter. This hyperlink is also passing two parameters to track_banner.cgi; *url* whose value is in $url (and subsequently the URL we are linking to) and *img*, which is the image being displayed. The track_banner.cgi script will use these parameters to update the database record for this image.

On its own, the preceding script can be very useful. It shows how to use a simple database table to store information about an image and display that information. It also showed you a good strategy to retrieve a random record from a database. But in the next section we will look at extending this script with another, track_banner.cgi. By combining these scripts the examples become a more complete and viable application.

8.4 Example Script: Click Tracking (Reprise)

The following example is almost exactly like that in Section 8.1. This script takes the input sent to it from show_banner.cgi, updates the database and redirects the browser to the URL the user really wants to get to.

```
01: #!/usr/bin/perl -wT
02: # track_banner.cgi
03: use strict;
04: use DBI;
05: use CGI qw(:standard);
06: use POSIX;
07: my $dbname = 'book';
08: my $dbhost = 'localhost';
09: my $dsn = "DBI:mysql:database=$dbname;host=$dbhost";
10: my $dbh=DBI->connect($dsn,"user","password");
11: if (!defined($dbh)) {
12:   print header;
13:   print "\nerror: There is a problem connecting to the
            MySQL database:\n";
14:   print DBI->errmsg;
15:   print "-" x 25;
16:   exit;
17: }
18: my $url = param('url');
19: my $image = param('img');
20: my $time = strftime("%Y-%m-%d %I:%M:%S", localtime);
```

Lines 1–20 all do things that have been seen earlier in the chapter.

```
21: my $query = qq(update image_tracker set CLICKS=CLICKS+1,
                LAST_CLICK='$time' where IMAGE='$image'
                and URL='$url');
```

Line 21 defines $query with SQL that will update the appropriate record by incrementing the COUNT field by 1 and updating the LAST_CLICK field with the new date-time information.

```
22: my $sth = $dbh->prepare($query);
23: $sth->execute;
24: $dbh->disconnect;
25: print redirect($url);
```

Lines 22–25 prepare the query from **line 21**, execute that query, disconnect from the database, and finally, redirect the browser to the desired URL.

With these two scripts working in conjunction, you now have a Web-based application to display rotating banner ads as well as track their impressions and click through ratio. It also has given you a framework with which to work to add more functionality as you may need it.

8.5 Reader Exercises

- One main functionality missing from the framework given for the rotating banner ads is a method that allows a user to add images, and image information, to the database. This first exercise is to create a Web page that allows someone to update the database by adding all needed image information. They will need to be able to upload a new image to the server, as well as add images that may already be on the server. Users would also need to be able to add a URL for the hyperlink and a description that will be used in the ALT attribute.

- After completing the previous exercise, add functionality to be able to edit the information for the images. This will be useful for making any needed changes to URLs as well as any nasty typos that may occur when creating the record.

- Modify the scripts to make sure that if there is an error connecting to the database, the user is none the wiser and is redirected to the URL desired.

- Finally, add functionality to delete record from the database.

8.6 Listings

Listing 8-5   **Full listing for track.cgi**

```
01: #!/usr/bin/perl -wT
02: # track.cgi
03: use strict;
04: use DBI;
05: use CGI qw(:standard);
06: use POSIX;
07: my $dbname = 'book';
08: my $dbhost = 'localhost';
09: my $dsn = "DBI:mysql:database=$dbname;host=$dbhost";
10: my $dbh=DBI->connect($dsn,"user","password");
11: if (!defined($dbh)) {
12:    print header;
13:    print "\nerror: There is a problem connecting to the MySQL
                database:\n";
14:    print DBI->errmsg;
15:    print "-" x 25;
16:    exit;
17: }
18: my $url = param('url');
19: my $time = strftime("%Y-%m/-%d %I:%M:%S", localtime);
20: my $query = qq(update click_tracker set COUNT=COUNT+1,
LAST_ACCESS='$time' where PAGE='$url');
21: my $sth = $dbh->prepare($query);
22: if ($sth->execute < 1) {
23:     $query = qq(insert into click_tracker (PAGE, COUNT,
LAST_ACCESS) Values ('$url', 1, '$time'));
24:     $sth = $dbh->prepare($query);
25:     $sth->execute;
26: }
27: $dbh->disconnect;
28: print redirect($url);
```

Listing 8-6   **Full listing for show_banner.cgi**

```
01: #!/usr/bin/perl -wT
02: # show_banner.cgi
03: use strict;
04: use DBI;
05: use CGI qw(:standard);
06: use POSIX;
07: use Image::Size qw(html_imgsize);
```
                                                            (continued)

```perl
08: my $dbname = 'book';
09: my $dbhost = 'localhost';
10: my $dsn = "DBI:mysql:database=$dbname;host=$dbhost";
11: my $dbh=DBI->connect($dsn,"user","password");
12: if (!defined($dbh)) {
13:   print header;
14:   print "\nerror: There is a problem connecting to the MySQL
            database:\n";
15:   print DBI->errmsg;
16:   print "-" x 25;
17:   exit;
18: }
19: my $time = strftime("%Y-%m-%d %I:%M:%S", localtime);
20: my $query = qq(select ID from image_tracker);
21: my $sth = $dbh->prepare($query);
22: $sth->execute;
23: my @num;
24: while (my $val = $sth->fetchrow_array) {
25:     push(@num, $val);
26: }
27: my $rand = int(rand(@num));
28: $query = "select IMAGE, URL, ALT from image_tracker where
              ID=" . $num[$rand];
29: $sth = $dbh->prepare($query);
30: $sth->execute;
31: my ($image, $url, $alt) = $sth->fetchrow_array;
32: $query = qq(update image_tracker set IMPRESSIONS=
IMPRESSIONS+1, LAST_IMPRESSION='$time' where IMAGE='$image');
33: $sth = $dbh->prepare($query);
34: $sth->execute;
35: $dbh->disconnect;
36: my $size = html_imgsize($image);
37: print qq(<A HREF="track_banner.cgi?url=$url&img=
              $image"><IMG SRC="$image" $size ALT="$alt"></A>);
```

Listing 8-7   Full listing for track_banner.cgi

```
01: #!/usr/bin/perl -wT
02: # track_banner.cgi
03: use strict;
04: use DBI;
05: use CGI qw(:standard);
06: use POSIX;
07: my $dbname = 'book';
08: my $dbhost = 'localhost';
09: my $dsn = "DBI:mysql:database=$dbname;host=$dbhost";
10: my $dbh=DBI->connect($dsn,"user","password");
11: if (!defined($dbh)) {
12:   print header;
13:   print "\nerror: There is a problem connecting to the
            MySQL database:\n";
14:   print DBI->errmsg;
15:   print "-" x 25;
16:   exit;
17: }
18: my $url = param('url');
19: my $image = param('img');
20: my $time = strftime("%Y-%m-%d %I:%M:%S", localtime);
21: my $query = qq(update image_tracker set CLICKS=CLICKS+1,
    LAST_CLICK='$time' where IMAGE='$image' and URL='$url');
22: my $sth = $dbh->prepare($query);
23: $sth->execute;
24: $dbh->disconnect;
25: print redirect($url);
```

Chapter 9

Using mod_perl

9.1 What Is mod_perl?

mod_perl is an Apache module that allows the Web server itself to execute Perl code. This means that the Perl interpreter is actually embedded into Apache so Perl scripts can be executed without needing to start an external process (the Perl interpreter). Normally when the Web server is to run a CGI script, it runs the script in the shell and returns the output. This does create speed penalties with CGI scripts because they are actually being parsed on the host system. However, mod_perl resolves this by not having to start a new Perl interpreter process each time a CGI is run. This is accomplished by linking Perl's runtime library into the Apache server. This not only gives a developer the ability to speed up their CGI, but it also gives them an object-oriented way of interacting with the Apache server's API. Being able to interact with the Apache API gives a developer the ability to interact with most of the request phases of an HTTP request.

mod_perl's biggest advantage is speed. Because there is no overhead of starting a process to handle the CGI code, results are returned more expediently. As stated previously, the developer can put his hand in any of the HTTP request phases such as logging, authentication, preresponse processing, and URI translations. With all these tools at a programmer's disposal, a whole New World of CGI scripting becomes available.

Of course, there are caveats to using mod_perl, one of the biggest being that it increases the size of the HTTPD process. This happens because the HTTPD now has the Perl interpreter embedded into it. This is a trade-off between speed and process size. There are a few ways to help get around this problem, one of which is by upgrading your system's RAM! If that isn't feasible, the Web server can be configured in a way that there are fewer child processes that are idle or by limiting the number of clients who can simultaneously connect. The documentation for the Web server is the best way to be confident that you know the latest idiomatic methods used to accomplish this. Another way to keep down the size is by using a startup script to preload Perl modules that are most frequently used. By doing this, these modules will be compiled only once when the server starts instead of each time a script *use()*s them. We will show an example of a startup script in the following section.

It is highly recommended that you read the mod_perl documentation that comes with the distribution, as well as the documentation and FAQ pointed to on the mod_perl Web site located at *http://perl.apache.org*. The documentation will show you various ways to configure and use mod_perl, as well as help you decide if mod_perl is really what you want to use.

Some of the modules used in this chapter are not included with the mod_perl distribution and can be found on the CPAN. The modules can be installed just as any other Perl module, since they are simply Perl modules. It is important that you read the documentation for the module to learn how to configure and use the module.

These are the pragmas and modules used in this chapter.

- strict
- lib
- Apache.pm
- Apache::Constants
- Apache::Registry
- Apache::Album
- Apache::AuthDBI
- Apache::MyLog
- Apache::Sandwich
- CGI.pm
- Untaint.pm
- Image::Magik

9.2 Configuring mod_perl

mod_perl can be configured in various ways, which you will see by reading the documentation. For the most part, basic configuration is simple and straightforward. Listing 9-1 shows an example configuration entry that would be inserted into httpd.conf.

Listing 9-1   Example of a basic mod_perl configuration

```
PerlTaintCheck On
PerlRequire /usr/local/apache/perllib/startup.perl
<Directory /usr/local/apache/htdocs/perl-cgi>
    SetHandler perl-script
    PerlHandler Apache::Registry
    PerlSendHeader On
    AllowOverride None
    Options +ExecCGI
</Directory>
```

Let's skip past the PerlRequire and PerlTaintCheck lines for the moment. The rest of the preceding example demonstrates how to enable a directory for use under mod_perl. The configuration data is contained within the Directory directive, with that directory being /usr/local/apache/htdocs/perl-cgi. The SetHandler directive is set to perl-script, which tells Apache to use mod_perl to employ the requests to /usr/local/apache/htdocs/perl-cgi. The PerlHandler directive tells mod_perl that you want the Apache::Registry module to actually handle the request before a response is sent to the browser. Right now, we will not be delving into what a PerlHandler module exactly does. Just keep in mind that it (or they) handles the HTTP request phase.

Listing 9-1 also introduces Apache::Registry. This module is useful for running Perl CGI scripts (hopefully) unaltered under mod_perl. In Listing 9-1, whenever a request is made to *http://www.you.com/perl-cgi/script. cgi*, the script will be compiled once *per* HTTPD child and cached by the Apache::Registry module. This can considerably speed up your CGI because for every request to the script after the initial request, which is compiled and cached, the results are shown from the code saved in the cache as opposed to being recompiled. The code is recompiled only if the script has been modified. The Apache::Registry module will be explained in more detail later in the chapter.

The PerlSendHeader's directive tells Apache if you want it to send the HTTP headers for you. This is generally a good idea. When this directive is enabled, the mod_perl enabled Web server checks scripts to see if they are sending an HTTP header, and if so, it sends the appropriate one.

Now let's visit the PerlTaintCheck directive. Apache::Registry only recognizes the -w switch when it examines a scripts #! line. When it notices that the #! line wants warnings turned on, the module appropriately sets the $^W variable to 1. However, at the time of this writing there is no special Perl variable used to turn on taint checking. So to turn on taint checking (which you want to do) a developer must use the PerlTaintCheck directive. By turning it *On*, mod_perl knows that you want to run your CGI in taint mode and does its magic to ensure that this happens. If you have -T on your #! line but do not have PerlTaintCheck set to *On*, an error will be shown in the Web server log, but the script will still run without being in taint mode.

We should now visit the PerlRequire directive. When a mod_perl-enabled Web server is started, it will "load" a startup file if one is named with PerlRequire. What it does is *require()* the startup file and compile the modules *use()*d in the file. The *use()*d modules are then available for all mod_perl-enabled CGI scripts to *use()* and only needed to be compiled on the first initialization. Listing 9-2 is an example startup.perl file.

Listing 9-2   An example startup.perl script

```
#!/usr/bin/perl -w
use strict;
use lib "/usr/local/apache/perllib";
use Apache::Registry ();
use CGI ();
CGI->compile(':all');
use CGI::Carp ();
use DBI ();
use DBD::mysql ();
use Untaint ();
1;
```

This startup script *use()*s all the modules it is told to and then it puts the compiled code for those modules into the HTTPD process. It does not import any methods from those modules, so a developer will still need to *use()* these modules from your scripts. However, Perl will know not to recompile the code for the modules, since it has already done so. The compiled code is also in every child HTTPD process, so it is really only compiled once!

Another helpful thing you can do in a startup file, which we just did, *is use lib '/path'* in the startup file. This means you do not have to *use lib '/path'* in every file, such as we have been doing for Untaint.pm. When you do this, you can simply drop any new modules into that directory, and they will be made available for all your scripts to *use()*. This could be most helpful when developing new modules because new revisions can be put in this directory for testing.

9.3 Apache::Registry

Earlier in this chapter we briefly touched on the Apache::Registry module, but it would be more useful to delve into it a bit deeper. This module comes with the mod_perl distribution and is extremely useful when developing CGI. One benefit of this module is that it simulates a CGI environment. This means that when it compiles the source code, it creates an environment that the script would expect if it were running in a CGI environment. Apache::Registry is also a benefit, since it caches that compiled code so it won't have to recompile the code each and every time the script is requested. Instead, the module checks the cache to see when the file was last modified. If the file was modified after it was last cached, the script is recompiled and recached. Another benefit of Apache::Registry is that it allows a programmer to choose how they want to write their scripts. Programmers can write CGI scripts the usual way or use the Apache Perl API. Also, both can be used.

It is up to the developer which style is most appropriate to use. If an application heavily uses the Apache Perl API, this could make it less portable since it will need to be modified if moved to a non-mod_perl-enabled Web server. If this is not likely to happen, it would greatly benefit developers to be able to use the API to do things that can't be done via regular CGI, such as easily logging and manipulating the request before the response is sent. To illustrate the use of Apache::Registry in the two different ways, Listing 9-3 shows a script written as a regular CGI, and Listing 9-4 shows the same script using only the Apache Perl API.

Listing 9-3   **Example CGI script using Apache::Registry**

```perl
#!/usr/bin/perl -wT
use strict;
print "Content-type: text/html\n\n";
my $request_time = scalar localtime;
print<<HTML;
     <HTML>
     <HEAD>
          <TITLE>Apache::Registry Example</TITLE>
     </HEAD>
     <BODY>
          Hello $ENV{REMOTE_ADDR}, on $request_time you
          requested that I send you
          $ENV{REQUEST_URI} with the $ENV{SERVER_PROTOCOL}
          protocol. Well, this is it! Thank you for
          playing.
     </BODY>
     </HTML>
HTML
```

As you can see in Listing 9-3, this CGI looks like any other CGI. The only difference is that it is being controlled by Apache::Registry (assuming it falls under your Apache configuration to do so).

Listing 9-4   Example script using Apache Perl API

```
01: #!/usr/bin/perl -wT
02: use strict;
03: use Apache::Constants qw(OK);
04: my $r = Apache->request;
05: $r->content_type('text/html');
06: $r->send_http_header;
07: return OK if $r->header_only;
08: my $remote_host = $r->get_remote_host;
09: my $request_time = scalar localtime $r->request_time;
10: my $uri = $r->uri;
11: my $protocol = $r->protocol;
12: $r->print(<<HTML);
13:          <HTML>
14:          <HEAD>
15:              <TITLE>Apache::Registry Example</TITLE>
16:          </HEAD>
17:          <BODY>
18:          Hello $remote_host, on $request_time you
             requested that I send you
19:          $uri with the $protocol protocol. Well,
             this is it! Thank you for playing.
20:     </BODY>
21:     </HTML>
22: HTML
```

The script shown in Listing 9-4 offers some new concepts, so it is worth doing a line-by-line explanation.

Lines 1 and 2 tell where the Perl interpreter is and turns on compiler warnings with the *strict* pragma.

Line 3 *use()*s the Apache::Constants module and imports its **OK** constant. The Apache::Constants module imports the constants found in the Apache header files. This allows a programmer to easily return server response codes such as OK, DECLINED, FORBIDDEN, and so forth. We only need to import the OK constant for this script.

Line 4 initialized $r to hold a reference to the Apache request object. The Apache.pm module has an object that holds all the information the server needs to process a request. By calling the *request()* method, we can hold a reference to this object; in this case it is held in $r. Generally, you will see $r being used this way in many programs with the Apache Perl API. Using the letter *r* for the object reference is a good way to tell both yourself and others that it is the *request* object. You will also see $s used in scripts to represent the *server* object, but you don't need to concern yourself with that right now. By having a reference to the request object, a developer can now access all the goodies that object holds.

Line 5 uses the *content_type()* method via our Apache request object to define the content type of the document.

Line 6 sends the response header to the browser via the *send_http_header()* method. One thing you will notice about the Apache Perl API is that the method names, for the most part, are named such that the name closely resembles the action it performs.

Line 7 returns the OK (200) server response to the browser if all it wanted was the response header and not the content. If this is so, the script ends when this response is sent.

Line 8 uses the *get_remote_host()* method to fetch the browsers DNS hostname. If the hostname is not known, *undef* is returned. If the HostName-Lookups directive is not turned on in the Apache configuration, the IP address of the client will be returned. If this directive is enabled, the DNS name will be returned. Many people choose not to enable this directive (it is not on by default) because it can mean a speed penalty when the server has to attempt to do reverse DNS on all incoming clients. Whatever the returned value is, it is stored in $remote_host.

Line 9 initializes $request_time with the scalar representation of the time the request was made to the server.

Line 10 fetches the URI from the request object with the *uri()* method. The value returned is stored in $uri.

Line 11 uses the *protocol()* method to find the HTTP protocol used to request this document. $protocol holds this returned value.

Lines 12–22 use the Apache request objects *print()* method to send the text to the browser. This can be used instead of Perl built-in *print()* function. In the background the Apache::print method sets a timeout before it actually sends the data to the client. Perl's built-in function does not do this.

It is a good idea to get familiar with the Apache.pm methods by reading its documentation carefully. When using mod_perl you will surely want to know all that it can do for you. This is especially true when you write your own content handler, which we will do later in this chapter.

One thing to remember is that Apache::Registry should only be used on executable files. Basically, if it isn't a Perl script, don't have Apache::Registry handling it. The reason for this is the module expects to be handling Perl scripts and it evaluates the contents of the requested file as if it were a subroutine. If it tries to compile an HTML file, for example, an error would occur. To ensure this is not an issue, make sure to configure Apache to only use Apache::Registry as a handler for files with a certain extension or directories of CGI scripts. For example, Listing 9-5 shows a configuration entry that will have Apache::Registry all files on the Web tree with a .rpl extension, which means that the .rpl files will need to be executable Perl scripts. The example shown in Listing 9-1 demonstrated how to enable everything in a directory to be managed by Apache::Registry.

Listing 9-5   Example configuration entry for Apache::Registry

```
<Files *.rpl$>
  SetHandler perl-script
  PerlHandler Apache::Registry
  PerlSendHeader On
  Options +ExecCGI
</Files>
```

In this section you learned about what Apache::Registry does and how to use it. You also learned how to use some of the Apache Perl API to boost up your code. In the next sections you will see other modules and uses for mod_perl.

9.4 Automatic Headers and Footers with Apache::Sandwich

Most, if not all, professional Web sites have a consistent look and feel aimed to please visitors as well as to create a brand image. The consistency between pages is done with color schemes, similar graphics, and page headers and footers. When developing a Web site, the question of how this consistency will be done and maintained is always a concern. An easily maintainable system for adding and modifying things such as headers and footers should be thought out. The following example deals with having an easily maintainable header and footer on your Web pages, using mod_perl and Apache::Sandwich.

When we talk about page headers, we are referring to the top section of a Web page that may contain a company logo, <BODY> information, banner ads and so on. The footer is generally the bottom section that may contain text links and copyright information. The best way to easily add this information to each and every Web page is to add the text to each and every page on the site. This can somewhat easily be done if a template is created and all pages are created from that template. Well, maybe it is easy to use the template to create a few hundred pages, but what happens when you need to add a new link to the footer? Your options include doing every page by hand, using a script to modify each page, or using an application that can do large search and replace operations. All of these options are time consuming and not very developer friendly. Not only is the process tedious, but you would probably want to view many (if not all) of the pages to make sure the script or application did not make any mistakes. I don't know about you, but this doesn't seem like a viable option.

Another way to add a header and footer to each page is by using SSIs. An SSI could be included at the top and bottom of every Web page. This would be a solution similar to the one previously given, except there would be only a few lines of text to worry about. But what happens when you have an SSI that displays the company logo, but you then decide to add a banner ad underneath that? You again would need to modify each and every page to which you want to add this. This raises the same issues as having the header and footer done in HTML within each and every page. This is maybe a better option, but it is still not a viable one.

A viable solution would be to use mod_perl and Apache::Sandwich. The Apache::Sandwich module, which is easy to use, will add a header and/or footer to all your Web pages automatically. It can do this because it is a module that acts as a content handler for Apache and is able to modify content before it is sent back to the browser in the HTTP response phase. This is what is so exciting about using mod_perl. It allows a Perl module to step in between the request from the client and the Web server. What the Apache::Sandwich module does is act as that go-between and sandwich your content between a predefined header and footer.

Let's take a look at how to accomplish this. First, there needs to be a configuration entry in httpd.conf that will tell Apache to use Apache::Sandwich as the request handler for a certain file type. For our example, we will be using .html files, but this could also be used for directories and other file types depending on your needs.

Listing 9-6   **Example configuration entry for Apache::Sandwich**

```
<FilesMatch "\.html$">
        SetHandler perl-script
        PerlHandler Apache::Sandwich
        PerlSetVar HEADER "/pbj/sandwich/header.txt"
        PerlSetVar FOOTER "/pbj/sandwich/footer.txt"
</FilesMatch>
```

Listing 9-6 illustrates how to instruct Apache that when it receives a request for a file with .html as an extension to have Apache::Sandwich handle that request. This begins by setting the SetHandler to *perl-script* that tells Apache that mod_perl is to be given control of the request. The PerlHandler directive then tells mod_perl that the Apache::Sandwich module will handle the request. The two PerlSetVar lines are used by the Apache::Sandwich module. They define two variables, HEADER and FOOTER, whose values are set to the path of the appropriate files. The path to these files is not a full server path, but the directory path from the Web server's Document-Root. You will notice that the files to be used as a header and footer are simply text files.

Listing 9-7   **Contents of header.txt**

```
<HTML>
<HEAD>
    <TITLE>Apache::Sandwich Example</TITLE>
</HEAD>
<BODY>
<CENTER>
<H1>Hello! I am the header!</H1>
</CENTER>
```

Listing 9-8   **Contents of footer.txt**

```
<CENTER>
<H3>Bye! I am the footer!</H3>
Copyright &copy; 19100, XYZZY Inc. Ltd. LLC. Corp.
</CENTER>
    </BODY>
</HTML>
```

Listings 9-7 and 9-8 show the contents of the header.txt and footer.txt files, respectively. As you can see they are simply HTML. With the configuration done and these files set in place, any file with an .html will have a header and footer from these files. Listing 9-9 shows index.html, which when requested will be sandwiched by Apache::Sandwich. The result is show in Figure 9-1.

Listing 9-9   **Contents of index.html**

```
<HR NOSHADE>
<P>
<CENTER>
Welcome to the body of the page.
</CENTER>
<P>
<HR NOSHADE>
```

Figure 9-1   Our sandwich

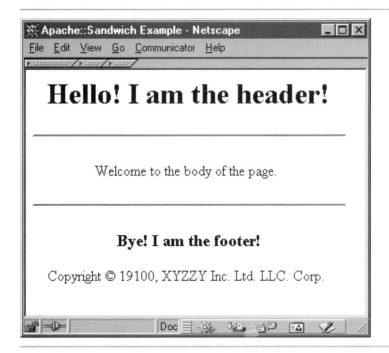

Apache::Sandwich also allows you to *stack* headers and footers. This means that a developer can have a series of files used as headers or footers. For example, let's assume that we wanted to add a rotating banner ad onto every page. We could now do this by stacking on another header file. If this was the case, we could use the banner ad script from Chapter 9, show_banner.cgi. In order to stack another header into the mix, we would change the configuration entry to look like Listing 9-10.

Listing 9-10   Two header files stacked together

```
<FilesMatch "\.html$">
    SetHandler perl-script
    PerlHandler Apache::Sandwich
    PerlSetVar HEADER "/pbj/sandwich/header.txt /cgi-bin/
    show_banner.cgi"
    PerlSetVar FOOTER "/pbj/sandwich/footer.txt"
</FilesMatch>
```

When adding more than one file to be used as a header or footer, the files will be executed in the order you listed in the configuration. Based on what is in Listing 9-10, the result would be as shown in Figure 9-2. The only modification to show_banner.cgi would be that a line printing the proper content line needs to be added.

Figure 9-2   Double-decker sandwich (on rye please)

One caveat of Apache::Sandwich is that if you attempt to use it with CGI scripts, it will not work properly. This is because on the inside of the module it needs to print a text/html HTTP header to have the header display. So if a CGI script is meant to be the body, the contents of the file will simply be displayed and not evaluated. The default way of using the module expects the body to be a static page of text. However, starting with version 2.04 of Apache::Sandwich, there is a helper method, *insert_parts()*, that can be used to add the header and footer. One caveat of using this is that each script has to call this method. But although its default usage isn't as nice as it is for nonexecutable files, the CGI scripts can benefit from having the header and footer added, as well as being able to utilize Apache::Registry. Listing 9-11 shows a configuration entry that will enable Apache::Registry to handle the HTTP requests for files with a .cgi extension. It also defines the HEADER and FOOTER, which Apache::Sandwich uses to know which files to use as the header(s) and footer(s). Stacking header/footer files also with a .cgi extension would cause freaky things.

Listing 9-11   Configuration for .cgi files to use Apache::Registry

```
<FilesMatch "*\.cgi">
    SetHandler  perl-script
    PerlHandler Apache::Registry
    PerlSetVar HEADER "/book/c10/header.txt"
    PerlSetVar FOOTER "/book/c10/footer.txt"
</FilesMatch>
```

Listing 9-12 shows an example CGI script that uses the *Apache::Sandwich::show_parts()* method.

Listing 9-12   Example CGI using the show_parts() method

```
01: #!/usr/bin/perl -wT
02: use strict;
03: use CGI qw(:standard);
04: use Apache::Sandwich;
05: print header;
06: Apache::Sandwich::insert_parts('HEADER');
07: print hr;
08: print p({align=>'center'},"Hello, world!");
09: print hr;
10: Apache::Sandwich::insert_parts('FOOTER');
```

Lines 6 and 10 directly call the *show_parts()* method. This needs to be done because the method is not imported when Apache::Sandwich is *use()*d. Scripts that use this method also must *use()* the Apache::Sandwich module, as well as run in a mod_perl environment. The module will not work in a non-mod_perl environment but requires that an Apache request object be available.

You have now learned how to easily add a header and footer inserted onto all the Web pages and CGI scripts on your site. This can save developers a lot of time when developing a site, as well as keep the site more maintainable.

9.5 A mod_perl Photo Album with Apache::Album

Many companies, large and small, have a graphics library available to the marketing department and to those who develop the company Web site and marketing materials. Also, many people use the Web to share pictures with family and friends. One of the problems is having these images organized in a way that makes browsing easy for people. I have seen companies with literally dozens of directories filled with images and no easy way to view them without actually opening each image or using third-party software to view them as thumbnails. This isn't a very productive situation, and I have heard graphic designers and developers alike complain that they cannot browse the images easily.

The Apache::Album module helps take care of this problem. This module will allow a developer to use directories filled with image files as photo albums. The module handles the displaying of the images, creating not only thumbnails (using ImageMagick) but different-sized images for various screen sizes, as well as handle the titles of images in two ways. It also proves itself as an application disguised as a module by allowing a user to create new albums *and* upload images via the Web. But enough talk about the module! Let's move on to discussing its implementation.

The Apache::Album module provides a healthy amount of configuration options. We highly suggest that if you are going to use this module (as with all modules), you should read the documentation to see what new features and configuration options are available. In this section we will go through a basic configuration that will display image albums, create and display thumbnails, and create thumbnails for various screen resolutions. The terrific thing about all this is there is no programming involved. Simply having the appropriate entry in the Web server configuration file and directory structure is all that is needed.

The first step is to create a directory structure with the image albums. Consider the structure shown in Listing 9-13.

Listing 9-13   Example directory structure for Apache::Album

```
/usr/local/apache/htdocs/albums
                        /kyla
                            /albums_loc
                                    /vol1
                                    /vol2
```

The directories *vol1* and *vol2* would be the photo albums and would contain the actual image files. These directories would need to have the proper write because Apache::Album will create a directory in each of the album directories to store the thumbnail images that will be generated. By default, it creates a directory named *thumbs*, and we will be using this (unless, of course, you also have a lot of images of thumbs and want to name it something else). Listing 9-14 shows the configuration we will be using.

Listing 9-14   httpd.conf entry for Apache::Album

```
01: Alias /kyla /usr/local/apache/htdocs/albums/kyla/
02: <Location /kyla/albums>
03:     SetHandler perl-script
04:     AllowOverride None
```

```
05:     Options None
06:     PerlHandler Apache::Album
07:     PerlSetVar AlbumDir /kyla/albums_loc
08:     PerlSetVar OutsideTableBorder 1
09:     PerlSetVar InsideTablesBorder 1
10:     PerlSetVar BodyArgs BGCOLOR=white
11:     PerlSetVar AllowFinalResize 1
12:     PerlSetVar FinalResizeDir thumbs
13: </Location>
```

Line 1 creates an alias for the */usr/local/apache/htdocs/albums/kyla* directory. Now when people access *http://www.me.com/kyla,* they are really seeing what is in the *albums/kyla/* directory.

Line 2 starts the configuration section for */kyla/albums*. The *Location* directive is used with an arbitrary directory path. This will tell Apache that when
a request comes to *http://www.me.com/kyla/albums*, it should take the information nested in this directive and act accordingly.

Line 3 tells Apache to use mod_perl to control this request—in this case, to
handle anything that is requested within */kyla/albums*.

Line 4 makes sure that any subdirectories can't override options given
in this configuration block. This could be tailored to your needs, but
Apache::Album manages everything you will need done in this directory
tree.

Line 5 sets *Options* to *None*, which tells Apache not to allow things like
CGI, directory indexing, and so forth to be done from within this location.
Options should not be needed because this directory tree should only con-
tain image files and an optional text file, which will be discussed later.

Line 6 tells mod_perl to use the Apache::Album module to be the handler
for incoming requests.

Line 7 sets a variable named *AlbumDir* to the physical location (from the
Web server's DocumentRoot) of the directory containing the album directories. The Apache::Album module uses this to know where the physical directory containing the photo albums is located. *PerlSetVar* is part of the
Apache Perl API that easily allows a programmer to pass variables from the
Web server's configuration file to the CGI script. We will see this better illustrated later when we cover how to write a mod_perl handler later in this
chapter.

Line 8 also sets a variable for the Apache::Album module to access. This
specific one is a setting to have the outer HTML table of the resulting display have a border.

Line 9 is much like **line 8** except this sets the border for inner HTML tables. This can be seen in Figure 9-4.

Line 10 tells Apache::Album that the background is to be white.

Line 11 sets a variable that tells Apache::Album that we want to allow different sizes of the image to be created. Normally, there would just be a thumbnail image made, but using this option allows the module to create images for alternate screen sizes. It will create images for 640x480, 800x600, or 1024x758 screen sizes when appropriate. For example, if an image has a width of 900, Apache::Album will create the thumbnail as well as images suitable for viewing on a 640x480 and 800x600 screens. When the page is generated, the viewer will have the choice to see the full-size image (by clicking on the thumbnail), as well as any images generated for alternate screen sizes.

Line 12 sets a variable, which lets the module know in which directory to create the various alternative-sized images. Here the *thumbs* directory is specified, so they are in the same location as the thumbnail images.

Line 13 ends this configuration block.

That's all! Now when I point my browser to *http://www.me.com/kyla/ albums*, I will be presented with a list of available photo albums, as seen in Figure 9-3. When I choose one of these albums, I am shown the thumbnails of the images in that directory, as shown in Figure 9-4. And finally, when I choose one of the images, I see the full-sized version, as illustrated in Figure 9-5.

Figure 9-3   List of photo albums

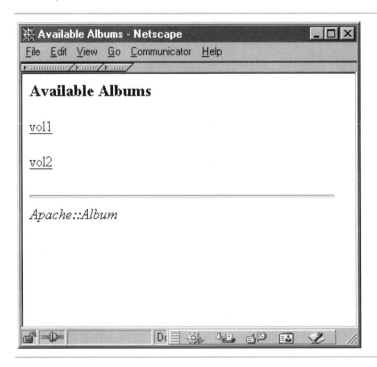

Figure 9-4   Viewing thumbnails

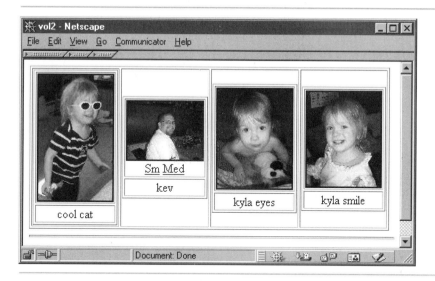

Figure 9-5   Viewing a full-sized image

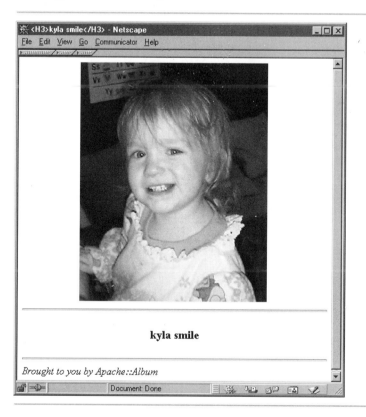

So far, so good. You now know how to take image directories and have them appear as photo albums with thumbnails and images for various screen sizes. You may also have noticed that the caption given to a photo is a slightly modified version of that file's name. This is a very nice feature that Apache::Album does for you. However, files may have more ambiguous names, so it might be more prudent to provide your own captions for some or all of the photos. Also, you may want to spiff up the top portion of your album page with descriptions, such as where the photos were taken, "My Birthday Party," or their genre, like "Psychedelic Images." Apache::Album provides a developer with an extremely simple way to do this by using a text file, *caption.txt*. After creating this text file, a developer places it in the directory for which it is meant, and the result will be custom captions. Listing 9-15 shows a caption.txt file that will be placed in the *vol2* directory.

Listing 9-15   **caption.txt file for the vol2 directory**

```
<CENTER><H2>Kyla Volume 2</H2></CENTER>
__END__
cool_cat.jpg: I am so cooool
kev.jpg: Dad
kyla_smile.jpg: &quot;Cheeeese&quot;
```

This file is very simple to set up, as you can see. Everything before the __END__ token will be used as a header for the page. Below this is the name of the image file, a colon, and the desired caption. You do not need to create a caption for each image if an image in the directory does not have an entry in the content.txt file. In that case, the name of the file will be used as it was before. After putting this file in the *vol2* directory, its view via the Web looks like Figure 9-6.

Now that people can see the photo albums, we need to have an easy way for those who have control over them to be able to create new albums and upload images in an easy manner. Apache::Album, the application disguised as a module, already has taken care of this. In order to allow an *edit mode* with this module, one line must be added to the configuration block.

```
PerlSetVar EditMode 1
```

When that is added and the server is restarted, people will be allowed to create new albums from the main page listing the available albums (refer to Figure 9-3) and have the ability to upload images into albums from their browser. However, you really do not want to simply give this ability to everyone. There would be security implications if you were to just allow everyone to create directories and upload files. To make sure this feature is "locked down" to only those you trust, some authentication must be added. But we can't just go and password protect */kyla/albums*, since that would hinder those without passwords from viewing the images. Since Apache::Album

Figure 9-6   vol2 directory with a content.txt file

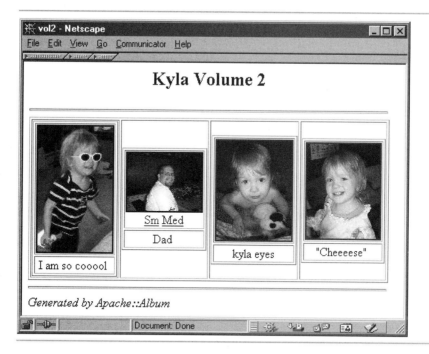

simply uses whatever directory you send it in AlbumDir to do its background magic, we can create another configuration block to another arbitrary directory and wrap Basic Authentication around it. This way the masses can view the images, and the authorized can update the albums. Listing 9-16 shows the new configuration block.

Listing 9-16   Configuration block with authentication

```
01: <Location /kyla/secure>
02:   SetHandler perl-script
03:   AllowOverride None
04:   AuthName "Edit Albums"
05:   AuthType Basic
06:   AuthUserFile /usr/local/apache/htdocs/albums/
      .kyla_access
07:   <Limit GET POST PUT>
08:       require valid-user
09:   </Limit>
10:   PerlSetVar EditMode 1
11:   Options None
12:   PerlHandler Apache::Album
13:   PerlSetVar AlbumDir /kyla/albums_loc
```

(continued)

```
14:    PerlSetVar OutsideTableBorder 1
15:    PerlSetVar InsideTablesBorder 1
16:    PerlSetVar BodyArgs BGCOLOR=white
17:    PerlSetVar AllowFinalResize 1
18:    PerlSetVar FinalResizeDir thumbs
19: </Location>
```

The only added lines from the configuration shown in Listing 9-16 are **lines 4–10**, so we will concentrate on them. You will notice that **line 1** is pointing to */kyla/secure,* which is an arbitrary directory. So this block will come into play when someone uses the URL *http://www. me.com/kyla/secure.*

Line 4 sets the AuthName for our secure area. This name will be displayed in the dialog box shown to anyone attempting to get into this section while still unauthorized. Figure 9-7 shows an example.

Figure 9-7   Dialog box for authentication

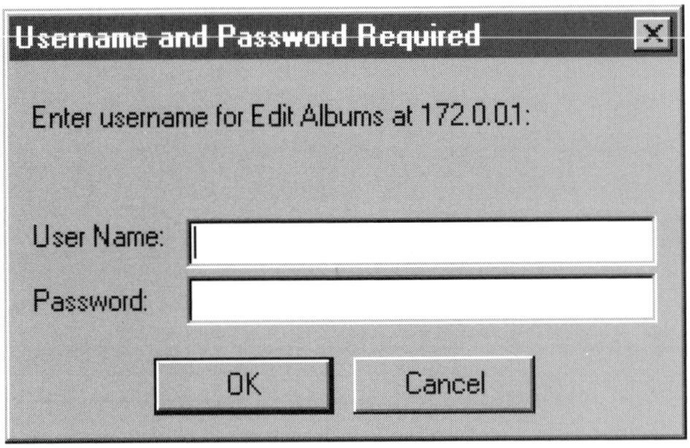

Line 5 sets the authorization type to Basic.

Line 6 uses the *AuthUserFile*directive to tell Apache to find the username/password combinations in the file */usr/local/apache/htdocs/albums/.kyla_access*.

Lines 7–9 use the *Limit* directive to restrict requests of the types GET, POST, and PUT to those who are valid users. Someone is considered a valid user only if they successfully log in.

Figure 9-8 shows the album listing after being authenticated into the new secure section. Notice the text box that will allow someone to create a new album. When a new album is created, it is really creating a directory in the AlbumDir directory. It is suggested that you make sure PerlTaintCheck is On when enabling edit mode. Apache::Album does untaint directory names to ensure they are as safe as possible, but it is always safer to be in taint mode with CGI.

Figure 9-8   **Album listing in edit mode**

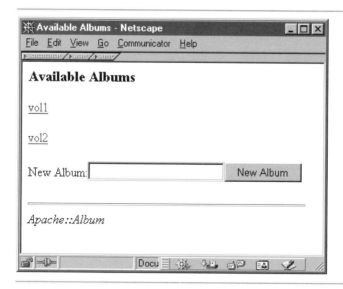

Now you have, with no programming at all, a viable application to share albums of images with friends, family, and co-workers. With the Web-based album creation and file uploading, it is easy to maintain from anywhere. We do suggest, again, that you read the documentation to see what other configuration options would be useful to you.

9.6 Authentication with Apache::AuthDBI

In the last section we password protected a directory in a non-mod_perl fashion. But we can also use mod_perl to do authentication with a database instead of using a flat file to store the usernames and passwords. This can be accomplished with the Apache::AuthDBI module, which is another mod_perl handler that deals with authentication and authorization. In this section we will use this module to password protect the photo album edit directory instead of using the method shown previously.

The first thing we need is a database table that will house the usernames and passwords. This table will be called *album_users* and will be very basic with only two columns. In your applications you could make this table however you like. You may want it to not only hold username and password information but also possibly some personal information on the user. Listing 9-17 shows the schema we will be using for this example.

Listing 9-17   Simple schema for Apache::AuthDBI table

```
create table album_users (
    user varchar(50),
    password varchar(50)
)
```

The next step is to configure Apache to use Apache::AuthDBI for handling authentication. As with Apache::Album, there is no scripting needed to use this, only configuration. Listing 9-18 shows the configuration block we will be using

Listing 9-18   Configuration block for Apache::AuthDBI

```
01: PerlModule Apache::AuthDBI
02: <Location /kyla/secure>
03:   SetHandler perl-script
04:   AllowOverride None
05:   AuthName "Edit Albums"
06:   AuthType Basic
07:   PerlAuthenHandler Apache::AuthDBI::authen
08:   PerlSetVar Auth_DBI_data_source
          dbi:mysql:database=book;host=localhost
09:   PerlSetVar Auth_DBI_username      public
10:   PerlSetVar Auth_DBI_password      foobar
11:   PerlSetVar Auth_DBI_pwd_table     album_users
12:   PerlSetVar Auth_DBI_uid_field     user
13:   PerlSetVar Auth_DBI_pwd_field     password
14:   PerlSetVar Auth_DBI_placeholder   on
15:   PerlSetVar Auth_DBI_nopasswd      on
16:   require valid-user
17:   Options None
18:   PerlHandler Apache::Album
19:   PerlSetVar EditMode 1
20:   PerlSetVar AlbumDir /kyla/albums_loc
21:   PerlSetVar OutsideTableBorder 1
22:   PerlSetVar InsideTablesBorder 1
23: </Location>
```

The only new lines in the configuration block are **line 1** and **lines 7–15**, which configure Apache to use Apache::AuthDBI and configure the module itself.

Line 1 tells Apache to load the Apache::AuthDBI module when it starts. This can also be done by adding a *use Apache::AuthDBI* line in startup.perl, but we chose to keep it with the configuration block for clarity and a reminder that it is being used.

Line 7 uses the *PerlAuthenHandler* directive to tell Apache to use Apache::AuthDBI::authen to handle any incoming requests to the password protected directory. Since we are using this directive within a Location directive, it will only be used when requests are made to this directory tree.

Line 8 initialized a variable, *Auth_DBI_data_source*, which Apache::AuthDBI uses to know what DSN to connect to. The value used is just that, a DSN that DBI.pm will use to make the database connection.

Line 9 sets *Auth_DBI_username*, which is the username DBI.pm will use to connect to the database.

Line 10 then sets *Auth_DBI_password*, which is the password to use to connect to the database. Do *not* use a username and password here for a database account that has full privileges to the database. Because the httpd.conf file is readable by anyone who has an account on the machine, you want to be sure that the user you use to connect only has a minimum set of privileges. For this scenario, that user only needs read access, since AuthDBI.pm is only being used for reading. If you wish for AuthDBI.pm to update any fields (which is not covered in this book, but the module documentation explains how to have it update a field for logging), make sure the account has the appropriate privileges only. The documentation for Apache::AuthDBI also shows a way to get and set *Auth_DBI_username* and *Auth_DBI_password* without displaying them in plain text.

Line 11 defines *Auth_DBI_pwd_table*, which is the database table the module will use to look up the usernames and passwords.

Lines 12 and 13 define *Auth_DBI_uid_field* and *Auth_DBI_pwd_field*, whose values are the database field to find the usernames and the passwords, respectively.

Line 14 is turning on the *Auth_DBI_placeholder* option for AuthDBI.pm. When using a database that supports placeholders, as MySQL does, turning on this option can help performance. By turning on this option, Apache::AuthDBI will use a placeholder for the username in the query used to fetch a password. By using the placeholder, this query can be prepared once instead of every time it is needed, which will save time when authenticating users.

Line 15 isn't something you would likely want to use for this application (photo album), but we feel it is important to show this feature of AuthDBI.pm. *Auth_DBI_nopasswd*, when enabled, will allow any username without a password to be able to log in with any password entered. This is something that can be useful if you have a secure application, or directory, but wish to allow a guest limited access. Of course, the programmer would have to limit the access based on the name of the user logged in (from $ENV{REMOTE_USER}), but this feature can be very useful to accomplish that.

Apache::AuthDBI checks passwords that are encrypted with the Perl *crypt()* function. By default, the salt for the *crypt()* is the password. So when the username and password are submitted, a sequence of events occurs, such as illustrated in Listing 9-19.

Listing 9-19   Flow of authentication

```
01: SELECT password FROM table WHERE username = user
02: if password eq crypt("password", "user"), login OK
03: otherwise, access is denied.
```

The module provides two other options that will give the username precedence over the password or just use plain text passwords. To do this, the following line must be added to the configuration block.

```
PerlSetVar Auth_DBI_encryption_salt userid
```

If you wanted to use plain text passwords, the following line must be added.

```
PerlSetVar Auth_DBI_encrypted off
```

In our example, we want to use encrypted passwords with the password as the salt for the *crypt()* function. We will be leaving it as an exercise for the reader to create a Web-based application to add usernames to the database or a command line tool. This will be explained more at the end of the chapter.

9.7 Writing a mod_perl Handler

So far you have learned how to do basic configuration of mod_perl, as well as use some Apache modules as handlers. In this section we will discuss writing your own mod_perl handler with Perl. Writing a mod_perl handler is basically the same as writing other Perl modules, except they can directly use the Apache Perl API, and the main method is generally named *handler()*. By default, when a module is used as a *Perl*Handler*, the method *handler()* is used to manage the request, or action. Other considerations are being careful of lexically and globally scoped variables. Global variables in an Apache module are shared throughout the life of a HTTPD process. In other words, if a child process is to manage 40 requests and uses a global variable called *$global*, when one of the requests changes this, all the requests to that child process will have that value available. Until you are able to get a real feel for this concept by trial and error, it is best to keep global variables that are not being used as constants to a minimum.

The example mod_perl handler we will cover is going to control the logging phase of a request. There is a lot of useful information that goes into a Web server's access log, but you generally need a piece of third-party software to parse it into something readily accessible. Having the information that goes into the access log put into a database can make the data readily available to access. This is exactly what Apache::MyLog does. The first thing is to decide what information should be logged. Here logging is done for the remote host, user (if it is an authenticated user), time stamp, requested URI, request status (200, 404, and so forth), the number of bytes sent to the client, the method of the request (GET, POST, and so forth), referrer, and the type of browser. Now that we know what information will be logged, a database table that will house this data is needed (see Listing 9-20).

Listing 9-20 **SQL to create request_log table for Apache::MyLog**

```
CREATE TABLE request_log (
  remote_host varchar(255) DEFAULT '' NOT NULL,
  user varchar(50),
  time_stamp datetime DEFAULT '0000-00-00 00:00:00' NOT NULL,
  requested varchar(255) DEFAULT '' NOT NULL,
  status smallint(3) DEFAULT '0',
  bytes int(8),
  method varchar(8) DEFAULT '' NOT NULL,
  referer varchar(255),
  browser varchar(255)
)
```

The table is named *request_log* and has the appropriate fields for the data that is to be saved. Next the module itself is needed. We will walk you through this module, which introduces some of the Apache Perl API. Before this is done, however, it is important to see the configuration block that is used in order to initialize this module to handling the logging phase to help put the module in context. Listing 9-21 shows this block.

Listing 9-21 **Configuration block for using Apache::MyLog**

```
PerlLogHandler Apache::MyLog
PerlSetVar MyLog_dsn dbi:mysql:database=book;host=localhost
PerlSetVar MyLog_user public
PerlSetVar MyLog_pwd foobar
PerlSetVar MyLog_table request_log
```

Since this module is to be used to control the logging phase of the request, we need to apprise mod_perl and Apache of this by declaring it as so using the *PerlLogHandler* directive. The lines following that directive should look familiar. Configuration variables are being set, much like Apache::AuthDBI does, so the module can get the DSN information, database login information, and the name of the table to use. This is not hard coded into the module to allow for the same module to connect to multiple databases on multiple servers or use a different database table for directory trees. This block can be placed within *Location* or *Directory* directives or used globally. Now on with the code!

```
01: package Apache::MyLog;
```

Line 1 defines the name of the package. Apache modules, which are used as handlers, are generally located in the Apache::* namespace, and the name of this module is MyLog.pm. Not all modules that can be used with mod_perl are in the Apache::* namespace, such as HTML::Mason, but those that are Apache/mod_perl specific usually are (or should be!).

```
02: use strict;
03: use Apache ();
04: use DBI ();
05: use Apache::Constants qw(:common);
06: use POSIX;
```

Lines 2–6 pull in the modules needed for the rest of MyLog.pm. The Apache.pm module will import the Perl Apache API methods; DBI.pm allows for easy connections to the database; Apache::Constants imports the common HTTP constants used (OK, DECLINED, and so forth); and the POSIX.pm module will be used to format the date and time.

```
07: $Apache::MyLog::VERSION = '0.01';
```

Line 7 defines a scalar variable, which holds the version number of this module. When creating a module for distribution, the MakeMaker.pm module creates a make file for use in installing the distribution. MakeMaker uses the *$Package::VERSION* scalar to know the version of the module that is being installed. We chose to directly assign this global scalar into the namespace in this fashion instead of declaring $VERSION a global variable with the *var* pragma, again for clarity.

```
08: sub handler {
09:    my $r = shift;
```

Lines 8 and 9 begin the *handler()* method and initialize the scalar *$r* as a reference to the request object. The request object is always passed to the *handler()* method as the first argument. This is equivalent to getting *$self* in OO Perl modules. A programmer will be able to access the Apache Perl API via the *$r* variable.

```
10:        return DECLINED unless ($r->is_main);
```

Line 10 uses the Apache Perl API method *is_main()* to check to see if this is the main piece of the HTTP request, as opposed to subrequests like redirects and included files. The main request is the only one of concern, so if this isn't it, DECLINED is returned and the processing of the request continues elsewhere.

```
11:        my %Config = ('dsn'=> $r->dir_config('MyLog_dsn'),
12:                      'user'=> $r->dir_config('MyLog_user'),
13:                      'pwd'=> $r->dir_config('MyLog_pwd'),
14:                      'table'=> $r->dir_config('MyLog_table')
15:                 );
```

Lines 11–15 initialize the hash *%Config*. This hash has four keys that will be used later in the module. The values of this hash are retrieved from the variables set in the configuration block. By using the *dir_config()* method and passing it an argument that is the name of the configuration variable you wish to retrieve, a programmer can now possess the values that were set in the configuration file.

```
16:      if (!$Config{dsn} ||
            !$Config{user} ||
            !$Config{pwd} ||
            !$Config{table}) {
17:           $r->log_error("MyLog.pm not properly configured.");
18:           return DECLINED;
19:      }
```

Lines 16–19 do a sanity check to make sure all the configuration variables expected were actually passed. If any of these four values were not set up in the configuration file, DECLINED is returned and nothing will be logged via the module.

```
20:      my $dbh = DBI->connect($Config{dsn}, $Config{user},
                                $Config{pwd});
```

Line 20 makes the connection to the database, using the information retrieved from the configuration file.

```
21:     if (!$dbh) {
22:         $r->log_error("Connection to database failed.
                            DBI::errstr");
23:         return DECLINED;
24:     }
```

Lines 21–24 check to make sure that the connection to the database was a success. If it was not, an error message is logged into the Web server's error log, including the error returned from the *DBI.pm* module. **Line 23** then returns DECLINED and nothing is logged by the module.

```
25:     my @INFO = ($r->get_remote_host,
26:                 $r->connection->user,
27:                 strftime("%Y-%m-%d %I:%M:%S", localtime),
28:                 $r->uri,
29:                 $r->status,
30:                 $r->bytes_sent,
31:                 $r->method,
32:                 $r->header_in('Referer'),
33:                 $r->header_in('User-Agent')
34:                 );
```

Lines 25–34 creates the *@INFO* array. This array contains all the information that will be inserted into the database in the correct order in which the table fields are set up. All but one of the elements is being initialized with the Apache Perl API. **Line 25** uses the *get_remote_host()* method to fetch the address from which the client is connecting. This is the same value a CGI script would see in $ENV{REMOTE_HOST}. **Line 26** uses the *connection->user()* method to retrieve what would be the equivalent to $ENV{REMOTE_USER}. This will only return a value if the client has been authenticated in a password-protected area. Next **line 27** uses *POSIX::strftime()* to format the date-time string to be inserted into the database's *time_stamp* field. **Line 28** uses the *uri()* method to bring in the value of the requested URI. The status of the request is then retrieved in **line 29** using the *status()* method. The status will be the numeric equivalent of OK, NOT_FOUND, and so on. So a successfully served document would return a 200, for example. A full list of the status codes is found in Appendix A. Because the logging phase is only followed by the cleanup phase, the client has already received the document it requested and the status is made available. **Line 30** retrieved the number of bytes sent to the client. Seeing this value as a 0 in the database may surprise you, since you know the file has some size to it. This is because the document may be requested, but the page is being served from a cache and isn't really being served by sending the physical file to the client again. The *method()* method in **line 31** returns the method used when the client made the request. This is generally GET, POST, HEAD, or PUT. **Line 32** passes the argument Referer to the *header_in()* method so it will return the URL of the Web page that sent the client to the one being requested. There will be no Referer and, subsequently, a NULL entry in the database if the client is going directly to the requested page from a bookmark or from typing directly into the Location (or equivalent) field on the browser. Finally, the argument User-Agent is passed to the *header_in()* method to fetch the browser information. The *header_in()* method is used to fetch information from the request header by passing the name of the header field to it as an argument. That being said, the *@INFO* array is complete.

```
35:      my $query = "insert into $Config{table} (remote_host,
                     user,
                     time_stamp, requested, status,
36:                  bytes, method, referer,
                     browser) values (" . (join(",", ("?") x
                     @INFO)) . ")";
```

Lines 35 and 36 initialize the *$query* variable with the SQL insert statement that will be used to add a record to the database. The table that is to be inserted is being defined by using $Config{table}, whose value was retrieved from the configuration file in **line 14** . The SQL statement is going to use placeholders, so **line 36** prints the appropriate number of comma separated question marks by joining ?s with commas.

```
37:      my $sth;
38:      unless ($sth = $dbh->prepare($query)) {
39:            $r->log_error("Can not prepare statement:
                             $DBI::errstr");
40:            $dbh->disconnect;
41:            return DECLINED;
42:      }
```

Lines 37–42 *prepare()*'s the SQL query. If the *prepare()* fails, an error, including the error from *DBI.pm* by way of $DBI::errstr, is put into the Web server's error log. The *log_error()* method takes whatever string it receives as an argument and appends it to the Web server's error log. **Line 40** then closes the database connection, and **line 41** returns a DECLINED.

```
43:      $sth->execute(@INFO);
44:      $dbh->disconnect;
45:      return OK;
46: }
47: 1;
48: __END__
```

Lines 43–48 finish off the module. **Line 43** *execute()*s the prepared query by passing the @*INFO* array that has the values that will be used to replace the placeholders in the prepared statement. **Line 44** then disconnects from the database, and a status of **OK** is returned in **line 45**. The *hander()* method is ended on **line 46**, while **line 47** returns a true value for when the module is *use()*d. **Line 48** is the __END__ token after which documentation should follow.

In this chapter you learned what mod_perl is and how to do a basic configuration. You also learned how to use various modules with Apache to accomplish caching, sandwiching documents, authentication using a database, creating photo albums, and writing a mod_perl handler. With these tools you can now work with mod_perl to create Web-based CGI applications with Perl. Doing the Reader Exercises in Section 9.8 of this chapter will help you learn even more by using what you already know.

9.8 Reader Exercises

- Visit CPAN and browse the available mod_perl handlers. Find one that looks interesting and useful and install it.
- Take the idea of Apache::Sandwich and write a handler that will display random, rotating images. Use the scripts from Chapter 9 as a framework to accomplish this.
- Look at the Apache::DBI module and modify MyLog.pm to use it for a persistent database connection.

9.9 Listings

Listing 9-22   MyLog.pm

```
01: package Apache::MyLog;
02: use strict;
03: use Apache ();
04: use DBI ();
05: use Apache::Constants qw(:common);
06: use POSIX;
07: $Apache::MyLog::VERSION = '0.01';
08: sub handler {
09:     my $r = shift;
10:     return DECLINED unless ($r->is_main);
11:     my %Config = ('dsn'    => $r->dir_config('MyLog_dsn'),
12:                   'user'   => $r->dir_config('MyLog_user'),
13:                   'pwd'    => $r->dir_config('MyLog_pwd'),
```

```
14:                         'table'    => $r->dir_config('MyLog_table')
15:                    );
16:     if (!$Config{dsn} ||
             !$Config{user} ||
             !$Config{pwd} ||
             !$Config{table}) {
17:             $r->log_error("MyLog.pm not properly configured.");
18:             return DECLINED;
19:     }
20:     my $dbh = DBI->connect($Config{dsn}, $Config{user},
                                $Config{pwd});
21:     if (!$dbh) {
22:             $r->log_reason("Connection to database failed.",
                                $r->uri);
23:             return DECLINED;
24:     }
25:     my @INFO = ($r->get_remote_host,
26:                     $r->connection->user,
27:                     strftime("%Y-%m-%d %I:%M:%S", localtime),
28:                     $r->uri,
29:                     $r->status,
30:                     $r->bytes_sent,
31:                     $r->method,
32:                     $r->header_in('Referer'),
33:                     $r->header_in('User-Agent')
34:             );
35:     my $query = "insert into $Config{table} (remote_host, user,
                     time_stamp, requested, status,
36:                  bytes, method, referer, browser) values
                     (" . (join(",", ("?") x @INFO)) . ")";
37:     my $sth;
38:     unless ($sth = $dbh->prepare($query)) {
39:             $r->log_reason("Can not prepare statement:
                                 $DBI::errstr", $r->uri);
40:             $dbh->disconnect;
41:             return DECLINED;
42:     }
43:     $sth->execute(@INFO);
44:     $dbh->disconnect;
45:     return OK;
46: }
47: 1;
48: __END__
```

10 Chapter

Web-Based E-mail

10.1 Introduction

It seems that everyone these days wants to check their e-mail from the Web. Being able to check your e-mail from any computer with Web access can be both convenient and useful. Services such as Hotmail, Yahoo!, Lycos and countless others give people a free interface for doing this, but these services have their drawbacks. One of them is that you need to have them save your POP account information such as username and password so they can check your POP account. In 1999 one popular free e-mail service was compromised by a hole in its software that made it possible to view anyone's e-mail just by knowing the login name to their account. Another drawback is that you cannot send e-mail *from* your POP account, only from your "free service" account. These days with all the SPAM that comes from these services, sending e-mail from these accounts can seem somewhat unprofessional. When a prospective employer, your boss, or family member sends mail to you@you.com, it is sometimes more prudent to reply to that e-mail from you.com and not from one of these free accounts. These services do indeed have their merits.[1] Wouldn't it be better to check your POP e-mail and send e-mail from your own POP account more easily? Wouldn't it be

---

1. They do have many features that are not included in this framework application. However, you will be able to add them with what you learn in this book.

nice to be able to offer your customers a way to check their e-mail via the Web? This chapter will give you the tools to do just that.

In this chapter you will learn how to use Perl to create a Web application to check, read, reply to, and compose e-mail. The application will also allow for adding attachments to your e-mail, as well as view and retrieve attachments from e-mail sent to your POP account.

Soon you will be introduced to some new modules, and you will also use some you should now be familiar with. The modules we will examine will handle all of the socket connections to the POP and SMTP server. They will also handle the sending and receiving of attachments and all the ugly details that you should not have to concern yourself with. We will be using the following pragmas and modules.

- strict
- lib
- CGI
- Mail::POP3Client
- Untaint
- URI::Escape
- Net::SMTP
- CGI::Carp
- MIME::Parser
- Mail::Address

10.2 Example Script: Checking POP3 Mail via the Web

The first thing we need to do is provide a way for the users to log in to the "system." During this login process, we will need to find out three things: the username, the password, and the POP server from which to retrieve the e-mail. What might be the best way to do this authentication? Of course, Basic Authentication comes to mind first when doing any per user authentication. But the user doesn't need to be authenticated to view the Web pages, which is what Basic Authentication does, but only to log into a POP server. And if Basic Authentication was used, you could only pass a username and password to the script, not what the POP server is. You could use Basic Authentication and make the usernames something like user@pop_server, with the password the password for the POP account user. If you change your POP account password (doesn't everyone change all their passwords regularly?), you will need to use htpasswd or a front end to it to change the password on the system. Also, if you have multiple POP accounts, you will need to create a new user for this Web application as well. Of course, these things are not difficult with Perl, but in this case, we do not want to save any information about the user at all. Thus, this is a single instance of this application that is easily shared by multiple users if desired. So how can we retrieve POP username, password, and server information and store it temporarily on the Web client? We do it with a Web form and a temporary cookie, of course!

NOTE   When you do anything that involves passwords being passed over the Internet in plain text, take extra precautions. We suggest that if this type of site were on the Internet, that it either use SSL or you encrypt the password, then decrypt within the script. We will leave it as an exercise to the reader to choose the best way to secure things like this. We do suggest sending an encrypted password that was encrypted using Perl's *crypt()* function or your favorite encryption scheme.

By providing a form that requests these three pieces of information, the entire authentication is actually handled by the POP server itself, and the client has this information saved. During the rest of the end user's "session" using this system, he or she does not have to fill out the login form again, assuming accurate information has been provided. This also makes it easy for someone to log into many POP accounts from the same set of scripts.

Listing 10-1, pop-login.html, shows the HTML for the Web form we will be using. A regular HTML file is sufficient for this, so we do not need to do it dynamically with a Perl script.

Listing 10-1   HTML Web form

```
<HTML>
<HEAD>
    <TITLE>POP Email Login</TITLE>
</HEAD>
<BODY>
<CENTER>
<TABLE CELLPADDING=4 CELLSPACING=4>
<TD ALIGN=center COLSPAN=2><B>Email Login</B></TD><TR>
<FORM METHOD=POST ACTION="index.cgi">
    <TD ALIGN=right>Username:</TD><TD ALIGN=left><INPUT
                        TYPE="text"
                        NAME="username" size=25></TD><TR>
    <TD ALIGN=right>Password:</TD><TD ALIGN=left><INPUT
                        TYPE="password"
                        NAME="password" size=25></TD><TR>
    <TD ALIGN=right>Server:</TD><TD ALIGN=left><INPUT
                        TYPE="text"
                        NAME="server" size=25></TD><TR>
    <TD ALIGN=center COLSPAN=2><INPUT TYPE=submit
                        VALUE="Login"></TD>
```

(continued)

```
</FORM>
</TABLE>
</CENTER>
</BODY>
</HTML>
```

The only thing you really need to keep in mind from this form is that it passes three form values: username, password, and server. Figure 10-1 is a screenshot of how this will look. Now we'll move on to the fun stuff!

Figure 10-1   Login form

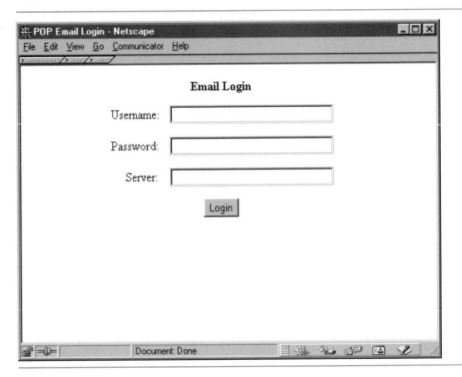

The first example script, **index.cgi** , will connect to the POP server via the Mail::POP3Client module, which will then parse the header of any e-mail messages from the POP server and display a list of the e-mail on the server.

```
01: #!/usr/bin/perl -wT
02: # index.cgi
03: $|=1;
04: use strict;
05: use Mail::POP3Client;
```

```
06: use CGI qw(:standard :netscape *table);
07: use CGI::Carp qw(fatalsToBrowser);
08: use Untaint;
```

Lines 1–8 should all be familiar now. In these lines we turn on warnings, taint checking, autoflush the output buffer, and pull in the modules we will be using. Mail::POP3Client is the only new module being used in this script and will be explained in detail as we progress through the chapter.

```
09: my $cookie = cookie('WebMail') || 0;
```

Line 9 uses the CGI.pm *cookie()* method to see if the cookie named 'Web-Mail' exists. If it does, it assigns the value of the cookie from the browser to the variable $cookie. If it does not exist, then the left side of the logical or (||) will fail and assign $cookie to 0. This is important because we are using the cookie to get the user's information to connect to the POP server. Near the end of the chapter we will incorporate the ability to "log out," which will be setting the value of the cookie to "0."[2] This is why we set the value of $cookie to "0." If we do not receive a value for the cookie (if one does not exist), we know someone is not logged into a session because $cookie will be 0.

```
10: my $user = param('username');
11: my $pass = param('password');
12: my $server = param('server');
```

Lines 10–12 check for form input. These lines look for incoming form values for the username, password, and server. Recall that the login form has three form elements named *username,* password, and *server.* Any values sent from these form elements are set to $user, $pass, and $server, respectively. If there is no input (the user isn't coming from the login page), these will have no value.

```
13: if ((!$user || !$pass || !$server) && !$cookie) {
14:     print redirect("pop-login.html"); exit;
15: }
```

Lines 13–15 make sure that either all the form input was given or the cookie exists. **Line 13** begins with a conditional check to see if there is not (signified with !) a value for $user or (using the logical or ||) $pass or $server. These three things are surrounded by parentheses, so they will be evaluated together, and the final yea or nay (true or false) from this will

---

2. The only issue here is if someone has a password of "0." However, the larger issue would be someone using "0" as their POP mail password. This is the equivalent of your bank-card's PIN being "1234."

then be used. If it returns false, meaning that there is indeed a value in $user, $pass, and $server, then this conditional will fail and the script will continue on. If it is found that one of these variables does not have a true value, then we check to see if there is also (represented by the logical and &&) no value for the cookie. If all of the form data is not present, then the user did not complete the form properly and will be redirected with the CGI.pm *redirect()* method. If there is form data, the user may have already logged in, and this will be verified by the existence of the cookie. If the cookie also does not exist, then the user has not yet logged on, and the user is then redirected to the login page, again using the *redirect()* function of CGI.pm. Also on **line 14** we *exit()*. This is put on the same line here to reinforce that when you do a *redirect()*, you should also *exit()*. This is because even though you have sent an instruction to *redirect()*, it can be possible to have the script continue and display garbage.

```
16: if (!$cookie) {
17:     $cookie = cookie(-name => 'WebMail',
18:                     -value => "$user $pass $server",
                        -path => '/'
19:     );
20:     print header(-cookie=>$cookie);
```

Lines 16–20 are checking to see if the user does not already have a session cookie in place. The scenario, which will make this conditional true, is when the user is coming from the login page. If this conditional is indeed true, then the session cookie will now be set. The cookie name is 'WebMail', and the value is the provided username, password, and server name, all separated by spaces and set in **line 18** . **Line 18** also sets the path information for the cookie. By setting the path for a cookie, the browser will check the URL of the script, asking for the cookie. If the URL does not contain the path set for the cookie, the cookie will not be sent from the browser back to the server. This is a temporary cookie, so when the browser session is complete (the user closes the browser), the cookie will no longer exist.

```
21: }else{
22:     print header;
23:     ($user, $pass, $server) = split(" ",$cookie);
24: }
```

Lines 21–24 do the appropriate action if the previous conditional shown in **lines 16–20** fail. If it has failed, this means that the user is already within a session. The HTTP header is printed with CGI.pm's *header()* method, and the login information is then parsed out of the cookie's value. By simply splitting the cookie value by spaces, the proper variables are assigned their counterpart values.

```
25: $server = untaint(qr(.*), $server);
26: $user = untaint(qr(^\w{1,8}$), $user);
27: $pass = untaint(qr(^\w{1,8}$), $pass);
```

Lines 25, 26, and 27 launder the variables given to us by either the cookie
or the Web form. No matter how we received the data, it is considered
tainted, since it came from outside our program and must be laundered.
The laundering is done by Untaint.pm's *untaint()* method. You will notice
that the pattern being passed to *untaint()* for the username and password
will match any 1 to 8 alphanumeric character string. The match for the
server is allowing anything to pass. This is being done for example sake,
and the patterns should be changed to meet your own needs.

```
28: system("/bin/rm","-rf","./$user-$server") unless
           $user !~ /^\w/;              # UNIX
28: system("delete","$user-$server"); # Windows
```

Line 28 is a "safe" *system()* call to delete anything that is in the user directory. You may now be asking yourself, "What user directory?" Later on in
the example, when we get to the script that parses an e-mail message for
viewing, we will discuss the MIME::Parser module. MIME::Parser uses a
temporary directory where it places all the parts of an e-mail message, such
as the message body and attachments, while it parses it. This directory is
being set to the name of the user logged in, a dash, and the name of the
POP server. This is where the user directory comes from. We delete everything out of this directory because we know that the user is not currently
viewing a message or retrieving any attachments. It is good to remove any
files that may be hanging around in that directory so no one can read them.
There will be more discussion on this directory later in the chapter. If you
are using Perl for Win32 systems, you would want to use the **line 28** denoted for Windows.

```
29: my $pop = new Mail::POP3Client(HOST        => $server
                                   AUTH_MODE => 'PASS');
```

Line 29 is where the real fun begins. A new Mail::POP3Client object is created, and the server information into that object is saved. The $pop variable
will be used to access the object. When constructing the object there are
two parameters being set: the HOST and AUTH_MODE. The HOST is the
server to check for e-mail, and the AUTH_MODE is the type of authorization to use on the POP server. PASS is the default (although we explicitly set
it here for clarity), but it may also be set to APOP to attempt APOP (MD5)
authorization.

```
30: $pop->User($user);
31: $pop->Pass($pass);
```

Lines 30 and 31 pass the username and password provided by the user to our Mail::POP3Client object via the *User()* and *Pass()* methods, respectively. At this point, the object has all of the connection information, and we are ready to roll!

```
32: $pop->Connect || error($pop->Message);
```

Line 32 does the actual connection to the POP server. This statement is really a sort of conditional statement. It is like saying, "Make a connection to the POP3 server. Otherwise, call the *error()* subroutine." If the *Connect()* method fails, this means that the connection to the POP server couldn't happen. If this occurs, the failure message is sent to our *error()* subroutine, which will be covered in a little while. If the connection is a success, which we hope it is, the script continues on. One of the caveats of this method is that when it fails, it is (at the time of this writing) impossible to distinguish between a failure due to a timeout or login failure.

```
33: my $count = $pop->Count;
```

Line 33 retrieves the number of messages on the server using the *Count()* method and assigns this value to the $count variable. This number will be used later on to create hyperlinks to the messages for viewing as well as deleting.

```
34: my %deleted;
```

Line 34 defines a hash, %deleted, which will be used to make sure we do not include messages in our listing that are being deleted. This is explained in more detail throughout the next few lines.

```
35: if (param('delete')) {
36:     ($pop->Delete($_) && $deleted{$_}++)
         foreach (param('mess'));
37: }
```

Lines 35–37 handle the deletion of messages. You will soon see that when a user wishes to delete a message, two name/value pairs are passed to the script: delete/1 and mess/message number. When the delete action is to be taken, the delete parameter has a value of 1, which is what **line 35** is specifically checking for. If this condition is true, **line 36** handles the actions needed by doing two things. First, it deletes the given message from the server with the *Delete()* method. Actually, that is a small fib. The *Delete()*

function actually just marks a message for deletion, and the actual deletion occurs when the connection to the POP server is closed. This will be explained in more depth in this chapter. Second, it adds an entry into the %deleted hash with the key being the message number that is being deleted. The hash value is simply a 1. An array certainly could have been used here, but hash lookups are not only fast and easy but will also nicely fit into an upcoming routine. **Line 36** does these two things while looping through the values of the "mess", where the current value is stored in $_. One little line can really do a lot!

Line 36 may be better explained if it were written out in a less "compact" way. That line is certainly doing a lot and may look confusing, even after knowing what it is doing! The following snippet of code is **line 36** in a longer format.

```perl
my @messages = param('mess');
for (@messages) {
    $pop->Delete($_);
    $deleted{$_}++;
}
```

You may choose to use the preceding style in much of your code for readability, but it is important that you can recognize that it has the same functionality as the one line above in **line 36**. Now it may be clearer what is happening. The returned value of *param('mess')* is an array because its values come from a list of selected checkboxes on the submitted form. This array is looped through, and the *Delete()* method is called, being passed the current array element, and the %deleted hash is being updated to keep track of which messages are marked for deletion.

```perl
38: print start_html({-title=>'Web Email Client Example',
39:                    -BGCOLOR=>'white'}),
40: p({-align=>'center'},
41:       start_table({-border=>1,
42:                    -cellpadding=>4,
43:                    -cellspacing=>4}),
44:       Tr,
45:       td({-align=>'CENTER',-colspan=>4},[strong("Email
              Example")]),
46:       Tr,
47:       th({-align=>'CENTER'},['Delete','From',
                                 'Subject','Date']),
48:       Tr,
49:       start_form({-method=>'POST',-action=>'index.cgi'}),
50:       hidden({-name=>'delete',-value=>'1'}))
51: ;
```

Lines 38–51 starts the HTML for the page that will be listing the messages on the server, using methods from CGI.pm. **Lines 38 and 39** print the start of the HTML, including the title and background color. **Line 40** starts a <P ALIGN='CENTER'> to start centering the upcoming table. **Lines 41–48** are the start of the table, in which the message information will be displayed. Next a form is started that will submit to index.cgi (itself) and a hidden tag with the name of 'delete', and value of '1' is added to the form. You will see in a moment that when the information of each message is displayed, there will be a checkbox next to it. These checkboxes are part of this form and will be used to help with deletion. As you saw back in **line 35** , the delete action is kicked off when the script sees a form element named 'delete' with a value of '1', which is what **line 50** is setting.

```
52: my $c = 1;
```

Line 52 initializes the variable $c to the value of 1, which is going to be used in the following loop to keep track of the message being parsed. If you quickly glance at the loop that is coming up, you may wonder why you need a counter. Why not just use $count or the current value of $i? Well, it is because of deletions. When this script checks the server for e-mail, it will see X messages, numbered A through X. But when you add in deleting, it will delete the messages but not recheck the server for the current list of e-mail. Why? Well, when *Delete()* is called, the message is really only being marked for deletion, not actually deleted. The message is truly deleted when the connection to the server is closed. Because of how this works there is no good reason to connect to the server, check the e-mail, make deletions, then check the server again. This explanation may sound a little confusing, so let's take a look at an example.

Let us assume that you have five e-mail messages on the server, and you are trying to delete messages numbered 2 and 4. Since the same script handles displaying the list of e-mail as well as deleting e-mail, we need to be able to handle the renumbering of the five e-mail messages when the deletions occur. When index.cgi is called, it first fetches the list of e-mail and the count on the server. In this case that count will be 5. Then we want to delete messages 2 and 4, which is done by *Delete()*. Actually, as just explained, the deletion hasn't happened, but those two messages are now marked for deletion. For all intents and purposes, we can consider them deleted. Next we will be displaying the list of messages to the browser again, but it has to be the new list of messages with the messages that were originally 2 and 4 removed. This means that messages 3 and 5 need to be shifted down in the display to resemble how the messages will look on the server when the connection is closed and the messages are actually deleted. Table 10-1 illustrates how the message number works at all three of these stages.

Table 10-1   Flow of Message Deletion

Original	In Progress	After Connection Closed
Message 1	Message 1	Message 1
Message 2	DELETED	Message 2 (was 3)
Message 3	Message 3	Message 3 (was 5)
Message 4	DELETED	
Message 5	Message 5	

That was certainly a lot of discussion based on the initialization of one little scalar! Now we can move on to the loop we have been describing and everything else it is doing.

```
53: for my $i (1..$count-1) {
```

Line 53 begins the loop. We initialize the variable $i, which will be our counter as we go through the loop. The number assigned to $i will hold the message number to retrieve next.

```
54:     next if exists $deleted{$i};
```

Line 54 checks to see if there is an entry in our %deleted hash for the current message number. If you recall way back in **line 36**, when a message was deleted, the %deleted hash was assigned a key value for that message number. Here in **line 54**, if there is indeed a record in the hash for the current message number, we know it was deleted and should not be part of what is displayed to the screen and goes ahead to the next message number in the loop.

```
55:     my @head;
```

Line 55 initializes the array @head. You will see what this is used for in a minute.

```
56:     foreach($pop->Head($i)) {
```

Line 56 is an inner loop that fetched the e-mail messages header elements with MIME::POP3Client's *Head()* method. As you can see, $i is passed to this method so it knows which message number to fetch. The loop continues.

```
57:            if(s/^From:\s+//i) {
                   $head[0] = qq(<td align=center>
                   <input type="checkbox" name="mess" value="$c">
                   </td>\n<td align=center>
                   <a href="pop-view.cgi?mess=$c">$_</a></td>\n);
           }
58:            if (s/^Subject:\s+//i) {
                   $head[1] = qq(<td align=center>
                   <a href="pop-view.cgi?mess=$c">$_</a></td>\n);
           }
59:            if (/^Date:\s+/i && $_ =~ s/^Date:\s+(.*?)
                   (?:\s+[+-]\d+(?:\s+.*?)?)?$/$1/i) {
                   $head[2] = qq(<td align=center>$_</td><tr>\n);
60: }
```

Lines 57–60 parse the header lines as the loop occurs. The elements we are interested in are the From, Subject, and Date for our example. **Lines 57 and 58** do a substitution to see if the current line (stored in $_) of the message header matches what that line is looking for (whom the e-mail is From and the Subject, in this case). If the substitution succeeds, the desired text is displayed. **Line 59** first checks if the line matches a pattern, and if it does, it performs the needed substitution. For example, these three header elements look something similar to this.

```
From: "Meltzer, Kevin" <kevin@xxxxx.xxx>
Subject: I am a subject!
Date: Mon, 10 Jan 2000 10:01:02 -0500
```

When the list of e-mail messages is displayed, we do not need to print the name of the header line to the browser. To remedy the fact that they are there, we strip out the words 'From', 'Subject', and 'Date'. The next action taken when this line is being processed is the HTML generation to print out the line, which constitutes one table row consisting of four cells. When the From is found, the line also adds the checkbox needed to accomplish a delete. The HTML is then assigned to the @head array in its proper order. $array[0] will always be the From information, while $array[1] and $array[2] are the Subject and Date, respectively. This array is needed because sometimes you may get an e-mail client who does not send the header elements in the same order. This became painfully obvious while testing this script. You will see in pop-view.cgi how to use MIME::Parser to parse an e-mail header, but we felt it is important for you to see how you would also do it on your own.

By the time this loop has gone through a header, the @head array will look like this.

```
@head = ('"<td align=center><input type="checkbox" name="mess"
        value="1"></td>\n<td align=center><a href="pop-
        view.cgi?mess=1">Meltzer, Kevin" <kevin@xxxxx.xxx></a>
        </td>\n"',
        '"<td align=center><a href="pop-view.cgi?mess=1">I am a
        subject!</a></td>\n"',
        '"<td align=center>Mon, 10 Jan 2000 10:01:02</td><tr>\n"'
    );
```

Now this inner loop ends for the moment and moves back to the outer loop.

```
61:     $c++;
```

Line 61 increments our count of what the next message number will be. As you could see from **lines 57–60** , this variable is used to help create the hyperlinks to the scripts to view and delete messages.

```
62:     print @head;
63: }
```

Line 62 prints the information from the last message header to the client. It then continues on to the next element in the outer loop. **Line 63** ends the outer loop.

```
64: $c--;
```

Line 64 de-increments $c by one because of how the preceding loop behaves. When the loop is going to finish, $c is incriminated one more time, and we need to de-increment it so it has the correct count.

```
65: print td({-colspan=>4,-align=>'LEFT'},
66:         submit(-value=>'Delete') . " You Have <b>$c</b>
                    Messages"),
67:end_form,
68:end_table,
69: end_html;
```

Lines 65–69 are a big *print()* statement put on multiple lines for readability. It starts off by beginning another table data tag (<TD>), on which **line 65** places a submit button as well as some text. The submit button, when clicked, will pass along all the message numbers back to this script for deletion. The message numbers that are passed along are obtained from the values of any checkboxes that were checked. **Lines 66, 67, and 68** print the closing tags for a FORM, TABLE, and HTML, respectively. This completes the display to the user!

```
70: $pop->Close;
```

Line 70 closed the connection to the POP server. In the background, a QUIT command is sent to the server. When this happens, any messages that were marked for deletion are officially deleted, and the socket is closed.

```
71: sub error {
72:     my $err = shift;
73:     print h3("There was an error connecting to the server ($err).
                  Please try again"),p,
74:     a({-href=>'index.cgi'},"Home");
75:     exit;
76: }
```

Lines 71–76 are an error reporting subroutine. This is called in **line 32** if the connection to the POP server fails. It reports to the user any trouble in the connection, based on the server response. After printing the error, it also gives a link back to the index.cgi script. Finally, it issues an *exit* so the script will stop and not attempt to display messages that aren't there. Figure 10-2 shows an example of this error when the script is unable to connect to the POP server.

Figure 10-2   Screenshot of a failed connection to the POP server

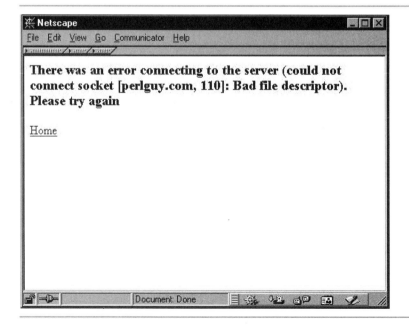

Now we have the base of our application that allows for logging into a POP server and displaying the e-mail messages on that server. We also have the ability to delete any unwanted messages. Figure 10-3 shows what the screen looks like when it is displaying messages.

Figure 10-3   Screenshot of checked e-mail

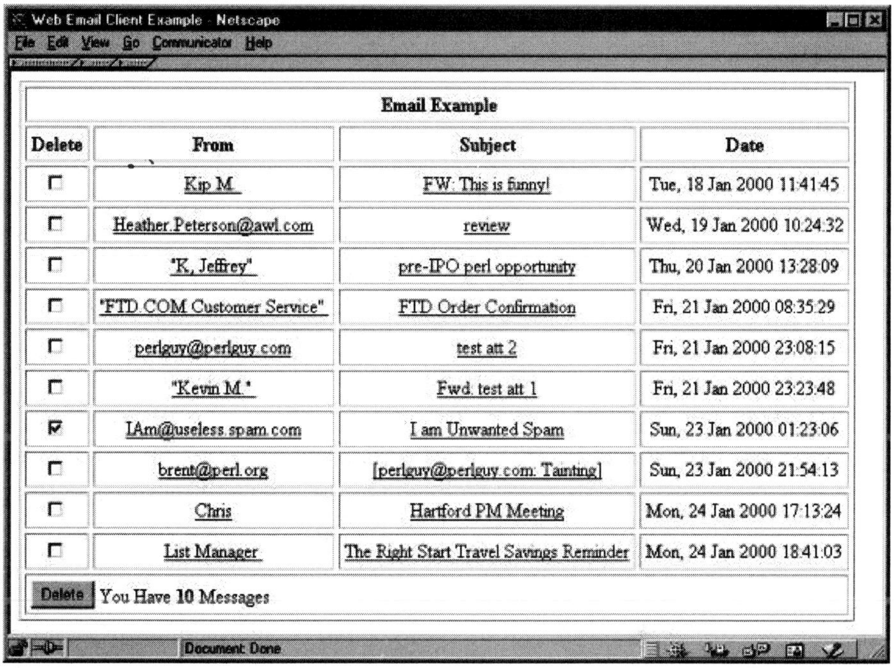

If you notice in Figure 10-3, I seem to have received some SPAM! You will also note that I have already checked the delete checkbox for that message, which happens to be message 7 entitled "I am Unwanted Spam." I want to get rid of that SPAM, and since it is checked and ready to be deleted, that's what I will do. Figure 10-4 shows the screen after it has deleted message 7. Recall the process that is happening in the background as well. As explained, while the page is being generated, it is numbering the messages not as they are currently but emulating what the numbering will be when the messages marked for deletion (in this case, message 7) are officially deleted.

Figure 10-4   **SPAM has been deleted!**

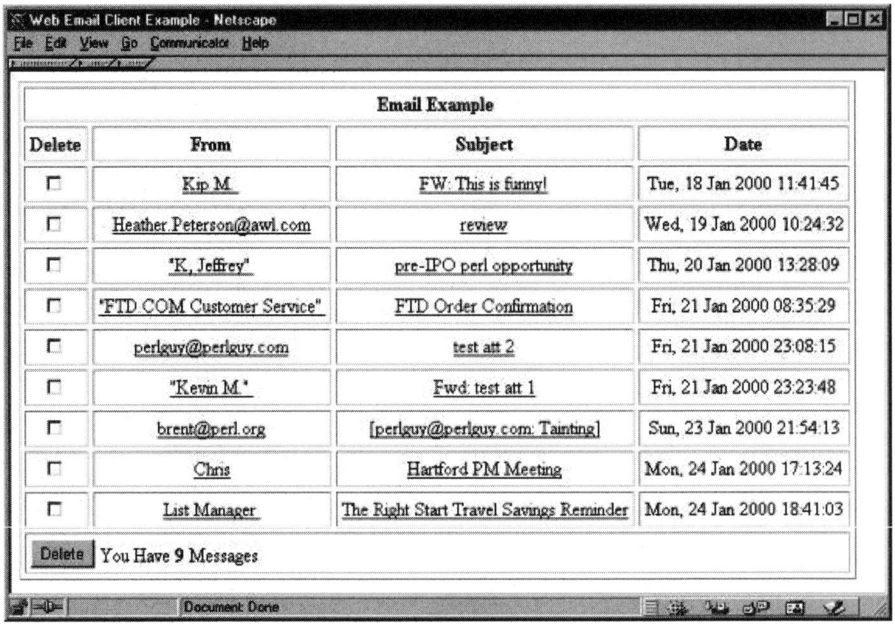

10.3 Example Script: Reading E-mail via the Web

So far so good, but we still need to read the e-mail. We can list and delete e-mail so far, which is good, but e-mail is best utilized when it can be read! As you know, the From and Subject fields on the display screen are linked to the pop-view.cgi script. Assuming we are looking at the link for message 5, the link would look like this.

```
<a href="pop-view.cgi?mess=5">
```

Let's now take a look at the pop-view.cgi script.

```
01: #!/usr/bin/perl -wT
02: # pop-view.cgi
03: $| = 1;
04: use strict;
05: use Mail::POP3Client;
06: use CGI qw(:standard);
07: use CGI::Carp qw(fatalsToBrowser);
08: use MIME::Parser;
```

```
09: use URI::Escape;
10: use Untaint;
```

Lines 1–10 should be old hat to you by now.

```
11: my $cookie = cookie('WebMail') || 0;
12: my ($user, $pass, $server);
13: if (!$cookie) {
14:     print redirect("pop-login.html"); exit;
15: }else{
16:     print header;
17:     ($user, $pass, $server) = split(" ",$cookie);
18: }
```

Lines 11–18 are very similar to **lines 9–24** in the index.cgi script. We look to see if the WebMail cookie exists. If it does not, the user is sent to the login page, and if it does, we continue on.

```
19: my $message = param('mess');
```

Line 19 uses CGI.pm's *param()* method to get the message number being passed in the URL by the request being sent to the Web server from the form. If you recall from earlier in the chapter, the links to this script include a name value pair that has *mess* as the name and the number of the message as the value. This value will be used to fetch that particular message from the POP server.

```
20: $server = untaint(qr(.*), $server);
21: $user = untaint(qr(^\w{1,8}$), $user);
22: $pass = untaint(qr(^\w{1,8}$), $pass);
```

Lines 20, 21, and 22 do the laundering. You will notice we are passing a *very* liberal pattern to match here. At this point, the user should have a valid cookie set from index.cgi, but it is better to be paranoid and change the patterns to something more restrictive later on. Now we may continue since we nicely laundered variables.

```
23: my $pop = new Mail::POP3Client(HOST   => $server);
24: $pop->User($user);
25: $pop->Pass($pass);
26: $pop->Connect || error($pop->Message);
```

Lines 23–26 create a new Mail::POP3Client object, pass it the connection information, and make the connection. This is the same as in the preceding index.cgi script.

```
27: my $parser = new MIME::Parser;
```

Line 27 creates a new MIME::Parser object into the variable $parser. We will be using this object to access the methods in MIME::Parser to parse the e-mail message.

```
28: if (!(-d "./$user-$server")) {
29: system("/bin/mkdir", "-m","0777", "$user-$server"); # UNIX
29: system("mkdir", "$user-$server");                    #Windows
30: }
```

Lines 28–30 create a directory to store the files that MIME::Parser will use to store its output. Remember **line 28** in index.cgi where we removed everything from this directory? Well, this is where we create it, if it doesn't already exist. The existence of the directory is first checked with -d, and if it is not there, it is created with a safe *system()* call (refer back to Chapter 2 about safe uses of *system()* and Unix permissions). MIME::Parser creates files as it parses through a message, such as a file for the message body, and files for any attachments. In case you are using the same script for many users or multiple POP accounts of your own, having each POP login ID, combined with the server name, should help make sure that e-mails of two users do not cross paths. We use a username/servername combination because it should be unique, since there can only be one username on a server.

```
31: $parser->output_dir("./$user-$server");
```

Line 31 tells the MIME::Parser object that we will put all the output to the directory we are giving as an argument. The files that MIME::Parser creates are generally deleted when they are done being used, but, attachments are not deleted. We do not want to delete the attached files until the user leaves the page (and returns to index.cgi, which does the deleting), in case they wish to view the attached file(s).

```
32: my $mail = $pop->Retrieve($message);
```

Line 32 uses the Mail::POP3Client::Retrieve method ($pop being a Mail::POP3Client object, which has the *Retrieve()* method) to fetch the wanted message. The numeric value in $message, which we got from the 'mess' form value, tells this method which e-mail message to retrieve from the server. The full text of the e-mail message, including the header, body, and encoded attachments, is then assigned to the $mail variable.

```
33: my $entity = $parser->parse_data($mail);
```

Line 33 is somewhat important and does a bit in the background. Let's read this line from right to left. As you can see, $mail (which is the full text of the e-mail message in a scalar) is being passed as an argument to the *parse_data()* method. The parse_data method is part of the $parser (MIME::Parser) object. Actually, it is a method of MIME::ParserBase, the base class of which MIME::Parser is a subclass, but we don't have to worry about that now. What it returns and saves the value into $entity is a MIME::Entity, which may be a single entity or an arbitrarily nested multi-part entity. Basically, what this means is we have another object, $entity, whose data structure is such that the entity, or entities, it contains are now easily separated and retrievable for our use.

```
34: my $head = $entity->head;
```

Line 34 fetches the header of the message from our $entity object. The value of the variable $head is now a data structure much like $entity, but is a subset of it. It is an object filled with the message header information.

```
35: print qq(To: ) . text_to_html($head->get('To',0));
36: print qq(CC: ) . text_to_html($head->get('Cc', 0))
                     if $head->get('Cc', 0);
37: print qq(Subject: ) . text_to_html($head->get('Subject',0));
38: print qq(From: ) . text_to_html($head->get('From', 0));
39: print qq(Date: ) . $head->get('Date', 0) . qq(<br>\n);
```

Lines 35–39 deal with the message header elements. The values retrieved by using the *get()* method of the $head object (it is a Mail::Header object) are printed out to the client. Each element is passed through the *text_to_html()* subroutine, which we will be discussing later in this chapter.

```
40: my $parts = $entity->parts;
```

Line 40 finds the number of parts of the message entity. If this message has no parts, which would be an attachment, the value if $parts will be 0.

```
41: print p;
```

Line 41 is a simple one! It prints out an HTML <P> tag using CGI.pm's *p()* method. Because we imported all of CGI.pm's *standard* methods, this included many methods for writing HTML, including the *p()* method, which writes this tag.

```
42: if (!$parts) {
43:     print text_to_html($entity->body_as_string);
44:     $entity->purge;
```

Lines 42–44 begin by checking if there were any parts returned from the result of **line 40** . If there are none ($parts is not a true value), then we print out the body of the message by getting the body returned as a string with the *body_as_string()* method from our MIME::Entity object, $entity. This is passed through a subroutine, *text_to_html()*, which we will see later in this chapter. Finally, on **line 44** , all external body parts (on disk) are deleted with the *purge()* method. As stated earlier, when MIME::Parser parses a message, it breaks up the message into separate files for the body and any other parts (such as attachments), and the call to *purge()* here deleted them. Since we are in an if/else that is entered when there is *only* a message body, that is all that will be purged.

```
45: }else{
46:     print text_to_html($entity->parts(0)->bodyhandle-
                          >as_string);
```

Lines 45 and 46 start the "other side" of the conditional. If we are here, then there have been multiple parts detected in the e-mail message. Similar to **line 43** , **line 46** fetches the body part of the message entity and passes it to the *text_to_html()* subroutine to be printed. The number "0" is passed to the *body()* method to retrieve the 0th element of the body, which is going to be the body of the message.

```
47:     print h3("Attachments:");
```

Line 47 simply prints out a level 3 header with the text "Attachments".

```
48:     for (my $i=1; $i<$entity->parts;$i++) {
```

Line 48 starts looping through the parts of the message entity. As you can see, the loop starts with the index, $i, at 1 because the zero element was the body of the message, which we just printed, and we want all parts after that.

```
49:         (my $temp_file_name =
            $entity->parts($i)->bodyhandle->path)
            =~ s!^.*$user-$server/!!;
50:         my $uri_file = uri_escape($temp_file_name);
```

Lines 49 and 50 deal with the "temp" file, which is really the attachment file. **Line 49** gets the name of the attached file by substituting everything *ex-*

cept the name of the file from *$entity->parts($i)->bodyhandle->path()*, which holds the server path to the attachment file. For example, using the paths as we are in these examples, all attachments will be created as ./user-server-name/attachment.ext, which is the value *$entity->parts($i)->bodyhandle ->path()* holds. We need to substitute the "./user servername/" out of that. Why? Because in the following lines we will be displaying that filename to the client, and we want it to look nice. Also, if the attachment is an image, we will want to display the name. **Line 50** URI encodes the name of the attachment because we will be making a hyperlink to it, and hyperlinks should be URI encoded to deal with spaces and odd characters. The name of the attachment file is assigned to $temp_file_name, and its URI encoded counterpart is stored in $uri_file.

```
51:        if ($temp_file_name=~/\.(gif|jpg|png)$/i) {
52:            print qq(File: <img src="$user-$server/
                         $temp_file_name">);
```

Lines 51 and 52 do a quick match on the name of the attachment file, $temp_file_name, to see if it happens to be a GIF, JPG, or PNG file. If it is, **line 52** then prints the appropriate HTML to display that image to the browser. Because the browser can inherently handle these file types, it makes sense to simply display these images rather than make a user download the image first.

```
53:        } else {
54:            print qq(File: <a href="view_att.cgi?att=$uri_file">
                     $temp_file_name</a><BR>);
```

Lines 53 and 54 handle the display of the attachment if it is *not* an image. **Line 54** prints the appropriate HTML to make a link to the attachment. You will notice it is linking to view_att.cgi and passing the $uri_file with the name "att" to display the attachment. We will be visiting the view_att.cgi script later in the chapter, and you will see an explanation for having another script display the attachment rather than directly link to it.

```
55:            }
56:        }
57: }
```

Lines 55–57 close the conditional (if the attachment is an image or not), the loop (looping through the parts of the e-mail message), and the conditional that checked to see if there were more parts to this message than just the body.

```
58: print p({-align=>'center'},
59: a({-href=>"index.cgi?delete=1&mess=$message"},
              "Delete Message"), " | ",
60: a({-href=>"index.cgi"}, "Back to Mail"), " | ",
61: a({-href=>"pop-logout.cgi"}, "Log Out"));
```

Lines 58–61 display our "footer" information to the client. This currently consists of three links: one to delete this message, another to return back to the listing of e-mail, and a third to log out of the system.

```
62: $pop->Close;
```

Line 62 closes the connection to the POP server.

```
63: sub text_to_html {
64:     my $raw = shift;
```

Lines 63 and 64 start off the *text_to_html()* subroutine. This subroutine takes the input, which is assigned to $raw in **line 65** and does four things. The following four lines explain these four tasks.

```
65:     $raw =~ s!([<>])!($1 eq '<') ? "&lt;" : "&gt\;"!eg;
```

Line 65 substitutes all greater than signs (>) with the proper HTML notation of ">" and all less than signs (<) with its corresponding "<" HTML tag. This could be done in two lines, but we do it here in a single regular expression. On the left side of the substitution we have a character class consisting of two characters, the less than (<) and greater than (>) signs. We put parentheses around this character class so we can access the matched character on the right side of the substitution. Now on the right side we have a conditional. If $1, which holds the value of the matched character from the left side, is the less than sign, then it is substituted with its HTML counterpart, "<". If that condition is not true, then it must be the greater than sign, which is then substituted with the corresponding HTML, ">". We are able to do this conditional expression on the right side of the substitution because we are using the /e modifier, which allows for Perl to be evaluated on the right side. This line is important because when you have e-mail that contains these two signs, you want to be sure that you can see them! Because we are displaying e-mail on a Web browser, consider what would happen if the e-mail contained "<hello world>." Well, nothing would happen, at least not that you would see. This is because the browser would interpret that as being an HTML tag, thus not displaying anything to the client. Of course, there are other times when these characters will appear in e-mail and are now taken care of!

```
66:        $raw =~ s!((ht|f)tps?://)([\w-]*)((\..[^\s]*)+)!
                <a href="$1$3$4" target="external">$1$3$4</a>!g;
```

Line 66 translates any occurrences of http, https, and ftp links in the e-mail text into hyperlinks. Because there are a few forward slashes (/) in regular expression, I have used an explanation point as the substitution delimiter to help with clarity. This regular expression begins by searching for the http://, https://, or ftp://. If any of these patterns is matched, the value is stored in $1, which is what is contained in the outer pair of parentheses. The inner pair of the first set of parentheses ((ht|f)) would match either "ht" or "f", and that value would be saved to $2, although we won't be using that. The next pair of parentheses is a character class that will match any alphanumeric characters and the dash character. These are the common and allowable characters in a domain name. This match continues until it comes to a dot, and then the matched characters are stored in $3. The last set of parentheses looks to match the dot and any characters that are not spaces and match this at least one time up to many times. What this matches is stored in $4. On the right side of the substitution, you can see that these values are used to create a hyperlink. This may a bit much to swallow right away if you are not too familiar with regular expressions or at least quasi-complex ones, so let's walk through what is happening.

For an example, let us consider the text string "http://www.geekstuff. com carries the Perl Monger line of shirts." The first pair of parentheses, ((ht|f)tps?://), will match the "http://" portion of the string and store the value in $1. Because inner parentheses store their values in special variables higher in number, $2 would equal the string "ht." So far, so good. The next pattern, ([\w-]*), is looking for all alphanumeric characters (represented by \w) and dashes. This will match all these characters until it comes across a character not in this character class, such as a dot. Pertaining to our string, this will match "www" and store that value in $3. The last pattern, ((\..[^\s]*)+), attempts to match a dot, followed by any and all characters that are not a space. The "+" then makes the pattern repeat and match a dot, followed by anything but a space one to many times. This will match ".geekstuff.com" and not the rest of the string because it matches that pattern multiple times and ends at the space—in fact, twice: ".geekstuff" and ".com." This value is stored in $4, and our match is complete!

```
67:        $raw =~ s!([\w\-.]+)\@([\w-]+)((\.[\w-]+)*)!
                <a href=\"pop-compose.cgi?to=$1\@$2$3\">$1\@$2$3</a>!g;
```

Line 67 is similar to **line 66** except it matches e-mail addresses[3] and converts them to hypertext mailto links. On the right side of the substitution

---

3.   This is one solution for matching most e-mail addresses.

we try to match any alphanumeric character, as well as a dash, one to many times until we happen across a "@". This would match the "who" of an e-mail address and store the matched value in $1. The next two sets of parentheses after the "@" match the rest of the e-mail address. Much like the match for a hyperlink in **line 66**, it first matches alphanumeric characters and the dash after the "@" and before a dot, and it stores the result in $2. Finally, it attempts to match dot-alphanumeric-or-dash sequences one to many times. If it succeeds, the result is stored in $3. That's it! One question that may arise at this point is why the two patterns for matching, namely the third set of parentheses, are different. After all, the domain name of a URL and of an e-mail address should be the same, right? Well, not exactly. Say, for example, someone sends you e-mail containing a URL with a query string, such as "http://search.cpan.org/search?mode=module&query=Apache." Obviously, everything after "http://search.cpan.org/search" contains characters that are not alphanumeric, and you would not have the desired results. On the contrary, an e-mail address would not contain non-alphanumeric characters, so we match only valid characters, as opposed to matching until the string is complete, marked by a space.

```
68:     $raw =~ s/\n/<br>/g;
69:     return $raw;
70: }
```

Lines 68–70 starts by substituting all newlines into an HTML
 (line break) tag. Since Web clients do not account for newlines, we need to make sure that line breaks occur where intended. Finally, **line 69** returns our HTMLized e-mail message, and **line 70** ends the *text_to_html()* subroutine. At this point, whatever text was fed to this subroutine should be nicely converted to look good in a browser.

```
71: sub error {
72:     my $err = shift;
73:     print h3("There was an error connecting to the server
                ($err). Please try again"),p,
74:     a({-href=>'index.cgi'},"Home");
75:     exit;
76: }
```

Lines 71–76 finish off the script. This subroutine should look familiar since it is the same as the *error()* subroutine in index.cgi. You may be thinking to yourself, "Why not have a module to share this subroutine?" I don't want to ruin the surprise, but you will see that in the exercises at the end of the chapter. The screenshot is shown in Figure 10-5.

Figure 10-5   Viewing a message

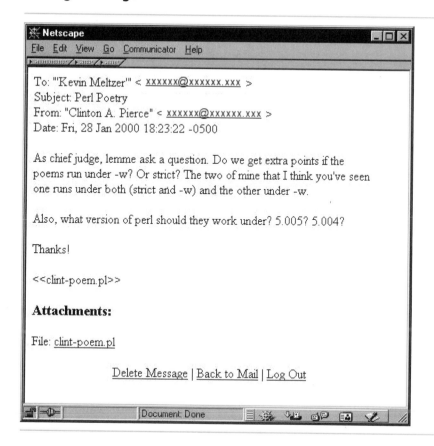

Let's recap what we have so far. Thus far we have the ability to log into a POP server, fetch the e-mail on it, and display it. We can also delete messages as well as read them, and we can also view attachments. Well, that isn't really true yet. We can see that there is an attachment and make a link to view it but not actually view it. So let's tackle that functionality next.

10.4 Example Script: Displaying Attachments

The script in Listing 10-2, view_att.cgi, handles sending an attachment to the client. This is a small script, and it should mostly be self-explanatory. The script takes the name of the attachment file as a parameter, then checks for the cookie information, just as in other scripts. If the cookie doesn't exist, the user is sent to the login page, again like the other scripts. The important part here is **line 7** and **lines 11–17** .

Listing 10-2   **Script that handles displaying attachments**

```
01: #!/usr/bin/perl -wT
02: # view_att.cgi
03: use CGI qw(:cgi);
04: use strict;
05: use URI::Escape;
06: use File::Basename;
07: my $id = basename(param('att'));
08: my $cookie = cookie('WebMail') || 0;
09: if ($cookie) {
10:     my ($user, $pass, $server) = split(" ",$cookie);
11:      print "Content-Type: application/x-unknown\n";
12:      print "Content-Disposition: attachment; filename=$id\n\n";
13:     open(FILE,"./$user-$server/$id");
14:            local $/ = undef;
15:            my $content = <FILE>;
16:        close FILE;
17:        return print $content;
18: }else{
19:     print redirect("pop-login.html"); exit;
20: }
```

Line 7 is there as a security precaution. As you will see, the following lines allow for the functionality of having the temporary files that MIME::Parser uses to be created out of the Web server tree. This line uses the *basename()* method imported by File::Basename in **line 5** . This method will ensure that the only thing in the $id variable is an actual file name and not a directory path. By doing this we will make sure that nobody tries to send a relative path to this script to download a file that they should not. As a security precaution, you should never blindly open any files based on terms passed to your script from a client. For these example scripts, we know that all we want from the client is a filename because we have defined the directory it will be in. So anything passed to the script that is not a filename should not be trusted and discarded like yesterday's trash.

Line 11 sends a header to the browser, saying that the content of what is coming is from an unknown filetype. This will cause the browser to pop open a box asking what you want to do with the upcoming data (Save, Open, and so forth).

Line 12 tells the browser that an attached file is coming and the name of the upcoming file. When a Web server sends a reply to a client for any file, it sends a MIME type as part of the header that sort of says to the client, "Hey, I am sending you a file, and this is the type of data it contains." This gives the client an advance notice on how it will want to handle the upcoming file. We are telling the client that we don't know what type of file this is. When a client doesn't know what the type of file is coming, it doesn't know how to handle it, so it pops up a window asking the user how they would like it to be handled. From there, they choose to save the file or open it with the appropriate application.

Lines 13–16 open the file, read the entire file into a scalar (by undefining $/), then close the filehandle.

Line 17 prints the string that is the contents of the file to the client.[4]

Now that you can see the how, let me explain the why. It would be very easy to simply link directly to the attachment file itself and simply let the Web server handle it directly. However, you may decide that for security reasons, you want to have the temporary directory that MIME::Parser uses omitted from the Web server tree. We did not do that in this example for simplicity's sake, but you can make the changes to do so by changing "./$user-$server" to something like "/tmp/$user-$server" and slightly modifying the regular expression in pop-view.cgi to show only what you want it to. Now back to the why. First, this script makes sure that the client supplies the appropriate cookie. If it does not, the attachment will not be seen. It also provides for the functionality explained above with moving the directory out of the Web server tree. If the directory was not in the Web server tree, trying to *redirect()* the browser to the file will not work. However, with the above, it opens up a file *somewhere* on the server (the machine the Web server is running on) and sends the contents of that file back to the client. This is actually a neat trick to be able to safely send files to the client when you have validated that this particular client is allowed to see that file. We do this validation by using the cookie and naming the temporary directory based on that cookie, which is really based on the POP server and POP account names that are unique.

When an attachment is sent to the browser, a dialog box is displayed, asking the user what to do with the incoming file. From here the file can be opened or saved (see Figure 10-6).

Figure 10-6   Popup to save attachment

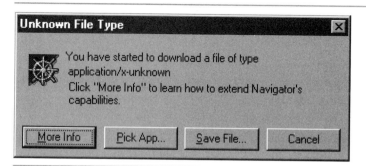

---

4. Unix systems don't know if a file is text or binary. However, on other Operating Systems you should use *binmode()* appropriately.

10.5 Example Script: Composing E-mail

What kind of an example would this be if we didn't show you how to compose e-mail? Not a very good one! So in the next section we cover how to compose and send e-mail. Listing 10-3 shows pop-compose.cgi, which will be the front end to composing and sending the e-mail.

Listing 10-3 **pop-compose.cgi, which displays the composition form**

```
01: #!/usr/bin/perl -wT
02: # pop-compose.cgi
03: use strict;
04: use CGI qw(:standard);
05: use Untaint;
06: my $cookie = cookie('WebMail') || 0;
07: my ($user, $pass, $server);
08: if (!$cookie) {
09:     print redirect("pop-login.html"); exit;
10: }else{
11:     print header;
12:     ($user, $pass, $server) = split(" ",$cookie);
13: }
14: $server = untaint(qr(.*), $server);
15: $user = untaint(qr(^\w{1,8}$), $user);
16: $pass = untaint(qr(^\w{1,8}$), $pass);
17: print start_html('Compose An Email Message'),
18:               h1('Compose An Email Message'),
20:               start_form({-method=>'POST',-action=>'
                            pop-send.cgi'}),
21:             "To: ",textfield('to'),p,
22:             "Cc: ",textfield('cc'),p,
23:             "Subject: ",textfield('subject'),p,
24:             "Message: ",p,textarea({-name=>'body',-rows=>15,
                            -cols=>70,-wrap=>'soft'}),p,
25:             submit({-value=>'Send Mail'}),
26:             end_form,
27:             hr;
```

The preceding script does nothing that should be new to you. It checks for the cookie, as does every script in this chapter, and displays a form that will be used to enter the e-mail To, Cc, Subject, and Body. This form submits to another script, pop-send.cgi, whose description is following.

```
01: #!/usr/bin/perl -wT
02: # pop-send.cgi
```

```
03: use strict;
04: use CGI qw(:standard);
05: use MIME::Parser;
06: use Net::SMTP;
07: use Untaint;
08: use CGI::Carp qw(fatalsToBrowser);
09: my $cookie = cookie('WebMail') || 0;
10: my ($user, $pass, $server);
11: if (!$cookie) {
12:     print redirect("pop-login.html"); exit;
13: }else{
14:     ($user, $pass, $server) = split(" ",$cookie);
15: }
16: $server = untaint(qr(.*), $server);
17: $user = untaint(qr(^\w{1,8}$), $user);
18: $pass = untaint(qr(^\w{1,8}$), $pass);
```

Lines 1–18 contain only one new item. Everything else you have seen in previous examples. **Line 6** pulls Net::SMTP into our mix of modules being used, which is the new item. This module will be used to do the actual sending of the e-mail.

```
19: my @to = split(/;\s+/,param('to'));
20: my @cc = split(/;\s+/,param('cc'));
21: my $subject = param('subject');
22: my @body = split(/\n/,param('body'));
```

Lines 19–22 handle retrieving the input from the form. We put the To and Cc data into arrays by splitting the form parameters on the semicolon and at least one space. For this example, we are going to assume that multiple To and Cc addresses are going to be separated by a semicolon and at least one space. This can, of course, be changed to split on whatever character or characters you wish. The Subject does not need to be split into an array because it is one text string, so it is stored into a scalar. And finally, **line 22** splits the Body information on newline characters. This will store each line of the message body in array elements.

```
23: my $top = build MIME::Entity ('X-Mailer' => 'WebMail',
24:                                -From     => "$user\@$server",
25:                                -To       => \@to,
26:                                -Cc       => \@cc,
27:                                -Subject  => $subject,
28:                                Data      => \@body
29:                   );
```

Lines 23–29 *build()* a MIME::Entity object. The result stored in $top will contain all the needed information of the e-mail message ready to be e-mailed! **Line 23** defines the mail client being used, which we are calling WebMail. **Line 24** defines from whom this e-mail is sent. This is somewhat of a simple way to do this, and we are assuming that it is coming from the same account name and server, which is used to check the e-mail. Next **line 25** tells the *build()* method who this e-mail is To by passing it a reference to the @to array created in **line 19**. **Line 26** does the same as **line 25**, except that it sets the values of any Cc addresses to also receive the e-mail. The Subject of the e-mail is created in **line 27**, while **line 28** passes the body of the message to the method by sending it a reference to our @body array. When this is all complete, our e-mail message is properly formatted and ready to be sent.

```
30: my $smtp = new Net::SMTP ('smtp.host.com');
```

Line 30 creates a new Net::SMTP object, as well as defines what SMTP server we will be using. If the machine on which this script is running is also your SMTP server, you can change this value to 'localhost'.

```
31: $smtp->mail("$user\@$server");
```

Line 31 tells our Net::SMTP object whom this e-mail is from.

```
32: $smtp->to(@to, @cc);
```

Line 32 tells the object to whom this e-mail is to be sent. This does seem a little redundant, since we already defined this information in the MIME:: Entity object, but it is again needed by the Net::SMTP object to do the proper handshaking with the SMTP server.

```
33: $smtp->data;
```

Line 33 calls the *data()* method, telling Net::SMTP that we are about to start sending actual e-mail data.

```
34: $smtp->datasend($top->stringify);
```

Line 34 sends our MIME::Entity object to our SMTP object as the body of the message. You can see that we *stringify()* the information so it is passed to $smtp as a string of data.

```
35: $smtp->dataend;
36: $smtp->quit;
```

Lines 35 and 36 start by calling the *dataend()* method to our Net::SMTP object (although this method actually resided in Net::Cmd). This tells the object that we are done sending data and to inform the SMTP we are done. **Line 36** tells Net::SMTP to send the QUIT command to the SMTP server and close the socket connection. As you can tell, Net::SMTP handles all the server handshaking and SMTP commands to send the e-mail so you don't have to!

```
37: print redirect('index.cgi');
38: exit;
```

Line 37 sends the browser back to the e-mail listing when the sending of the e-mail message is complete! Finally, **line 38** *exit()*s to make sure the script does stop running. See the screenshot in Figure 10-7.

Figure 10-7   **Compose e-mail form**

Whew! We have covered a lot of new information in this chapter. Everything for the example is almost complete. We have only one thing left, which is logging out. Any Web-based application that you can log in to, you should also be able to log out of. This is mainly for security reasons. You surely don't want to be logged into your e-mail and step out to lunch, allowing anyone to sit at your computer and read your e-mail or, worse yet, send e-mail in your name!

The script in Listing 10-4, pop-logout.cgi, is the small and final script that will log the user out of the system. When someone is logged out, they will not be able to check e-mail again until logging in.

Listing 10-4   pop-logout.cgi script

```
01: #!/usr/bin/perl -wT
02: # pop-logout.cgi
03: use CGI qw(:standard);
04: $cookie = cookie(-name => 'WebMail',
05:                  -value => 0
06:                 );
07: print header(-cookie=>$cookie);
08: print start_html(-title=>'Logged Out',
09:                  -BGCOLOR=>'white'
10:                 );
11: print qq(You are now logged out of WebMail. You can return to
12:     the login by clicking <A HREF="pop-login.html">here
        </A>.);
```

Nothing in this script is new. The main point of the script is what we set the new cookie value to. **Line 4** sets this value to "0," which will not pass any of the tests in the other scripts that check to make sure someone is logged into the system, hence, logging them out! Because this cookie is, and has been, a temporary cookie, when the user closes his or her browser (all of their browser processes), the cookie will go away. This is a good safety feature because if someone was to not log out properly and the cookie was permanent, anyone could view their cookie file and see the values that contain their user/password information. By making the cookie temporary, this won't happen!

10.6 Reader Exercises

■ There are a few occurrences of code that appear in each script, such as the *error()* subroutine and connection to the POP server. Try to take these functions and any others you find to be common, and move them into a separate module to be used by all the scripts.

- One omission from the script that sends/composes e-mail is that there is no functionality to send attachments! Take what you learned from the examples in Chapter 7 and add that functionality. A hint is to read the documentation for MIME::Entity.

- Another omission is the functionality to "Reply To" an e-mail message. However, all the pieces of that puzzle are found within the examples contained in this chapter. You have seen how to parse a header, get the body parts of a message, create a MIME entity, and e-mail it. By putting all these things together, you can accomplish this task.

10.7 Listings

Listing 10-5 **Full listing of index.cgi**

```
01: #!/usr/bin/perl -wT
02: # index.cgi
03: $|=1;
04: use strict;
05: use Mail::POP3Client;
06: use CGI qw(:standard :netscape *table);
07: use CGI::Carp qw(fatalsToBrowser);
08: use Untaint;
09: my $cookie = cookie('WebMail') || 0;
10: my $user = param('username') || 0;
11: my $pass = param('password');
12: my $server = param('server');
13: if ((!$user || !$pass || !$server) && !$cookie) {
14:     print redirect("pop-login.html"); exit;
15: }
16: if (!$cookie) {
17:     $cookie = cookie(-name => 'WebMail',
18:                      -value => "$user $pass $server",
                         -path  => '/'
19:                      );
20:     print header(-cookie=>$cookie);
21: }else{
22:     print header;
23:     ($user, $pass, $server) = split(" ",$cookie);
24: }
25: $server = untaint(qr(.*), $server);
26: $user = untaint(qr(^\w{1,8}$), $user);
27: $pass = untaint(qr(^\w{1,8}$), $pass);
```

(continued)

```
28: system("/bin/rm","-rf","./$user-$server") unless $user !~ /^\w/;
29: my $pop = new Mail::POP3Client(HOST   => $server);
30: $pop->User($user);
31: $pop->Pass($pass);
32: $pop->Connect() || &error($pop->Message);
33: my $count = $pop->Count;
34: my %deleted;
35: if (param('delete')) {
36:     ($pop->Delete($_) && $deleted{$_}++) foreach (param('mess'));
37: }
38: print start_html({-title=>'Web Email Client Example',
39:                    -BGCOLOR=>'white'}),
40: center,
41: start_table({-border=>1,
42:               -cellpadding=>4,
43:               -cellspacing=>4}),
44:     Tr,
45:     td({-align=>'CENTER',-colspan=>4},[strong("Email
                                             Example")]),
46:     Tr,
47:     th({-align=>'CENTER'},['Delete','From','Subject','Date']),
48:     Tr,
49:     start_form({-method=>'POST',-action=>'index.cgi'}),
50:     hidden({-name=>'delete',-value=>'1'})
51:     ;
52: my $c = 1;
53: for my $i (1..$count) {
54:     next if exists $deleted{$i};
55:     my @head;
56:     foreach($pop->Head($i)) {
57:         if(s/^From:\s+//i) {
                head[0] = qq(<td align=center>
                <input type="checkbox" name="mess" value="$c">
                </td>\n<td align=center>
                <a href="pop-view.cgi?mess=$c">$_</a></td>\n);
            }
58:         if (s/^Subject:\s+//i) {
                $head[1] = qq(<td align=center>
                <a href="pop-view.cgi?mess=$c">$_</a></td>\n);
             }
59:         if (/^Date:\s+/i && $_ =~ s/^Date:\s+(.*?)(?:\s+
                                     [+-]\d+(?:\s+.*?)?)?$/i)
             {
                $head[2] = qq(<td align=center>$_</td><tr>\n);
             }
60:     }
```

(continued)

```
61:     $c++;
62:     print @head;
63: }
64: $c--;
65: print td({-colspan=>4,-align=>'LEFT'},
66:     submit(-value=>'Delete') . " You Have <b>$c</b> Messages"),
67:     end_form,
68:     end_table,
69:     end_html;
70: $pop->Close();
71: sub error {
72:     my $err = shift;
73:     print h3("There was an error connecting to the server ($err).
                 Please try again"),p,
74:     a({-href=>'index.cgi'},"Home");
75:     exit;
76: }
```

Listing 10-6   pop-view.cgi full listing

```
01: #!/usr/bin/perl -wT
02: # pop-view.cgi
03: $| = 1;
04: use strict;
05: use Mail::POP3Client;
06: use CGI qw(:standard);
07: use CGI::Carp qw(fatalsToBrowser);
08: use MIME::Parser;
09: use URI::Escape;
10: use Untaint;
11: my $cookie = cookie('WebMail') || 0;
12: my ($user, $pass, $server);
13: if (!$cookie) {
14:     print redirect("pop-login.html"); exit;
15: }else{
16:     print header;
17:     ($user, $pass, $server) = split(" ",$cookie);
18: }
19: my $message = param('mess');
20: $server = untaint(qr(.*), $server);
21: $user = untaint(qr(^\w{1,8}$), $user);
22: $pass = untaint(qr(^\w{1,8}$), $pass);
23: my $pop = new Mail::POP3Client(HOST   => "$server");
```

(continued)

```
24: $pop->User($user);
25: $pop->Pass($pass);
26: $pop->Connect() || &error($pop->Message);
27: my $parser = new MIME::Parser;
28: if (!(-d "./$user-$server")) {
29:     system("/bin/mkdir", "-m","0777", "$user-$server");
30: }
31: $parser->output_dir("./$user-$server");
32: my $mail = $pop->Retrieve($message);
33: my $entity = $parser->parse_data($mail);
34: my $head = $entity->head;
35: print qq(To: ) . text_to_html($head->get('To',0));
36: print qq(CC: ) . text_to_html($head->get('Cc', 0)) if
                     $head->get('Cc', 0);
37: print qq(Subject: ) . text_to_html($head->get('Subject',0));
38: print qq(From: ) . text_to_html($head->get('From', 0));
39: print qq(Date: ) . $head->get('Date', 0) . qq(<br>\n);
40: my $parts = $entity->parts;
41: print p;
42: if (!$parts) {
43:     print text_to_html($entity->body_as_string);
44:     $entity->purge;
45: }else{
46:     print text_to_html($entity->parts(0)->bodyhandle->as_string);
47:     print h3("Attachments:");
48:     for (my $i=1; $i<$entity->parts;$i++) {
49:         (my $temp_file_name = $entity->parts($i)->
            bodyhandle->path) =~ s!^.*$user-$server/!!;
50:         my $uri_file = uri_escape($temp_file_name);
51:         if ($temp_file_name=~/\.(gif|jpg|png)$/i) {
52:             print qq(File: <img src="$user-$server/
                $temp_file_name"><br>);
53:         } else {
54:             print qq(File: <a href="view_att.cgi?att=$uri_file">
                         $temp_file_name</a><br>);
55:         }
56:     }
57: }
58: print p({-align=>'center'},
59:     a({-href=>"index.cgi?delete=1&mess=$message"},"Delete
                 Message"), " | ",
60:     a({-href=>"index.cgi"}, "Back to Mail"), " | ",
61:     a({-href=>"pop-logout.cgi"}, "Log Out"));
62: $pop->Close;
```

(continued)

```
63: sub text_to_html {
64:     my $raw = shift;
65:     $raw =~ s/([<>])/($1 eq '<') ? "&lt;" : "&gt\;"/eg;
66:     $raw =~ s!((ht|f)tps?://)([\w-]*)((\..[^\s]*)+)!<a href=
                "$1$3$4" target="external">$1$3$4</a>!g;
67:     $raw =~ s!([\w\-.]+)\@([\w-]+)((\.[\w-]+)*)!
                <a href=\"compose.isp?to_address=$1\@$2$3\
                ">$1\@$2$3</a>!g;
68:     $raw =~ s/\n/<br>/g;
69:     return $raw;
70: }
71: sub error {
72:     my $err = shift;
73:     print h3("There was an error connecting to the server ($err).
                Please try again"),p,
74:     a({-href=>'index.cgi'},"Home");
75:     exit;
76: }
```

Listing 10-7 **pop-send.cgi full listing**

```
01: #!/usr/bin/perl -wT
02: # pop-send.cgi
03: use strict;
04: use CGI qw(:standard);
05: use MIME::Parser;
06: use Net::SMTP;
07: use Untaint;
08: use CGI::Carp qw(fatalsToBrowser);
09: my $cookie = cookie('WebMail') || 0;
10: my ($user, $pass, $server);
11: if (!$cookie) {
12:     print redirect("pop-login.html"); exit;
13: }else{
14:     ($user, $pass, $server) = split(" u,$cookie);
15: }
16: $server = untaint(qr(.*), $server);
17: $user = untaint(qr(^\w{1,8}$), $user);
18: $pass = untaint(qr(^\w{1,8}$), $pass);
19: my @to = split(/;\s+/,param('to'));
20: my @cc = split(/;\s+/,param('cc'));
21: my $subject = param('subject');
22: my @body = split(/\n/,param('body'));
```

(continued)

```
23: my $top = build MIME::Entity ('X-Mailer' => 'WebMail',
24:                                   -From    => "$user\@$server",
25:                                   -To      => \@to,
26:                                   -Cc      => \@cc,
27:                                   -Subject => $subject,
28:                                   Data     => \@body
29:                               );
30: my $smtp = new Net::SMTP ('smtp.host.com');
31: $smtp->mail("$user\@$server");
32: $smtp->to(@to, @cc);
33: $smtp->data();
34: $smtp->datasend($top->stringify);
35: $smtp->dataend();
36: $smtp->quit;
37: print redirect('index.cgi');
38: exit;
```

11 Chapter

Introduction to DBI and Databases on the Web

11.1 Introduction

Databases are probably the most useful thing to put on the Web. Without databases, most of the pages on the Web would be static—and static pages get old fast. Today, all of the best sites have some sort of database behind the scenes driving the content viewed by visitors to the site.

In this chapter, you will learn how to use the DBI/DBD interface. DBI means DataBase Independent. It is named this because this is the module that is used for all databases; it is independent of the database. DBD means DataBase Driver or DataBase Dependent, depending on whom you ask (both terms are used). The DBD is the portion that is database specific, and you will need to download the appropriate driver for your database. We will be using MySQL as the database for the examples because it is a very good database and it is free. Perl and the DBI/DBD interface will work with many different databases. Check the DBI home page at *http://www.symbolstone.org/technology/perl/DBI* or *http://search.cpan.org* to find out if there is an interface for the database that you want to use. Chances are that there is already an interface for it.

To do the examples in this chapter, you need to have a database installed, the DBI module, and the appropriate DBD module for your database. You also need at least a basic understanding of SQL. The SQL statements in this chapter are pretty easy, and if you pick up on things quickly, you will probably be able to get by. However, a good reference book on SQL would also be a great help.

The examples in this chapter start out by getting you familiar with the DBI interface. The first few examples are not even Web-based, but once you have some of the basics down, we will move on to creating a CGI application that will search a product database. We are not covering all of the methods in the DBI module. There are too many options and choices to cover in this book. *MySQL & mSQL* by Randy Jay Yarger, et al. is a good book that covers much more than we can here.

To begin, we must have the tables in the database. Listing 11-1 is the table structure that is used for this chapter. Create these tables in your database and add a few records to each so that you have some data with which to work.

Listing 11-1   Table creation for chapter examples

```
CREATE TABLE products (
  sku        VARCHAR(20) NOT NULL PRIMARY KEY,
  mfg_pn     VARCHAR(30),
  mfg_pn     VARCHAR(30),
  name       VARCHAR(50),
  descr      VARCHAR(255),
  stock      INT,
  unit       VARCHAR(10),
  image      VARCHAR(50),
  vend_num   INT,
  price      VARCHAR(15)
);
CREATE TABLE vendors (
  vend_num   INT NOT NULL PRIMARY KEY AUTO_INCREMENT,
  address    VARCHAR(50),
  address2   VARCHAR(50),
  city       VARCHAR(50),
  state      VARCHAR(2),
  zip        VARCHAR(10),
  phone      VARCHAR(25),
  email      VARCHAR(150),
  url        VARCHAR(150),
  vname      VARCHAR(100)
);
```

11.2 Using the Perl DBI

Our first example is very short and has no interaction with the tables that we will be using, but shows us what drivers are installed on the server. This is very useful because you need to know what is available to work with on your system. Also, this example will generate an error if the DBI module is not loaded, so you can tell right away if you need to load the DBI module onto the server.

```
01: #!/usr/bin/perl -wT
02: # example_11-1
```

Line 1 has been used in almost every example up to now. It tells the system where to find Perl and turns on Taint checking and warnings.

Line 2 is simply a comment with the program name.

```
03: use strict;
04: use DBI;
```

Line 3 tells the program to use strict. Strict has also been used in every example so far, and it should be used in all of your programs as well.

Line 4 loads the DBI module. This is the one that this chapter is all about.

```
05: my @drivers = DBI->available_drivers();
```

Line 5 creates an array called @drivers and loads it with the result of a call to the *available_drivers()* method from the DBI module. This will load the array with all of the database drivers, or DBDs, that the system knows about.

```
06: print "The drivers loaded on this server are:\n\n";
07: print join("\n", @drivers);
08: print "\n";
```

Line 6 begins the output for the program.

Line 7 is a little different—it prints out the entire contents of the @drivers array but via a *join()* call. Since the *join()* call used "\n" as the item with which to join the text, it will print out each item on a separate line.

Line 8 prints an extra line feed to separate the output (see Listing 11-2).

Listing 11-2   **Listing for example 11-1 script**

```
01: #!/usr/bin/perl -wT
02: # example_11-1
03: use strict;
04: use DBI;
05: my @drivers = DBI->available_drivers();
06: print "The drivers loaded on this server are:\n\n";
07: print join("\n", @drivers);
08: print "\n";
```

The output of the program should look something like Listing 11-3 (the actual output will depend on what drivers are actually loaded on your server). This shows that, first of all, DBI is loaded on this server. The DBD drivers that are loaded are ADO, ExampleP, Proxy, and mysql. Case matters when telling your programs which driver to use, so make sure that you pay attention to the case and spelling of the drivers.

Listing 11-3   **Output of example script**

```
The drivers loaded on this server are:
ADO
ExampleP
Proxy
mysql
```

11.3 Connecting to the Database

The next DBI method we'll cover is a rather important one. The *connect()* method is used to open a connection to a database so that the program can begin using it. Its operation is pretty simple, and it will be used in all of the examples that access a database, so you will get very familiar with it. Let's take a look at the connect method so you know what each part does when you see it in our examples.

```
$DBH =
    DBI->connect(source:host:port, username, password, \%attributes)
    or die "Cannot connect! $DBI::errstr\n";
```

The *source* and its syntax are very important; the *host* and *port* are optional. If they are not provided, the default is the localhost. By using the *host* and *port*, you can connect to and use the DBI methods on one server, whereas the database resides on an entirely different server.

To use the MySQL database called book on the localhost, the *connect()* method would look like this.

```
$DBH = DBI->connect("DBI:mysql:book", "username", "password")
                    or die "Error: $DBI::errstr\n";
```

To use the MySQL database called book on a host named www.myserver.com and port 333, the connect method would look like this.

```
$DBH = DBI->connect("DBI:mysql:book:www.myserver.com:333", "username",
                    "password") or die "Error: $DBI::errstr\n";
```

You can't connect to just any database server. The permissions must be set up so that the machine and user with which you are connecting are authorized to do so. To set up the database permissions you will need to consult the documentation for the database to which you are connecting.

The $data_source is broken down into DBI, followed by the driver name (mysql), the database to connect to (book), and then the hostname and port (if you are connecting to a remote machine). The username and password may be needed, depending on how the rights to the database to which you are connecting are configured.

11.3.1 Disconnecting from the Database

With every good connect, there must be a disconnect. (After that poor attempt at humor, we'll move on.) The *disconnect()* method is used to disconnect from the database. You should always call the *disconnect()* method when your program terminates. Also, remember to call it in error handling routines so that there is always a disconnect before the program terminates, even after errors.

If you are using a server that supports transactions, you must be extra sure that you call the *disconnect()* method to avoid database errors and unanticipated rollbacks. Also, if you fail to call the *disconnect()* method, some databases will maintain an active process until the process times out, which could take a while. If you end up with several processes that are doing nothing, you are just wasting resources and degrading your server's performance. The *disconnect()* method is very simple. Here is an example.

```
$result = $DBH->disconnect;
```

disconnect() will return a nonzero value if there was an error. The return value ($result) is not needed, but if you want to check for a successful close, it is available.

11.4 Preparing and Executing an SQL Query

Next we'll cover two DBI methods. The reason we are covering both of these together is because they are a pair, like peanut butter and jelly. Take a look, and you will see what I mean.

The *prepare()* method is used to store an SQL statement into an internal, compiled form. In MySQL and mSQL, this internal compiling is not supported, but the SQL statement *is stored* and thus still useful. The *execute()* method is then used to perform, or run, an SQL statement that was prepared. Any arguments passed in the *execute()* method call are used to substitute the values for the placeholders. An example should help you understand what all of this does.

```
01: #!/usr/bin/perl -wT
02: # example 11-2
03: use strict;
04: use DBI;
```

Line 1 tells the program where to find Perl and turns on warnings and Taint checking.

Line 2 is a comment with the program name.

Line 3 brings in the strict module.

Line 4 brings in the DBI module so that we can manipulate databases.

```
05: my $dbh = DBI->connct("DBI:mysql:book","book","addison")
06:             or die "Error: $DBI::errstr\n";
```

Lines 5 and 6 are actually a single Perl line. These lines create a my variable called $dbh. $dbh is a scalar that will store the return value from the connect method—a handle to the database. We are connecting to a mysql database called book on the local host (since the host and port are not specified) Also, the username is *book,* and the password is *addison.* Simply put, this connects the program to the database and stores a reference to the connection in $dbh.

```
07: my $sql = "SELECT mfg_pn, name, price FROM products
                WHERE vend_num = ?";
08: my $sth = $dbh->prepare($sql);
```

Line 7 creates a new my variable that is simply a string containing a SQL statement. Notice at the end of this particular SQL statement that there is a question mark (?). This is called a **placeholder**. It is used like a variable that allows the program to pass data to the SQL statement when it is executed.

Line 8 then calls the *prepare()* method to store the SQL statement into a precompiled form on databases that support it or on databases that don't. It stores a reference to the statement in $sth.

```
09: $sth->execute("31");
10: print DBI::dump_results($sth);
```

Line 9 calls the *execute()* method. Notice that we did not call it using the database handle ($dbh). Instead we used the statement handle ($sth). Also notice that we passed an argument to the *execute()* method. This argument, 31, will replace the placeholder that was used above. The SQL statement will then be executed using the 31. The number of arguments passed to the *execute()* method *must* match the number of placeholders in the prepared SQL statement or you will get an error.

Line 10 prints out the results of the query that was just executed. The DBI::dump_results method is not normally used for output to the user, since the data is dumped in a rather unformatted way. We use it here just so you can see that the SQL statement actually did work.

```
11: print "\n\n";
```

Line 11 simply prints out two linefeeds so that the different SQL calls can be easily differentiated.

```
12: $sth->execute("5");
13: print DBI::dump_results($sth);
```

Lines 12–13 are exactly like **lines 9–10**, with the exception of the value that gets passed into the *execute()* method.

```
14: $dbh->disconnect;
```

And since all good things must come to an end, on **line 14** we call the disconnect method to gracefully terminate our connection to the database.

When this program is run, the output should be somewhat similar to Listing 11-4.

Listing 11-4   **Program output**

```
0 rows
0
'Raq3-128', 'RaQ 3', '2379.99'
'CPD-G500', 'Sony Monitor', '1139'
'CPD-G400', 'Sony Monitor', '679.99'
'E400', 'Sony Monitor', '635'
'CPD-G200', 'Sony Monitor', '439.99'
5 rows
5
```

The first time the SQL statement was executed, 31 was passed. There were no matches for 31, so 0 rows were returned. The second statement was passed 5, and there were 5 matches returned. It was just a coincidence that the number of matches happened to match the number of rows returned. The 5 rows of data that matched the query were printed out via the *dump_results()* method.

So we are now able to connect to and disconnect from a database as well as get data from a database. Let's now learn how to do some more advanced queries and get into fetching the data in a manner that makes formatting our output in HTML much easier.

11.5 Fetching Data

The ability to fetch the data you want is obviously very important. Also, being able to do this easily is very important to the developers. Luckily, with Perl and the DBI module, getting the data is pretty easy to do.

11.5.1 The fetchall_arrayref() Method

The first method for fetching data we will cover is *fetchall_arrayref()*. This method returns all remaining data in the statement handle as a reference to an array of arrays. Each item in the reference that is returned is an array that contains a row of data. If there is no data to be returned, it will return undef. Also, if you have previously used any of the other fetchrow functions (which we'll cover shortly), *fetchall_arrayref()* will return all of the *remaining* records, not the records that have already been fetched.

In all of the following examples, we use the database tables shown at the beginning of the chapter.

```
01: #!/usr/bin/perl -wT
02: # example 11-3
03: use strict;
04: use DBI;
```

Lines 1–4 are the same lines we've been using in all of our programs so far.

```
05: my $dbh = DBI->connect("DBI:mysql:book","book","addison")
06:             or die "Error: $DBI::errstr\n";
```

Lines 5–6 are a single statement that creates a my variable called $dbh. These lines create a connection to the database and store the result of the *connect()* method in the $dbh variable. The value that gets stored is a reference, or handle, to the database.

```
07: my $sql = "SELECT sku, name, descr, stock FROM products";
08: my $sth = $dbh->prepare($sql);
09: $sth->execute;
```

Line 7 creates the SQL statement and stores the string in the $sql variable. It also is perfectly legal to pass a string directly into the *prepare()* method. But storing the SQL strings into variables makes them easier to work with. For example, you could have a hash or an array that contains the SQL statements and then just pass a reference to the particular SQL statement you wish to use into the *prepare()* method.

Line 8 prepares the SQL statement and stores the prepared SQL statement in $sth.

Line 9 calls the *execute()* method to perform the SQL statement on the database.

```
10: my $data = $sth->fetchall_arrayref;
```

Line 10 is the call to the *fetchall_arrayref()* method. This will fetch all of the remaining records that were returned from the SQL command that was executed on **line 9** .

```
11: foreach (@$data){
12:     print join(' * ', @$_), "\n";
13: }
```

Lines 11–13 are used to print out all the data that was retreived. We stored the reference to the returned data on **line 10** into a variable called $data. $data should now hold a reference to several arrays. Since $data itself is an array, we need to refer to it as an array.

Line 11 refers to the $data variable as an array. By placing the @ in front of the variable name, it is the same as writing @{$data}. This causes the array to become the array of whatever value is stored in $data, so basically the array name is like a variable.

Line 12 prints out the current line of data by using the *join()* function. Normally when you simply print an array, each element in the array is printed with no line breaks or spaces between the records. By using the *join()* function, we can put the data together using any characters as separators that we choose to. In this case, we chose to use the asterisk surrounded by spaces to join the data. The *join()* function expects to be passed a list, and that is what we are doing. The *foreach()* loop stores the current value of the array we are looping through in $_. By putting the @ in front of it, we accomplish the same thing that we did on **line 11** . The @$_ on **line 12** could also be written @{$_}.

Line 13 simply closes the *foreach()* block.

```
14: print "\n\n";
```

Line 14 prints out two blank lines so that the program output is more readable.

```
15: print "Below is the 2nd record, 3rd column:\n";
16: print $data->[1][2], "\n\n";
```

Line 15 just prints out some descriptional text.

Line 16 prints out a specific row and column from the SQL query results.

```
17: $dbh->disconnect;
```

Line 17 disconnects the program from the database.

That is really all there is to using the *fetchall_arrayref()* method. This method is commonly used when you want to get all, or the rest, of the data fetched from the database.

Many times you don't want *all* of the data but rather a record, or row, at a time. To do this, you have a few options: *fetchrow_arrayref()* and *fetchrow_hashref()*. Since we have already been talking about arrays, we'll cover the *fetchrow_arrayref()* method first.

11.5.2 The fetchrow_arrayref() Method

The *fetchrow_arrayref()* method will get a single row of data and store the individual fields in the array structure. Each time you call the function, the contents of the array are overwritten with the new data. This means that you cannot simply call the third field of the fourth record; you need to program so that you work with one row at a time. This may sound very restrictive but, it really is not a bad thing.

The following is an example of how to deal with the data one row at a time. With this example, we will also be moving from a command-line interface to a true CGI.

```
01: #!/usr/bin/perl -wT
02: # example 11-4
03: use strict;
04: use DBI;
05: use CGI qw(:standard);
```

Lines 1–5 are the same as in the previous examples, except since the output is going to a Web browser, we also use the CGI module, which is included on **line 5**.

```
06: my $data;
07: my $dbh = DBI->connect("DBI:mysql:book","book","addison")
08:             or die "Error: $DBI::errstr\n";
```

Line 6 creates a my variable so that we can use it later on without the strict pragma complaining to us.

Lines 7 and 8 connect us to the database and check to make sure that there were no errors.

```
09: my $sql = "SELECT sku, name, descr, stock, price
                FROM products";
10: my $sth = $dbh->prepare($sql);
```

Line 9 is the SQL statement that we'll use to get the data from the database.

Line 10 prepares the SQL statement so that it is ready for the database to use.

```
11: $sth->execute;
```

Line 11 executes the SQL statement.

```
12: print header;
```

Line 12 prints out the HTTP content type header. This is a function from CGI.pm that is simply used to save some typing and help prevent typographical errors.

```
13: print <<HTML;
14:   <HTML>
15:     <HEAD><TITLE>Example 11-4 Output</TITLE></HEAD>
16:     <BODY>
17:      <CENTER>
18:       <TABLE BORDER="1" CELLSPACING="0">
19:         <TR>
20:           <TD><B>SKU</B></TD>
21:           <TD><B>Product</B></TD>
22:           <TD><B>Description</B></TD>
23:           <TD><B># in Stock</B></TD>
24:           <TD><B>Price</B></TD>
25:         </TR>
26: HTML
```

Lines 13–26 are a here document that prints out the beginning HTML content for the page that the program is generating. It also begins a table and prints the column headings.

```
27: while($data = $sth->fetchrow_arrayref){
28:     print qq(<TR>\n);
```

Line 27 begins a *while()* loop that reads in a row of data that matched the SQL statement. By putting this in a *while()* loop, the program will loop until there are no more rows of data to fetch. Once it runs out of data to fetch, the *while()* loop will fall through to the next part of the code.

Line 28 prints an HTML <TR> tag. Each time through this *while()* loop, we create a new row of data. This line makes the HTML table display the data as we intended it to be displayed.

```
29:     foreach(@$data){
30:         print qq(<TD>$_</TD>\n);
31:     }
```

Line 29 is a *foreach()* loop that prints out each element from a row of data. The way this works is that the variable called $data is a reference to an array. By placing the @ in front of the variable, we dereference it and cause it to act as an array instead of a reference. Each time through the *foreach()* loop, it places the current record into the $_ variable.

Line 30 prints out the HTML required for each element of data and also the data itself.

Line 31 closes the foreach loop.

```
32:      print qq(</TR>\n);
33: }
```

Line 32 prints out the closing table row tag. This causes this item to end, and the new item will be on a new line.

Line 33 ends the *while()* loop.

```
34: print qq(</TABLE></CENTER></BODY></HTML>);
35: $dbh->disconnect;
```

Line 34 prints out the HTML to end the page.

Finally, **line 35** disconnects from the database. Remember to *disconnect()* from the database to prevent having open connections waiting for something to do and eating up resources when the program that opened them has already ended.

11.5.3 The fetchrow_hashref() Method

All right, now we are on to an even easier method for accessing data from the database. This section is going to be very short though because accessing the data is almost identical to the previous method (*fetchrow_arrayref()*). We can pick up the previous program at line 27, and all we really need to talk about is the while loop that is used to display the data that matched the query.

```
27: while($data = $sth->fetchrow_hashref){
28:      print qq(<TR>\n);
29:      print qq(<TD>$data->{sku}</TD>\n);
30:      print qq(<TD>$data->{name}</TD>\n);
31:      print qq(<TD>$data->{descr}</TD>\n);
32:      print qq(<TD>$data->{stock}</TD>\n);
33:      print qq(<TD>$data->{price}</TD>\n);
34:      print qq(</TR>\n);
35: }
```

Line 27 begins the while loop that fetches the data that matched the SQL statement. The call to *fetchrow_hashref()* creates a *hash* that contains one row of data with the names of the fields as the keys of the hash. *This* is the very reason that this method should be easier. By using a hash and having the keys be the field names, you always know exactly what field you are working with. With the *fetchrow_arrayref()* method, all of the field names are abstracted by array indexes, and it is easy to forget exactly which array index is which data element.

Line 28 begins a new row of data.

Lines 29–33 print out the individual data elements in the row.

Line 34 ends the current row.

Finally, **line 35** ends the *while()* loop.

After this, the rest of the program is the same as our previous example. As you can see, the only difference between *fetchrow_arrayref()* and *fetchrow_hashref()* is that the results row is returned in a different data structure, and therefore the values are retrieved from that data structure accordingly.

11.5.4 The bind_columns() Method

One of the great things about writing a book is that you are forced to go back and read documentation so that you can make sure your information is accurate. A benefit of this is that instead of just programming merrily along as usual, you get to read about more things than you normally do. The *fetchrow_hashref() was* my favorite method of accessing data, and I used it all the time in my programs. I was happy with it, so I didn't search for any alternatives.

Well, things have changed now. The *bind_columns()* method is now tied with *fetchrow_hashref()* favorite because it saves typing *and* it still keeps perfectly clear what data is being worked with.

We'll cover the important bits in this section, with the complete program listing at the end of the chapter. There really isn't much different from the other methods of access, except for the few lines we'll cover here.

```
09: my $sql = "SELECT sku, name, descr, stock, price
                   FROM products";
10: my $sth = $dbh->prepare($sql);
11: $sth->execute;
12: my ($sku,$prod,$desc,$stock,$price);
13: $sth->bind_columns(undef, \($sku, $prod, $desc, $stock,
                                $price));
```

Lines 9–11 are identical to the previous methods for accessing the data.

Line 12 simply declares the variables that we'll use for accessing the data.

Line 13 is the line that does the *magic. We call the bind_columns()* method and pass it two arguments. The first is used to pass arguments to the database and is unused in MySQL and mSQL (which is why it is *undef*). The second argument that we pass is a list of scalar *references* to the fields that we are fetching. The references that we pass *must* be in the order that they are fetched, and there *must* be exactly the same number of scalar references as there is data returned from the SQL select statement.

Now for the best part of the *bind_columns()* method. When the data is accessed via the fetch method, the variables that were bound "magically" contain the data for the current row of data. No more having to reference an array index or hash. Simply use the variable name!

The rest of the program is the same as the previous example programs. The only difference is the *bind_colums()* method call, and the while loop to access the data is easier to manage because there is less typing to mistype.

11.6 Putting It All Together

Well, we now have all this new knowledge, and we have even created some programs that access data from a database. But we really don't have anything that has user-interaction. In this book, we are not going to leave you hanging out to dry! Let's create a small Web application, using what we've covered so far, that will allow a user to go to the Web site and search for products. We will also tie both the products table and the vendor table into this application to make it even more realistic.

With this sample application, we'll allow the user to enter a string to search on and a field to sort on; then the application will display the data that the user was looking for. An application like this is a great beginning to a real product database that could be used for an online shopping site.

```
01: #!/usr/bin/perl -wT
02: # example 11-7
03: use strict;
04: use DBI;
05: use CGI qw(:standard);
06: use CGI::Carp qw(fatalsToBrowser);
```

Lines 1–6 are basically the standard lines we've been using for CGI programs. The difference here is the inclusion of the Carp module on **line 6** to display any errors to the browser.

```
07: my ($Data, $prod_sth, $vend_sth);
08: my $Search_String = param('search_for');
09: my $Sort_Field    = param('sort_by');
```

Line 7 creates a few variables that we'll be using. We create a $Data variable that will hold a reference to the current line of data and two statement handles ($prod_sth, $vend_sth) for the statements that we use in this program.

Lines 8–9 create my variables and gather the information from the HTML form that calls this program.

```
10: my $dbh = DBI->connect("DBI:mysql:book","book","addison")
11:             or die "Error: $DBI::errstr\n";
```

Lines 10–11 are a single Perl statement that connects us to the database and stores the database handle in the $dbh variable.

```
12: print header;
13: get_products();
14: print_output();
```

Line 12 prints out the HTTP header needed for all CGI programs that send any sort of output back to the browser.

Line 13 calls the *get_products()* subroutine, which is used to get the products from the database.

Line 14 calls the *print_output()* subroutine so that we can present the users with the data that they are looking for.

```
15: sub get_products{
16:     my $sql   = "SELECT * FROM products WHERE
17:                  descr LIKE ? ORDER BY ?";
```

Line 15 begins the *get_products()* subroutine. This subroutine is called to get all of the products that match what the user is looking for.

Line 16–17 are the SQL statement that fetches the matching records. Inside the SQL statement are two placeholders (denoted with question marks), one for the text that is being searched for and one to determine the field on which the results should be sorted.

```
18:     $prod_sth = $dbh->prepare($sql);
19:     $prod_sth->execute("%$Search_String%", $Sort_Field);
20: }
```

Line 18 prepares the SQL statement that was created on **lines 16 and 17**.

Line 19 executes the SQL statement. Inside of the *execute()* call two parameters were passed. You must pass a parameter for each placeholder that is in the prepared SQL statement. Here we pass $Search_String, but notice that we also surrounded it with %'s. This was done because the % is the wildcard character in SQL, so it will match anything followed by the string we are searching for with anything after it. If we did not do this, the matches would have to be exact matches. For example, without the %'s, *base* would not match *baseball*, but with the %'s, it matches.

Finally, **line 20** closes out the subroutine.

```
21: sub get_vendor{
22:     my $vendor = shift;
```

Line 21 begins the *get_vendor()* subroutine. This subroutine is called each time a row is fetched in the while loop so that we can get the name of the vendor from the vendors table. This allows us to translate the vendor number, which is stored in the products table, into the actual vendor name.

Line 22 creates a my variable called $vendor and shifts the item that was passed in the function call into it.

```
23:     my $sql    = "SELECT vname FROM vendors WHERE
24:                    vend_num = ?";
```

Lines 23–24 are the SQL statement that we'll use to grab the vendor name. We use a placeholder again. This time we use the placeholder to get the vendor number passed from the current product record.

```
25:     $vend_sth  = $dbh->prepare($sql);
26:     $vend_sth->execute($vendor);
27: }
```

Line 25 prepares the SQL statement from **lines 23 and 24** .

Line 26 executes the SQL statement and passes the vendor to the execute method.

Line 27 ends the *get_vendor()* subroutine.

So we now have just about everything we need. We can get the products from the database and get the vendor name from the database. The only thing left is to print out the results so that the user can see what they were searching for.

```
28: sub print_output{
29:     print <<HTML;
30:       <HTML>
31:        <HEAD><TITLE>Example 11-7 Output</TITLE></HEAD>
32:        <BODY>
33:         <CENTER>
34:          <TABLE BORDER="1" CELLSPACING="0">
35:           <TR>
36:            <TD><B>SKU</B></TD>
37:            <TD><B>Vendor</B></TD>
38:            <TD><B>Name</B></TD>
39:            <TD><B>Description</B></TD>
40:            <TD><B># in Stock</B></TD>
41:            <TD><B>Price</B></TD>
42:           </TR>
43: HTML
```

Line 28 begins the *print_output()* subroutine.

Line 29 begins a here document that is used to print out the HTML needed to start the results screen.

Lines 30–42 are the HTML used to create the top of the output page.

Line 43 closes the here document.

```
44:     while($Data = $prod_sth->fetchrow_hashref){
45:         get_vendor($Data->{vend_num});
46:         my $vendor = $vend_sth->fetch->[0];
```

Line 44 begins the *while()* loop for printing out the rows of data that matched the query. This is very similar to the *while()* loop from the previous examples. In this example, we use the *fetchrow_hashref()* method to access the data.

Line 45 calls the *get_vendor()* subroutine and passes it the current vendor number, which we get from $Data->{vend_num}.

Line 46 creates a my variable called $vendor in which we store the current vendor name.

To get the vendor name, we make a few assumptions about the data integrity of the database with which we are dealing. We are assuming that there is only one vendor name associated with each vendor number. Since the vendor number is the primary key for the table, and it is an auto-increment variable, we can be pretty sure that each one is unique. To write a bullet-proof program, add more error checking to ensure without a doubt that each value is unique.

Now that we know what assumptions were made, we get the data from the vendor table using the fetch method. The fetch method and the *fetchrow_arrayref()* method are actually aliases of each other, so you can use either one and they will do the same thing. Since the data comes to us in an array and we only should have one match, any match will be in element 0 of the array. That is how we come up with the line

```
my $vendor = $vend_sth->fetch->[0];
```

This tells the program to create a my variable named $vendor and set it to the value returned from element 0 of the *fetch* method when performed on the $vend_sth statement handle. Whew!

```
47:              print<<HTML;
48:               <TR>
49:                <TD>$Data->{sku}</TD>
50:                <TD>$vendor</TD>
51:                <TD>$Data->{name}</TD>
52:                <TD>$Data->{descr}</TD>
53:                <TD>$Data->{stock}</TD>
54:                <TD>$Data->{price}</TD>
55:               </TR>
56: HTML
57:       }
```

Lines 47–56 are a here document that prints out each element of data in the table.

Line 57 closes the *while()* loop. The *while()* loop from **line 44** to **line 57** will loop once for each match that was returned, call the *get_vendor()* subroutine each time through the loop, and print out the data. When the *while()* loop is finished, all of the matching data should be printed, and the only thing left is to finish up the HTML for the page.

```
58:     print qq(</TABLE>);
59:     print qq(<A HREF="/book/db/example_11-7.html">
                Search Again</A>);
60:     print qq(</CENTER></BODY></HTML>);
```

Line 58 closes the HTML for the table.

Line 59 prints out a link in case the user wants to go back and search again.

Line 60 prints out the remaining HTML tags needed to end the output screen.

```
61:    $dbh->disconnect;
62: }
```

Line 61 disconnects us from the database.

Line 62 ends the *print_results()* subroutine.

That is it for this example—62 lines of code, many of which are simply HTML, and we end up with a CGI application that will search through a database table, perform lookups in a different database table, and print the results out to the screen in an easy-to-read format for the user. Not too shabby!

11.6.1 The do() Method

There is one more method that deserves mention before we move on to the reader exercises. If desired, you can even use this method to complete the exercises.

The *do()* method is used for SQL statements that *do not* return any data. To use it, simply pass it an SQL statement, and it is executed. The *do()* method takes the place of the *prepare()* and the *execute()* methods. It is your choice to use it or not. *prepare()* and *execute()* work fine, but by using the *do()* method, you cut out the overhead of an extra function call. Here is a quick example of using the *do()* method. It is a very straightforward method to use in your applications.

```
$sth->do("INSERT INTO products VALUES ('a','b','c','d')");
```

11.6.2 Wrapping It Up

Using the DBI module with Perl is a very effective and easy way to connect databases to the Web. The DBI module is robust and full-featured. It was written with portability in mind. If you change the database that you are on, there is no problem: Simply download the new DBD for that database, install it, change the connect string, and you are off and running again.

There are still several DBI methods that were not covered in this chapter. The documentation that comes with the DBI module is excellent, and there are also several Web sites that have more examples and cover all of the available methods.

11.7 Reader Exercises

- Create a Web interface to add new records to the vendor and product tables.
- Use the *do()* method in an application.
- Create a Web-based phonebook.

11.8 Listings

Listing 11-5   **Example script 11-2**

```
01: #!/usr/bin/perl -wT
02: # example 11-2
03: use strict;
04: use DBI;
05: my $dbh = DBI->connect("DBI:mysql:book","book","addison")
06:              or die "Error: $DBI::errstr\n";
07: my $sql = "SELECT mfg_pn, name, price FROM products WHERE
                  vend_num = ?";
08: my $sth = $dbh->prepare($sql);
09: $sth->execute("31");
10: print DBI::dump_results($sth);
11: print "\n\n";
12: $sth->execute("5");
13: print DBI::dump_results($sth);
14: $dbh->disconnect;
```

Listing 11-6   **Program 11-3**

```
01: #!/usr/bin/perl -wT
02: # example 11-3
03: use strict;
04: use DBI;
05: my $dbh = DBI->connect("DBI:mysql:book","book","addison")
06:               or die "Error: $DBI::errstr\n";
07: my $sql = "SELECT sku, name, descr, stock FROM products";
08: my $sth = $dbh->prepare($sql);
09: $sth->execute;
10: my $data = $sth->fetchall_arrayref;
11: foreach (@$data){
```

(continued)

```
12:      print join(' * ', @$_), "\n";
13: }
14: print "\n\n";
15: print "Below is the 2nd record, 3rd column:\n";
16: print $data->[1][2], "\n\n";
17: $dbh->disconnect;
```

Listing 11-7 **Program 11-4**

```
01: #!/usr/bin/perl -wT
02: # example 11-4
03: use strict;
04: use DBI;
05: use CGI qw(:standard);
06: my $data;
07: my $dbh = DBI->connect("DBI:mysql:book","book","addison")
08:              or die "Error: $DBI::errstr\n";
09: my $sql = "SELECT sku, name, descr, stock, price FROM products";
10: my $sth = $dbh->prepare($sql);
11: $sth->execute;
12: print header;
13: print <<HTML;
14:   <HTML>
15:   <HEAD><TITLE>Example 11-4 Output</TITLE></HEAD>
16:   <BODY>
17:    <CENTER>
18:     <TABLE BORDER="1" CELLSPACING="0">
19:      <TR>
20:       <TD><B>SKU</B></TD>
21:       <TD><B>Product</B></TD>
22:       <TD><B>Description</B></TD>
23:       <TD><B># in Stock</B></TD>
24:       <TD><B>Price</B></TD>
25:      </TR>
26: HTML
27: while($data = $sth->fetchrow_arrayref){
28:     print qq(<TR>\n);
29:     foreach(@$data){
30:         print qq(<TD>$_</TD>\n);
31:     }
32:     print qq(</TR>\n);
33: }
34: print qq(</TABLE></CENTER></BODY></HTML>);
35: $dbh->disconnect;
```

Listing 11-8   Program 11-5

```
01: #!/usr/bin/perl -wT
02: # example 11-5
03: use strict;
04: use DBI;
05: use CGI qw(:standard);
06: my $data;
07: my $dbh = DBI->connect("DBI:mysql:book","book","addison")
08:             or die "Error: $DBI::errstr\n";
09: my $sql = "SELECT sku, name, descr, stock, price FROM products";
10: my $sth = $dbh->prepare($sql);
11: $sth->execute;
12: print header;
13: print <<HTML;
14:   <HTML>
15:    <HEAD><TITLE>Example 11-5 Output</TITLE></HEAD>
16:    <BODY>
17:     <CENTER>
18:      <TABLE BORDER="1" CELLSPACING="0">
19:       <TR>
20:        <TD><B>SKU</B></TD>
21:        <TD><B>Product</B></TD>
22:        <TD><B>Description</B></TD>
23:        <TD><B># in Stock</B></TD>
24:        <TD><B>Price</B></TD>
25:       </TR>
26: HTML
27: while($data = $sth->fetchrow_hashref){
28:     print qq(<TR>\n);
29:     print qq(<TD>$data->{sku}</TD>\n);
30:     print qq(<TD>$data->{name}</TD>\n);
31:     print qq(<TD>$data->{descr}</TD>\n);
32:     print qq(<TD>$data->{stock}</TD>\n);
33:     print qq(<TD>$data->{price}</TD>\n);
34:     print qq(</TR>\n);
35: }
36: print qq(</TABLE></CENTER></BODY></HTML>);
37: $dbh->disconnect;
```

Listing 11-9   **Program 11-6**

```perl
01: #!/usr/bin/perl -wT
02: # example 11-6
03: use strict;
04: use DBI;
05: use CGI qw(:standard);
06: my $data;
07: my $dbh = DBI->connect("DBI:mysql:book","book","addison")
08:           or die "Error: $DBI::errstr\n";
09: my $sql = "SELECT sku, name, descr, stock, price FROM products";
10: my $sth = $dbh->prepare($sql);
11: $sth->execute;
12: my ($sku,$prod,$desc,$stock,$price);
13: $sth->bind_columns(undef, \($sku, $prod, $desc, $stock, $price));
14: print header;
15: print <<HTML;
16:  <HTML>
17:   <HEAD><TITLE>Example 11-6 Output</TITLE></HEAD>
18:   <BODY>
19:    <CENTER>
20:     <TABLE BORDER="1" CELLSPACING="0">
21:      <TR>
22:       <TD><B>SKU</B></TD>
23:       <TD><B>Product</B></TD>
24:       <TD><B>Description</B></TD>
25:       <TD><B># in Stock</B></TD>
26:       <TD><B>Price</B></TD>
27:      </TR>
28: HTML
29: while($data = $sth->fetch){
30:     print qq(<TR>\n);
31:      print qq(<TD>$sku</TD>\n);
32:      print qq(<TD>$prod</TD>\n);
33:      print qq(<TD>$desc</TD>\n);
34:      print qq(<TD>$stock</TD>\n);
35:      print qq(<TD>$price</TD>\n);
36:     print qq(</TR>\n);
37: }
38: print qq(</TABLE></CENTER></BODY></HTML>);
39: $dbh->disconnect;
```

Listing 11-10   Program 11-7

```perl
01: #!/usr/bin/perl -wT
02: # example 11-7
03: use strict;
04: use DBI;
05: use CGI qw(:standard);
06: use CGI::Carp qw(fatalsToBrowser);
07: my ($Data, $prod_sth, $vend_sth);
08: my $Search_String = param('search_for');
09: my $Sort_Field    = param('sort_by');
10: my $dbh = DBI->connect("DBI:mysql:book","book","addison")
11:             or die "Error: $DBI::errstr\n";
12: print header;
13: get_products();
14: print_output();
15: sub get_products{
16:     my $sql    = "SELECT * FROM products WHERE
17:                     descr LIKE ? ORDER BY ?";
18:     $prod_sth = $dbh->prepare($sql);
19:     $prod_sth->execute("%$Search_String%", "$Sort_Field");
20: }
21: sub get_vendor{
22:     my $vendor = shift;
23:     my $sql    = "SELECT vname FROM vendors WHERE
24:                     vend_num = ?";
25:     $vend_sth = $dbh->prepare($sql);
26:     $vend_sth->execute($vendor);
27: }
28: sub print_output{
29:     print <<HTML;
30:      <HTML>
31:       <HEAD><TITLE>Example 11-7 Output</TITLE></HEAD>
32:       <BODY>
33:        <CENTER>
34:         <TABLE BORDER="1" CELLSPACING="0">
35:          <TR>
36:           <TD><B>SKU</B></TD>
37:            <TD><B>Vendor</B></TD>
38:            <TD><B>Name</B></TD>
39:            <TD><B>Description</B></TD>
40:            <TD><B># in Stock</B></TD>
41:            <TD><B>Price</B></TD>
42:          </TR>
```

(continued)

```
43: HTML
44:     while($Data = $prod_sth->fetchrow_hashref){
45:         get_vendor($Data->{vend_num});
46:         my $vendor = $vend_sth->fetch->[0];
47:         print<<HTML;
48:          <TR>
49:            <TD>$Data->{sku}</TD>
50:            <TD>$vendor</TD>
51:            <TD>$Data->{name}</TD>
52:            <TD>$Data->{descr}</TD>
53:            <TD>$Data->{stock}</TD>
54:            <TD>$Data->{price}</TD>
55:          </TR>
56: HTML
57:     }
58:     print qq(</TABLE>);
59:     print qq(<A HREF="/book/db/example_11-7.html">Search Again</A>);
60:     print qq(</CENTER></BODY></HTML>);
61:     $dbh->disconnect;
62: }
```

12 Chapter

Tied Variables

12.1 Introduction

You may find at times that you have to do things over and over, or that you want to make things easier to do when you are writing a program. Tied variables can help you out in many different situations.

Are tied variables magical variables that can perform powerful tasks? Actually, tied variables are simply variables that have certain methods assigned to the various tasks that can be performed on them. This power does come at the cost of some up-front work. But when you are finished, you have a powerful tool that can be used again and again.

For example, you want your table rows to have alternating colors, but you are tired of having to recode all of the color values each time you need to change the color scheme. Or you want to change from two colors to three colors, so you are forced to go through the HTML and fix *all* the color tags for the table rows. There *must* be an easier way! A tied variable is perfect in a case like this.

Scalars, arrays, hashes, and filehandles can be tied. While the concept is basically the same for all types, the methods that need to be created differ for each type. We'll talk about tying a scalar and a hash in this chapter. The way tied variables work is that when the various actions are performed on the tied variable, instead of acting the way a normal variable would, it uses methods that you, the programmer, created. This is kind of hard to explain, so let's try a simple example to help us out. Let's say that you create a variable and set its value to 9.

```
$myvar = 9;
```

When you do this, you STORE the value of 9 in the variable called $myvar. Now when you want to print it out, you do something like this.

```
print "The value is: $myvar\n";
```

You probably expected the output to look exactly like this.

```
The value is: 9
```

But what if it printed this instead?

```
The value is: 99
```

How could this happen? Well, when a variable is tied, you can alter how it behaves. When the variable was being printed, you were FETCHing the value from the $myvar variable.

It just so happens that FETCH and STORE are two of the methods that can be redefined in tied scalars. In this case, the FETCH method may have had something like this.

```
sub FETCH {
    my $self = shift;
    my $data = shift;
    return ($data * 11);
}
```

Granted, this is a very basic example, but hopefully it helped you to grasp the concept. We'll get into the gory details in a bit. We have some code to look at—lots and lots of code! Another example of a tied scalar would be a variable that increments itself every time it is accessed. A variable tied like this would make a great counter!

Scalars are the easiest variable type to tie. They have the TIESCALAR, FETCH, STORE, and DESTROY methods.

Arrays have TIEARRAY, FETCH, STORE, DESTROY, FETCHSIZE, and STORESIZE as tied methods. You can also define POP, PUSH, SHIFT, UNSHIFT, SPLICE, CLEAR, EXTEND, DELETE, and EXISTS. Hashes have TIEHASH, FETCH, STORE, DELETE, CLEAR, EXISTS, FIRSTKEY, NEXTKEY, and DESTROY as tied methods. Filehandles have TIEHANDLE, PRINT, PRINTF, WRITE, READLINE, GETC, READ, and DESTROY. You can also define BINMODE, OPEN, CLOSE, EOF, FILENO, SEEK, and TELL. The tied method/function names *must* be in all upper case and use these names.

Thankfully, if you want to tie a variable, you don't have to define *all* these methods yourself. There are Perl modules for each variable type that define the basic functionality of each method required. This allows you to override only those methods that you wish. The modules are called Tie::Scalar, Tie::Hash, Tie::Array, and Tie::Handle. If you would like more information than is provided in this chapter, perldoc perltie is a great place to look.

12.2 Setting It All Up

Since we are going to be doing quite a bit in this chapter, there is some setup involved if you want to try these examples out for yourself. Hopefully, you still have a database setup on your server. We'll be using MySQL again for these examples. There are a few tables that need to be created before we begin. We need a *cart* table, a *products* table, and a *session* table. Here is the information needed to create the tables in MySQL.

```
# Table structure for table 'cart'
CREATE TABLE cart (
  sku varchar(25),
  qty int(11),
  modified varchar(25),
  session varchar(25)
);
# Table structure for table 'products'
CREATE TABLE products (
  sku varchar(20) DEFAULT '' NOT NULL,   # The SKU of the item
  mfg_pn varchar(30),                    # Manufacture Part number
  name varchar(50),                      # Item name
  descr varchar(255),                    # Item description
  stock int(11),                         # Quantity in stock
  unit varchar(10),                      # Unit (that is: ea, gal, box)
  image varchar(50),                     # Image name (not yet used)
  vend_num int(11),                      # Vendor number, used to link
  price varchar(15),                     # Price, no dollar signs
  PRIMARY KEY (sku)                      # Tells MySQL sku is primary key
);
# Table structure for table 'session'
```

(continued)

```
CREATE TABLE session (
  UID int(11) DEFAULT '0' NOT NULL auto_increment,
  expires varchar(25),
  PRIMARY KEY (UID)
);
# Table structure for table 'vendors'
CREATE TABLE vendors (
  vend_num int(11) DEFAULT '0' NOT NULL auto_increment, # Vendor number
  address varchar(50),          # Address line 1
  address2 varchar(50),         # Address line 2
  city varchar(50),             # City
  state char(2),                # State
  zip varchar(10),              # Zip code
  phone varchar(25),            # Phone number
  email varchar(150),           # Email address
  url varchar(150),             # URL, if known
  vname varchar(100),           # Vendor name
  PRIMARY KEY (vend_num)        # Tells MySQL vend_num is primary key
);
```

Once you have these tables created, enter some data into the products table and the vendors table so that you have some data to search on and work with. You can just make up items for these examples, but put in at least ten so that you can see how everything works together.

12.3 Getting Started

We will be building on what you have learned so far in this book, particularly the chapter dealing with database access. The example program we'll be building is quite complex, but give it a chance. It is easy to look at the code and let your eyes glaze over while you think, "This is too hard!" Honest—while some of this code is quite complex, our goal is for you to understand exactly what is happening each step of the way.

We will be creating three separate files in this chapter: cart.cgi, which will be our main program; product_search.cgi, which is used to fetch data from the database and display it to the user; and ShopCart.pm, which will contain the methods needed for our tied variables.

The first item we are going to build is the interface that will allow the user to search for products. We'll build a simple cart.cgi program, all of the product_search.cgi program, and begin the ShopCart.pm module.

12.4 Diving In

Okay, let's dive into the first program. This will be the beginning of cart.cgi. When we are done with the chapter, cart.cgi will look very different, but the code that we create now will remain nearly unchanged inside of the file, although it just may be moved around a bit.

```
01: #!/usr/bin/perl -w
02: use strict;
03: use CGI qw(:standard);
04: use lib qw(.);
05: use ShopCart;
06: $|=1;
```

Lines 1–3 are the standard lines we've been using in just about all our programs so far.

Line 4 adds the current directory, represented by the dot (.), to @INC. This makes it so that we can use modules in the program that are in the current directory and have Perl still find them. Normally, the modules would have to be installed in one of Perl's standard locations.

Line 5 uses the ShopCart.pm module. This module, which we'll create soon, will be stored in the same directory as this program, which is why we needed **line 4** .

Line 6 tells Perl to autoflush the buffer. If we don't do this, Perl will wait until the output is complete before sending it to the browser. By autoflushing the buffer, the output is sent directly to the browser without having to wait for the entire program to finish.

```
07: my ($color);
08: tie $color, 'Colors', qw(ffffff e0e0e0);
```

Line 7 creates a my variable that we'll use in the program. All variables must be declared because we are programming under the strict pragma.

Line 8 ties the variable $color to the Colors class and passes it a list of data containing the colors that we want to alternate between. We are not limited to just two colors. We could put ten in here just as easily, although the resulting table would probably look strange. Now if you want to change the colors or add new colors, this is the only thing that you need to change!

```
09: Display_Search_Page();
10: exit;
```

Line 9 calls the *Display_Search_Page()* subroutine, which will simply display the HTML form needed to perform the search on the products database.

Line 10 exits the program. This is not entirely needed, but many people like to include an *exit()* where the program should logically end so that they can see that nothing below that line should execute without being called via a function call. It allows the programmer to easily look and say that anything below the *exit()* should be subroutines.

```
11: sub Display_Search_Page{
12:   print header;
13:   print<<HTML;
14:     <HTML><HEAD><TITLE>Product Search</TITLE></HEAD>
15:     <BODY BGCOLOR="#FFFFFF">
16:     <CENTER>
17:     <FORM ACTION="/cgi-bin/tie/product_search.cgi" METHOD="POST">
18:     <H2>Tied Hash Shopping Cart</H2>
19:     <TABLE BORDER="1" CELLSPACING="0">
20:      <TR><TD>
21:        <INPUT TYPE="text" NAME="search_for">
22:      </TD><TD>
23:        <INPUT TYPE="submit" VALUE="Begin Search">
24:      </TD></TR>
25:     </TABLE></FORM>
26:     <P>
27:     <A HREF="/cgi-bin/tie/cart.cgi?action=view"
28:      METHOD="POST">View Cart/Checkout</A>
29:     </CENTER></BODY></HTML>
30: HTML
31: } # End of Display_Search_Page
```

Lines 11–30 are the complete *Display_Search_Page()* subroutine. This subroutine is nothing special; it simply contains the HTML needed to display the search form, and it is printed via our old friend, the here document.

Note that the link on **line 27** does not actually do anything but send us back to the search page again. The cart.cgi program will be modified to act differently depending on what is passed in the action variable.

That wasn't too bad. Everything except **line 8** should be old hat to you by now. Figure 12-1 is what the output of this program should look like once we write the ShopCart.pm module. Note that cart.cgi will not run properly until we create the ShopCart.pm module, which is what we'll cover next.

Figure 12-1   Searching the Shopping Cart

This is nice, but the HTML form points to a file that does not exist yet, and cart.cgi uses a module that has yet to be created. Let's get down to business and create the module that allows us to tie the scalar. Once you have the module created, the cart.cgi program should run and display a page similar to Figure 12-1 without any errors.

Beginning the Module

Now we are ready to start putting together the module that we'll use for this chapter. Although the first part of the module we create deals with colors, we will name the module ShopCart.pm because that will end up being its main purpose.

```
01: package Colors;
02: use Tie::Scalar;
03: sub TIESCALAR{
04:     my ($class, @values) = @_;
05:     bless \@values, $class;
06:     return \@values;
07: }
```

Line 1 tells Perl that this is now the Colors package. This means that for items in this block, they belong to the Colors namespace. This is a way for Perl to keep things organized. If you were to refer to the $class variable, you are referring to the value that is in the Colors namespace. Therefore, if there is another $class variable elsewhere in the program, they are actually entirely different variables to Perl.

Line 2 uses the Tie::Scalar module. Since we don't want to be responsible for defining *all* of the methods for the scalar we are tying, this line brings in the default values for us so that we can redefine only the methods that we want to.

Line 3 begins the TIESCALAR subroutine. Remember that the name must be all upper case, and the name must be TIESCALAR.

Line 4 creates two my variables. $class is a reference to the class itself, and @values is the list of values that was passed when the *tie()* method was invoked.

Line 5 uses the *bless()* function to "bless" the reference to the tied variable. *bless()*ing turns the class into an object. An object is simply a reference that knows which class it belongs to. In our case, it would be the Colors class.

Line 6 returns a *bless()*ed reference to the @values array. So we now have a reference to an array that knows it belongs to the Colors class.

Line 7 closes the TIESCALAR subroutine.

```
08: sub FETCH {
09:     my $self = shift;
10:     push(@$self, shift(@$self));
11:     return $self->[-1];
12: }
13: 1;
```

Line 8 begins the FETCH subroutine. We only need to define this one subroutine because for what we are doing with the data, that is all that will be required.

Line 9 creates a reference to the object and calls it $self. Remember, this is a reference to an array that has been blessed.

Line 10 pushes the value returned by the *shift()* function. This effectively shifts a variable off the end of the array and places it onto the beginning of the array.

Line 11 returns the last element of the array. When you use a negative index, Perl begins at the end of the array and works toward the beginning of the array. By doing this, you can have as many values as you want in the array and always return the last element of the array without having to figure out how many elements are in the array first.

Line 12 ends the FETCH subroutine.

Line 13 returns true. All modules that you import into your program must return a true value.

The credit for this wonderful use of a tied scalar goes to Tom Christiansen and Nathan Torkington, who had an example like this in *The Perl Cookbook*.

It is such an obvious and useful way to use a tied scalar. It had never occurred to tie a scalar for table colors! Their example had a bit more functionality, but we just pulled off the bits that we needed.

That is all there is to our initial ShopCart.pm module. What can we do at this point? Well, you can display the initial page for searching as shown in Figure 12-1. We *still* can't do anything that is truly useful, so we will write a script that will fetch the data from the database for us and return it to the program.

Product Searching

Since this is going to be a shopping cart program, the user must be able to search for items to buy. We'll be creating a separate program that will handle the searching and displaying results for us. All of the other functions will be handled inside of the cart.cgi program. This is a choice that you have to make as a programmer. In our case, we decided that the product search program was distinct enough and large enough to warrant being a separate program.

The product search program will take the value that the user wants to search on and check the descriptions field of our MySQL database to see if it can find any matches. The program will then display a table of the records that matched the search criteria and provide the user with a means to add an item to their cart.

```
01: #!/usr/bin/perl -wT
02: use strict;
03: use DBI;
04: use CGI qw(:standard);
05: use lib qw(.);
06: use ShopCart;
```

Lines 1–6 should be pretty familiar.

Line 5 adds the current directory to the @INC array so that Perl will be able to find the ShopCart module in the directory that the program is in.

Line 6 tells the program to use the ShopCart module.

```
07: my ($Data, $prod_sth, $vend_sth, $color);
08: my $Search_String = param('search_for');
```

Line 7 creates some my variables that will be used throughout the program.

Line 8 creates a variable that reads the value passed from the "search_for" textbox on the HTML page that called the program.

```
09: my $dbh = DBI->connect("DBI:mysql:book","book","addison")
10:            or die "Error: $DBI::errstr\n";
```

Lines 9–10 are a single command on two lines. Here we create a my variable called $dbh and call the *DBI>connect()* method to make a connection to the database. This should be familiar if you read the database chapter.

```
11: tie $color, 'Colors', qw(ffffff e0e0e0);
```

Line 11 is where we *tie()* the scalar variable. We call the *tie()* function followed by the variable to which we are tying the new methods, the name of the class that we are using to tie the variable (case is important) and finally a list of data that is passed to the class. In this case, we are passing two hexidecimal color values that will be used for our table rows. Remember that qw means quote word and will quote each item inside of the parentheses.

```
12: print header;
13: get_products();
14: print_output();
```

Line 12 prints out the HTTP header using the header function from the CGI module.

Line 13 calls the *get_products()* subroutine to get all the products that match what the user searched for.

Line 14 calls the *print_output()* subroutine to display the results to the user.

```
15: sub get_products{
16:     $prod_sth = $dbh->prepare( qq{ SELECT * FROM products
17:                                    WHERE descr LIKE ?
18:                                    ORDER BY name });
```

Line 15 begins the *get_products()* subroutine.

Lines 16–18 are a single statement spanning multiple lines. On **line 16** we are setting the $prod_sth variable. It will hold a reference to the SQL statement that we pass the *$dbh->prepare()* method. Inside the prepare method, we use the *qq()* function that will quote the entire string for us and even let us put quotes inside because it takes care of escaping them for us.

```
19:     $prod_sth->execute("%$Search_String%");
20: }
```

Line 19 executes the SQL statement. In the *execute()* method call, we pass some data. This data replaces the placeholder (?) in the SQL statement on **line 17** . The percent signs on each side of the string are the SQL wildcard characters. We don't want to do an exact match but want to match any portion of the string in the field we are searching, so the wildcards on each side of the text we are looking for help us to do this.

Line 20 ends the *get_products()* subroutine.

```
21: sub get_vendor{
22:     my $vendor = shift;
```

Line 21 begins the *get_vendor()* subroutine.

Line 22 creates a my variable called $vendor that gets whatever value was passed to the function shifted into it. In this case, a vendor number is passed in the function call so that we know which vendor information to get.

```
23:     $vend_sth = $dbh->prepare( qw{ SELECT vname FROM vendors
24:                                       WHERE vend_num = ? });
```

Lines 23–24 are the equivalents of **lines 16–18** except for the vendor table rather than the product table. We are simply getting an SQL statement ready to perform a search on the database table.

```
25:     $vend_sth->execute($vendor);
26: }
```

Line 25 executes the SQL statement from **lines 23–24** .

Line 26 closes the *get_vendor()* subroutine.

```
27: sub print_output{
28:     print <<HTML;
29:      <HTML>
30:       <HEAD><TITLE>Product Search Results</TITLE></HEAD>
31:       <BODY><CENTER>
32:        <TABLE BORDER="1" CELLSPACING="0">
33:         <TR BGCOLOR="#c0c0c0">
34:          <TD><B>Buy</B></TD>
35:          <TD><B>Vendor</B></TD>
36:          <TD><B>Name</B></TD>
37:          <TD><B>Description</B></TD>
38:          <TD><B># in Stock</B></TD>
39:          <TD><B>Price</B></TD>
40:         </TR>
41: HTML
```

Line 27 begins the *print_output()* subroutine.

Line 28 begins a here document that will be used to print out the HTML needed to begin our output page.

Lines 29–40 are simply HTML for the result page.

Line 41 closes the here document.

```
42:      while($Data = $prod_sth->fetchrow_hashref){
43:          get_vendor($Data->{vend_num});
44:          my $vendor = $vend_sth->fetch->[0];
45:          my $cart_link;
```

Line 42 begins a *while()* loop that will loop through all the data that was returned from the query on the product table. We use *fetchrow_hashref()* to get the data, one row at a time. Each time through the while loop, $Data gets populated and holds a reference to the hash containing the data.

Line 43 calls the *get_vendor()* subroutine and passes the vendor number to it.

Line 44 creates a my variable called $vendor and uses the *fetch()* method to get the first element in the resulting array. Since we are only fetching one field in the SQL statement and since the vendor number is the primary key, we should only ever get one value in the array, the 0th element.

Line 45 creates a my variable called $cart_link, which will be used to build up the HTML link needed so the user can add the item to their cart.

```
46:      if($Data->{stock} > 0){
47:          $cart_link  = qq(<A HREF="cart.cgi?);
48:          $cart_link .= qq(action=add&sku=$Data->{sku});
49:          $cart_link .= qq(">Add to Cart</A>);
50:      }
```

Line 46 begins an if . . . else structure that builds up the link to the shopping cart for the current item. We first check to see if there are more than 0 of the item in stock. If there is, then we enter the block and build a clickable link.

Lines 47–49 build the text for the link. The .= is an easy way to concatenate onto a string. It will append the values onto the end of the present string. On line 48 we add an action variable and set it to add and also add an sku variable and set it to the value stored in $Data->{sku}. This passes the data to the cart.cgi program in the form of an HTTP GET. The action and sku variables are not used yet in the cart.cgi program. They will be soon.

Line 50 closes the if portion of the if . . . else block.

```
51:          else{
52:              $cart_link = qq(Add to Cart);
53:          }
```

Lines 51–53 are the else portion of our if . . . else block. This is where we get if there are not any of the current item in stock. If this is the case, we still keep the text the same but do not create a clickable link.

Line 53 ends the if . . . else structure.

```
54:          my $price = sprintf("%.2f", $Data->{price});
```

Line 54 creates a my variable called $price and uses the *sprintf()* function to make it round to two decimal places.

```
55:          print<<HTML;
56:           <TR BGCOLOR="$color">
57:            <TD>$cart_link</TD>
58:            <TD>$vendor</TD>
59:            <TD>$Data->{name}</TD>
60:            <TD>$Data->{descr}</TD>
61:            <TD>$Data->{stock}</TD>
62:            <TD>$price</TD>
63:           </TR>
64: HTML
65:      }
```

Line 55 begins a here document that will print out the current row of data.

Line 56 sets the background color of the table row. This variable $color is our tied scalar! Since we passed it two colors when we tied it, those will be the colors that the table rows will alternate between. If you want ten colors, simply pass ten color values when you tie the variable! Could it be any simpler?

Lines 57–63 print out the individual table cells. Some of the cells use regular variables, and some are using the hash reference $Data to get their data; it all depends on where the data is stored.

Line 64 closes the here document.

Line 65 ends the *while()* loop that began on **line 42,** which prints out a row of data for each matching item.

```
66:      print qq(</TABLE>);
67:      print qq(<P><A HREF="cart.cgi">Link back to cart</A>);
68:      print qq(</CENTER></BODY></HTML>);
```

Lines 66–68 finish off the HTML needed for the search results screen.

```
69:     $vend_sth->finish;
70:     $prod_sth->finish;
71:     $dbh->disconnect;
72: }
```

Lines 69–71 clean up the database statement handles that we created earlier.

Line 71 *disconnects()* from the database.

Line 72 ends the *print_output()* subroutine.

Now that we have something that will produce some output, let's give it a test run and see it in action before we move on to the meat and potatoes of this chapter!

When you call cart.cgi with no arguments, you should get the search screen that looks something like the one in Figure 12-1.

Now enter something to search for, and hit the Begin Search button. Depending on the data that is in the database, you should get something similar to Figure 12-2.

Figure 12-2   Search Results

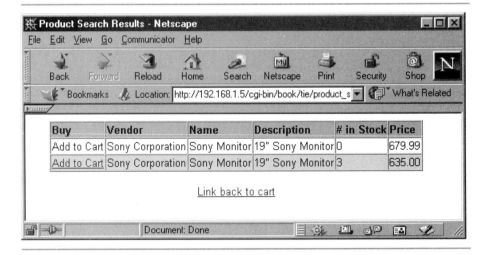

Notice that there is an underlined link for the second monitor, but the first one does not have a link. This is because the number in stock for the first one is 0, so we did not put a link for the item. Also notice that the row colors are different; we are alternating between white and a medium gray. The header field, which is a darker gray, was hand coded to be that color; it does not come from the tied scalar.

Think you are ready to take on the shopping cart project? First we need to determine what features we need in our shopping cart. Here is a list of features that are a good start.

Features

- Session management, so users can come back and cart will still contain items
- Ability to change quantities of items
- Ability to remove items from shopping cart
- Use a tied hash in a cool way

This shopping cart will not be a full-fledged model that you can actually make purchases from because we don't have it integrated with billing and credit card software. However, it is a tool that will help you gain the knowledge needed to tackle larger projects. Before you know it, you'll be ready to code on some major programs!

When deciding whether to choose between covering the cart.cgi program first or the ShopCart.pm module, we chose to cover the cart.cgi program first because with the ShopCart.pm module, we would have been writing a number of functions that we didn't yet know anything about. By covering cart.cgi first, we see *what* is supposed to happen, and then when we get to ShopCart.pm, we'll actually cover *how* we are going to make it happen.

On to the cart.cgi program, which is the program that does the most work. Remember, some of the code in the cart.cgi program relies on code that is not yet in the ShopCart.pm module. This will make some things seem a little strange when we first cover them. Keep in mind that these features will be completed when we write the rest of the ShopCart.pm module.

12.5 The Main Program

```
01: #!/usr/bin/perl -w
02: use strict;
03: use CGI qw(:standard);
04: use lib qw(.);
05: use ShopCart;
06: $|=1;
```

Lines 1–6 are how we begin many of our programs.

Line 4 tells Perl to add the current directory to the @INC array so that it can find the ShopCart module that we load on **line 5** .

Line 6 tells Perl to autoflush the buffers so that data is sent directly to the browser rather than storing it in a buffer until the program finishes running.

```
07: my $action     = param('action');
08: my $Session_ID = Check_Session();
09: my (%cart, $color);
```

Line 7 creates a my variable and uses the param function from the CGI modules to read in the data passed on the URL and named *action*. This is the data that follows the ? in the URL. For example: http://www.mysite.com/cart.cgi?action=view.

Line 8 creates a my variable called $Session_ID and stores the results of a call to *Check_Session()* into it.

Line 9 simply creates a couple my variables that we will use later.

```
10: tie %cart, 'ShopCart';
11: tie $color, 'Colors', qw(ffffff e0e0e0);
```

Line 10 ties the hash %cart to the ShopCart class.

Line 11 ties the scalar $color to the class Colors and passes a list of data (colors) to the class.

```
12: if($action     =~ /view/)    { View_Cart(); }
13:   elsif($action =~ /update/)  { Update_Cart(); }
14:   elsif($action =~ /add/)     { Add_Item(); }
15: else                          { Display_Search_Page(); }
16: exit;
```

Line 12 begins an if . . . elsif . . . else structure that we use to figure out what action the user wanted to perform and then calls the appropriate function. This line checks to see if the user wanted to view the cart.

Lines 13–14 check for *update* or *add,* respectively, and send the user to the appropriate subroutine.

Line 15 sends the user to the *Display_Search_Page()* subroutine if nothing else matched.

Line 16 uses the *exit()* function to stop the program. This is not required, but it is nice to put in so that if you ever need to go back and read the code, you can easily see where the program should end and subroutines should begin. This also can help if you are cutting and pasting code around in a program and some code gets accidentally left outside a subroutine. If this happens, the program would try to execute it, and you will be left trying to figure out why more code is getting executed when the program should have ended.

```
17: sub Add_Item{
18:     my $sku = param('sku');
19:     $cart{$sku} = '1';
20:     Print_Added($sku);
21: } # End of Add_Item
```

Line 17 begins the *Add_Item()* subroutine.

Line 18 creates a my variable called $sku and reads the sku in from the calling Web page with the *param()* function.

Line 19 sets the %cart hash with a key of $sku to a value of 1. Remember that $cart is our tied hash, so some "magical" things are going to occur that don't happen with "normal" hashes. In this case, if there is already an item in the cart with the same sku by the same user, it will add 1 to the quantity rather than setting it to 1.

Line 20 sends the user to the *Print_Added()* subroutine and passes the $sku. This subroutine creates a simple HTML page that lets the user know that they have successfully added the item to their cart.

Line 21 closes the *Add_Item()* subroutine.

```
22: sub Print_Added{
23:     my $sku = shift;
```

Line 22 begins the *Print_Added()* subroutine. This subroutine creates an HTML page that tells the user that they have successfully added an item to their cart. For our example it is not fancy, so feel free to play with the HTML and make the page as elegant as you want.

Line 23 creates a my variable called $sku and shifts the item passed to the subroutine into it.

```
24:     print<<HTML;
25:        <HTML><HEAD><TITLE>Item $sku Added</TITLE></HEAD>
26:         <BODY BGCOLOR="#ffffff">
27:          <CENTER>
28:           <H3>Item $sku added</H3>
29:   [ <A HREF="/cgi-bin/book/tie/cart.cgi">Search Again</A> ]
30:   [ <A HREF="/cgi-bin/book/tie/cart.cgi?action=view">View
        Cart</A> ]
31:          </CENTER>
32:         </BODY>
33:        </HTML>
34: HTML
35: } # End of Print_Added
```

Lines 24–34 are a here document that creates the HTML page.

Line 35 ends the *Print_Added()* subroutine.

```
36: sub Check_Session{
37:     my $session = cookie('session');
```

Line 36 begins the *Check_Session()* subroutine. This subroutine is used to check if the user currently has a session cookie set. If not, it will set one for them. This type of system has a drawback because if a user has cookies turned off, they will not be able to store anything in their shopping cart. If this were a real store site, we could put a notice on the main page telling the user that cookies must be turned on and also display a message telling them to turn cookies on if they still have them off when they try to order something.

Line 37 creates a my variable called $session and then uses *CGI.pm's cookie()* subroutine to see if there is a cookie set named session.

```
38:     if($session){
39:         print header();
40:         return $session;
41:     }
```

Line 38 checks to see if $session contains some data. If it does, the user already has a session cookie set so we enter this block of code.

Line 39 prints the standard HTTP header. The user already has a cookie, so we don't want to set it again.

Line 40 returns the $session variable.

Line 41 closes this portion of the *if()* structure.

```
42:     else{
43:         $session    = time() . $$;
44:         my $cookie  = cookie( -name    => 'session',
45:                               -value   => $session,
46:                               -expires => '3h' );
```

Line 42 is where we go if there is no cookie set.

Line 43 creates a $session variable by taking the current time (in seconds since the epoch) and appending the process ID, or PID, of the current program. This number should always end up unique.

Lines 44–46 create the cookie and store the data in the $cookie variable. For this cookie, we set the name to *session*, the *value* to whatever value was created and stored in the $session variable and set the cookie to expire in three hours. The time you want it to expire is up to you. You can set it to something like one minute (1m) to see what happens when you have items in your cart and the cookie expires.

```
47:          print header( -cookie => $cookie );
48:          return $session;
49:     }
50: } # End of Check_Session
```

Line 47 prints the HTTP header and passes the cookie in the header so that it gets set on the users browser.

Line 48 returns the $session value.

Line 49 closes the if . . . else block.

Line 50 closes the *Check_Session()* subroutine.

```
51: sub Update_Cart{
52:     my $sku = param('sku');
53:     my $qty = param('qty');
```

Line 51 begins the *Update_Cart()* subroutine. This subroutine is used when the user enters a specific number for the quantity of items they want. When a user goes to the "View Cart" page, they can change quantities for items and then update the cart. This feature will become clearer when we have finished and can run the program.

Lines 52–53 create two my variables and read in the data that was passed from the HTML form. The sku and new quantity should have been passed from the form.

```
54:     $cart{$sku} = $qty;
```

Line 54 sets the %cart hash with the key $sku to the new quantity, $qty.

```
55:     View_Cart();
56:     exit;
57: } # End of Update_Cart
```

Line 55 calls the *View_Cart()* subroutine. Once the user has updated the quantity, we make the changes and then send them to the "View Cart" page.

Line 56 calls the *exit()* function to make sure that the program is done. Again, this is not required but can save debugging time later on.

Line 57 closes the *Update_Cart()* subroutine.

```
58: sub Session{
59:     return $Session_ID;
60: } # End of Session
```

Lines 58–60 look like a pretty useless subroutine, but with our tied hash, we need a way to get the $Session_ID from the main program. The $Session_ID variable is a my variable that has a scope within the main program. We need to access this value inside of the ShopCart namespace. This subroutine allows us to do just that because we can call the subroutine from the ShopCart namespace, and the subroutine will return the value to us.

```
61: sub View_Cart{
62:     print <<HTML;
63:      <HTML>
64:       <HEAD><TITLE>Checkout Page</TITLE></HEAD>
65:       <BODY><CENTER>
66:        <TABLE BORDER="1" CELLSPACING="0">
67:         <TR BGCOLOR="#c0c0c0"><TD ALIGN="CENTER">
68:          <H1>Checkout Page</H1>
69:         </TD></TR>
70:         <TR><TD>
71:          <B>Ship To:</B></BR>
72:          Amelia A. Camel<BR>
73:          321 Desert Dr.<BR>
74:          Sahara, CA 90220<BR>
75:         </TD></TR>
76:         <TR><TD>
77:          <TABLE BORDER="1" CELLSPACING="0">
78:           <TR BGCOLOR="#c0c0c0">
79:            <TD><B>SKU</B></TD>
80:            <TD><B>Item</B></TD>
81:            <TD><B>Qty</B></TD>
82:            <TD><B>Price</B></TD>
83:            <TD><B>Total</B></TD>
84:            <TD><B>Update</B></TD>
85:           </TR>
86: HTML
```

Line 61 begins the *View_Cart()* subroutine, which is used to display the contents of the shopping cart to the user.

Lines 62–86 are a here document that create the top of the page and begin the table that is used to display the shopping cart contents. The "Ship To" name is hardcoded in this example, but in the real world you would want to get that information from the user or a user database.

```
87:      my $grand_total = 0;
```

Line 87 creates a my variable called $grand_total and sets it initially to 0. This variable will be used to keep the total cost for all items in the shopping cart.

```
88:      while( my($sku, $qty)  = each %cart){
89:          my($name, $price) = Get_Product_Info($sku);
90:          my $total         = sprintf("%.2f", ($price * $qty));
91:          $price            = sprintf("%.2f", $price);
92:          $grand_total      += $total;
```

Line 88 begins a *while()* loop that cycles through each item in the %cart hash. The key/value pairs are stored in the my variables named $sku and $qty.

Line 89 calls the *Get_Product_Info()* subroutine and passes it the $sku of the current item. The name and price will be returned from this subroutine and stored in the $name and $price my variables.

Line 90 creates a my variable called $total and uses *sprintf()* to round the number to two decimal places. The value that gets set is $price * $qty, which is the total cost for the *current* item.

Line 91 uses the *sprintf()* function to round the $price variable to two decimal places.

Line 92 adds the $total onto the current value of $grand_total.

```
93:          print<<HTML;
94:            <TR BGCOLOR="#$color">
95:             <FORM METHOD="POST">
96:             <INPUT TYPE="hidden" NAME="action" VALUE="update">
97:             <INPUT TYPE="hidden" NAME="sku" VALUE="$sku">
98:             <TD ALIGN="left">
99:               $sku
100:            </TD>
101:            <TD ALIGN="left">$name</TD>
102:            <TD ALIGN="center">
103:             <INPUT TYPE=TEXT SIZE="2" NAME="qty" VALUE="$qty">
104:            </TD>
105:            <TD ALIGN="right">\$$price</TD>
106:            <TD ALIGN="right">\$$total</TD>
107:            <TD ALIGN="center"><INPUT TYPE="SUBMIT"
                                  VALUE="Update"></TD>
108:            </FORM>
109:            </TR>
110: HTML
111:    }
```

Lines 93–110 are a here document that prints out one row of information that contains the data for the current item in the shopping cart. Notice on line 94 that we are using our $color tied scalar. We are also filling in some information dynamically (with variables) on lines 97, 99, 101, 103, 105, and 106.

Line 111 closes the *while()* loop. The program will continue looping until it runs out of items in the shopping cart, and then it will continue onto **line 112**.

```
112:     $grand_total = sprintf("%.2f", $grand_total);
```

Line 112 uses the *sprintf()* function to round the $grand_total to two decimal places. This is done outside of the *while()* loop, so the program should be through all the items in the cart, and the final cost should be stored in the $grand_total variable.

```
113:     print<<HTML;
114:         </TABLE>
115:         <TR><TD ALIGN="RIGHT">
116:          <B>Total:</B> \$$grand_total
117:         </TD></TR>
118:         </TD></TR></TABLE>
119:         <P><A HREF="cart.cgi">Link back to cart</A>
120:         <P>To remove an item, set it's qty to 0 and
121:             click it's "Update" button.
122:         </CENTER></BODY></HTML>
123: HTML
124: } # End of View_Cart
```

Lines 113–123 are a here document that finishes off the HTML page. On **line 116** we display the grand total for the page.

Line 124 closes the *View_Cart()* subroutine.

```
125: sub Get_Product_Info{
126:     my $sku = shift;
127:     my $dbh = DBI->connect("DBI:mysql:book", "book", "addison")
128:               or die "Error: $DBI::errstr\n";
```

Line 125 begins the *Get_Product_Info()* subroutine. This subroutine gets passed the sku of an item, and then it looks up the item in the products database. It returns the items name and price.

Line 126 gets the sku that was passed to the subroutine and stores it in $sku.

Lines 127–128 connect us to the database and store the database handle in $dbh. We also check to make sure that we actually got a connection. If we did not, we generate an error message.

```
129:      my $SQL = "select * from products where sku = ?";
130:      my $sth = $dbh->prepare($SQL);
```

Line 129 creates the SQL statement that we need to fetch the product information and stores the string in $SQL.

Line 130 calls the *prepare()* method on the SQL statement in $SQL and stores the result in $sth.

```
131:      $sth->execute($sku);
```

Line 131 calls the *execute()* function and passes $sku to it so that it can replace the placeholder (?) in the SQL statement from **line 129** .

```
132:      my $p     = $sth->fetchrow_hashref;
133:      my $price = $p->{price};
134:      my $name  = $p->{name};
```

Line 132 creates a my variable called $p, which we will use as a pointer. We set it to the value returned by the *fetchrow_hashref()* call. This will create a pointer to the data returned by *fetchrow_hashref()*. Since we searched on the sku, and the sku is unique, we should always get only one value. Therefore, we don't have to put the *fetchrow_hashref()* inside of a loop.

Lines 133–134 get the values of price and name and store them in the $price and $name my variables.

```
135:      $sth->finish();
136:      $dbh->disconnect();
```

Line 135 calls the *finish()* method to release the data in the statement handle.

Line 136 calls the *disconnect()* method to disconnect us from the database.

```
137:      return ($name, $price);
138: } # End of Get_Product_Info
```

Line 137 returns the $name and $price.

Line 138 closes the *Get_Product_Info()* subroutine.

```
139: sub Display_Search_Page{
140:    print<<HTML;
141:       <HTML><HEAD><TITLE>Product Search</TITLE></HEAD>
142:       <BODY BGCOLOR="#FFFFFF">
143:       <CENTER>
144:        <FORM ACTION="/cgi-bin/book/tie/product_search.cgi"
METHOD="POST">
145:        <H2>Tied Hash Shopping Cart</H2>
146:        <TABLE BORDER="1" CELLSPACING="0">
147:         <TR><TD>
148:           <INPUT TYPE="text" NAME="search_for">
149:         </TD><TD>
150:           <INPUT TYPE="submit" VALUE="Begin Search">
151:         </TD></TR>
152:        </TABLE></FORM>
153:        <P>
154:        <A HREF="/cgi-bin/book/tie/cart.cgi?action=view"
155:         METHOD="POST">View Cart/Checkout</A>
156:       </CENTER></BODY></HTML>
157: HTML
158: } # End of Display_Search_Page
```

Lines 139–158 are simply a here document that displays the search page. The search page is the default page that is displayed if nothing was passed on the URL of the cart.cgi call. That is it for the cart.cgi program. Now that the cart.cgi program is done, we have just one more thing to finish to make our shopping cart functional! It has been a lot of work so far, but when you are dealing with something as complex as a shopping cart, things can get pretty complex. Overall, we have less than 350 lines of code, and over 80 of those lines are dedicated to HTML output, not Perl! (Put that in your Java pipe and smoke it.)

12.6 Finishing the ShopCart Module

When this chapter began, we created a small module called ShopCart.pm. We used that module to hold the subroutines for our tied scalar example. Now we are going to rearrange things in the module and add a bunch of code so that we can handle a hash that is tied to a database.

```
01: use Tie::Hash;
02: use DBI;
```

Lines 1–2 bring in some modules that we will need. We are using the Tie::Hash module because we don't want to have to write *all* of the methods for our hash, just the ones we want to override. We use DBI for our database access. Notice that the module does not need to begin with the #!/usr/bin/perl line. A module is not executable by itself but must be called by another Perl program.

```
03: my $dbh = DBI->connect("DBI:mysql:book","book","addison")
04:               or die "Error: $DBI::errstr\n";
05: my @KEYS;
```

Lines 3–4 connect us to the database and store the database handle in $dbh.

Line 5 declares a my variable called @KEYS.

```
06: package ShopCart;
07: @ISA = qw(Tie::StdHash);
```

Line 6 creates a new package called ShopCart. This will create a new namespace for all the methods below it.

Line 7 tells Perl that we want to inherit the methods from the Tie::StdHash module.

```
08: sub STORE {
09:     my ($self, $key, $val) = @_;
```

Line 8 creates the STORE method for our tied hash.

Line 9 stores the values from the @_ array into their respective variables. $self is a reference to the package itself, $key is the key that was passed and $val contains the value that was passed.

```
10:     my $modified = time();
11:     my $session  = main::Session();
12:     my $existed  = $self->EXISTS($key); # Already exist?
13:     my $action   = main::param('action');
14:     my $new_qty;
```

Line 10 creates a my variable called $modified and stores the current time in it. We will add this to the database to make it easier to clean up data that does not need to be stored in the database anymore.

Line 11 creates our $session variable.

Notice that the function from which we get the value is called like *main::Session()*. The reason for this is that we are now in the ShopCart namespace, so if we just call the *Session()* subroutine, Perl would look for the *Session()* subroutine in the ShopCart namespace—and it doesn't exist there because it exists in the main namespace. By default, programs run in the main namespace, so specifying package main is unnecessary in your Perl programs. Preceding a subroutine with ::namespace is how you can get to them if they are in a different namespace.

Line 12 creates a my variable called $existed and calls the *$self->EXISTS ($key)()* method on it. By doing this, we call the EXISTS subroutine inside of the current package. We will be creating the EXISTS subroutine in a little bit.

Line 13 creates a my variable called $action and sets it to the value that is returned from the *param('action')()* function call, which is in the main namespace.

Line 14 simply creates a my variable that we'll use later.

```
15:      unless($val){
16:          $self->DELETE($key);
17:          return;
18:      }
```

Line 15 uses the *unless()* function to check and see if $val contains anything. unless is the same as "if not." So in this case, we are checking to see if $val contains 0.

Line 16 calls the *$self->DELETE($key)()* method, which will delete the record matching $key.

Line 17 returns us to where we called the subroutine.

Line 18 closes the subroutine block.

```
19:      if($existed) {
20:          if($action eq "update"){
21:              $new_qty = $val;
22:          }
23:          else{
24:              $new_qty = $existed + $val;
25:          }
```

Line 19 begins an if . . . else block that checks to see if the $key already existed. If it did, we enter the block.

Line 20 begins another if . . . else block. This one checks to see if the value of $action is "update." If it is, on **line 21,** we set the new value of the hash element to the value that the user entered.

Line 22 closes the first part of the if . . . else block.

Line 23 begins the *else()* portion. We enter this block if the $action was not "update." This means that the user clicked on the link to add the item to the shopping cart.

Line 24 creates the $new_qty by adding $val to the currently existing value, $existed. When a user adds an item to their cart by clicking the link on the search results screen, a value of 1 is sent. So we are simply adding 1 to the existing quantity.

Line 25 closes the current if . . . else block.

```
26:          my $sth = $dbh->prepare( qq{ UPDATE cart
27:                                       SET     qty = '$new_qty'
28:                                       WHERE   session = ?
29:                                       AND     sku = ? });
```

Lines 26–29 create and prepare the SQL statement needed to update the cart table.

Remember when we created a separate $SQL variable and just passed that to the *$dhh->prepare()* statement? Well, with Perl there's more than one way to do it (TMTOWTDI). By using the qq function, our string gets quoted for us, and we don't have to worry about escaping any special characters.

```
30:          $sth->execute($session, $key);
31:       }
```

Line 30 executes the SQL statement and passes the $session and $key variables. These are important because the $session variable tells us which user in the database we need to work with, and the $key variable tells us which item for that user we need to work on.

Line 31 closes the if portion of the if . . . else block.

```
32:       else{
33:          my $sth = $dbh->prepare( qq{ INSERT INTO cart
34:                                       VALUES (?,?,?,?) });
```

Line 32 begins the *else()* portion of the if . . . else block.

Lines 33–34 create and prepare the SQL needed to insert a new item into the shopping cart. We use four placeholders to represent the values that we will be passing when we *execute()* the SQL statement.

```
35:            $sth->execute($key, $val, $modified, $session);
36:        } # End of if . . . else
37: } # End of STORE
```

Line 35 executes the SQL statement and passes the key, value, modification time, and session ID.

Line 36 ends the current if . . . else block.

Line 37 ends the *STORE()* subroutine.

```
38: sub EXISTS{
39:     my($self, $key) = @_;
40:     my $session     = main::Session();
```

Line 38 begins the *EXIST()* subroutine. This subroutine returns 0 if the value did not exist or something other than 0 if it did exist.

Line 39 creates our $self and $key my variables.

Line 40 creates the $session my variable and populates it with the return result of the *main::Session()* subroutine.

```
41:     my $sth = $dbh->prepare( qq{ SELECT qty FROM cart
42:                                  WHERE   session = ?
43:                                  AND     sku = ? });
```

Lines 41–43 create and prepare the SQL statement that will attempt to see if there is any qty data for the record we are searching for.

```
44:     $sth->execute($session, $key);
45:     my $temp = $sth->fetch;
```

Line 44 executes the SQL statement. $session and $key replace the two placeholders in the SQL statement.

Line 45 fetches the data from the database and returns an array reference which gets stored in $temp.

```
46:     return $temp->[0] ? $temp->[0] : 0;
47: } # End of EXISTS
```

Line 46 uses the trinary operator to determine the return value. Perl evaluates the value to the left of the ?. If it is true/non-zero, the first value gets returned. If it is false/zero, then the second value gets returned.

Line 47 closes the *EXISTS()* subroutine.

```
48: sub DELETE{
49:     my ($self, $key) = @_;
50:     my $session      = main::Session();
```

Line 48 begins the *DELETE()* subroutine.

Line 49 creates our $self and *$key my()* variables.

Line 50 creates our *$session my()* variable and populates it with the value returned from the *main::Session()* subroutine.

```
51:     my $sth = $dbh->prepare( qq{ DELETE FROM cart
52:                                  WHERE  session = ?
53:                                  AND    sku = ? });
```

Lines 51–53 create and prepare the SQL statement to delete an item from the shopping cart.

```
54:     $sth->execute($session, $key);
55: } # End of DELETE
```

Line 54 executes the SQL statement to delete the item from the shopping cart.

Line 55 closes the *DELETE()* subroutine.

```
56: sub FETCH{
57:     my ($self, $key) = @_;
58:     my $session      = main::Session();
```

Line 56 begins the *FETCH()* subroutine.

Line 57 creates our $self and $key my variables.

Line 58 creates our $session my variable and populates it with the value returned from the *main::Session()* subroutine.

```
59:     my $sth = $dbh->prepare( qq{ SELECT qty FROM cart
60:                                  WHERE session = ?
61:                                  AND sku = ? });
```

Lines 59–61 create and prepare the SQL statement to fetch an item from the cart database.

```
62:     $sth->execute($session, $key);
63:     my $temp = $sth->fetch;
```

Line 62 executes the SQL statement to get an item from the cart database.

Line 63 creates a my variable called $temp that holds a pointer to the date returned by the *$sth->fetch()* function.

```
64:      return $temp->[0];
65: } # End of FETCH
```

Line 64 returns the value stored at $temp->[0]. Since we only requested the qty in the SQL statement, there will only be one item returned in the array that *fetch()* creates. So if a value is returned, that is how many are currently in the shopping cart. If nothing is returned, there is nothing in the cart for that key.

Line 65 closes the FETCH subroutine.

```
66: sub FIRSTKEY{
67:      my $self    = shift;
68:      my $session = main::Session();
```

Line 66 begins the *FIRSTKEY()* subroutine. This subroutine is used to get the first key in the hash.

Line 67 creates a my variable that points to the current package.

Line 68 creates our session variable and populates it.

```
69:      my $sth     = $dbh->prepare( qq{ SELECT qty, sku
70:                                       FROM   cart
71:                                       WHERE  session = ? });
```

Lines 69–71 create and prepare the SQL statement to select all of the qty and sku from the cart for all items matching the current session.

```
72:      $sth->execute($session);
```

Line 72 executes the SQL statement and passes the current $session value to the SQL statement.

```
73:      $self->{DATA}  = $sth->fetchall_arrayref;
74:      $self->{INDEX} = 0;
75:      my $val        = $self->{DATA}->[0][0];
76:      my $key        = $self->{DATA}->[0][1];
```

Line 73 creates a hash element with a key named DATA that stores a reference to the data returned by the *fetchall_arrayref()* function call.

Line 74 creates a hash element with a key named INDEX and initializes it to 0. We will be using this to keep track of an arrays indexes later on.

Line 75 creates a my variable called $val and stores the value from $self->{DATA}[0][0] in it.

This is where things get a little tricky. *fetchall_arrayref()* returns a reference to an array and that array contains arrays that make up the data returned by the SQL statement. So by saying $self->{DATA}[0][0], we are saying the first item of the first element in the array pointed to by $self{DATA}. And the $self->{DATA}[0][1] means the second item of the first element in the array pointed to by $self{DATA}.

Line 76 creates a my variable called $key and stores it in the value from $self->{DATA}[0][1] in it.

```
77:      return if !@{$self->{DATA}};  # No data, return.
```

Line 77 will cause the subroutine to return if there was no data. There is no point in going on if there is no data, so we don't.

```
78:      foreach(@{$self->{DATA}}){
79:          my $key = $_->[1];
80:          my $val = $_->[0];
81:          $self->{LIST}{$key} = $val;
82:      }
```

Line 78 begins a *foreach()* loop that will go through all of the records stored in the array referenced by $self->{DATA}

Line 79 creates a my variable called $key and sets it to the second element of the current record.

Line 80 creates a my variable called $val and sets it to the first element of the current record.

Line 81 creates a hash called $self->{LIST} and puts the current key and value into it. Don't let the $self->{LIST}{$key} get you confused. $self->{LIST} is just like a regular variable name, such as $foo{$key}, but in this case it is a dynamically generated variable.

Line 82 closes the *foreach()* loop.

```
83:      @KEYS              = keys ( %{$self->{LIST}} );
```

Line 83 creates an array called @KEYS that contains all the keys that are in the hash that we just created.

```
84:      $self->{FIRSTKEY} = $key;
85:      return ($val, $key);
86: } # End of FIRSTKEY
```

Line 84 sets $self->{FIRSTKEY} to the value in $key.

Line 85 returns the key and value.

Line 86 ends the *FIRSTKEY()* subroutine.

```
87: sub NEXTKEY{
88:      my $self    = shift;
89:      my $lastkey = shift;
```

Line 87 begins the *NEXTKEY()* subroutine. This subroutine fetches the next key in the hash.

Line 88 creates the $self my variable.

Line 89 creates the $lastkey variable and shifts it from @_. This value is automagically passed by Perl to the subroutine.

```
90:      $key = $KEYS[$self->{INDEX}++];
```

Line 90 takes the next value from the @KEYS array and stores it in the $key variable. The ++ on the end of the $self->{INDEX} will increment the $self->{INDEX} variable so the next time through, you get the next item. ++ is kind of neat because it not only increments but also returns the current value before the item gets incremented.

```
91:      next if($key eq $self->{FIRSTKEY});
92:      return($key);
93: } # End of NEXTKEY
```

Line 91 causes the program to go to the next item in the array. We do this because if the current key is the same as the $self->{FIRSTKEY}, then we don't want to return it again.

Line 92 returns the $key for the current value.

Line 93 ends the *NEXTKEY()* subroutine.

```
94: sub DESTROY {
95:      $dbh->disconnect();
96: } # End of DESTROY
```

Lines 94–96 are the *DESTROY()* subroutine. You must remember to clean up your database connections, so this subroutine closes our connection to the database.

```
97: package Colors;
```

Line 97 creates a different package. Whatever is below this line is in the Colors package—until another package is encountered. Remember that a package is really just a namespace in Perl.

```
98: use Tie::Scalar;
```

Line 98 tells Perl to use the Tie::Scalar module. This will import the basic functionality for a scalar. We are free to override only the methods we choose instead of all of the methods.

```
 99: sub TIESCALAR{
100:     my ($class, @values) = @_;
101:     bless \@values, $class;
102:     return \@values;
103: }
```

Line 99 begins the *TIESCALAR()* subroutine. Remember that the name must be all upper case and the name must be TIESCALAR.

Line 100 creates two my variables. $class is a reference to the class itself, and @values is the list of values that was passed when the *tie()* method was invoked.

Line 101 uses the *bless()* function to "bless" the reference to the tied variable. *bless()*ing turns the class into an object. An object is simply a reference that knows which class it belongs to. In our case, it would be the Colors class.

Line 102 returns a *bless()*ed reference to the @values array. So we now have a reference to an array that knows it belongs to the Colors class.

Line 103 closes the *TIESCALAR()* subroutine.

```
104: sub FETCH {
105:     my $self = shift;
106:     push(@$self, shift(@$self));
107:     return $self->[-1];
108: }
109: 1;
```

Line 104 begins the *FETCH()* subroutine. We only need to define this one other subroutine because for what we are doing with the data, that is all that will be required. We are only fetching data from this scalar, so we don't need to store data.

Line 105 creates a reference to the object. Remember, this is a reference to an array that has been blessed.

Line 106 pushes the value returned by the *shift()* function. This effectively shifts a variable off the end of the array and places it onto the beginning of the array.

Line 107 returns the last element of the array.

When you use a negative index, Perl begins at the end of the array and works toward the beginning of the array. You can have as many values as you want in the array and always return the last element of the array without having to figure out how many elements are in the array first.

Line 108 ends the *FETCH()* subroutine.

Line 109 returns true. Remember that all modules that you import into your program must return a true value.

12.7 Running the Program

Finally! We have the module created. We have the shopping cart and product search programs listed. Now let's take a look at the application. The main program that needs to be executed is the cart.cgi program. When you first start cart.cgi, you will get a screen that looks similar to Figure 12-1. Enter some text to search on. I searched on the word *monitor* and got a screen that looked like Figure 12-3. Your results will be different depending on what data you entered into the database.

Figure 12-3   **Search Results**

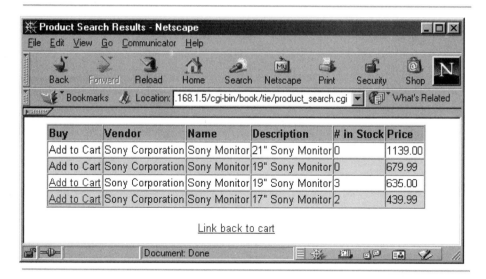

This called our product_search.cgi program, and it searched the database and returned the results in a nice table. The table rows alternate colors because we used our $color tied scalar as the color for the table row. Now you can add an item to your shopping cart by clicking on one of the links under the "Buy" column header. The URL of the links looks like this.

http://www.mysite.com/cgi-bin/cart.cgi?action=add&sku=52973

You can see that it calls the cart.cgi program and passes some data in the form of a GET to the program. Here we passed an action of add and a sku of 52973. This will tell the cart.cgi program to add item 52973 to the shopping cart.

Once you have clicked on the link, the item is added to your shopping cart and you get a screen that should look like Figure 12-4. This simply tells the user that the item was added to the cart. Now you can either click the "Search Again" link, or the "View Cart" link. Try adding a few more items to the cart before you click the "View Cart" link.

Figure 12-4   Add Item Confirmation Page

Once you have a few items in your cart, click on the "View Cart" link.
You should see a page similar to Figure 12-5.

Figure 12-5   Cart Checkout Page

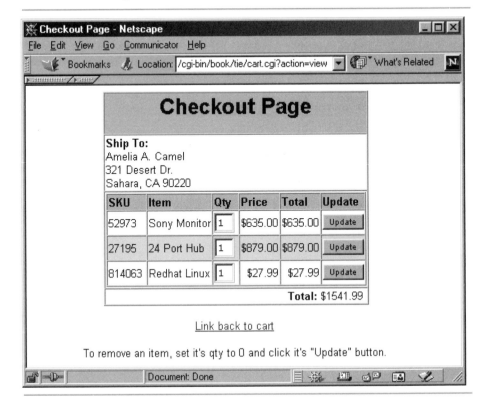

If you look at the URL, it should now look like this:

http://www.mysite.com/cgi-bin/cart.cgi?action=view

We called the cart.cgi program again, but this time we changed the action to view. This will cause a different section of the cart.cgi program to run. The output is like an order review page—the name is hardcoded into this one, but on a real site that would be dynamic also.

Notice that the program seemed to "remember" what you had in your shopping cart. This is because we set the session cookie on the browser, and the session is unique, so only you have that session number.

Change one of the items to a different quantity, then press the "Update" button. The screen should refresh, and the totals should change to reflect the new quantity. The screen will still look like Figure 12-5 except for the quantity. When we did that, we sent a value to the tied hash. The tie functions checked to see if that item already existed in the shopping cart, and since it did, it updated the record to reflect the new quantity.

Now set one of the values to 0 and hit the "Update" button. Again the screen will refresh, but this time the item that you set to a quantity of 0 is gone! When you did this, it caused the tie subroutines to execute the *DELETE()* function.

When you add things to the cart or change quantities, the cart.cgi program will go back to the methods that we created to manage the tied variable. You can even shut down your browser and come back to the page and your items will remain in the cart as long as the cookie still exists on your system. That is about it for functionality. We've accomplished our objectives for this project.

Features

■ Session management, so users can come back and cart will still contain items

■ Ability to change quantities of items

■ Ability to remove items from shopping cart

■ Use a tied hash in a cool way

Not too bad for a chapter!

12.8 Wrapping It Up

Some things you may want to consider when creating something like this for a real site.

■ You will want to create a script and set it up as a cron event to remove old entries from the database.

■ Create a way for users to enter their name and address information.

■ Make the view page display the user's name dynamically.

■ Make the user screens match your site's layout and design.

12.9 Program Listings

Listing 12-1 **cart.cgi**

```
01: #!/usr/bin/perl -w
02: # cart.cgi
03: use strict;
04: use CGI qw(:standard);
05: use lib qw(.);
06: use ShopCart;
07: $|=1;
08: my $action    = param('action');
09: my $Session_ID = Check_Session();
10: my (%cart, $color);
11: tie %cart, 'ShopCart';
12: tie $color, 'Colors', qw(ffffff e0e0e0);
13: if($action     =~ /view/)     { View_Cart(); }
14:   elsif($action =~ /update/)   { Update_Cart(); }
15:   elsif($action =~ /add/)      { Add_Item(); }
16: else                          { Display_Search_Page(); }
17: exit;
18: sub Add_Item{
19:     my $sku = param('sku');
20:     $cart{$sku} = '1';
21:     Print_Added($sku);
22: }
23: sub Print_Added{
24:     my $sku = shift;
25:     print<<HTML;
26:      <HTML><HEAD><TITLE>Item $sku Added</TITLE></HEAD>
27:       <BODY BGCOLOR="#ffffff">
28:        <CENTER>
29:         <H3>Item $sku added</H3>
30:   [ <A HREF="/cgi-bin/book/tie/cart.cgi">Search Again</A> ]
31:   [ <A HREF="/cgi-bin/book/tie/cart.cgi?action=view">View Cart</A> ]
32:         </CENTER>
33:        </BODY>
34:       </HTML>
35: HTML
36: } # End of Print_Added
37: sub Check_Session{
38:     my $session = cookie('session');
39:     if($session){
40:        print header();
41:        return $session;
42:     }
```

(continued)

```
43:     else{
44:         $session    = time() . $$;
45:         my $cookie = cookie( -name    => 'session',
46:                                -value  => $session,
47:                                -expires => '3h' );
48:         print header( -cookie => $cookie );
49:         return $session;
50:     }
51: } # End of Check_Session
52: sub Update_Cart{
53:     my $sku = param('sku');
54:     my $qty = param('qty');
55:     $cart{$sku} = $qty;
56:     View_Cart();
57:     exit;
58: } # End of Update_Cart
59: sub Session{
60:     return $Session_ID;
61: } # End of Session
62: sub View_Cart{
63:     print <<HTML;
64:      <HTML>
65:       <HEAD><TITLE>Checkout Page</TITLE></HEAD>
66:        <BODY><CENTER>
67:         <TABLE BORDER="1" CELLSPACING="0">
68:         <TR BGCOLOR="#c0c0c0"><TD ALIGN="CENTER">
69:          <H1>Checkout Page</H1>
70:         </TD></TR>
71:         <TR><TD>
72:          <B>Ship To:</B></BR>
73:          Amelia A. Camel<BR>
74:          321 Desert Dr.<BR>
75:          Sahara, CA 90220<BR>
76:         </TD></TR>
77:         <TR><TD>
78:          <TABLE BORDER="1" CELLSPACING="0">
79:           <TR BGCOLOR="#c0c0c0">
80:            <TD><B>SKU</B></TD>
81:            <TD><B>Item</B></TD>
82:            <TD><B>Qty</B></TD>
83:            <TD><B>Price</B></TD>
84:            <TD><B>Total</B></TD>
85:            <TD><B>Update</B></TD>
86:           </TR>
```

(continued)

```
 87: HTML
 88:     my $grand_total = 0;
 89:     while(my($sku, $qty)  = each %cart){
 90:         my($name, $price) = Get_Product_Info($sku);
 91:         my $total          = sprintf("%.2f", ($price * $qty));
 92:         $price             = sprintf("%.2f", $price);
 93:         $grand_total      += $total;
 94:         print<<HTML;
 95:           <TR BGCOLOR="#$color">
 96:            <FORM METHOD="POST">
 97:            <INPUT TYPE="hidden" NAME="action" VALUE="update">
 98:            <INPUT TYPE="hidden" NAME="sku" VALUE="$sku">
 99:            <TD ALIGN="left">
100:               $sku
101:            </TD>
102:            <TD ALIGN="left">$name</TD>
103:            <TD ALIGN="center">
104:             <INPUT TYPE=TEXT SIZE="2" NAME="qty" VALUE="$qty">
105:            </TD>
106:            <TD ALIGN="right">\$$price</TD>
107:            <TD ALIGN="right">\$$total</TD>
108:            <TD ALIGN="center"><INPUT TYPE="SUBMIT"
                                    VALUE="Update"></TD>
109:           </FORM>
110:          </TR>
111: HTML
112:     }
113:     $grand_total = sprintf("%.2f", $grand_total);
114:     print<<HTML;
115:         </TABLE>
116:         <TR><TD ALIGN="RIGHT">
117:          <B>Total:</B> \$$grand_total
118:        </TD></TR>
119:        </TD></TR></TABLE>
120:        <P><A HREF="cart.cgi">Link back to cart</A>
121:        <P>To remove an item, set it's qty to 0 and
122:            click it's "Update" button.
123:        </CENTER></BODY></HTML>
124: HTML
125: }
126: sub Get_Product_Info{
127:     my $sku = shift;
128:     my $dbh = DBI->connect("DBI:mysql:book", "book", "addison")
129:                 or die "Error: $DBI::errstr\n";
```

(continued)

```
130:     my $SQL = "select * from products where sku = ?";
131:     my $sth = $dbh->prepare($SQL);
132:     $sth->execute($sku);
133:     my $p     = $sth->fetchrow_hashref;
134:     my $price = $p->{price};
135:     my $name  = $p->{name};
136:     $sth->finish();
137:     $dbh->disconnect();
138:     return ($name, $price);
139: }
140: sub Display_Search_Page{
141:   print<<HTML;
142:     <HTML><HEAD><TITLE>Product Search</TITLE></HEAD>
143:     <BODY BGCOLOR="#FFFFFF">
144:     <CENTER>
145:      <FORM ACTION="/cgi-bin/book/tie/product_search.cgi"
METHOD="POST">
146:      <H2>Tied Hash Shopping Cart</H2>
147:      <TABLE BORDER="1" CELLSPACING="0">
148:       <TR><TD>
149:         <INPUT TYPE="text" NAME="search_for">
150:       </TD><TD>
151:         <INPUT TYPE="submit" VALUE="Begin Search">
152:       </TD></TR>
153:      </TABLE></FORM>
154:      <P>
155:      <A HREF="/cgi-bin/book/tie/cart.cgi?action=view"
156:       METHOD="POST">View Cart/Checkout</A>
157:     </CENTER></BODY></HTML>
158: HTML
159: } # End of Display_Search_Page
```

Listing 12-2 **product_search.cgi**

```
01: #!/usr/bin/perl -wT
02: # product_search.cgi
03: use strict;
04: use DBI;
05: use CGI qw(:standard);
06: use lib qw(.);
07: use ShopCart;
08: my ($Data, $prod_sth, $vend_sth, $color);
09: my $Search_String = param('search_for');
10: my $dbh = DBI->connect("DBI:mysql:book","book","addison")
11:             or die "Error: $DBI::errstr\n";
12: tie $color, 'Colors', qw(ffffff e0e0e0);
13: print header;
14: get_products();
15: print_output();
16: sub get_products{
17:     $prod_sth = $dbh->prepare( qq{ SELECT * FROM products
18:                                    WHERE descr LIKE ?
19:                                    ORDER BY name });
20:     $prod_sth->execute("%$Search_String%");
21: }
22: sub get_vendor{
23:     my $vendor = shift;
24:     $vend_sth  = $dbh->prepare( qq{ SELECT vname FROM vendors
25:                                     WHERE vend_num = ? });
26:     $vend_sth->execute($vendor);
27: }
28: sub print_output{
29:     print <<HTML;
30:      <HTML>
31:       <HEAD><TITLE>Product Search Results</TITLE></HEAD>
32:        <BODY><CENTER>
33:         <TABLE BORDER="1" CELLSPACING="0">
34:          <TR BGCOLOR="#c0c0c0">
35:           <TD><B>Buy</B></TD>
36:           <TD><B>Vendor</B></TD>
37:           <TD><B>Name</B></TD>
38:           <TD><B>Description</B></TD>
39:           <TD><B># in Stock</B></TD>
40:           <TD><B>Price</B></TD>
41:          </TR>
42: HTML
43:     while($Data = $prod_sth->fetchrow_hashref){
44:         get_vendor($Data->{vend_num});                    (continued)
```

```perl
45:          my $vendor = $vend_sth->fetch->[0];
46:          my $cart_link;
47:          if($Data->{stock} > 0){
48:              $cart_link  = qq(<A HREF="cart.cgi?);
49:              $cart_link .= qq(action=add&sku=$Data->{sku});
50:              $cart_link .= qq(">Add to Cart</A>);
51:          }
52:          else{
53:              $cart_link = qq(Add to Cart);
54:          }
55:          my $price = sprintf("%.2f", $Data->{price});
56:          print<<HTML;
57:           <TR BGCOLOR="$color">
58:             <TD>$cart_link</TD>
59:             <TD>$vendor</TD>
60:             <TD>$Data->{name}</TD>
61:             <TD>$Data->{descr}</TD>
62:             <TD>$Data->{stock}</TD>
63:             <TD>$price</TD>
64:           </TR>
65: HTML
66:      }
67:      print qq(</TABLE>);
68:      print qq(<P><A HREF="cart.cgi">Link back to cart</A>);
69:      print qq(</CENTER></BODY></HTML>);
70:      $vend_sth->finish;
71:      $prod_sth->finish;
72:      $dbh->disconnect;
73: }
```

Listing 12-3   ShopCart.pm

```
01: use Tie::Hash;
02: use DBI;
03: my $dbh = DBI->connect("DBI:mysql:book","book","addison")
04:           or die "Error: $DBI::errstr\n";
05: my @KEYS;
06: package ShopCart;
07: @ISA = qw(Tie::StdHash);
08: sub STORE {
09:     my ($self, $key, $val) = @_;
10:     my $modified = time();
11:     my $session  = main::Session();
12:     my $existed  = $self->EXISTS($key); # Already exist?
13:     my $action   = main::param('action');
14:     my $new_qty;
15:     unless($val){
16:         $self->DELETE($key);
17:         return;
18:     }
19:     if($existed) {
20:         if($action eq "update"){
21:             $new_qty = $val;
22:         }
23:         else{
24:             $new_qty = $existed + $val;
25:         }
26:         my $sth = $dbh->prepare( qq{ UPDATE cart
27:                                      SET   qty = '$new_qty'
28:                                      WHERE session = ?
29:                                      AND   sku = ? });
30:         $sth->execute($session, $key);
31:     }
32:     else{
33:         my $sth = $dbh->prepare( qq{ INSERT INTO cart
34:                                      VALUES (?,?,?,?) });
35:         $sth->execute($key, $val, $modified, $session);
36:     } # End of if . . . else
37: } # End of STORE
38: sub EXISTS{
39:     my($self, $key) = @_;
40:     my $session     = main::Session();
41:     my $sth = $dbh->prepare( qq{ SELECT qty FROM cart
42:                                  WHERE session = ?
43:                                  AND   sku = ? });
```

(continued)

```
44:      $sth->execute($session, $key);
45:      my $temp = $sth->fetch;
46:      return $temp->[0] ? $temp->[0] : 0;
47: } # End of EXISTS
48: sub DELETE{
49:      my ($self, $key) = @_;
50:      my $session      = main::Session();
51:      my $sth = $dbh->prepare( qq{ DELETE FROM cart
52:                                   WHERE  session = ?
53:                                   AND    sku = ? });
54:      $sth->execute($session, $key);
55: } # End of DELETE
56: sub FETCH{
57:      my ($self, $key) = @_;
58:      my $session      = main::Session();
59:      my $sth = $dbh->prepare( qq{ SELECT qty FROM cart
60:                                   WHERE session = ?
61:                                   AND sku = ? });
62:      $sth->execute($session, $key);
63:      my $temp = $sth->fetch;
64:      return $temp->[0];
65: } # End of FETCH
66: sub FIRSTKEY{
67:      my $self     = shift;
68:      my $session = main::Session();
69:      my $sth      = $dbh->prepare( qq{ SELECT qty, sku
70:                                        FROM   cart
71:                                        WHERE  session = ? });
72:      $sth->execute($session);
73:      $self->{DATA}   = $sth->fetchall_arrayref;
74:      $self->{INDEX} = 0;
75:      my $val         = $self->{DATA}->[0][0];
76:      my $key         = $self->{DATA}->[0][1];
77:      return if !@{$self->{DATA}};  # No data, return.
78:      foreach(@{$self->{DATA}}){
79:          my $key = $_->[1];
80:          my $val = $_->[0];
81:          $self->{LIST}{$key} = $val;
82:      }
83:      @KEYS            = keys ( %{$self->{LIST}} );
84:      $self->{FIRSTKEY} = $key;
85:      return ($val, $key);
86: } # End of FIRSTKEY
```

(continued)

```
87: sub NEXTKEY{
88:     my $self    = shift;
89:     my $lastkey = shift;
90:     $key = $KEYS[$self->{INDEX}++];
91:     next if($key eq $self->{FIRSTKEY});
92:     return($key);
93: } # End of NEXTKEY
94: sub DESTROY {
95:     $dbh->disconnect();
96: } # End of DESTROY
97: package Colors;
98: use Tie::Scalar;
99: sub TIESCALAR{
100:     my ($class, @values) = @_;
101:     return bless \@values, $class;
102: }
103: sub FETCH {
104:     my $self = shift;
105:     push(@$self, shift(@$self));
106:     return $self->[-1];
107: }
108: 1;
```

13 Chapter

Embedding Perl in HTML with Mason

13.1 Introduction

Mason is a tool for embedding Perl inside of your HTML documents and for creating sites based on components. Mason runs on the Apache Web server with mod_perl installed. Using Mason allows you to build powerful, dynamic Web sites with minimum effort.

Mason uses a "component" architecture in which you build small pieces of Perl code that are embedded into the HTML and then piece together the Web page from these components. With Mason, components can call other components that, in turn, call other components. For example, you can have a component for the header, the footer, a couple for navigation, and one for the body. Then to display a page, you create an HTML file that pieces the components together. Mason has a component called an autohandler that applies a certain style to all the pages in a directory. You can also easily make a custom error message instead of showing your users a boring 404 error.

Mason has a lot of exciting possibilities. Recently Brent chose Mason to develop a new project, and he was thoroughly impressed with it. Brent's project will also be spun off and "co-branded" for other owners. Co-branding is when the look of a site is changed to match the owner's designs but the functionality is kept the same. Co-branding with the Mason solution will be very easy.

In fact, when Brent got the HTML from the design firm, he had to clean it up quite a bit to make it readable. The design firm had used an HTML editor that didn't believe in white space. It took a full day to get the HTML cleaned up and human-readable. Then came the task of setting up all the pages with the look and feel of a Mason approach. Less than an hour later, the entire site of around 20 pages was done! Once the layout for the site was completed, dropping other pages into the site was a breeze.

The tools that Mason provides are quite simple, yet Mason is extremely powerful because it allows you to embed Perl right into the HTML. Enough hyping Mason! Mason does a good job at that just by doing what it was designed for. In our example, we will redesign a Web site. The Web site chosen was the site at *http://www.perlguy.net*. This site was picked for particular reasons: It needed updating, it was pretty bland, and it needed more features.

13.2 Installation

Setting up mod_perl and Mason is not all that difficult, but you need to be sure that you read the documentation on how to install it. Installing mod_perl or Mason won't be covered here because the documentation covering both is quite extensive. Plus, the installation documentation is the most up-to-date information you can find for setup instructions. For Mason to run, you need at a minimum an Apache Web server running mod_perl and with the HTML::Mason Perl module installed.

13.3 The Strategy

When Brent set off to create the new site, the first thing he did was to sketch out a rough design of how the site was to be laid out. A basic page design consisting of a header, a footer, the body, and on the homepage a couple of news boxes. With the site design in hand, the next step is to come up with a strategy of how it was going to be laid out. Since Brent hates frames, tables were the obvious choice to use for positioning elements on the pages. Now that we have our basic design and layout, it is probably a good idea to cover some of Mason's syntax.

13.4 Mason Syntax

We won't cover all the Mason syntax. That could easily be a book in itself. However, we will cover enough to get you off to a great head start. One thing that may be a small hurdle is the methodology that Mason uses. If you have been developing Web sites for quite a while and have become very used to the regular CGI way of doing things, Mason will challenge you to think a little differently.

With Mason you don't have a bunch of the print statements and here documents making up the pages. Instead, whatever code is to be executed is preceded by one of Mason's tags, and everything else simply gets processed as standard HTML. There is no more need for a cgi-bin directory because any code that you need to process is handled directly by Mason.

component

The first thing you will hear a lot is the term *component*. A component is nothing more that a file containing HTML, Perl code, or both. Try not to get hung up on terminology. Since Mason uses many small pieces, component is the perfect choice to describe the pieces.

Components are nice because they truly reap the benefits of reusability. Components can be self-contained pieces of code that perform specific tasks—or just a few simple HTML tags. Components don't have to be large, and you will probably benefit most by having several small components that perform specific tasks rather than one large one that tries to do everything.

If there are several developers working on a site, it is much easier to divide up the work because individual components can be assigned to the different workers. This eliminates some of the problems of having multiple developers try to work on the same site at the same time. Each programmer can be assigned a component to work on, rather than assigning a large piece that may require the work of more people.

<%perl> . . . </%perl>

The <%perl> tag is a way to enclose larger blocks of Perl code in a component. Whatever is between the opening and closing tag is treated as regular Perl code. As you can see, this tag, like most of the other Mason tags, is very HTML-like.

%

Lines that begin with % are also treated as Perl code. The % *must* be at the beginning of the line or else the line will be treated as a regular HTML line. The % is a nice way to throw a couple of lines of Perl code into a document without having to make a <%perl> block.

<% . . . %>

The <% . . . %> syntax allows you to put Perl code directly into a line of HTML. When the Mason parser sees the <% %> tag, it will execute whatever is inside the tag. If it is a scalar variable holding a string, the string will replace the variable in the actual HTML that gets produced. If it is a function call, such as a call to the localtime function, whatever is returned by the function gets displayed. This is the tag that is probably most often forgotten when writing Mason pages. It is easy to just put a variable on a line and expect it to print out even though the <% %> tags were forgotten. So you would get something like this, which is not what you were looking for.

$title

But this would print out the value of $title and center it. That's more like it!

<% $title %>

The spaces between the % and the variable name are not needed, but you may find that it makes things easier to read. <% $variable %> is easier to read than <%$variable%>. The spaces will not be included in the output, so use them to make your programs easier to read.

<%init> . . . </%init>

An <%init> block is executed as soon as the component is called. This allows you to set up variables and execute code before any of the component HTML is printed. The <%init> block is effectively the same as a <%perl> block, but a <%perl> block gets parsed at the point where it is in the component, whereas an <%init> block gets parsed first, even if it is at the end of the component.

It is a common practice to put the <%init> blocks at the *end* of the components. That way, when changes to the HTML need to be made, the people making the changes don't have to look at a bunch of code that may be unfamiliar to them.

<%cleanup> . . . </cleanup>

This tag set creates a block of code that gets executed just before the component exits. They are rarely needed because Perl is so good at cleaning up after itself. But in case you need to do something at the very end of a component, this is what you would use.

<%once> . . . </%once>

The code in this block gets executed once when the component is loaded. Any variables created will be available for the life of the component. When components are used, they get cached by Mason. Using a <%once> block will make the portion of code that it contains only get executed in the parent process and make it available to all child processes.

<%shared> . . . </%shared>

The <%shared> block contains code, such as variables, that you want to be seen in all the components code, as well as subcomponents.

<%def name> . . . </%def>

This is how you can define a subcomponent inside of a component. It is like a named subroutine in Perl, where the name is the name you use to call it. You are allowed to use Mason tags inside of a <%def name> block, but you are not allowed to use the <%def>, <%method>, <%once>, or <%shared> tags.

The scope of a <%def name> block is different from the scope of the component it is in. Its variables and scope are private and only meant to be called from within the component that it is in. This means that you cannot create a subcomponent and call it from a different component. You may, however, only call it from the component that it is in.

<%method name> . . . </%method>

Methods are named the same way as the <%def name> blocks. The big difference here is that <%method name>'s are meant to be called from other components. They are much like Perl subroutines.

<%attr> . . . </attr>

The <%attr> block is used to assign key/value pairs that can be read by other components.

<%filter>(regular expression)</%filter>

A filter is used to filter the output of the component that it is in.

This may sound useless because why would you want to produce output and then filter it? In the example code, we'll show a <%filter> that checks what page we are currently on and updates the menu automatically based on this.

<%doc> . . . </%doc>

This is used for commenting large blocks of text. It is simply a comment and is ignored by Mason. Also, these comments do *not* show up in the final HTML document.

<%text> . . . </%text>

This block is used to pass through blocks of text untouched by Mason. This makes it so that you can write blocks that have Mason tags in them, such as documentation, and they will simply pass through and get displayed.

<%args> . . . </%args>

The <%args> section is used for generating a list of arguments expected by a component, as well as setting default values.

If a variable with no default value is in an <%args> block and nothing is passed to the component, an error will be generated. If there is a default value, then the default is the value that gets used if nothing is passed.

The <%args> blocks are excellent for HTML forms. If a form has a text box called first_name, in your <%args> block you could put $first_name if it is a required field or $first_name=>foobar to make foobar the default value if nothing is passed.

That is pretty much it for the extra tags you should be familiar with. Be aware that Mason is still in progress, so don't be surprised if more tags are created. However, remember that Mason *is* stable and is a good choice for creating Web sites.

13.5 Special Mason Components

Mason has some components that are "special" because they automatically performs tasks when certain events occur.

autohandler

The autohandler gets executed *before* the component executes. An autohandler will work on a per-directory basis, so all files in the directory *and* its subdirectories will be affected by it. Autohandlers are great for wrapping a header and footer around all the pages in a site. We'll use an autohandler like this in our example.

dhandler

The dhandler is the *default handler* that gets called if there are no components that match what was called in the URI. dhandlers are nice because they allow you to create custom error messages or perform tasks if a URL is not found. To make a dhandler, just create a component called dhandler.

$m

$m is the Mason request object. It provides an API for Mason that provides access to all of the Mason features not activated by a tag. $m is available to all components.

13.6 Cascading Execution

When you request an HTML document from a Mason server, the actual document is put together in a cascading style. No, we don't mean cascading stylesheets, but the components cascade to create the document. When a top-level component is requested—say, index.html—the first thing that happens is the system will check to see if the file exists. If it does, then it will check to see if an autohandler file exists in the current directory. If there is an autohandler, then the code up to the $m->call_next method call is executed. It won't be until this point that the actual file requested (index.html) is executed. The system will then go through each line of the component requested and call any components that it requests. Those components can in turn call other components and so on.

Once the entire top-level component (the component that was requested) has been processed, the server goes back to the autohandler component and executes any remaining code. This is what makes adding a header and footer easy. Since the autohandler executes its code up to the call_next method, then the component that was requested and then, finally, whatever is after the component call, the component requested gets "sandwiched" by the autohandler. Let's say that the user requests the foo.html file. The process would look something like this.

User:

request foo.html

Server:

autohandler (everything up to $m->call_next)

foo.html

autohandler (everything after the $m->call_next)

All this "component sandwiching" happens very fast. Many of the components are cached to speed things up even more. But with all the components calling components calling components and so on, you can see how the system cascades through the different components to generate the document requested.

13.7 Moving Right Along

We have talked briefly about the syntax of Mason. Next we will begin creating a site using Mason. Though there are still some concepts that we need to cover, we'll cover them in the code so that you can see everything in action.

Let's begin by showing my new index.html file (see Listing 13-1). The main file that is called is named the *top-level component*. The top-level component acts as the duct tape to bind together all the components that make up the requested page. Usually the top-level component is the HTML file that the URL points to.

Listing 13-1   **index.html**

```
1: <& menu_start &>
2:    <& rss2html, site=>"perl-news" &>
3:    <& rss2html, site=>"perl.com" &>
4: <& menu_end &>
5: <& body_start &>
6:    <& my_news &>
7:    <& pictures &>
8:    <& links &>
9: <& body_end &>
```

That is the whole index.html file! The resulting page looks like Figure 13-1.

Figure 13-1   **index.html screenshot**

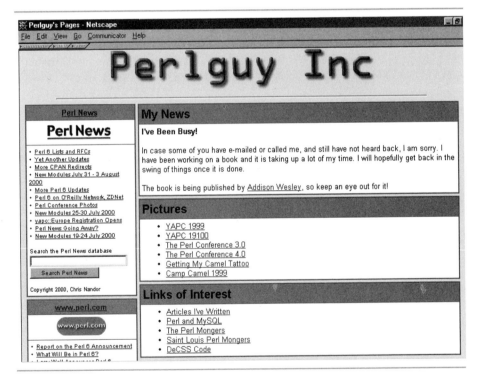

Wow! That is a pretty nice looking page considering that there are only nine lines in the index.html file! How is this possible? With Mason, of course!

Recall that with Mason you build the HTML pages by piecing together components. In the index.html file, eight components are called (one is used twice). Let's check out the components and see what they do. Some are very simple, but others are quite complex.

The first thing that happens is the server tries to open the page that was referenced. Since index.html does indeed exist, we can continue. Since Mason is set up, Mason is going to handle all the requests first and pass them to the appropriate handlers as necessary. Next, Mason will check for the existence of a file named autohandler. If the autohandler file exists, the code inside it will get executed *before* the index.html file that we referenced. On this site, we are using an autohandler, so let's take a look at it first because it is what gets executed first. The autohandler script is also quite short. You may also notice that several of the components are used more than once throughout the site. Reusability is a key strength for Mason.

```
01: <HTML><HEAD><TITLE><& SELF:title &></TITLE></HEAD>
```

Line 1 Creates the beginning HTML for the pages. The <& SELF:title &> is new, although it is a Mason directive. Like the old way of calling a subroutine in Perl (&subname), in Mason when you have the & sign, you are calling a function or external component. Here, we call the *title* method from the current component. The autohandler has a method called *title* (on **lines 11–13**), but if your top-level component also contains a method called *title*, it will override the autohandler's. The overriding is nice because with the autohandler, you can create a default title, and in your top-level components you can place a specific page title if you choose to. The use of SELF ensures that we get the title method from this component (autohandler) rather than one from the top-level component.

```
02:   <BODY BGCOLOR="<% $color %>">
```

Line 2 sets the HTML page's background color. The variable $color was initialized inside of the <%init> block on lines 14–16. Anything inside of the <% %> tag is treated as Perl, and the output gets printed. So if you put a variable in there, it will get printed. If you put something like 10–3, 7 would get printed.

```
03:   <CENTER>
04:    <img src="/images/new_header.gif" width="475" height="74">
05:   </CENTER>
06:   <HR WIDTH=85%>
07: <center>
08:  <table width="100%" border="0" cellspacing="0" cellpadding="0">
```

Lines 3–8 are simply HTML, and they get sent to the browser exactly as you would expect them to.

```
09:   <% $m->call_next %>
```

Line 9 is kind of special. We have not seen anything like it yet. Remember that $m is the Mason request object, and it is available to all components. $m provides an API to the Mason features that are not provided by syntactic tags. The *$m->call_next()* tells Mason to call the next component in the chain. This would actually call the HTML file that was requested, index.html in our case. Once the HTML file is finished with all of its work, we return to the line just after the *$m->call_next()*. This allows us to create a "wrapper" for all the pages simply using the autohandler.

```
10: <& footer &>
```

Line 10 calls the footer component. The footer component is the one that contains the HTML that finishes off the page. In our example site, it also puts a list of links at the bottom of the page as well as links to the Perl ring.

```
11: <%method title>
12:   Perlguy's Pages
13: </%method>
```

Lines 11–13 create a method called title. A method is like a subroutine in Perl. Here it simply returns the default title for all of the pages.

```
14: <%init>
15:   my $color = "#f1edd3";
16: </%init>
```

Lines 14–16 are our <%init> block. This is where we initialize any variables that we may need for the autohandler component—or actually any component. A variable named $title could have gone here and stored the default title, but then I wouldn't have been able to talk about methods!

So that is it for the autohandler component. Only 16 lines, but it creates a wrapper for all of the pages on the site. A developer can simply generate an HTML page and, without having to worry about putting header and footer code in the pages, will automatically have the proper header and footer.

index.html

Now when the index.html file kicks in, we are at line 9 of the autohandler component.

Line 1 of index.html calls the menu_start component. Listing 13-2 is a listing of the menu_start component.

Listing 13-2   menu_start component

```
<tr>
  <td width="15%" valign="top">
```

That is it, just two lines! As I said before, components do not have to be big. The menu_start component should be self-explanatory.

Lines 2–3 of index.html call a component named rss2html and pass it a key named site with a value associated with it. We'll cover all of these components in a moment after we get through index.html.

Line 4 calls the menu_end component. This too is a very small component; it simply contains "<td>."

Now why bother putting a single tag inside a component? You actually have to type *more* characters to reference it now! The answer to that is easy: *flexibility*. If you decide to make changes to the layout of your site, it is much easier to change a single component rather than change the same thing in several HTML files.

Line 5 calls the body_start component. Again, this component is very small with only two lines of HTML.

```
<td width="85%" valign="top">
    <center>
```

This is used to create a table that the body of the document will reside in.

Lines 6–8 contain calls to components that produce the three main boxes on the page. Each one is self-contained so they can be edited or removed very easily.

Line 9 calls the body_end component. This component contains a whopping three lines of HTML.

```
</center>
  </td>
  </tr>
```

That is all there is in the index.html file.

Next, the autohandler component would take control again and put the menu and the links to the Perl ring on the bottom of the page. They don't even have to be referenced in any way. Mason auto-magically looks for the autohandler component and executes it, so the programmer doesn't even have to remember to put it in the page.

13.8 rss2html

Now let's take a look at the rss2html component. This is a great component that takes in an RSS/RDF file and formats it to look nice. RSS/RDF files are XML files that are in a standard format for distributing news and information. The code for rss2html was adapted from the code in the XML::RSS module by Jonathan Eisenzopf.

The original version of rss2html used the LWP::Simple module and retrieved the RSS/RDF file each time someone hit the page. That is much slower because for each section desired, a separate request must go out and get the XML document. It just took too much time!

Instead, we created a small script that goes out and fetches the RSS/RDF documents and stores them in a MySQL database. The script runs as a cron event, so no further action is required to get the content. Changing to the database version greatly decreased the load time of the page, and it eased much of the load on the sites that provide the RSS/RDF files.

The rss2html component is a great one to look at because it shows how Perl code plus HTML can be integrated to produce something very nice with Mason.

```
01: <%perl>
02:     $sth->execute($site);
03:     $content = $sth->fetch->[0];
04:     # parse the RSS content
05:     $rss->parse($content);
06: </%perl>
```

Line 1 begins a <%perl> block. Anything inside this block, until the closing tag, is handled just like Perl code.

Line 2 executes an SQL command on the MySQL database. This may be kind of confusing because the connection to the database and the SQL statement are actually at the bottom of the file. With Mason, it is generally accepted to put as much of the Perl code at the end of the component as possible. Doing so makes it easier on the Web designer's eyes. They don't have to look at confusing code and can concentrate more on the HTML.

Line 3 calls the fetch method on the database and fetches the first item returned. We are only fetching one item, so hard-coding the 0th element of the array is fine here.

Line 4 is simply a comment.

Line 5 calls the parse method from the XML::RSS module. This is the module that parses the content of the RSS/RDF file and loads the data into a structure that is easy for Perl to work with.

Line 6 closes the </%perl> block.

```
07: <table bgcolor="#996600" border="0" width="200">
08:  <tr>
09:   <td>
10:    <table cellspacing="1" cellpadding="4" bgcolor="#FFFFFF"
11:     border=0 width="100%" >
12:     <tr>
13:      <td valign="middle" align="center" bgcolor="#cc9900">
14:       <font color="#000000" face="Arial,Helvetica">
15:        <b>
```

Lines 7–15 are simply HTML with no code embedded in it.

```
16: <a href="<% $rss->{'channel'}->{'link'} %>">
        <% $rss->{'channel'}->{'title'} %></a>
```

Line 16 is split into two lines here. It creates a link to the channel. If you look on the Web page, the title of each RSS/RDF box is linked. This is what creates the link. Inside of this line, you will also see two blocks that use the <% %> tags. This creates in-line Perl and whatever the result of the enclosed code is becomes the value that is placed there.

```
17:         </b>
18:        </font>
19:       </td>
20:      </tr>
21:      <tr>
22:       <td align="center">
```

Lines 17–22 are again just HTML with no embedded code.

```
23: %       # print channel image
24: %       if ($rss->{'image'}->{'link'}) {
```

Line 23 is a comment. Notice how the line begins with %. Because of this, everything on the line is treated as Perl, even comments. You can be generous with comments, too, because anything that is Perl code will not end up in the final HTML document, just HTML.

Line 24 checks to see if a link to an image exists. If one does, the if block is entered.

```
25:         <a href="<% $rss->{'image'}->{'link'} %>"><img
26:            src="<% $rss->{'image'}->{'url'} %>"
27:            alt="<% $rss->{'image'}->{'title'} %>" border="0"
```

Line 25 begins an html link so that the image is hyperlinked and beings an img tag.

Line 26 sets the src attribute of the img tag.

Line 27 sets an alt attribute for the img tag.

```
28: %      if($rss->{'image'}->{'width'}){
29:            width="<% $rss->{'image'}->{'width'} %>"
30: %      }
```

Line 28 checks to see if a width was passed with the image. If a width was passed, line 29 creates the width attribute and then line 30 closes the if block.

Notice on these lines that lines 28 and 30 begin with the %, but line 29 does not. Even though line 29 does not begin with a %, it will be skipped if line 28 was false because it is inside an *if()* block.

Line 29 embeds the Perl inside it because it also outputs some text.

```
31: %      if($rss->{'image'}->{'height'}){
32:            height="<% $rss->{'image'}->{'height'} %>"
33: %      }
```

Lines 31–33 do the same thing that lines 28–30 did, except this time for the height attribute instead of the width attribute.

```
34: ></a>
35: %      }
```

Line 34 finishes off the HTML link.

Line 35 ends the *if()* block that began on line 24.

```
36:      </td>
37:      </tr>
38:      <tr>
39:      <td><font face="arial,helvetica" size="2">
40:      <p>
```

Lines 36 –40 are simply HTML.

```
41: %  # print the channel items
42: %     foreach my $item (@{$rss->{'items'}}) {
43: %        next unless defined($item->{'title'}) &&
defined($item->{'link'});
```

```
44:             <li><a href="<% $item->{'link'} %>"><% $item->
{'title'} %></a><BR>
45: %     }
```

Line 41 is a comment.

Line 42 begins a *foreach()* loop that will go through each element in the array *@{$rss->{'items'}*.

Line 43 goes to the next iteration of the loop if there is no title and link defined.

Line 44 creates the link to the article.

Line 45 ends the *foreach()* loop that we began on line 42.

```
46: %    # if there's a textinput element
47: %    if ($rss->{'textinput'}->{'title'}) {
```

Line 46 is a comment.

Line 47 checks to see if there is a textinput field in the RSS document. If so, we need to add a form to the page so that the appropriate input box can be created.

```
48: <form method="get" action="<% $rss->{'textinput'}->{'link'}
%>">
49: <% $rss->{'textinput'}->{'description'} %><br />
50: <input type="text" name="<% $rss->{'textinput'}->{'name'}
%>"><br />
51: <input type="submit" value="<% $rss->{'textinput'}->
{'title'} %>">
52: </form>
```

Line 48 creates an HTML form and sets the action to the value stored in *$rss->{'textinput'}->{'link'}*.

Line 49 gets the description for the form field, prints it, and then prints an HTML break tag.

Line 50 creates the actual form text input field.

Line 51 creates and names the submit button for the form.

Line 52 closes the HTML form.

Lines 48–52 can appear rather confusing because it looks like there is so much happening. Let's take a look at the same lines but with all of the "noise" removed.

```
48: <form method="get" action="link_name">
49: Field title<br />
50: <input type="text" name="field_name"><br />
51: <input type="submit" value="button_text">
52: </form>
```

See—if you can get past the initial shock of the code *looking* like it is confusing and try to think of it in simpler terms, it really doesn't come out being all that hard. The descriptions we used above apply to these lines also. Nothing has really been changed, only simplified so you can see what is really going on.

```
53: %      }
54: %      # if there's a copyright element
55: %      if ($rss->{'channel'}->{'copyright'}) {
56:        <p><sub><% $rss->{'channel'}->{'copyright'} %></sub></p>
57: %      }
```

Line 53 closes the *if()* block that was opened on line 47. So the form field only gets printed out if it exists.

Line 54 is a comment.

Line 55 begins an *if()* block to check and see if there is copyright information associated with this RSS file. If there is, then the block is entered.

Line 56 prints out the copyright information.

Line 57 closes the *if()* block.

```
58:        </font></td>
59:        </tr>
60:      </table>
61:      </td>
62:    </tr>
63: </table>
```

Lines 58–63 are simply HTML that gets sent to the browser.

```
64: <%args>
65:  $site
66: </%args>
```

Lines 64–66 are the <%args> block that contains variables that are expected to be passed in when the component is called. On **line 65** , if no default value is given, error is generated if a value for $site is not passed.

In the index.html file, we have lines <& rss2html, site=>"perl.com" &>, which call the rss2html component and pass the site name as an argument. The argument name that is passed and the name in the <%args> block must match.

```
67: <%once>
68:  my $dbh;
69:  $dbh  = DBI->connect("DBI:mysql:book","book","addison")
70:                  || die "Cannot connect: $DBI::errstr\n" unless $dbh;
71:  my $sth = $dbh->prepare(qq{SELECT data FROM rss WHERE site = ?});
72: </%once>
```

Lines 67–72 are a <%once> block. Code inside a <%once> block is executed only once and survives for the duration of the component.

Lines 69–70 create a database handle. The database handle will not go away after we have used the module; instead it will be maintained in memory until the component no longer exists. This speeds things up since a new database connection and handle is not needed each time.

Line 71 creates and prepares an SQL statement. Since we don't want to recreate this over and over either, we also put it inside of the <%once> block.

Remember that components function differently from regular CGI programs. In a regular CGI program, the program gets called, the Perl interpreter starts, the program gets interpreted and executed, then the program closes and it all starts over again the next time it is accessed. In a Mason application, the Perl interpreter is constantly running, and components are cached to make things even faster. So just because a user has finished with a script, the script may still be loaded into memory waiting to be used again.

```
73: <%init>
74:  my $content;
75:  my $file;
76:  my $rss;
```

Line 73 begins our <%init> block. This block is used to declare variables and run code as soon as the component is called.

Lines 74–76 declare some my variables that will be used by the component.

Mason components run in strict mode, so you must declare variables with my before you can use them.

```
77:  $rss = new XML::RSS;
78: </%init>
```

Line 77 creates a new instance of the XML::RSS module and stores the handle in $rss. Even though we only need one instance of XML::RSS, we need a new instance each time the component is called. If we don't do this, you will be re-using a handle and stepping all over any code that was previously generated.

Line 78 closes the <%init> block and is the end of the component. Because of the way that Mason pages cascade, it is hard to really list the components used in order. If it seems like we are skipping around a bit. We are— but that is exactly what Mason does, too!

13.9 my_news

The my_news component reads a text file that contains news and information, wraps it, and then displays it. On the home page, it is the block on the top with the title "My News."

```
01: <& wrap_top, width=>'100%' &>
```

Line 1 calls the wrap_top component and passes it the width that you want the main "wrapper table" to have.

```
02:     <table cellspacing="1" cellpadding="4" border="0"
bgcolor="#ffffff"
03:      width="100%">
04:      <tr bgcolor="#cc9900">
05:       <td valign="top" align="left">
06:        <font face="Arial,Helvetica" size="5">
07:         <b> My News</b>
08:        </font>
09:       </td>
10:      </tr>
11:      <tr>
12:       <td><font face="arial,helvetica" size="3">
13:        <p>
```

Lines 2–13 are simply HTML that generate the nice box that wraps the news items.

```
14: % my $news = $m->file('news_text');
```

Line 14 is something that we have not seen yet. Remember that $m is the Mason request object and is an API to get at some of the Mason functions that are not represented by tags. *$m->file(filename)* will read in a file and return it as a string. You don't have to open the file or close it; just make sure that it exists or you will get an error.

So this line reads the contents of the file news_text and stores it in the $news variable. news_text simply is a text file that contains the HTML for the text area of the "My News" block.

```
15:    <% $news %>
```

Line 15 then prints out the data that was read in from the news_text file.

```
16:      </p>
17:      </td>
18:      </font>
19:      </tr>
20:    </table>
```

Lines 16–20 finish off the HTML table for the inner portion of the My News box.

```
21: <& wrap_bottom &>
```

Line 21 calls the wrap_bottom component. This component finishes off the outer table that wraps the entire My News box. That is it for the my_news component. The components used to create the links section and the pictures section is basically the same as this file except that the HTML is slightly different.

13.10 footer

The footer component is the last one that we are going to cover in detail. It contains a good example of a <%filter> and how they can be used.

```
01:   </tr>
02:   <tr>
03:    <td colspan="2" align="center">
04: <br><br>
05:     <center>
06:     <hr width="85%">
07: <br><br>
08:     <font face=arial size=2>
```

(continued)

```
09:    [
10:      <a href="/index.html">Home</a> |
11:      <a href="/articles.html">Articles</a> |
12:      <a href="/sql/index.html">DBI/SQL Tutorial</a> |
13:      <a href="/services.html">My Services</a> |
14:      <a href="/campcamel/index.html">Camp Camel</a> |
15:      <a href="/bbq/index.html">BBQ Anyone?</a> |
16:      <a href="/tattoo/index.html">Camel Tattoo</a>
17:    ]
18:    </font>
19:    <br><br>
20:    </center>
21:   </td>
22:  </tr>
23:  <tr>
24:   <td colspan="2" align="center">
```

Lines 1–24 are just the HTML that makes up the links section that is on the bottom of each of the pages on the site.

```
25:    <& perl_ring &>
```

Line 25 calls the perl_ring component. This component adds the links to the Perl Ring sites to the very bottom of my pages.

```
26:   </td>
27:  </tr>
28: </table>
29: </center>
30: </body>
31: </html>
```

Lines 26–31 finish off the HTML for the page.

```
32: <%filter>
33:  my $uri = $r->uri;
34:  s{<a href="$uri/?">(.*?)</a>} {<b>$1</b>}i;
35: </%filter>
```

Lines 32–35 are the <%filter> block that changes the output from this component.

On **line 33** you will see the *$r->uri()* referenced. $r is basically the same as the $m we've seen before except the $r is an API into mod_perl rather than Mason. This line gets the URI of the page called.

Line 34 is a regular expression that does a search-and-replace. Let's break it down. First of all, the output of a component is stored in $_ and a <%filter> block performs its regular expression on the $_ variable. Here is the regex that we used.

```
s
 {<a href="$uri/?">(.*?)</a>}
 {<b>$1</b>}
i;
```

The s is the substitution operator, so we are going to attempt to make a substitution. The next part looks for the link that we are currently at based on the URI. It also captures the text between the <a href> and </a> tags. The captured data is stored in $1. Next, the link tag, <a href">, is removed and replaced with just bold tags with the value of $1 in between them. This should then be the text only link name. The final line just has the i to make it case-insensitive. So to put it all together again, the filter looks at what page we are currently on via the $r->uri API function from mod_perl. Then it performs a search-and-replace to un-link the HTML link for the page we are on. In Figure 13-2, we are on the home page. Notice that the "Home" link is not active.

Figure 13-2   **On the home page**

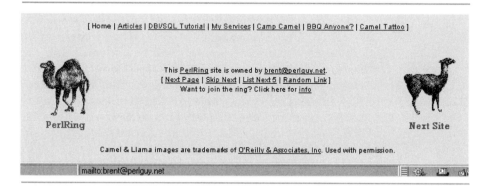

Now look at Figure 13-3. It was taken from the articles.html page. Notice that the "Home" link is now active again and that the "Articles" link is now inactive.

Figure 13-3   On the articles page

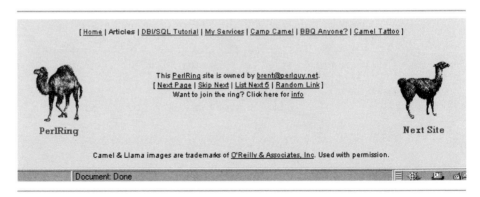

This is all done with that simple, one line regular expression in the <%filter> block!

Hopefully you can see that filters are a powerful tool that can make things a lot easier. Sure, we could have created an if . . . elsif . . . else block and checked the current page manually and then displayed either an active link or inactive text, but this would have added several lines of code. Also, each time you added a link, you would have to add on to the if . . . elsif . . . else structure. By using a filter, all you need to do is add the new link in the HTML, and the filter will take care of the rest!

13.11 Wrapping It Up: The Code for the Example Site

Hopefully you have now been turned on to the wonderful world of Mason. Mason is truly is an excellent tool to design sites with. Mason is still in development and more features will be added as they are thought of. The Mason author, Jonathan Swartz, has done an excellent job of not letting Mason get "feature creep." This means that he has not added more and more features to try and make Mason do *everything*. Many of us know how software can become bloated and slow by trying to add every feature known to man to it. Jonathan has kept Mason quite simple and yet has been able to create a very powerful tool.

This chapter ends with listings of all the code that makes up the front page of the example site (see Listings 13-3 to 13-18). Not all components were covered in detail because several of the components are so simple. They speak for themselves. The listings will not be in any real order. I am going to start with the top-level component and then list the rest of the components alphabetically.

Listing 13-3   **index.html, the top-level component**

```
01: <& menu_start &>
02:  <& rss2html, site=>"perl-news" &>
03:  <& rss2html, site=>"perl.com" &>
04: <& menu_end &>
05: <& body_start &>
06:  <& my_news &>
07:  <& pictures &>
08:  <& links &>
09: <& body_end &>
```

Listing 13-4   **autohandler, the script that runs automatically for every page served**

```
01: <HTML><HEAD><TITLE><& SELF:title &></TITLE></HEAD>
02:  <BODY BGCOLOR="<% $color %>">
03:    <CENTER>
04:      <img src="/images/new_header.gif" width="475"
         height="74">
05:    </CENTER>
06:    <HR WIDTH=85%>
07: <center>
08:  <table width="100%" border="0" cellspacing="0"
       cellpadding="0">
09:    <% $m->call_next %>
10: <& footer &>
11: <%method title>
12:  Perlguy's Pages
13: </%method>
14: <%init>
15:    my $color = "#f1edd3";
16: </%init>
```

Listing 13-5   **body_end, used to end the table that makes up the body of the document**

```
01:    </center>
02:    </td>
03:  </tr>
```

Listing 13-6   **body_start, used to begin the table that makes up the body of the document**

```
01:    <td width="85%" valign="top">
02:      <center>
```

Listing 13-7 **dhandler, the component that gets called if the page referred to did not exist**

```
01: <font face="arial,helvetica">
02:  <font size="7">
03:   <center>
04:    Oops!
05:   </center>
06:  </font>
07:  <font size="5">
08:   I didn't find the page you were looking for!<P>
09:   Please check the URL and try again.
10:  </font>
11: </font>
```

Listing 13-8 **footer, used to print the links, Perl Ring data, and end the document**

```
01:  </tr>
02:  <tr>
03:   <td colspan="2" align="center">
04: <br><br>
05:    <center>
06:    <hr width="85%">
07: <br><br>
08:    <font face=arial size=2>
09:    [
10:     <a href="/index.html">Home</a> |
11:     <a href="/articles.html">Articles</a> |
12:     <a href="/sql/index.html">DBI/SQL Tutorial</a> |
13:     <a href="/services.html">My Services</a> |
14:     <a href="/campcamel/index.html">Camp Camel</a> |
15:     <a href="/bbq/index.html">BBQ Anyone?</a> |
16:     <a href="/tattoo/index.html">Camel Tattoo</a>
17:    ]
18:    </font>
19:    <br><br>
20:   </center>
21:   </td>
22:  </tr>
23:  <tr>
24:   <td colspan="2" align="center">
25:    <& perl_ring &>
26:   </td>
```

```
27:  </tr>
28: </table>
29: </center>
30: </body>
31: </html>
32: <%filter>
33:  my $uri = $r->uri;
34:  s{<a href="$uri/?">(.*?)</a>} {<b>$1</b>}i;
35: </%filter>
```

Listing 13-9   **links, used to create the Links of Interest section**

```
01: <& wrap_top, width=>'100%' &>
02:     <table cellspacing="1" cellpadding="4" border="0"
bgcolor="#ffffff"
03:     width="100%">
04:     <tr bgcolor="#cc9900">
05:      <td valign="top" align="left">
06:       <font face="Arial,Helvetica" size="5">
07:        <b> Links of Interest </b>
08:       </font>
09:      </td>
10:     </tr>
11:     <tr>
12:      <td><font face="arial,helvetica" size="3">
13:       <p>
14:        <ul>
15:         <li><a href="articles.html">Articles I've Written</a>
16:         <li><a href="/sql/">Perl and MySQL</a>
17:         <li><a href="http://www.pm.org">The Perl Mongers</a>
18:         <li><a href="http://stlouis.pm.org">Saint Louis Perl
Mongers</a>
19:         <li><a href="decss.html">DeCSS Code</a>
20:        </ul>
21:      </font></td>
22:     </tr>
23:    </table>
24: <& wrap_bottom &>
```

Listing 13-10   **menu_end, used to end the menu section**

```
01: </td>
```

Listing 13-11   menu_start, used to begin the menu section

```
01:  <tr>
02:   <td width="15%" valign="top">
```

Listing 13-12   my_news, used to create the My News section

```
01: <& wrap_top, width=>'100%' &>
02:    <table cellspacing="1" cellpadding="4" border="0"
bgcolor="#ffffff"
03:     width="100%">
04:    <tr bgcolor="#cc9900">
05:     <td valign="top" align="left">
06:      <font face="Arial,Helvetica" size="5">
07:       <b> My News</b>
08:      </font>
09:     </td>
10:    </tr>
11:    <tr>
12:     <td><font face="arial,helvetica" size="3">
13:      <p>
14: % my $news = $m->file('news_text');
15:    <% $news %>
16:      </p>
17:     </td>
18:    </font>
19:    </tr>
20:    </table>
21: <& wrap_bottom &>
```

Listing 13-13   news_text, the text for the My News section

```
01: <b>I've Been Busy!</b><br>
02: <p>
03: In case some of you have e-mailed or called me, and still
have not heard back, I am sorry.  I have been working on a book
and it is taking up a lot of my time. I will hopefully get back
in the swing of things once it is done.
04: </p>
05: <p>
06: The book is being published by <a href="http://www.awl.com">
Addison Wesley</a>, so keep an eye out for it!
07: </p>
```

Listing 13-14   page_header, used to create the top of the document

```
01: <%args>
02:   $color
03:   $title => "Perlguy's Pages"
04: </%args>
05: <HTML><HEAD><TITLE><% $title %></TITLE></HEAD>
06:   <BODY BGCOLOR="<% $color %>">
07:   <CENTER>
08:     <img src="/images/new_header.gif" width="475"
         height="74">
09:   </CENTER>
10:   <HR WIDTH=85% SIZE=1 noshade>
11: <table width="100%" border="0" cellspacing="0"
       cellpadding="0">
```

Listing 13-15   pictures, creates the Pictures box on the page

```
01:   <& wrap_top, width=>'100%' &>
02:     <table cellspacing="1" cellpadding="4" border="0"
         width="100%"
03:       bgcolor="#ffffff">
04:     <tr bgcolor="#cc9900">
05:     <td valign="top" align="left">
06:       <font face="Arial,Helvetica" size = "5">
07:         <b> Pictures </b>
08:       </font>
09:     </td>
10:     </tr>
11:     <tr>
12:     <td><font face="arial,helvetica" size="3">
13:     <p>
14:      <ul>
15:        <li><a href="/yapc">YAPC 1999</a>
16:        <li><a href="/yapc19100">YAPC 19100</a>
17:        <li><a href="/tpc3">The Perl Conference 3.0</a>
18:        <li><a href="/tpc4">The Perl Conference 4.0</a>
19:        <li><a href="/tattoo">Getting My Camel Tattoo</a>
20:        <li><a href="/campcamel/1999.html">Camp Camel 1999</a>
21:      </ul>
22:     </font></td>
23:     </tr>
24:     </table>
25:   <& wrap_bottom &>
```

Listing 13-16   **rss2html, used to get the RSS data from the database and then format it into a nice news block**

```
01: <%perl>
02:     $sth->execute($site);
03:     $content = $sth->fetch->[0];
04:     # parse the RSS content
05:     $rss->parse($content);
06: </%perl>
07: <table bgcolor="#996600" border="0" width="200">
08:  <tr>
09:   <td>
10:    <table cellspacing="1" cellpadding="4" bgcolor="#FFFFFF"
11:    border=0 width="100%" >
12:    <tr>
13:     <td valign="middle" align="center" bgcolor="#cc9900">
14:      <font color="#000000" face="Arial,Helvetica">
15:       <b>
16: <a href="<% $rss->{'channel'}->{'link'} %>"><% $rss->
    {'channel'}->{'title'} %></a>
17:       </b>
18:      </font>
19:     </td>
20:    </tr>
21:    <tr>
22:     <td align="center">
23: %     # print channel image
24: %     if ($rss->{'image'}->{'link'}) {
25:        <a href="<% $rss->{'image'}->{'link'} %>"><img
26:          src="<% $rss->{'image'}->{'url'} %>"
27:          alt="<% $rss->{'image'}->{'title'} %>" border="0"
28: %     if($rss->{'image'}->{'width'}){
29:          width="<% $rss->{'image'}->{'width'} %>"
30: %     }
31: %     if($rss->{'image'}->{'height'}){
32:          height="<% $rss->{'image'}->{'height'} %>"
33: %     }
34: ></a>
35: %     }
36:     </td>
37:    </tr>
38:    <tr>
39:     <td><font face="arial,helvetica" size="2">
40:      <p>
41: %  # print the channel items
42: %     foreach my $item (@{$rss->{'items'}}) {
```

(continued)

```
43: %       next unless defined($item->{'title'}) && defined
    ($item->{'link'});
44:           <li><a href="<% $item->{'link'} %>"><% $item->
    {'title'} %></a><BR>
45: %    }
46: %    # if there's a textinput element
47: %    if ($rss->{'textinput'}->{'title'}) {
48:       <form method="get" action="<% $rss->{'textinput'}
          ->{'link'} %>">
49:       <% $rss->{'textinput'}->{'description'} %><br />
50:        <input type="text" name="<% $rss->{'textinput'}
           ->{'name'} %>"><br />
51:        <input type="submit" value="<% $rss->{'textinput'}
           ->{'title'} %>">
52:       </form>
53: %    }
54: %    # if there's a copyright element
55: %    if ($rss->{'channel'}->{'copyright'}) {
56:       <p><sub><% $rss->{'channel'}->{'copyright'} %></sub></p>
57: %    }
58:        </font></td>
59:      </tr>
60:     </table>
61:   </td>
62:  </tr>
63: </table>
64: <%args>
65:  $site
66: </%args>
67: <%once>
68:  my $dbh;
69:  $dbh  = DBI->connect("DBI:mysql:book","root","c600go")
70:               || die "Cannot connect: $DBI::errstr\n" unless
                     $dbh;
71:  my $sth  = $dbh->prepare(qq{SELECT data FROM rss WHERE site
     = ?});
72: </%once>
73: <%init>
74:  my $content;
75:  my $file;
76:  my $rss;
77:  $rss = new XML::RSS;
78: </%init>
```

Listing 13-17 **wrap_bottom, used to finish the table that is used as a wrapper**

```
01:    </td>
02:    </tr>
03: </table>
```

Listing 13-18 **wrap_top, used to create the table that acts as a wrapper**

```
01: <%args>
02:   $bgcolor => "#996600"
03:   $width => ''
04: </%args>
05: <table bgcolor="<% $bgcolor %>" border="0" width="<%
$width %>">
06:   <tr>
07:     <td>
```

Chapter

Document Management via the Web

14.1 Introduction

If you have ever wanted to manage a group of documents for personal reasons or for something small at work, a simple file manager should do just fine. However, what if you work with 20 other people, and you need to have a central location for documents? Your simple file manager just became pretty useless because it only works on your desktop. Or if you have some directories shared, what is stopping user X from working on a document at the same time as user Y? If this happens, whoever saves the file last will wipe out any changes that the other made.

Also, drives that are shared are not as reliable as something as rock solid as a Web server. What if a directory is shared out on user Y's hard drive and user Y takes a one-month vacation to Antarctica? Oh, yes, user Y shut down their computer, thinking it would save electricity and forgot about the shared directory and for some reason is not answering their cell-phone.

Document management systems (DMS) were created to solve this and a slew of other problems, such as version control and backup of documents. Enterprise DMSs can cost hundreds of thousands of dollars, requiring expensive hardware and dedicated systems administrators to keep it all running.

Just because something costs a lot of money does not mean that it is good. When Brent worked at Boeing, they had purchased an expensive

DMS system and a separate Unix machine to run it on. Boeing had it for about six months before Brent got there, and they never did get it running properly. Brent came in and wrote a complete, custom-designed DMS for a project that ran on a single Windows NT machine, IIS, and Perl. It wasn't NT or IIS that made all of this possible, it was Perl; the OS and Web server software were irrelevant.

The DMS project was for a joint project, which means that there were direct competitors on the same system, and we obviously did not want them to see documents that were only meant for Boeing. The version developed at Boeing had features like this.

- File check in/out
- Security based on the user/groups rights
- Automatic e-mail reminders for documents checked out too long
- Version control
- Dynamic interface depending on rights

The application that we will be developing in this chapter is a scaled-down DMS. Actually, we'll be implementing the DMS in less than 500 lines of code! This is going to be another rather large application that we won't be able to really play with until we get it finished. The end result is definitely worth the work that it will take to get there, so let's get moving.

14.2 The Plan

The first thing that is needed when you create a project such as this is a plan. If you are developing for an environment where many others will use it, get some extra people involved at least in the interface design and list of features. The features that this DMS will have are the following.

- File upload
- File view
- User authentication
- Dynamic main page (based on rights)
- File check in/out
- Extended descriptions
- Security based on groups

Since we now have the features planned, here is what we are going to do next. We'll create a program called auth.cgi that will handle the authentication, main.cgi will display the main page, upload.cgi will handle the file uploading, and viewer.cgi will handle file viewing. We will also create a file called shared.pl that we will use to store any common functions that we may come up with.

We will also need a couple of database tables to store information. It seems as though we use databases a lot, and that is absolutely right. The Web is a great thing, but unless you have information to store and present, it really doesn't do much good. Databases natively store and present data, so databases and the Web complement each other very nicely.

We'll need one database table to store information about the users of the system. We need to know who is logged in and what group they belong to. We will need another table to store information about the files themselves. Two tables is enough for what we'll be doing in this application. If you plan on expanding the capabilities, then adding more tables would probably be something that you would need to do, depending on what your goals are. Here is the structure for our two tables, in MySQL format:

```
# Table structure for table 'dms_users'
CREATE TABLE dms_users (
  username    varchar(40) DEFAULT '' NOT NULL,
  password    varchar(25),
  e_mail      varchar(150),
  phone       varchar(25),
  group_id    varchar(25),
  PRIMARY KEY (username)
);
```

```
# Table structure for table 'dms_files'
CREATE TABLE dms_files (
  file_id int(11) DEFAULT '0' NOT NULL auto_increment,
  filename    varchar(255),
  description varchar(255),
  location    varchar(255),
  mime_type   varchar(50),
  group_id    varchar(25),
  who_to      varchar(40),
  out_date    varchar(20),
  PRIMARY KEY (file_id)
);
```

The first table is simply for storing some information about the users. In our DMS example, we did not create an admin interface to directly update this table. A simple input form would work just fine, but since we want to cover the core functionality of the DMS, we did not include an admin tool. An admin area would be a great add-on for the DMS, and by the time you finish this book, you'll have no problem creating one. Data is required in the dms_users table for the program to function, so populate it with some phony user information so we can test the DMS.

For the group_id in the examples, I created four groups: PEON, USER, PHB, and BOFH. PEON is the lowest-level group, and BOFH has access to everything. Some directories will also need to be created. The programs reside in the cgi-bin/dms directory and the data subdirectories are in the cgi-bin/dms/data directory. The data subdirectories are named the same as the group names, so the first one would be cgi-bin/dms/data/PEON, and so on. When finished, your subdirectory structure should look something like this.

```
cgi-bin
      /data
            /PEON
            /USER
            /PHB
            /BOFH
```

All the pages are dynamically generated, so we won't need any HTML forms in the regular Web server HTML directory. The data directory must have sufficient rights for the "Web user" to create files in it. The "Web user" is the user that the Web server runs as. For security purposes, you also want to make sure that the Web server does not serve pages directly from the cgi-bin directory. You would have to specifically turn this on, so it is probably okay, but to check it, put an HTML file in the cgi-bin/dms/data/PEON subdirectory and try to get to it from your browser. Even if you enter the proper path, the Web server should return a "forbidden" error or something similar.

14.3 auth.cgi

The first program we will create will be auth.cgi. This program will be used to log a user in or out, and it will also generate the login page.

```
01: #!/usr/bin/perl -wT
02: # auth.cgi
03: use DBI;
04: use strict;
05: use CGI qw(:standard);
06: require "./shared.pl" or die "Can't find file. $!\n";
```

Lines 1 and 2 tell the system where to find Perl, turn on warnings and taint checking, and tell us the name of the program. Including the program name makes it easier to keep things straight when you are looking at several printouts.

Line 3 brings in the DBI module so we can do easy database access.

Line 4 turns on strict mode, to force us to write cleaner programs.

Line 5 imports the CGI module and imports the standard functions.

Line 6 brings in the shared.pl file. This is the file in which we will store our common subroutines. I know many people who cringe at the *require()* function. They would rather have everything be a module. My philosophy is that *require()* is quick and simple, and if Larry is going to leave it in the language, I am going to use it. There is nothing wrong with using *require()* when you need it.

```
07: my $user     = param('username');
08: my $pass     = param('password');
09: my $action   = param('action');
10: my $dbh      = DB_Connect();
```

Lines 7–9 create some my variables and set them to the values passed from the HTML form.

Line 10 calls the *DB_Connect()* subroutine, which is in shared.pl. It will return a database handle, which we store in $dbh.

```
11: Logout()     if($action eq "logout");
12: Login_Page() unless($pass);
```

Line 11 calls the *Logout()* function if the action passed was "logout."

Line 12 calls the *Login_Page()* function if no password is present. Since all the users must have passwords, a password must be sent to log in. If no password is present, we simply display the login page again for the user. Remember that *unless()* is the same as "if not."

```
13: my $valid = Check_Login($user, $pass);
```

Line 13 calls the *Check_Login()* subroutine and sends it the username and password. The *Check_Login()* subroutine will return 0 on failure (bad username and/or password) and 1 if the username and password are good.

```
14: if($valid) {
15:     my $cookie = Create_Cookie("1h", $user);
16:     print redirect(-uri=>"main.cgi", -cookie=>$cookie);
17:     exit;
18: }
```

Line 14 begins an if . . . else block that decides what we should do with this user. We are checking to see if $valid contains any data.

Line 15 creates a cookie called $cookie using the *Create_Cookie()* subroutine. Here we are passing a value of "1h," which means 1 hour and the username. This creates a cookie that will be used to ensure that a user is authorized to be using our DMS system. The cookie is simply the username.

Line 16 redirects the user to the main.cgi program and sends the newly created cookie along so that it gets set on the user's Web browser. For this application, if cookies are not on, the user will never be able to do anything.

Line 17 exits the program. We are done if the program ended up here.

Line 18 closes this portion of the if . . . else block.

```
19: else{
20:     my $time = time();
21:     print redirect(-uri=>"auth.cgi?$time");
22:     exit;
23: }
```

Line 19 begins our else portion of the if . . . else block. This is where the user gets sent if the login was invalid for some reason.

Line 20 creates a variable called $time and sets it to the current time.

Line 21 redirects the user back to this program, auth.cgi. The time appended onto the end of the URL is only there because some browsers cache information from CGI pages. This will be a constantly changing value so the browser will see it as a different URL each time. This also solved another problem that we ran across. The CGI.pm module did not want to redirect back to itself, adding the time onto the URL solved this problem.

Line 22 exits the program. We are done if the program ended up here.

Line 23 closes the if . . . else block.

```
24: sub Logout{
25:     my $time   = time();
26:     my $cookie = Create_Cookie("-1h", "");
27:     print redirect(-uri=>"auth.cgi?$time", -cookie=>$cookie);
28:     exit;
29: }
```

Line 24 begins the *Logout()* subroutine. This subroutine is used to log out the user by simply setting the cookie value to nothing.

Line 25 creates a $time variable and sets it to the current time.

Line 26 creates a cookie using the *Create_Cookie()* subroutine. This cookie will have an empty value.

Line 27 redirects the user to the auth.cgi program again and resets the cookie.

Line 28 exits the program.

Line 29 closes the *Logout()* subroutine.

```
30: sub Create_Cookie{
31:     my $exp = shift;
32:     my $val = shift;
```

Line 30 begins the *Create_Cookie()* subroutine.

Lines 31 and 32 *shift()* off the values passed to the subroutine and store them in $exp and $val, respectively.

```
33:     my $cookie = cookie( -name    => 'dms',
34:                          -value   => $val,
35:                          -expires => $exp );
```

Lines 33–35 use *CGI.pm's cookie()* function to build a cookie. The name is hard coded into the program since that won't change, but the value($val) and expires($exp) variables can change so they are scalars.

```
36:     return($cookie);
37: }
```

Line 36 returns the cookie to the calling function.

Line 37 closes the *Create_Cookie()* subroutine.

```
38: sub Check_Login{
39:     my $user = shift;
40:     my $pass = shift;
41:     my $data;
```

Line 38 begins the *Check_Login()* subroutine. This subroutine is used to make sure that the username and password match what is stored in the database.

Lines 39–41 create some my variables that we'll be needing. $user and $pass are the username and password that were sent to the function when it was called.

```
42:     my $sth = $dbh->prepare( qq{ SELECT password
43:                                  FROM dms_users
44:                                  WHERE
45:                                  username = ?
46:                                  } );
```

Lines 42–46 create a statement handle $sth that is a prepared SQL statement, ready to be used on the database. In the parentheses we use the *qq()* function to quote the text. qq will interpolate variables, and it will also properly handle quotes in the string. Here we are creating a SQL statement to get the password from the dms_users table.

```
47:     $sth->execute($user);
48:     $data = $sth->fetch;
```

Line 47 executes the statement we prepared above. It also passes the $user variable so that it can be included in the SQL statement where the placeholder(?) is.

Line 48 stores the result of the *fetch()* method in the variable $data. The *fetch()* method returns a reference to an array. Each element in the array is a field for the row of data that was returned.

```
49:     $sth->finish;
50:     $dbh->disconnect;
```

Line 49 calls the *finish()* method. *finish()* releases the statement handle that helps to ensure that the database exits properly.

Line 50 calls the *disconnect()* method and disconnects us from the database.

```
51:     ($data->[0] eq $pass) ? return 1 : return 0;
52: }
```

Line 51 uses the trinary operator to check if *$data->[0]* matched what was in $pass. $pass is the password that the user sent from the Web page. *$data->[0]* is the first element of the row returned. Since we only asked for one field back, and there can only be one user per username, we should have the password here. In any case, if the password is wrong or was not returned due to some other problem, 0 is returned here. If the passwords match, we return 1.

The trinary, which is sometimes called the ternary operator, works like this. If the expression on the left of the ? returns true, then the first item gets returned. Otherwise, the last item gets returned. It is just an easier way to write this.

```
if($data->[0] eq $pass){
    return 1;
}
else{
    return 0;
}
```

The trinary operator makes this much easier for us!

Line 52 closes the *Check_Login()* subroutine.

```
53: sub Login_Page{
54:     print header();
```

Line 53 begins the *Login_Page()* subroutine. This subroutine is designed simply to create the HTML form used for logging in to the site.

Line 54 prints the HTTP header using CGI.pm's header function.

```
55:     print<<HTML;
56:       <html><head><title>DMS Example</title></head>
57:        <body bgcolor="#ffffff">
58:         <center>
59:          <form method="post">
60:           <p>
61:            <h2>Welcome to the DMS Example</h2>
62:           </p>
63:           <p>
64:            <table border="1" cellspacing="0">
65:             <tr>
66:              <td>Username:</td>
67:              <td><input type="text" name="username"></td>
68:             </tr>
69:             <tr>
70:              <td>Password:</td>
71:              <td><input type="password" name="password"></td>
72:             </tr>
73:            <tr align="center">
74:             <td colspan="2">
75:              <input type="submit" value="    Login    ">
76:             </td>
77:            </tr>
78:           </table>
79:          </p>
80:         </form>
81:        </center>
82:       </body>
83:      </html>
84: HTML
```

Lines 55–84 are a here document that makes up the HTML form for the login page.

```
85:      exit;
86: }
```

Line 85 exits the program.

Line 86 ends the *Create_Login()* subroutine. That is it for the first part of our DMS application. If you have some test users entered in the database, you can run this script. You should see a page similar to Figure 14-1.

Figure 14-1   DMS Login Screen

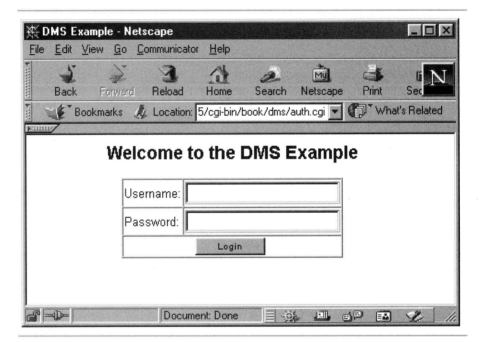

Enter the next program, shared.pl, and then you can test the auth.cgi program out. shared.pl is very short, so it won't take very long to enter. If you enter an invalid username and/or password, the program should just return you to the login page. If you enter a valid username and password, the program should send you to the main.cgi program. The main.cgi program does not exist yet, but you can at least check to see that the auth.cgi program is working.

14.4 shared.pl

The second program we'll cover is the shared.pl file. shared.pl contains the three subroutines that are needed in several of the DMS programs.

```
01: sub DB_Connect{
02:     my $dbh = DBI->connect("DBI:mysql:book", "book", "addison")
03:         or die "Error connecting to DB! $DBI::errstr\n";
04:     return($dbh);
05: }
```

Line 1 begins the *DB_Connect()* subroutine. Since this is just an included file and is not itself executable, we don't need the #!/usr/bin/perl line at the top.

Lines 2 and 3 create a connection to the database and store the database handle that is returned in the new my variable $dbh.

Line 4 returns the database handle.

Line 5 ends the *DB_Connect()* subroutine.

```
06: sub Check_Cookie{
07:     my $user = cookie('dms');
```

Line 6 begins the *Check_Cookie()* subroutine.

Line 7 creates a my variable called $user and sets it to the value returned by the *cookie()* subroutine. The cookie subroutine is passed the name of the cookie that we want to fetch, and it will return the cookie's value if one that we are allowed to see is found.

```
08:     if($user){
09:         return($user);
10:     }
```

Line 8 begins an if . . . else block. It checks to see if there is any value in the $user variable. If there is, then it means that the user already had a cookie set so we enter the block.

In **Line 9** the user had a cookie set, so we simply return the $user variable, which is the username of for the current user.

Line 10 closes this part of the if . . . else block.

```
11:     else{
12:         print redirect(-uri=>"auth.cgi");
13:         exit;
14:     }
15: }
```

Line 11 begins the else portion of the if . . . else block.

Line 12 redirects the user to the auth.cgi program. There was not a cookie set. The cookie either expired or there was some other error. In these cases, we simply send the user back to the auth.cgi program, and they can log in again.

Line 13 exits the program.

Line 14 closes the if . . . else block.

Line 15 ends the *Check_Cookie()* subroutine.

```
16: sub Get_Group{
17:     my $user = shift;
```

Line 16 begins the *Get_Group()* subroutine. This subroutine returns the group that the user belongs to.

Line 17 gets the variable passed to the subroutine and stores it in $user.

```
18:     my $dbh = DBI->connect("DBI:mysql:book", "book", "addison")
19:         or die "Error connecting to DB! $DBI::errstr\n";
```

Lines 18 and 19 create a database connection so that we can get the group from the database. We had to make a connection here because even though we made a connection in the main program, it is not in the scope of this subroutine.

```
20:     my $sth = $dbh->prepare( qq{ SELECT group_id
21:                                  FROM dms_users
22:                                  WHERE
23:                                  username = ?
24:                                  } );
```

Lines 20–24 create and prepare the SQL statement that we will use to get the group_id from the database table.

```
25:     $sth->execute($user);
26:     $group = $sth->fetch->[0];
27:     redirect(-uri=>"auth.cgi") unless $group;
```

Line 25 executes the SQL statement we just prepared.

Line 26 sets the $group variable to whatever was returned by a call to *fetch()*. Here we are calling *fetch()* and getting the 0th element of the array returned all in one line.

Line 27 redirects the user to the auth.cgi page if no group was returned.

```
28:      $sth->finish;
29:      $dbh->disconnect;
30:      return($group);
31: }
```

Line 28 calls the *finish()* method to release the $sth handle.

Line 29 calls the *disconnect()* method to disconnect us from the database.

Line 30 returns the value in $group.

Line 31 closes the *Get_Group()* subroutine.

```
32: 1;
```

Line 32 —finally! We have a lonely 1; at the end of this script. All files included must return a true value. "1;" is the most traditionally used method. You could also return some text or just about anything you wanted if you felt creative, just as long as it is a true value. Great—that was a short and sweet script. Now you will be able to run the auth.cgi program to verify that it is working. Once you are done with testing, we'll move on to the next scripts in our DMS.

14.5 main.cgi

The program that is going to get the most action will be main.cgi. This program will be used as the "home page" for the DMS application. main.cgi is also used to display links to all the documents that the user has rights to see.

Our main.cgi program is not going to be an overly fancy, do-everything program. Instead, it will be an excellent building block for a larger, more elaborate DMS application. Feel free to customize the page and build in some other cool features!

```
01: #!/usr/bin/perl -wT
02: # main.cgi
```

Lines 1–2 should be very familiar by now. We are simply telling the system where to find Perl on the system, turning on warnings and taint checking, and also a comment so that we can easily tell which program this is.

```
03: use strict;
04: use CGI qw(:standard);
05: use CGI::Carp qw(fatalsToBrowser);
06: use DBI;
07: require "./shared.pl" or die "Can't find file. $!\n";
```

Line 3 tells Perl to use the strict pragma.

Line 4 loads the CGI module and imports the standard functions.

Line 5 loads the Carp module. This module will display more specific error messages on the browser to aid in troubleshooting.

Line 6 loads the DBI module. This module is required for database access.

Line 7 is a require that will bring in the code from shared.pl, which is the program we just got finished with. *require()* is much like an include in C.

```
08: my $user    = Check_Cookie();
09: my $dbh     = DB_Connect();
10: my $group   = Get_Group($user);
```

Line 8 calls the *Check_Cookie()* subroutine to populate the $user variable, which should be the username.

Line 9 calls the *DB_Connect()* subroutine to create a connection to the database. A handle to the connection is then stored in the $dbh variable.

Line 10 calls the *Get_Group()* subroutine to access the database and get the group to which the current user belongs.

```
11: my $action = param('action');
12: my $file   = param('file');
13: my $out_to = param('out_to');
```

Lines 11–13 use CGI.pm's param function to fetch the data from the action, file, and out_to fields on the HTML form. The values are stored in their respective variables.

```
14: my %files;
```

Line 14 simply declares a hash called %files that we'll use at a later time in the program.

```
15: my @groups = qw(PEON USER PHB BOFH);
```

Line 15 creates an array called @groups that stores the names of each group for this DMS system. The order for these is important. The lowest level of access (PEON in our case) should come first, and the highest level should come last (BOFH).

```
16: foreach (@groups){
17:     $files{$_} = Get_Files($_);
18:     last if($group eq "$_");
19: }
```

Line 16 begins a foreach loop that cycles through the values in the @groups array. The purpose of this loop is to populate a hash that will contain a reference to an array of files for each different user group. This is kind of hard to picture, so let me try to make things a bit clearer for you. We are populating a hash called %files (we created it on line 14). Each time through the loop, $_ gets set to the current value in the array. The first time through $_ would get set to PEON and so on. For the value of that hash element, we call the *Get_Files()* subroutine, which returns a reference to the data it finds. So this subroutine gets the required data (we'll see how a bit later) and simply returns a reference.

Line 17 is the line that assigns the reference to the current hash value by calling the *Get_Files()* subroutine. Try to remember that a reference is really nothing more than a scalar variable. But instead of holding a "normal" value, such as a string or number, it contains an address that holds the location of a different variable. The variable it references can be of any data type.

Line 18 is used to break out of the *foreach()* loop if the $group is equal to the current value $_. This means that if a user belongs to the USER group, they will get the data for the PEON group, then the data for the USER group. However, since the values in $group and $_ would then match, the loop will be terminated. This makes it so that the user does not gain access to data that they are not supposed to see.

Line 19 ends the *foreach()* loop.

```
20: Display_Page();
```

Line 20 calls the *Display_Page()* subroutine. This subroutine will display the "home page."

```
21: sub Get_Files{
22:     my $group = shift;
23:     my @temp;
```

Line 21 begins the *Get_Files()* subroutine. This subroutine will get whatever files match the group name that is passed when the function is called.

Line 22 uses the *shift()* function to get the first—and only, in this case—item that was passed to the subroutine.

Line 23 creates a my variable called @temp.

```
24:     my $sth = $dbh->prepare( qq{ SELECT *
25:                                  FROM dms_files
26:                                  WHERE group_id = ? } );
```

Lines 24–26 make up the SQL statement needed to get all the fields from the dms_files table that match the group_id that was passed to the subroutine.

```
27:     $sth->execute($group);
```

Line 27 executes the SQL statement that we just prepared.

```
28:     while(my $ptr = $sth->fetchrow_hashref){
29:         push @temp, $ptr;
30:     }
```

Line 28 begins a *while()* loop that will continue looping as long as there is still data left to be retrieved. *fetchrow_hashref()* returns one row of data in a hash. Each time through the loop, the next row of data is retrieved. A *pointer* to the hash containing the data is stored in the variable $ptr.

Line 29 *push()*es the current value of $ptr onto the @temp array. Remember that $ptr is a reference to a hash, so we are creating an array where each element in the array is a reference to a hash that contains a row of data!

Line 30 ends the while loop.

```
31:     return \@temp;
32: }
```

Line 31 returns a reference to the @temp array. By putting a \ in front of the variable name, we create a reference to the variable. This way, instead of returning the entire array, we simply return one value that is a reference to the array.

Line 32 closes the *Get_Files()* subroutine.

```
33: sub Check_Status{
34:     my ($who_to, $date_out, $file_id) = @_;
35:     my $data;
```

Line 33 creates the *Check_Status()* subroutine. This subroutine is used to check whether the file passed to it is checked out. It then creates the HTML that will be displayed on the page to either show you who has the file checked out or it creates a link in which to check the file if you are the person who has it checked out.

Line 34 gets the values passed to the subroutine and stores them in three new my variables that we create.

Line 35 creates another my variable that we will be using later.

```
36:     return unless($who_to);
```

Line 36 returns if there was nothing in the $who_to variable. If the file is not checked out, the $who_to variable will have nothing in it. Since the file is not checked out, we don't need to do anything so we simply *return()*.

```
37:     my $sth = $dbh->prepare( qq{ SELECT phone, e_mail
38:                                  FROM   dms_users
39:                                  WHERE  username = ? } );
```

Lines 37–39 create the SQL needed to get the phone number and e-mail address from the user who has the file checked out.

```
40:     $sth->execute($who_to);
41:     my $ptr = $sth->fetch;
```

Line 40 executes the SQL statement we just created and passes the value of $who_to to the SQL statement.

Line 41 fetches a row of data and stores a reference to it in $ptr. Since the username is the primary key of the table, only one row can be retrieved when we search on that field. Because of this, we do not have to put the *fetch()* method into a loop.

```
42:     if($who_to eq $user){
43:         $data  = "<b>Checked Out:</b> ";
44:         $data .= "<a href='viewer.cgi?action=checkin";
45:         $data .= "&file=$file_id'>Check in</a><br>";
46:     }
```

Line 42 begins an if . . . else block that is used to see if the current user has the document checked out or if it is a different user. We compare the username of the person who has the item checked out ($who_to) to the username of the person currently using the DMS ($user). If $who_to and $user match, then the user currently using the DMS is also the person who has the file checked out. If this is the case, we enter the block and create an HTML link that will check the file back in to the DMS.

Lines 43–45 are the HTML needed for a link to check the item in. The HTML is stored as a string in $data.

Line 46 closes the first part of the if . . . else block.

```
47:     else{
48:         $data  = "<b>Checked Out To:</b> ";
49:         $data .= "<a href='mailto:$ptr->[1]'>$who_to</a> ";
50:         $data .= "- Phone: $ptr->[0]<br>";
51:     }
```

Line 47 begins the *else()* portion of the if . . . else block. We enter this block of code if the $user and $who_to are different. If they are different, it means that the current user and the person who has the file checked out are not the same person.

Lines 48–50 are the HTML needed to create a "mailto" link.

Line 51 closes the if . . . else block.

```
52:     return($data);
53: }
```

Line 52 returns the string $data.

Line 53 ends the *Check_Status()* subroutine.

```
54: sub Display_Page{
55: print header;
```

Line 54 begins the *Display_Page()* subroutine. This subroutine is used to display the main page for the DMS application. It contains a header and a list of all the files to which the user has access.

Line 55 prints the standard HTTP header using the *header()* function from the CGI module.

```
56:    print<<HTML;
57:       <html><head>
58:        <title>Document Management System</title>
```

```
59:     </head>
60:     <body bgcolor="#ffffff">
61:     <center>
62:      <table border="1" width="60%">
63:       <tr><td align="center">
64:        <h2>Simple Document Management System</h2>
65:        <b>Welcome $user!</b><br>
66:       </td></tr>
67:       <tr><td valign='top'>
68: HTML
```

Lines 56–68 are a here document that simply prints out the beginning of the HTML page that we are generating.

```
69:     foreach my $grp (keys %files){
70:         next unless(@{$files{$grp}});
```

Line 69 begins a large *foreach()* loop that is pretty much the heart of this program. It will loop through each of the keys that are in the %files hash. These keys will correspond to the groups PEON, USER, and so forth. We don't just want to loop through all the groups in the @groups hash because only the groups that the user belongs to will be in the %files hash.

Line 70 makes us skip to the *next()* iteration of the loop if there is nothing in the array. @{$files{$grp}} is another one of those variables that can make your eyes glaze over, so let's break it down. $files{$grp} would evaluate to something like this: $files{PEON}. Now that is not hard to deal with; it looks like the normal way to get a value from a hash.

Remember that the %files hash stores a reference to an array in its value. So $files{$grp} is a reference to an array. To get to that array, we need to access it properly. @{*array_reference*} is the proper way to do this, so @{$files{$grp}} is what we did. Sometimes things look really hard in Perl, but when you break them down into individual components, it is not nearly as difficult.

```
71:         print qq( <p><b>$grp Area</b><br>\n );
```

Line 71 is simply used to print the area out so that the user can tell to which area a group of files belongs.

```
72:         foreach my $ptr (@{$files{$grp}}){
73:             my $fname;
74:             my $checked_out = Check_Status($ptr->{who_to},
75:                                 $ptr->{out_date}, $ptr->
                                    {file_id});
```

Line 72 is again using the format that we talked about in detail on **line 70**. This time, since we are at this point, the @{$files{$grp}} *must* contain data. Each element of the array is a reference to a hash that contains a row of data. The $ptr variable will be set to the pointer to the hash so that we can reference the data that it contains.

Line 73 is simply declaring a my variable.

Lines 74–75 are used to check the status of the current file. The variable $checked_out is populated with the results of the *Check_Status()* subroutine. The *Check_Status()* subroutine is expecting to be passed three items: the username of the person who has the file checked out, the date that they checked out the file, and the file_id of the file that is checked out. The username and date could easily be empty, meaning that the file is not checked out.

Since $ptr is a *reference* to a hash and not a hash itself, we need to use the arrow operator "->" to *dereference* it and get to the data. So with $ptr->{file_id}, $ptr is the reference to the hash, -> dereferences the hash reference, and file_id is the key for the hash. This would be equivalent to $hash{file_id} if $ptr had actually been a hash rather than a reference to a hash. References are a difficult concept to explain in an easily understandable manner. References themselves are not that difficult, but when you start having hashes of arrays of references to hashes, things can get confusing.

To help others truly understand references, Mark Jason Dominus wrote an outstanding article titled "Understand References Today." It is a "references bible." It is available on his site at *http://www.plover.com/~mjd/perl/FAQs/references.html* and is definitely worth looking at.

```
76:          print qq( <table bgcolor="#e0e0e0" width="100%">
                         <tr><td> );
77:          print qq( <b>Filename:</b> );
```

Lines 76–77 create some of the HTML that we use to generate the listing of files.

```
78:          $fname  = qq(<a href="viewer.cgi?action=);
79:          $fname .= qq(view&file=$ptr->{file_id}">);
80:          $fname .= qq($ptr->{filename}</a>);
```

Lines 78–80 create the link to the file that is needed so the user can view the file. In this DMS application, we do not link directly to any document. Instead, we have a program called viewer.cgi that we use to fetch the file and send it to the user *after* we have verified that they have sufficient rights to view the file. Again, on lines 79 and 80 we are using the arrow operator to dereference and get to the values in the hash.

```
81:                    unless($checked_out){
82:                        $fname .= qq( [<a href="viewer.cgi?action=);
83:                        $fname .= qq(checkout&file=$ptr->
                                   {file_id}">);
84:                        $fname .= qq(Check Out</a>]);
85:                    }
```

Line 81 checks to see if $checked_out contains data. If it does *not,* then we enter this block and create the HTML that links to the viewer.cgi program and passes the file_id on the URL.

Lines 82–84 create the HTML and store it in the $fname variable.

Line 85 closes the unless block.

unless() is a function that makes you think a bit (well, it makes *me* think a bit). It is the same as *if not* but the Perlish way to represent it. Look at *unless(),* and then think, "Okay, this means if *not.*" Doing this should help out if you have problems remembering how *unless()* works.

```
86:                    print qq( $fname<br> );
87:                    print qq( <b>Description:</b> $ptr->
                                   {description}<br> );
88:                    print qq( $checked_out );
89:                    print qq( </td></tr></table> );
90:                }
91:            }
```

Lines 86–89 create the HTML that displays the information for one file. Here we see the arrow operator again on line 87, getting the description of the file.

Line 90 closes the *foreach()* loop that began on line 72.

Line 91 closes the *foreach()* loop that began on line 69.

```
 92:  print<<HTML;
 93:        </td></tr>
 94:        <tr><td>
 95:         <a href="upload.cgi?action=add">Add New Document
                   </a><br />
 96:         <a href="auth.cgi?action=logout">Logout</a>
 97:        </td></tr>
 98:       </table>
 99:      </body></html>
100: HTML
101: }
```

Lines 92–100 are a here document that print out the HTML, which ends the page we just generated.

Line 101 ends the *Display_Page()* subroutine. Now we have our main.cgi program. We can log in to the site via the auth.cgi script or by calling this program, main.cgi. If we are not logged in, it will redirect us to auth.cgi.

14.6 upload.cgi

We are getting close to having something very workable. We still need a program that will allow us to upload files to the DMS and another that will allow us to view the files that are in the DMS. Since it would not make much sense to create the viewer program before we could even upload any files to the system, we will do the upload.cgi program next and then the final program: viewer.cgi. The upload.cgi program is the largest program needed for our DMS system. However, it should not be too difficult. We covered file uploading in Chapter 7, and some of the code is taken directly from that code.

```
01: #!/usr/bin/perl -wT
02: # upload.cgi
```

Lines 1 and 2 are the same basic lines we've used for all programs thus far in this chapter.

```
03: use DBI;
04: use strict;
05: use File::Basename;
06: use CGI qw(:standard);
07: use CGI::Carp qw(fatalsToBrowser);
08: require "./shared.pl" or die "Can't find file. $!\n";
```

Lines 3–8 bring in the modules and files we need, and turn on the strict pragma. These lines should also be extremely familiar by now. The one exception here is that we are using the File::Basename module in this program.

```
09: my $user  = Check_Cookie();
10: my $dbh   = DB_Connect();
11: my $group = Get_Group($user);
```

Line 9 checks to see that the user has a valid cookie for this application. If they do not, the *Check_Cookie()* subroutine will redirect them to the auth.cgi program. If they do have a valid cookie, then it will get the value of the cookie and return it so that it can be stored in the $user variable.

Line 10 makes a connection to the database and stores the database handle in $dbh.

Line 11 calls the *Get_Group()* subroutine and stores the group returned in the $group variable.

```
12: param('filename') ? Process_File() : Default_Page();
```

Line 12 uses the trinary operator to determine what to do. If the value on the left side of the ? is true (true is anything but 0 or ""), then the first item to the right of the ? is executed. If the value on the left is false, then the last item gets executed. We are checking to see if anything was passed from the HTML form in the filename element.

```
13: exit;
```

Line 13 simply exits the program. Once we get to this line, we are done! You may be thinking, WOW, only 13 lines! And he said it was going to be a long program. Well, next we get to look at all the subroutines!

```
14: sub Get_File_Name{
```

Line 14 begins the *Get_File_Name()* subroutine. This subroutine was taken from the file uploading chapter. It gets rid of any path information and returns just the filename.

```
15:     if($ENV{HTTP_USER_AGENT} =~ /win/i){
16:         fileparse_set_fstype("MSDOS");
17:     }
```

Lines 15–17 begin an if . . . elsif block that checks to see what operating system the user is currently on. This first section looks to see if the user is on a Windows OS. If so, we enter the block and call the *fileparse_set_fstype()* function. This function is part of the File::Basename module.

```
18:     elsif($ENV{HTTP_USER_AGENT} =~ /mac/i){
19:         fileparse_set_fstype("MacOS");
20:     }
```

Lines 18–20 are the *elsif()* part of our block. This section checks to see if the user is on a Macintosh OS. If so, we enter the block and set the appropriate type with the *fileparse_set_fstype()* function. We do not have an *else()*

condition in this block. We used *if()* and *elsif()* but no else. This is perfectly legal in Perl. For this section, we only want to make changes if the HTTP_USER_AGENT is Windows or Macintosh. Otherwise, we just leave the default settings and continue.

```
21:     my $f_name = shift;
22:     $f_name    = basename($f_name);
23:     $f_name    =~ s!\s!\_!g;
```

Line 21 gets the filename that was passed to the subroutine via the *shift()* function.

Line 22 uses the basename function to get just the filename with no path information.

Line 23 replaces any spaces in the filename with underscores. Spaces create too many headaches, and by simply replacing them, you can eliminate problems such as having to explicitly quote every filename you wish to access.

```
24:     return($f_name);
25: }
```

Line 24 returns the filename with all the path information removed and all spaces replaced with _'s.

Line 25 ends the *Get_File_Name()* subroutine.

```
26: sub UnTaint{
27:     my $var = shift;
```

Line 26 begins the *UnTaint()* subroutine. This subroutine will ensure that the filename submitted doesn't contain any illegal characters.

Line 27 creates a my variable called $var and shifts in the value that was passed to the subroutine.

```
28:     if ($var =~ /^([-\@\w.]+)$/){
29:         $var = $1;
30:     }
```

Line 28 begins an if . . . else block. Here we are using a regular expression to filter out illegal characters. We are allowing word characters, -, @, and .

Line 29 sets $var to $1. $1 contains whatever matched in the parentheses. This untaints the variable.

Line 30 closes the *if()* part of the if . . . else block.

```
31:     else{
32:         die "Filename is tainted!\n";
33:     }
```

Line 31 begins the *else()* portion of the if . . . else block. We get here if there were illegal characters in the filename.

Line 32 ends the program and prints out an error message.

Line 33 ends the if . . . else block.

```
34:     return($var);
35: }
```

Line 34 returns the variable, which is now untainted.

Line 35 ends the *UnTaint()* subroutine.

```
36: sub Process_File{
37:     my $description = param('description');
38:     my $file_name   = param('filename');
39:     my $area        = param('area');
40:     my $mime        = uploadInfo($file_name)->{'Content-Type'};
41:     my $path        = "/usr/www/cgi-bin/dms/data";
```

Line 36 begins the *Process_File()* subroutine. This subroutine is used to handle the details of getting information about the file, making sure that the database gets updated properly and that the file gets uploaded.

Lines 37–39 create some my variables and set them to the information that was passed from the HTML form.

Line 40 uses the *uploadInfo()* function from CGI.pm to get the MIME type of the file that was uploaded. This will be saved in the database so that when we stream the file to the user, we send the proper MIME type back with the file.

Line 41 sets the path to where the files will be stored.

```
42:     my $file        = Get_File_Name($file_name);
```

Line 42 calls the *Get_File_Name()* function to get the filename without all the path details.

```
43:     $area = UnTaint($area);
44:     $file = UnTaint($file);
```

Lines 43–44 untaint the $area and $file variables.

```
45:     unless($mime){ $mime = "text/plain"; }
```

Line 45 sets the MIME type to "text/plain" if one was not received from the file.

```
46:     my $ptr = Get_File_Info($file, $area);
```

Line 46 gets the file information from the database and stores a pointer to the data in $ptr.

```
47:     unless($ptr->{file_id}){
```

Line 47 begins an unless . . . else block. Here we are checking to see if there is no file_id associated with this file. If not, then it must be a new file, so we upload it and *add* it to the database.

```
48:         Upload_File ($file, $area, $mime, $description);
49:         Add_New_File($file, $area, $mime, $description);
50:         print redirect(-uri=>"main.cgi");
51:         exit;
52:     }
```

Line 48 calls the *Upload_File()* subroutine and passes it the filename, area (or group) that the file goes in, the MIME type, and the file's description.

Line 49 calls the *Add_New_File()* subroutine and passes the same data that we passed to the *Upload_File()* subroutine.

Line 50 redirects the user to the main.cgi program. The file has now been uploaded and added to the database, so we can safely send the user back to the site's main page.

Line 51 exits the program.

Line 52 closes this part of the unless . . . else block.

```
53:     else{
```

Line 53 begins the *else()* portion of the unless . . . else block.

```
54:         unless($ptr->{who_to}){
55:             print redirect(-uri=>"main.cgi");
56:             exit;
57:         }
```

Line 54 begins another unless . . . else block. This one is checking to see if there is a user with the file checked out.

In **Line 55,** if the file is not checked out, we redirect the user back to the main.cgi page.

Line 56 exits the program. We should never get here, since we just redirected the user to another URL.

Line 57 closes this portion of the unless . . . else block.

```
58:          else{                    # File *is* checked out.
59:             if($ptr->{who_to} eq $user){
60:                 Upload_File ($file, $area, $mime,
                                    $description);
61:                 Check_File_In ($file, $area, $mime,
                                    $description);
62:                 print redirect(-uri=>"main.cgi");
63:                 exit;
64:             }
```

Line 58 is the *else()* part of our unless . . . else block. We enter this block if the file *is* checked out.

Line 59 then checks to see if the file is checked out to the user. If it is, we enter this block.

Line 60 calls the *Upload_File()* subroutine and passes the required data to the subroutine so that it can get all of the details correct in the database.

Line 61 calls the *Check_File_In()* subroutine. This updates the database so that the file is no longer in a checked-out status.

Line 62 redirects the user to the main.cgi program.

Line 63 exits the program.

Line 64 closes the *if()* portion of this if . . . else block.

```
65:          else{
66:              print redirect (-uri=>"main.cgi");
67:              exit;
68:             }
```

Line 65 begins the *else()* portion of the if . . . else block.

Line 66 redirects the user to the main.cgi program.

Line 67 exits the program.

Line 68 closes the if . . . else block.

```
69:            } # end of unless..else
70:       }
71:    exit;
72: }
```

Line 69 closes the inner unless . . . else block.

Line 70 closes the outer unless . . . else block.

Line 71 exits the program.

Line 72 ends the *Process_File()* subroutine.

```
73: sub Check_File_In{
74:     $dbh->do( " UPDATE TABLE dms_files SET
75:                 (filename, group_id, mime_type, description,
                    who_to, out_date)
76:                 VALUES
77:                 (?, ?, ?, ?, 'NULL', 'NULL') ", {}, (@_) );
78: }
```

Line 73 begins the *Check_File_In()* subroutine. This one will be used to update the file information in the database.

Lines 74–77 create and execute the SQL statement needed to do an update on the table. The (?, ?, ?, ?, 'NULL', 'NULL') ", {}, (@_) looks a bit odd, so let me explain. The question marks are simply database placeholders, which we have used many times before. The NULLs are the two fields we want to clear so that the program can tell that this file is checked in. The quotes close off the string portion that we pass to the do function. The {} is an empty hash. With MySQL these fields are not used, but they still must be provided. The @_ is the data that was passed to the subroutine. We passed four items: $file, $area, $mime, and $description. They all get stored in @_ when the subroutine begins. So what happens is that the four values get passed back in to the placeholders and we save ourselves from having to create variables and assign them values.

Line 78 ends the *Check_File_In()* subroutine.

```
79: sub Add_New_File{
80:     $dbh->do( " INSERT INTO dms_files
81:                 (filename, group_id, mime_type, description)
82:                 VALUES
83:                 (?, ?, ?, ?) ", {}, (@_) );
84: }
```

Lines 79–84 are the *Add_New_File()* subroutine. This subroutine functions almost exactly the same as the *Check_File_In()* subroutine. The only real difference here is that we do not have to pass the last two fields of data to the database because they will be NULL by default.

```
85: sub Upload_File{
86:     my ($file, $area, $mime, $description) = @_;
87:     my $file_name   = param('filename');
88:     my $path        = "/usr/www/cgi-bin/book/dms/data";
```

Line 85 begins the *Upload_File()* subroutine.

Line 86 reads in the data that was passed to the subroutine and stores it in some variables.

Line 87 gets the filename that was passed from the HTML form.

Line 88 sets the path to where we will be storing the uploaded files.

```
89:     my $data;
```

Line 89 creates a my variable called $data.

```
90:     $area = UnTaint($area);
91:     $file = UnTaint($file);
```

Lines 90–91 untaint the $area and $file variables.

```
92:     open(VAULT, ">$path/$area/$file")
93:        or die "Error opening file: $!\n";
```

Line 92 opens a filehandle for writing in the $path/$area subdirectory. The file is named whatever value is stored in $file.

Line 93 is our *or die()* statement that checks to make sure that we successfully opened the file.

```
94:     unless($mime =~ /text/){
95:         binmode ($file_name);
96:         binmode (VAULT);
97:     }
```

Line 94 checks to see if the MIME type contains the word text. If it does not, it is probably a binary file, so we set *binmode()* on the filehandles. *binmode()* has no effect on Unix systems; these lines are here for the Windows users.

Lines 95 and 96 set *binmode()* on the filehandles $file_name and VAULT.

Line 97 closes this *unless()* block.

```
98:     while( read($file_name, $data, 1024) ){
99:         print VAULT $data;
100:    }
```

Line 98 is a *while()* loop that reads through the file a 1024 byte chunk at a time. The data is stored temporarily in $data each time through the loop.

Line 99 prints the current chunk of data to the filehandle.

Line 100 ends the *while()* loop that we use for saving the file.

```
101:    close VAULT;
102: }
```

Line 101 closes the VAULT filehandle.

Line 102 ends the *Upload_File()* subroutine.

```
103: sub Get_File_Info{
104:    my ($file, $group) = @_;
```

Line 103 creates the *Get_File_Info()* subroutine that is used to get the information about the file from the database.

Line 104 reads in the values that were passed to the subroutine when it was called.

```
105:    my $sth = $dbh->prepare( qq{ SELECT * FROM dms_files
                    WHERE
106:                        ((filename = ?) AND (group_id =
                                                ?)) } );
```

Lines 105–106 create and *prepare()* the SQL statement needed to get the data about the file from the database.

```
107:    $sth->execute($file, $group);
```

Line 107 executes the SQL statement that we just created.

```
108:    my $ptr = $sth->fetchrow_hashref;
```

Line 108 gets a row of data. There should only be one row, and it stores a pointer to the hash returned in the $ptr variable.

```
109:     return($ptr);
110: }
```

Line 109 returns the pointer $ptr.

Line 110 ends the *Get_File_Info()* subroutine.

```
111: sub Default_Page{
112:     my $options;
```

Line 111 creates the *Default_Page()* subroutine.

Line 112 creates a variable named $options.

```
113:     {
114:         $options = qq{ <option value="PEON">Peon</option> };
115:             last if($group eq "PEON");
116:         $options .= qq{ <option value="USER">User</option> };
117:             last if($group eq "USER");
118:         $options .= qq{ <option value="PHB">Manager</option> };
119:             last if($group eq "PHB");
120:         $options .= qq{ <option value="BOFH">God</option> };
121:     }
```

Lines 113–121 are rather interesting. We only want to display the options in the dropdown box of the upload screen into which the user has rights to upload. What these lines do is start at the lowest level of access, create an option field, store it in a string, and then check to see if the user's $group is the same as the group we just processed. If it is, then we break out of the block. These items had to be included inside of a block; otherwise, the last function will not work. So these lines simply create a string that contains the values that will be put into the dropdown box on the upload screen.

```
122:     print header;
```

Line 122 prints out the standard HTTP header.

```
123:        print<<HTML;
124:        <html><head>
125:         <title>DMS Example - Uploading</title></head>
126:         <body bgcolor="#ffffff">
127:         <center>
128:          <form method="post" ENCTYPE="multipart/form-data">
129:           <p>
130:            <h2>Welcome to the DMS Example - Uploading</h2>
131:           </p>
132:           <p>
133:            <table border="1" cellspacing="0">
134:             <tr>
135:              <td>Filename:</td>
136:              <td><input type="file" name="filename"></td>
137:             </tr>
138:             <tr>
139:              <td>Area:</td>
140:              <td>
141:               <select name="area">
142: HTML
```

Lines 123–142 are a here document that prints the first part of the upload screen.

```
143:              print $options;
```

Line 143 prints out the $options variable. This is the variable that contains the options that go in the dropdown box.

```
144: print<<HTML;
145:               </select>
146:              </td>
147:             </tr>
148:             <tr>
149:              <td>Description:</td>
150:              <td>
151:         <textarea name="description" cols="40" rows="4"
                          wrap="physical"></textarea>
152:              </td>
153:             </tr>
154:             <tr align="center">
155:              <td colspan="2"><input type="submit" value=
                              "   Upload File   "></td>
156:             </tr>
157:            </table>
```

```
158:        </p>
159:      </form>
160:     </center>
161:    </body>
162:   </html>
163: HTML
```

Lines 144–163 are a here document that prints out the rest of the HTML for the upload page.

```
164: exit;
165: }
```

Line 164 exits the program.

Line 165 ends the *Default_Page()* subroutine.

Now we've finished the upload page! You can give this one a try now if you'd like. We have one more program to write before we finish up our DMS. The final script will be the one that allows the users to view the files that are on the DMS. It is called viewer.cgi and is a fairly short program, 75 lines.

14.7 viewer.cgi

The viewer.cgi program not only serves the files to the users but is also the program that is used to check a document in or out.

```
01: #!/usr/bin/perl -wT
02: # viewer.cgi
03: use DBI;
04: use strict;
05: use CGI qw(:standard);
06: require "./shared.pl" or die "Can't find file. $!\n";
```

Lines 1–6 we've seen many times before. They do the same thing that they have been doing in previous programs.

```
07: my $file   = param('file');
08: my $action = param('action');
```

Lines 7 and 8 get the data passed from HTML form and store them in some my variables.

```
09: my $user   = Check_Cookie();
10: my $dbh    = DB_Connect();
```

Line 09 checks the cookie to ensure that the user is logged in. The result is stored in the $user variable.

Line 10 creates a connection to the database and stores the database handle in the $dbh variable.

```
11: my $f_ptr  = Get_File_Info_ID($file);
12: my $group  = Get_Group($user);
```

Line 11 gets a pointer to the file information and saves it in the $f_ptr variable.

Line 12 gets the group that the user is in and stores it in the $group variable.

```
13: my %g_hash = ( 'BOFH' => 4, 'PHB'  => 3,
14:                'USER' => 2, 'PEON' => 1);
```

Lines 13–14 create a hash of the groups called %g_hash. These group names are given values that will be used to determine if a user has the proper permissions to view a file. The higher the number, the more rights the user has.

```
15: my $u_val = $g_hash{$group};
16: my $f_val = $g_hash{$f_ptr->{group_id}};
```

Line 15 gets the value of the group that the user is in. If a user is logged in and is in the PHB group, then the $u_val would be 3 for that user.

Line 16 gets the value of the group_id that is in the database for this file. This value will be stored in the $f_val variable.

```
17: print redirect(-uri=>"auth.cgi")
18:    unless($u_val >= $f_val);
```

Lines 17–18 redirect the user to the auth.cgi page if the user value is not greater than or equal to the file value. For a professional system, this would be a good place to add a screen informing the use of the problem.

```
19: if($action eq "view"){
20:     View_File();
21:     exit;
22: }
```

Line 19 begins an if . . . elsif . . . elsif . . . else block that checks to see what action needs to be performed. In this test condition, we are checking to see if the action was view.

Line 20 is if it was view; then we enter the block and call the *View_File()* subroutine.

Line 21 exits the program.

Line 22 closes this portion of the block.

```
23: elsif($action eq "checkout"){
24:     Check_Out();
25:     print redirect(-uri=>"main.cgi");
26:     exit;
27: }
```

Line 23 checks to see if the action was checkout. If it was, we enter this block.

Line 24 calls the *Check_Out()* subroutine to check the file out to the current user.

Line 25 redirects the user to the main.cgi program.

Line 26 exits the program.

Line 27 closes this portion of the block.

```
28: elsif($action eq "checkin"){
29:     Check_In();
30:     print redirect(-uri=>"main.cgi");
31:     exit;
32: }
```

Line 28 checks to see if the action was checkin. If it was, this portion of the block is entered.

Line 29 calls the *Check_In()* subroutine to update the database and check the file in.

Line 30 redirects the user to the main.cgi program.

Line 31 exits the program.

Line 32 closes this portion of the block.

```
33: else{
34:     print redirect(-uri=>"main.cgi");
35:     exit;
36: }
```

Line 33 is where we get if none of the other conditions were true.

Line 34 is if this was the case; we simply redirect the user back to the main page.

Line 35 exits the program.

Line 36 closes the if . . . elsif . . . elsif . . . else block.

```
37: sub Check_Out{
38:     my $time = time();
```

Line 37 begins the *Check_Out()* subroutine.

Line 38 grabs the current time and stores it in the $time variable.

```
39:     $dbh->do( qq{ UPDATE dms_files
40:                   SET
41:                   who_to   = '$user',
42:                   out_date = '$time'
43:                   WHERE
44:                   file_id  = '$file' } );
```

Lines 29–44 create the SQL and execute it for the update of the database table.

```
45:     print redirect(-uri=>"main.cgi");
46: }
```

Line 45 redirects the user to the main.cgi program.

Line 46 ends the *Check_Out()* subroutine.

```
47: sub Check_In{
```

Line 47 begins the *Check_In()* subroutine.

```
48:     $dbh->do( qq{ UPDATE dms_files
49:                   SET
50:                   who_to   = NULL,
51:                   out_date = NULL
52:                   WHERE
53:                   file_id  = '$file' } );
```

Lines 48–53 create and execute the SQL needed to update the database.

```
54:     print redirect(-uri=>"main.cgi");
55: }
```

Line 54 redirects the user to the main.cgi program.

Line 55 ends the *Check_In()* subroutine.

```
56: sub View_File{
57:     my $data;
58:     my $filepath = "data/$f_ptr->{group_id}/$f_ptr->{filename}";
```

Line 56 creates the *View_File()* subroutine. This subroutine is used to fetch the document requested and send it to the user.

Line 57 creates a my variable that we'll be using.

Line 58 creates the file path where the file is stored.

```
59:     print redirect(-uri=>"main.cgi") unless $f_ptr->{filename};
60:     open(FILE, $filepath) or die "Error opening file! $!\n";
```

Line 59 redirects the user to the main page if there is no filename.

Line 60 opens the file for reading.

```
61:     print header($f_ptr->{mime_type});
```

Line 61 prints the header that was captured when the file was uploaded.

```
62:     while( read(FILE, $data, 1024) ){
63:         print $data;
64:     }
```

Lines 62–64 are a *while()* loop that reads through the file 1024 bytes at a time and stores it to the $data variable, then prints out the data.

```
65:     close FILE;
66: }
```

Line 65 closes the file.

Line 66 ends the *View_File()* subroutine.

```
67: sub Get_File_Info_ID{
68:     my $file_id = shift;
```

Line 67 creates the *Get_File_Info_ID()* subroutine. This subroutine fetches a file's details based on the file id that is passed on the URL.

Line 68 creates a my variable called $file_id and stores the value that was passed to the subroutine in it.

```
69:      my $sth = $dbh->prepare( qq{ SELECT *
70:                                   FROM dms_files
71:                                   WHERE file_id = ? } );
```

Lines 69–71 create and prepare the SQL needed to select the information about a file from the table.

```
72:      $sth->execute($file_id);
```

Line 72 executes the SQL statement that we just created.

```
73:      my $ptr = $sth->fetchrow_hashref;
74:      return $ptr;
75: }
```

Line 73 fetches a row of data from the database and stores it in a new variable called $ptr.

Line 74 returns $ptr.

Line 75 ends the *Get_File_Info_ID()* subroutine.

14.8 Program Listings

Listing 14-1   **auth.cgi**

```
01: #!/usr/bin/perl -wT
02: # auth.cgi
03: use DBI;
04: use strict;
05: use CGI qw(:standard);
06: require "./shared.pl" or die "Can't find file. $!\n";
07: my $user    = param('username');
08: my $pass    = param('password');
09: my $action  = param('action');
10: my $dbh     = DB_Connect();
11: Logout()    if($action eq "logout");
```

```perl
12: Login_Page() unless($pass);
13: my $valid = Check_Login($user, $pass);
14: if($valid) {
15:     my $cookie = Create_Cookie("1h", $user);
16:     print redirect(-uri=>"main.cgi", -cookie=>$cookie);
17:     exit;
18: }
19: else{
20:     my $time = time();
21:     print redirect(-uri=>"auth.cgi?$time");
22:     exit;
23: }
24: sub Logout{
25:     my $time   = time();
26:     my $cookie = Create_Cookie("-1h", "");
27:     print redirect(-uri=>"auth.cgi?$time", -cookie=>$cookie);
28:     exit;
29: }
30: sub Create_Cookie{
31:     my $exp = shift;
32:     my $val = shift;
33:     my $cookie = cookie( -name    => 'dms',
34:                          -value   => $val,
35:                          -expires => $exp );
36:     return($cookie);
37: }
38: sub Check_Login{
39:     my $user = shift;
40:     my $pass = shift;
41:     my $data;
42:     my $sth = $dbh->prepare( qq{ SELECT password
43:                                  FROM dms_users
44:                                  WHERE
45:                                  username = ?
46:                                  } );
47:     $sth->execute($user);
48:     $data = $sth->fetch;
49:     $sth->finish;
50:     $dbh->disconnect;
51:     ($data->[0] eq $pass) ? return 1 : return 0;
52: }
```

(continued)

```
53: sub Login_Page{
54:     print header();
55:     print<<HTML;
56:       <html><head><title>DMS Example</title></head>
57:        <body bgcolor="#ffffff">
58:         <center>
59:          <form method="post">
60:           <p>
61:            <h2>Welcome to the DMS Example</h2>
62:           </p>
63:           <p>
64:            <table border="1" cellspacing="0">
65:             <tr>
66:              <td>Username:</td>
67:              <td><input type="text" name="username"></td>
68:             </tr>
69:             <tr>
70:              <td>Password:</td>
71:              <td><input type="password" name="password"></td>
72:             </tr>
73:            <tr align="center">
74:             <td colspan="2">
75:              <input type="submit" value="    Login    ">
76:             </td>
77:            </tr>
78:           </table>
79:          </p>
80:         </form>
81:        </center>
82:       </body>
83:      </html>
84: HTML
85:     exit;
86: }
```

Listing 14-2 **shared.pl**

```
01: sub DB_Connect{
02:     my $dbh = DBI->connect("DBI:mysql:book", "book", "addison")
03:       or die "Error connecting to DB! $DBI::errstr\n";
04:     return($dbh);
05: }
06: sub Check_Cookie{
07:     my $user = cookie('dms');
08:     if($user){
```

```
09:            return($user);
10:        }
11:        else{
12:            print redirect(-uri=>"auth.cgi");
13:            exit;
14:        }
15: }
16: sub Get_Group{
17:        my $user = shift;
18:        my $dbh = DBI->connect("DBI:mysql:book", "book", "addison")
19:          or die "Error connecting to DB! $DBI::errstr\n";
20:        my $sth = $dbh->prepare( qq{ SELECT group_id
21:                                    FROM dms_users
22:                                    WHERE
23:                                    username = ?
24:                                  } );
25:        $sth->execute($user);
26:        $group = $sth->fetch->[0];
27:        redirect(-uri=>"auth.cgi") unless $group;
28:        $sth->finish;
29:        $dbh->disconnect;
30:        return($group);
31: }
32: 1;
```

Listing 14-3   main.cgi

```
01: #!/usr/bin/perl -wT
02: # main.cgi
03: use strict;
04: use CGI qw(:standard);
05: use CGI::Carp qw(fatalsToBrowser);
06: use DBI;
07: require "./shared.pl" or die "Can't find file. $!\n";
08: my $user = Check_Cookie();
09: my $dbh  = DB_Connect();
10: my $group = Get_Group($user);
11: my $action = param('action');
12: my $file   = param('file');
13: my $out_to = param('out_to');
14: my %files;
15: my @groups = qw(PEON USER PHB BOFH);
16: foreach (@groups){
```

(continued)

```
17:        $files{$_} = Get_Files($_);
18:        last if($group eq "$_");
19: }
20: Display_Page();
21: sub Get_Files{
22:        my $group = shift;
23:        my @temp;
24:        my $sth = $dbh->prepare( qq{ SELECT *
25:                                      FROM dms_files
26:                                      WHERE group_id = ? } );
27:        $sth->execute($group);
28:        while(my $ptr = $sth->fetchrow_hashref){
29:            push @temp, $ptr;
30:        }
31:        return \@temp;
32: }
33: sub Check_Status{
34:        my ($who_to, $date_out, $file_id) = @_;
35:        my $data;
36:        return unless($who_to);
37:        my $sth = $dbh->prepare( qq{ SELECT phone, e_mail
38:                                      FROM   dms_users
39:                                      WHERE  username = ? } );
40:        $sth->execute($who_to);
41:        my $ptr = $sth->fetch;
42:        if($who_to eq $user){
43:            $data  = "<b>Checked Out:</b> ";
44:            $data .= "<a href='viewer.cgi?action=checkin";
45:            $data .= "&file=$file_id'>Check in</a><br>";
46:        }
47:        else{
48:            $data  = "<b>Checked Out To:</b> ";
49:            $data .= "<a href='mailto:$ptr->[1]'>$who_to</a> ";
50:            $data .= "- Phone: $ptr->[0]<br>";
51:        }
52:        return($data);
53: }
54: sub Display_Page{
55: print header;
56:  print<<HTML;
57:        <html><head>
58:        <title>Document Management System</title>
59:        </head>
60:        <body bgcolor="#ffffff">
```

(continued)

```
61:     <center>
62:      <table border="1" width="60%">
63:       <tr><td align="center">
64:        <h2>Simple Document Management System</h2>
65:        <b>Welcome $user!</b><br>
66:       </td></tr>
67:       <tr><td valign='top'>
68: HTML
69:    foreach my $grp (keys %files){
70:        next unless(@{$files{$grp}});
71:        print qq( <p><b>$grp Area</b><br>\n );
72:        foreach my $ptr (@{$files{$grp}}){
73:            my $fname;
74:            my $checked_out = Check_Status($ptr->{who_to},
75:                              $ptr->{out_date}, $ptr->{file_id});
76:          print qq( <table bgcolor="#e0e0e0" width="100%"><tr><td> );
77:            print qq( <b>Filename:</b> );
78:            $fname  = qq(<a href="viewer.cgi?action=);
79:            $fname .= qq(view&file=$ptr->{file_id}">);
80:            $fname .= qq($ptr->{filename}</a>);
81:            unless($checked_out){
82:                $fname .= qq( [<a href="viewer.cgi?action=);
83:                $fname .= qq(checkout&file=$ptr->{file_id}">);
84:                $fname .= qq(Check Out</a>]);
85:            }
86:            print qq( $fname<br> );
87:            print qq( <b>Description:</b> $ptr->{description}<br> );
88:            print qq( $checked_out );
89:            print qq( </td></tr></table> );
90:        }
91:    }
92: print<<HTML;
93:       </td></tr>
94:       <tr><td>
95:        <a href="upload.cgi?action=add">Add New Document</a><br />
96:        <a href="auth.cgi?action=logout">Logout</a>
97:       </td></tr>
98:      </table>
99:     </body></html>
100: HTML
101: }
```

Listing 14-4   upload.cgi

```perl
01: #!/usr/bin/perl -wT
02: # upload.cgi
03: use DBI;
04: use strict;
05: use File::Basename;
06: use CGI qw(:standard);
07: use CGI::Carp qw(fatalsToBrowser);
08: require "./shared.pl" or die "Can't find file. $!\n";
09: my $user  = Check_Cookie();
10: my $dbh   = DB_Connect();
11: my $group = Get_Group($user);
12: param('filename') ? Process_File() : Default_Page();
13: exit;
14: sub Get_File_Name{
15:     if($ENV{HTTP_USER_AGENT} =~ /win/i){
16:         fileparse_set_fstype("MSDOS");
17:     }
18:     elsif($ENV{HTTP_USER_AGENT} =~ /mac/i){
19:         fileparse_set_fstype("MacOS");
20:     }
21:     my $f_name = shift;
22:     $f_name    = basename($f_name);
23:     $f_name    =~ s!\s!\_!g;
24:     return($f_name);
25: }
26: sub UnTaint{
27:     my $var = shift;
28:     if ($var =~ /^([-\@\w.]+)$/){
29:         $var = $1;
30:     }
31:     else{
32:         die "Filename is tainted!\n";
33:     }
34:     return($var);
35: }
36: sub Process_File{
37:     my $description = param('description');
38:     my $file_name   = param('filename');
39:     my $area        = param('area');
40:     my $mime        = uploadInfo($file_name)->{'Content-Type'};
41:     my $path        = "/usr/www/cgi-bin/book/dms/data";
42:     my $file        = Get_File_Name($file_name);
43:     $area = UnTaint($area);
44:     $file = UnTaint($file);
```

(continued)

```
45:        unless($mime){ $mime = "text/plain"; }
46:        my $ptr = Get_File_Info($file, $area);
47:        unless($ptr->{file_id}){
48:            Upload_File ($file, $area, $mime, $description);
49:            Add_New_File($file, $area, $mime, $description);
50:            print redirect(-uri=>"main.cgi");
51:            exit;
52:        }
53:        else{
54:            unless($ptr->{who_to}){
55:                print redirect(-uri=>"main.cgi");
56:                exit;
57:            }
58:            else{                    # File *is* checked out.
59:                if($ptr->{who_to} eq $user){
60:                    Upload_File ($file, $area, $mime, $description);
61:                    Check_File_In($file, $area, $mime, $description);
62:                    print redirect(-uri=>"main.cgi");
63:                    exit;
64:                }
65:                else{
66:                    print redirect (-uri=>"main.cgi");
67:                    exit;
68:                }
69:            } # end of unless . . . else
70:        }
71:    exit;
72: }
73: sub Check_File_In{
74:     $dbh->do( " UPDATE TABLE dms_files SET
75:                 (filename, group_id, mime_type, description,
                    who_to, out_date)
76:                 VALUES
77:                 (?, ?, ?, ?, 'NULL', 'NULL') ", {}, (@_) );
78: }
79: sub Add_New_File{
80:     $dbh->do( " INSERT INTO dms_files
81:                 (filename, group_id, mime_type, description)
82:                 VALUES
83:                 (?, ?, ?, ?) ", {}, (@_) );
84: }
85: sub Upload_File{
86:     my ($file, $area, $mime, $description) = @_;
87:     my $file_name    = param('filename');
88:     my $path         = "/usr/www/cgi-bin/book/dms/data";
89:     my $data;
```

(continued)

```
90:        $area = UnTaint($area);
91:        $file = UnTaint($file);
92:        open(VAULT, ">$path/$area/$file")
93:          or die "Error opening file: $!\n";
94:        unless($mime =~ /text/){
95:            binmode ($file_name);
96:            binmode (VAULT);
97:        }
98:        while( read($file_name, $data, 1024) ){
99:            print VAULT $data;
100:       }
101:       close VAULT;
102: }
103: sub Get_File_Info{
104:       my ($file, $group) = @_;
105:       my $sth = $dbh->prepare( qq{ SELECT * FROM dms_files WHERE
106:                                 ((filename = ?) AND (group_id = ?)) } );
107:       $sth->execute($file, $group);
108:       my $ptr = $sth->fetchrow_hashref;
109:       return($ptr);
110: }
111: sub Default_Page{
112:       my $options;
113:       {
114:           $options = qq{ <option value="PEON">Peon</option> };
115:             last if($group eq "PEON");
116:           $options .= qq{ <option value="USER">User</option> };
117:             last if($group eq "USER");
118:           $options .= qq{ <option value="PHB">Manager</option> };
119:             last if($group eq "PHB");
120:           $options .= qq{ <option value="BOFH">God</option> };
121:       }
122:       print header;
123:       print<<HTML;
124:       <html><head>
125:        <title>DMS Example - Uploading</title></head>
126:        <body bgcolor="#ffffff">
127:        <center>
128:         <form method="post" ENCTYPE="multipart/form-data">
129:          <p>
130:           <h2>Welcome to the DMS Example - Uploading</h2>
131:          </p>
132:          <p>
133:           <table border="1" cellspacing="0">
```

```
134:          <tr>
135:           <td>Filename:</td>
136:           <td><input type="file" name="filename"></td>
137:          </tr>
138:          <tr>
139:           <td>Area:</td>
140:           <td>
141:            <select name="area">
142: HTML
143:          print $options;
144: print<<HTML;
145:            </select>
146:           </td>
147:          </tr>
148:          <tr>
149:           <td>Description:</td>
150:           <td>
151:      <textarea name="description" cols="40" rows="4" wrap=
           "physical"></textarea>
152:            </td>
153:          </tr>
154:          <tr align="center">
155:           <td colspan="2"><input type="submit" value="    Upload
    File  "></td>
156:           </tr>
157:          </table>
158:         </p>
159:        </form>
160:       </center>
161:      </body>
162:     </html>
163: HTML
164: exit;
165: }
```

Listing 14-5   viewer.cgi

```
01: #!/usr/bin/perl -wT
02: use DBI;
03: use strict;
04: use CGI qw(:standard);
```

(continued)

```
05: require "./shared.pl" or die "Can't find file. $!\n";
06: my $file   = param('file');
07: my $action = param('action');
08: my $user   = Check_Cookie();
09: my $dbh    = DB_Connect();
10: my $f_ptr  = Get_File_Info_ID($file);
11: my $group  = Get_Group($user);
12: my %g_hash = ( 'BOFH' => 4, 'PHB'  => 3,
13:                'USER' => 2, 'PEON' => 1);
14: my $u_val = $g_hash{$group};
15: my $f_val = $g_hash{$f_ptr->{group_id}};
16: print redirect(-uri=>"auth.cgi")
17:   unless($u_val >= $f_val);
18: if($action eq "view"){
19:     View_File();
20:     exit;
21: }
22: elsif($action eq "checkout"){
23:     Check_Out();
24:     print redirect(-uri=>"main.cgi");
25:     exit;
26: }
27: elsif($action eq "checkin"){
28:     Check_In();
29:     print redirect(-uri=>"main.cgi");
30:     exit;
31: }
32: else{
33:     print redirect(-uri=>"main.cgi");
34:     exit;
35: }
36: sub Check_Out{
37:     my $time = time();
38:     $dbh->do( qq{ UPDATE dms_files
39:                   SET
40:                   who_to   = '$user',
41:                   out_date = '$time'
42:                   WHERE
43:                   file_id  = '$file' } );
44:     print redirect(-uri=>"main.cgi");
45: }
46: sub Check_In{
47:     $dbh->do( qq{ UPDATE dms_files
48:                   SET
49:                   who_to   = NULL,
50:                   out_date = NULL
```

```
51:                        WHERE
52:                          file_id  = '$file' } );
53:      print redirect(-uri=>"main.cgi");
54: }
55: sub View_File{
56:      my $data;
57:      my $filepath = "data/$f_ptr->{group_id}/$f_ptr->
                         {filename}";
58:      print redirect(-uri=>"main.cgi") unless $f_ptr->
   {filename};
59:      open(FILE, $filepath) or die "Error opening file! $!\n";
60:      print header($f_ptr->{mime_type});
61:      while( read(FILE, $data, 1024) ){
62:          print $data;
63:      }
64:      close FILE;
65: }
66: sub Get_File_Info_ID{
67:      my $file_id = shift;
68:      my $sth = $dbh->prepare( qq{ SELECT *
69:                                   FROM dms_files
70:                                   WHERE file_id = ? } );
71:      $sth->execute($file_id);
72:      my $ptr = $sth->fetchrow_hashref;
73:      return $ptr;
74: }
```

15 Chapter

Dynamically Manipulating Images

15.1 Introduction

In this chapter we cover some basic image manipulation using Perl. Image manipulation can be done dynamically, as will be shown in examples, as well as by writing backend scripts to ready images for your Web site. The examples in this chapter cover some of the basic functions you may want to use to show how easy this task is to do in Perl. The examples will teach you how to create a chart on the fly, do thumbnails, run filters on images, create animated images, and add to an image with text and shapes onto images.

Concentration will be on the Perl modules **GD.pm**[1] and **Image:: Magick** .[2] The **GD** module is an API to the gd library, written Perl by Lincoln Stein. The gd library is a graphics library used to manipulate graphics, written in C by Thomas Boutell. gd provides developers with a way to create rudimentary shapes such as polygons, arcs, and lines as well as add text and color. It is not the be-all for image manipulation, but it is very useful for getting many tasks done. The **Image::Magick** module, on the other hand, provides an API to the Image Magick software suite. Image Magick is itself a graphics manipulation program and has more advanced

---

1. This requires gdlib being installed. Consult the documentation for current prerequisites.
2. This Perl module provides an API to the ImageMagick graphics suite. This free software can be obtained at *http://www.wizards.dupont.com/cristy/ImageMagick.html*, and the documentation should be consulted for installation instructions.

features, such as filters, and is intended to be a general purpose graphics manipulation program.

15.2 Adding Shapes and Text

There may be times when you may want to add text or shapes to preexisting images. A real-world example of this is software I recently developed. In this case I had a Web security[3] system whose administration screens are based off an image. The image happens to resemble, and is called, a remote control. This system allows for each virtual host to have its own remote control (all using one set of scripts), which could get confusing if you have many remotes open and no way to tell which is for what virtual host. To remedy this, text is dynamically overlaid on the remote control image, noting the domain name of the virtual host as well as the version of the security system. Now users can have multiple remotes open and easily be able to differentiate each of them. This is all done with the GD.pm Perl module.

The example script we will walk through doesn't have quite the serious usage as a Web security system, but it applies the same principles, concept, and methods. What we will be looking at is a script that opens an existing image file, then overlays some rudimentary shapes (circles) and places text within that. This script is called add_text.cgi. In this example an image of an adorable child[4] will be altered to add "thought bubbles" and text inside. It will teach you how to add a rudimentary shape as well as text to an image.

```
01: #!/usr/bin/perl -wT
02: use strict;
03: use GD;
04: no strict 'subs';
```

Lines 1–4 define the path to Perl as well as pull in the *strict* pragma and *GD* module. Line 4 tells the *strict* pragma not to complain about barewords that look like they may be subroutines. This needs to be done because of how we will be using a bareword, which will really be a filehandle, in line 6. If this is not done, *strict* would throw an error and terminate the script.

```
05: open (PNG,"kyla_smile.png") || die "$!";
06:    my $image = newFromPng GD::Image(PNG) || die "$!";
07: close PNG;
```

---

3. This is currently proprietary as a whole, and it would take a book in itself to explain.
4. Of course, this is a subjective statement.

Lines 5, 6, and 7 open the image that is to be manipulated—in this case, kyla_smile.png—and create a new image object with that open filehandle. **Line 6** is really where that magic happens. The *newFromPng()* method, which is imported by GD, is passed the argument GD::Image(PNG). PNG is the filehande to the open image file, and that filehandle is what is being passed to GD::Image. This is also where the bareword warning would come from if *strict 'subs'* was still enabled. So the filehandle is passed to GD::Image, which reads in the file data, and that is being passed to *newFromPng()*, which GD uses to decode the image. For example, if we were using an XBM image, we would use the *newFromXBM()* method so GD can properly handle the incoming data. The resulting object reference is stored in the variable $image.

```
08: my $white = $image->colorAllocate(255,255,255);
09: my $black = $image->colorAllocate(0,0,0);
```

Lines 8 and 9 allocate two colors, black and white. This was briefly introduced in Chapter 7. The *colorAllocate()* method adds colors to the images color table. The three arguments passed to it are the red, green, and blue (RGB) triplet for the color you wish to define. The returned value is the index of that color in the images color table and can be referred to with the variable on the left side of the = sign. A developer *must* allocate colors to the images color table when he or she wishes to use a color for the image.

```
10: $image->arc(50,50,95,75,0,360,$black);
11: $image->fillToBorder(50,50,$black, $white);
12: $image->arc(60,95,25,25,0,360,$black);
13: $image->fillToBorder(60,95,$black, $white);
14: $image->arc(70,125,20,20,0,360,$black);
15: $image->fillToBorder(70,125,$black, $white);
```

Lines 10–15 create three different ovals. Each of these shapes is created by two lines, one defining the boundaries of the ellipse and the color of that boundary. The other line is to fill in the shape with one color. In this case, the arcs will have black boundaries and be filled in with white to look like thought bubbles. To define the size and borders of the arc, the *arc()* method is used. This method is passed seven arguments. The first two are the XY coordinates for the center of the ellipse. The third and fourth arguments are the width and height, respectively, of the ellipse. Arguments five and six define what portion of the ellipse is covered by the arc. The top of the ellipse is 0, with angles increasing clockwise to 360. This example uses a complete ellipse, so the start is 0 and the end is 360. Finally, the seventh argument is the color of the ellipses border, which will be black. With this line alone, an ellipse with its black border will be drawn on the image.

Usually thought bubbles have a solid white background within its black border, so now the ellipse needs to be filled in. This is done with the *fillTo-Border()* method. This method takes four arguments. The first and second ones define the XY coordinates of where to begin doing a flood fill. The third argument is the color of the border to which it is to be filled. This method flood fills until it reaches the border color specified by this argument. The sister method of *fillToBorder()* is *fill()*, which will fill starting from the XY point you specify but only until a pixel of a different color is reached. By using *fillToBorder()*, a developer can easily flood fill ellipses and other shapes. The final argument passed is the color to flood fill with. This color, as well as the one used for the third argument, must be a color that you have added to the image's color table. When the three ellipses are complete, so are the thought bubbles.

```
16: $image->string(gdMediumBoldFont,10,45,"I Love Dad!",$black);
```

Line 16 adds a string of text onto the image. The *string()* method is used to place text onto the image. This object method takes five arguments, beginning with the type of font to use for the text. **Line 16** is using gdMedium-BoldFont, but other fonts include TinyFont, gdSmallFont, gdLargeFont, and gdGiantFont. The third and fourth are for the X and Y coordinates, which the text should *start* on the image. Next is the text string to be written and, finally, the color of the text.

```
17: print "Content-type: image/png\n\n";
```

Line 17 prints out the content type HTTP header. Since a PNG image is being sent to the browser, the MIME type of *image/png* is sent so the client will know how to handle it.

```
18: binmode STDOUT;
```

Line 18 sets STDOUT to be in binary mode with the Perl *binmode()* function. This makes sure that the data from the image is written in binary mode. Most systems do not care if a file is in text or binary form and read, as well as write, both types of files in the same manner. However, some systems such as Win32 systems do make a distinction between text and binary files. Because of this, adding this line helps portability of the script by taking into account that this may be run on either type of system.

```
19: print $image->png;
```

Line 19 writes the image data to STDOUT, which is the browser. The object method *png()* converts the image data into PNG format. In this example, we are displaying the image directly to STDOUT, so no new image file is created. A developer could, however, open a filehandle and write the data to a file or use the data in any way they want. The final result of this example is shown in Figure 15-1.

Figure 15-1   The output from the add_text.cgi script

15.3 Creating a Dynamic Graph

In the previous section you saw how to do basic image manipulation with GD, and in this section you will see how to use GD::Graph to make dynamic graphs. For the example script, a bar graph chart will be created, but a developer can also create line, point, pie, points with lines, area, and mixed graphs using this module. This module can be very useful for creating graphs quickly and easily. The example in this section will use a real-life example by using the data collected from a previous example in the book. In Chapter 9 you learned how to track impressions and clicks on banner advertisements. In this section we will extend on that application by using the data collected to create a graph showing the impressions and clicks for the top five clicked banners. This will demonstrate how to use information from a database to create a graph to show the data in a more useful manner. From our experience in the IT field, it is a fact that people like to see charts and graphs of some sort rather than text.

The following script is named hits.cgi and would be called directly via *http://www.you.com/cgi-bin/hits.cgi* and will then display the image directly to the browser. This is a dynamic image, and no physical image file is used or created in this script. After we finish explaining the script, we will show you how to save the image to a file so this script could also be used to create graphs and save them to do comparisons with multiple graphs at a later time.

```
01: #!/usr/bin/perl -wT
02: use strict;
03: use CGI qw(:standard);
04: use GD::Graph::bars;
05: use DBI;
06: my $dbname = 'book';
07: my $dbhost = 'localhost';
08: my @res;
09: my $dsn = "DBI:mysql:database=$dbname;host=$dbhost";
10: my $dbh=DBI->connect($dsn,"guest","cheese");
11: if (!defined($dbh)) {
12:   print header;
13:   print "\nerror: There is a problem connecting to the MySQL
              database:\n";
14:   print DBI->errmsg;
15:   print "-" x 25;
16:   exit;
17: }
```

Lines 1–17 should all be familiar now. After providing the path to Perl on the #! line, we *use()* the strict pragma, CGI.pm, GD::Graph::bars, and DBI.pm. This example is introducing the GD::Graph::bars module that will be used to create the graph. CGI.pm has a small role in this script that is only to display the HTTP header and may be overkill but good to use for its convenience. We will also be using DBI.pm in order to get the needed data from the database. You can see that the script attempts to make a connection to the database and displays an error if the connection fails.

```
18: my $sth = $dbh->prepare(qq{select IMAGE, CLICKS, IMPRESSIONS
                    from image_tracker order by CLICKS desc limit 5});
```

Line 18 uses the DBI.pm *prepare()* method to prepare the SQL statement. The SQL statement is going to select the image name, number of clicks, and number of impressions for the image. The data, which is coming from the image_tracker table,[5] is being ordered by the CLICKS field in descending order. This will ensure that we retrieve the records with the highest amount of clicks. Because we are only interested in the top five records, we limit the number of records being returned to five. The returned statement handle is initialized into the $sth object reference.

```
19: $sth->execute;
```

Line 19 executes the SQL query with *execute()* method.

```
20: while (my @results = $sth->fetchrow_array) {
21:     push @res, @results;
22: }
```

Lines 20, 21, and 22 fetch the returned rows from the database using the *fetchrow_array()* method. As this loop happens, the resulting row is stored in the @results array. On **line 21** those results are then added to the array @res, which was initialized in line 8, using the Perl *push* function. When this is complete, @res will have a total of 15 elements; each set of three will be the data for a different record. You will see how this structure is used in the coming lines.

```
23: $dbh->disconnect;
```

Line 23 disconnects from the database. We no longer need to keep the connection open, so we close it. It is worth repeating that it is generally a good idea to close a database connection as soon as you have received all the information from it that you need. In order to better understand how

---

5. Refer to Chapter 8 for the schema of this table.

this information will be used in the next few lines, it may be useful to see the structure of the @res array. Listing 15-1 shows, in pseudo-code, this data structure.

Listing 15-1   Data structure of @res

```
@res = ("foo.png", 150, 175,
        "bar.png", 100, 110,
        "baz.png", 75, 150,
        "zog.png", 72, 88,
        "xyzzy.png", 50, 99);
```

```
24: my @data = (
25:     [$res[0],$res[3],$res[6],$res[9],$res[12]],
26:     [$res[1],$res[4],$res[7],$res[10],$res[13]],
27:     [$res[2],$res[5],$res[8],$res[11],$res[14]],
28: );
```

Lines 24–28 create a new array called @data. The three elements of the array are three anonymous arrays. The first anonymous array contains the names of the images. These will be used to create the labels on the X axis of the graph. The second anonymous array contains the values for the clicks, and the third for the impressions. This array will be used by GD::Graph::bars to add the text for the X axis labels and knows what points the bars should end on the Y axis. This will make more sense when we cover the *GD::Graph::plot()* method later in this script.

```
29: my $my_graph = new GD::Graph::bars(640, 480);
```

Line 29 created a new GD::Graph::bars object reference, which is the variable $my_graph. We pass two arguments to the *new()* method, the width and height, respectively, to make the new image. If no arguments are passed to the *new()* method the new image will be 400x300 by default.

```
30: $my_graph->set_legend("Clicks", "Impressions");
```

Line 30 uses the object method *set_legend()* to define label names for the chart legend. Charts do not need to have legends, but this one is using two colors (which you will see momentarily) and comparing two pieces of data, clicks, and impressions. A legend tells those viewing the chart which bars are for Click and which are for Impressions. This also demonstrates how to add a legend. The two arguments here are the labels that will be used. The order is important. You will notice that the labels are being given in the same order as the anomalous arrays are put in @res, which has the click data as an element before the impression data. You will again see that this order is important when we define colors for the bars in the upcoming lines.

```
31: $my_graph->set(
```

Line 31 begins a call to the *set()* method. We will be passing a lot of key/value pairs to this methods as arguments, so we will do each on a separate line to better explain each of them. The *set()* method itself is used to set options for the chart. The options we will be using[6] are the following.

```
32:    dclrs              => [ qw(lgreen lyellow) ],
```

Line 32 sets the *dclrs*, which is short for datacolors, option. This option is given a reference to an array of color names to use for the data sets. Again, the order here is important because the first element of the array will be the color for the first data set (clicks in our case), and the next color will be for the next data set (impressions). For this chart, the bars for clicks will be a light green, denoted with *lgreen*, and the impressions will be light yellow, denoted with *lyellow*.[7]

```
33:    title              => "Top Banner Stats",
```

Line 33 defines, using the title option, the title of the chart. By default, this will be placed centered at the top of the chart image.

```
34:    x_label            => "Images",
```

Line 34 defines the text for the label to be on the X axis to be the string "Images", with the x_label option.

```
35:    y_label            => "Count",
```

Line 35 sets the y_label option to the string "Count". This does the same as x_label, except that this label will be for the Y axis.

```
36:    long_ticks         => 1,
```

---

6. Check the module documentation to read about all the options and about new ones.
7. To see all the colors available, type *perldoc GD::Graph::colour*. That module is installed with the GD::Graph package.

Line 36 defines the long_ticks option to 1. By setting this to a true value, ticks will be drawn the length of the axis.

```
37:     x_ticks            => 0,
```

Line 37 sets the x_ticks option to 0. When this option is set to 1, as it is by default, ticks will be drawn for the X axis.

```
38:     x_label_position => '.5',
```

Line 38 assigns the value .5 to the x_label_position option. This option sets the positioning of the label (x_label) for the X axis. The value for this option should be between 0 and 1, with 0 being the far left and 1 the far right. Here the label will be centered by using .5. The default position for the X axis label is .75.

```
39:     y_label_position => '.5',
```

Line 39 does the same as line 38 except for the Y axis label.

```
40:     bgclr              => 'white',
```

Line 40 sets the value for the *bgclr*, or background color, option. By setting this to the color 'white' the background of the chart will be white.

```
41:     transparent       => 0,
```

Line 41 sets the transparent option to 0. By default, this is true. When true, this option will mark the background color of the chart as transparent. This line is really here for illustration purposes, since the background color has already been defined as white.

```
42:     interlaced        => 1,
```

Line 42 defines the interlaced option to a true value. By doing this, GD::Graph will produce an interlaced image. When using graphics over the Web, it can be beneficial to use an interlaced image. When you are on a Web page and see an image loading that looks like it is dithering or becoming less and less fuzzy and filled in, that is an interlaced image. When an interlaced image is created, the pixels are saved in nonconsecutive order and then fed back to the browser in the same order it was saved. By using this technique, the person on the other end of the browser sees an effect of an image being filled in rather than the image filling in from top to bottom. Much of the time interlaced images may be larger in file size, but when developing an application for the Web, it can be a good trick to make users think the images are downloading faster than they are.

```
43:    x_labels_vertical=> 1,
```

Line 43 sets the x_labels_verticle option to 1. This option, when true, will display the labels on the X axis vertically instead of horizontally. This is something that can be extremely useful when you have X axis labels, which are long, such as URLs, filenames, or the full names of people.

```
44:    lg_cols           => 2,
```

Line 44 relates to the legend that was defined in line 30. Here the value is set to 2, which will create two columns for the legend. Since this example is using two legend elements, they will appear side by side in the columns. If this was set to 1, one would be shown above the other.

```
45:    bar_spacing       => 8,
```

Line 45 uses the bar_spacing option to define the number of pixels to have between the bars on the graph. By default, this is 0 and is only useful with bar graphs.[8] Here, we use eight pixels, which will leave only a small gap.

```
46:    shadow_depth      => 4,
```

Line 46 allows us to use the eight-pixel gap we created in an aesthetic way. The shadow_depth option, here being set to four pixels, will create a shadow from the bars in the graph. When this is a positive number, the shadow will fall to the right and down. When this is made a negative number, the shadow will fall to the left and upward.

```
47:    shadowclr         => 'red',
```

Line 47 makes the shadow that was created in line 46 the color red with the *shadowclr* option.

```
48: );
```

Line 48 ends the options being given to the *set()* method! We gave 16 options, which will help shape and define how the bar chart looks. These

---

8. After all, how many bars does a pie chart have?

may be more options than needed for a simple graph, but not all the options are available to a programmer to use. Some options are specific to the type of chart being created, and some are global. We strongly encourage you to take a few moments and read the module documentation to see all the options available, as they may grow over time. It is also a good idea (and can be fun) to take this example script and change, remove, and add options from this script to see how the chart changes.

```
49: my $format = $my_graph->export_format;
```

Line 49 uses the *export_format()* method to find the format of this image. It calls the GD library being used to create the image and returns the type of image being created. The format will be stored in $format and will be used in line 50.

```
50: print header("image/$format");
```

Line 50 prints out the HTTP header to show the image. As you can see, the $format variable is created in line 49 to write the header out. This needs to be done to let the browser know what type of file is coming and how to handle it.

```
51: binmode STDOUT;
```

Line 51 sets STDOUT to send data in binary mode because image data is binary data.

```
52: print $my_graph->plot(\@data)->$format();
```

Line 52 ends the script. This is the cumulation of all those options being set! In this line, the *plot()* method is passed a reference to the @data array, which contains all the data for plotting the graph. That is exactly what the *plot()* method does. It takes the coordinate data from lines 24 to 28 and creates the graph based on those coordinates, the type of graph, and the options. It writes the file out, to STDOUT in this case, which will send the data directly to the browser using the method that is the same as the format of the image. If the image is a PNG file, the method used will be *png()* in order to correctly write the data in the correct format. You cannot write out PNG data as, for example, a JPEG file. It will not work because the compression algorithms are different and not compatible. When this script is run, you will see output similar to that in Figure 15-2.

Figure 15-2   Dynamic graph output

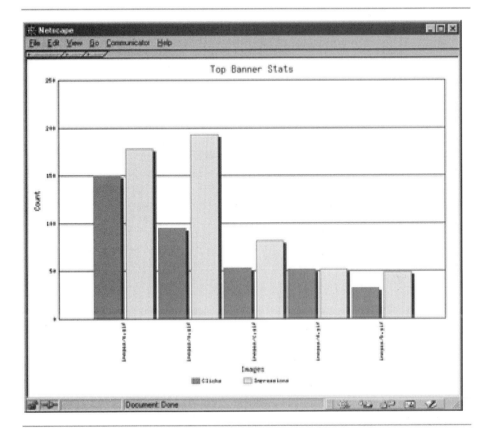

In Figure 15-2 you can see that from the hits.cgi script output, a nice bar graph is generated. All the labels are placed where we wanted, and you can see a two-column legend on the bottom center. As the legend shows, the green (darker[9]) bars show the clicks, and the yellow (lighter) bars show the impressions. The GD::Graph module, in our opinion, can really generate some cool graphs that can improve Web applications to display dynamic graphs based on log statistics, user date, sales information, traffic information, and whatever else may be needed for your application. Keep in mind while using this module in your application that these graphs can be saved to disk and used later. For example, a weekly cron job can create graphs based on weekly Web server logs and saved. At that point, there is a nice set of weekly graphs to view and use.

---

9.   Assuming you have a color monitor, you will see the green and yellow colors.

15.4 Creating Thumbnail Images

Back in Chapter 9 you learned how to use the Apache::Album module to create thumbnail images. In this section you will learn how this is done. The example script we will discuss, make_thumbnails.cgi, takes the heart of that module to show you how you can use a CGI script to create thumbnails for images in a directory and display them. It also shows you how to create thumbnails in general, in case you can also use this functionality from non-CGI Perl scripts.

This module depends on having the Image::Magick installed, which in turn needs the Image Magick software package installed. This is a freely available image creations and manipulation suite, and the Image::Magick Perl module is an interface to its API. This allows a developer to essentially use the software without actually "using" the software themselves. There are other Perl modules that interface with other image manipulation programs, such as GIMP, which will allow developers to do the same types of operations on images.

```
01: #!/usr/bin/perl -wT
02: use strict;
03: use CGI qw(:standard);
04: use Image::Magick;
```

Lines 1–4 begin the script with the path to Perl, turning warning and taint checking on as well as pulling in the strict pragma, CGI module and Image::Magick module.

```
05: print header,
06:     start_html('Thumbnails'),
07:     h1('Thumbnail Images');
```

Lines 5, 6, and 7 start off the HTML for the generated Web page. Line 5 uses the *header()* method from CGI.pm to display the HTTP header. Following that, lines 6 and 7 start the actual HTML and add a header line with the string 'Thumbnail Images.' This should be old hat to you by now!

```
08: unless(opendir(IN,"./")) {
09:     print "Couldn't open directory ($!)";
10:     exit;
11: }
```

Lines 8–11 are a conditional that accomplished two things. First, it attempts to open the current working directory, and second, it displays an error and exits the program if that filehandle cannot be opened. Assuming that the directory is in fact opened, we are left with the filehandle IN.

```
12: my @files = grep { !/^tn_/ and /\.jpe?g$/ } readdir(IN);
13: closedir(IN);
```

Line 12 creates an array of a subset of files in the directory. This is done by using the *grep()* function. The *grep()* function will run through the list of elements that *readdir()* returns, which will be all the files in the directory. The expression portion of the *grep()* looks for files that have a .jpeg or .jpg extension, while weeding out those that are prefixed with "tn_." You will see later in the script that we will be naming the thumbnails with a "tn_" prefix. This will allow us to know which images are the originals and which are the thumbnails. When this is complete, @files will be filled with the names of all the images that do not begin with "tn_" or end with .jpeg or .jpg. **Line 13** then closes the IN filehandle. We now know all the filenames to be concerned with.

```
14: foreach (@files) {
15:     unless (-e "tn_$_" && ((stat("./tn_$_"))[9] >
                              (stat($_))[9])) {
```

Line 14 begins a *foreach()* block that will iterate through the filenames in the @files array. **Line 15** starts an *unless()* conditional block that checks to see if the image already has a thumbnail image. As stated earlier, the thumbnail images are prefixed with "tn_." If the file does exist being checked with -e, then the last modified time is checked on both the original image and the thumbnail image. This is done by comparing the ninth indices of the array returned by the *stat()* function. The ninth indices of the returned array is the last modified time since the epoch. This side of the conditional is true if the last modified time of the thumbnail image is more recent than that of the original image. This would mean that the original image has not changed since the corresponding thumbnail was created. If this is true, then this entire block will end, the thumbnail will be displayed to the browser (this will happen on line 26), and the next image will be checked. If this conditional is true and there is a thumbnail image that has a lost modified time older than the original file, this block will continue.

```
16:     my $image = new Image::Magick;
```

Line 16 creates a new Image::Magick object. A new object will be created for each file that needs a thumbnail image created. A reference to this object is stored in the $image variable. We will use this object to call the methods to manipulate the image.

```
17:     print STDERR "Unable to Read() $_" if $image->Read($_);
```

Line 17 attempts to read in the image data using Image::Magick's *Read()* method. If this method fails, it will return a true value. If this occurs, the *Read()* couldn't get the needed data, and an error is printed to standard error (STDERR). The error is displaying to standard error to ensure that the error goes somewhere (likely the Web server error log) while not stopping the script from continuing. The *Read()* method can take a list of filenames, as well as a glob, such as "*.jpg" to read in. It can also accept an open filehandle by calling it in the form of "$image->Read(file => *FILEHANDLE)." The *Read()* method will get the images file format by reading the magic number in the file data, which precedes the image data. This allows for the functionality of passing an open filehandle to the method.

```
18:        my ($o_width, $o_height) = $image->Get('width',
                                                  'height');
```

Line 18 uses the *Get()* method to find the width and height of the original image. The width and height are then stored in the scalars $o_width and $o_height, respectively. The prefix "o_" in the variables denotes that it relates to the original image, and the prefix "tn_" denotes it relates to a thumbnail.

```
19:        my $tn_width = $o_width * .25;
```

Line 19 initializes the $tn_width variable. This defines the width, in pixels, that the thumbnail will be. The thumbnails we wreate will be one quarter the size of the originals, so here we take the width of the original image and multiply it by .25, which will give us ¼ scale for the width. Assuming that the original image has a width of 400 pixels, $tn_width would be 100.

```
20:        my $ratio = $o_width / $o_height;
```

Line 20 takes the width of the original image and divides it by the height of the original. The result of this is stored in the $ratio variable. Assuming the original image has a width of 400 pixels and a height of 200 pixels, $ratio would be 2.

```
21:        my $tn_height = $tn_width / $ratio;
```

Line 21 figures out the height of the thumbnail. The thumbnail width, 100, is divided by the ratio, 2, to give a height of 50. The final dimensions of the thumbnail to create will be 100 pixels wide and 50 pixels high.

```
22:        $image->Sample(width => $tn_width, height => $tn_height);
```

Line 22 uses the *Sample()* method, which creates the thumbnail image. Actually, it doesn't create an image; rather, the data of the original image is sampled down to the desired thumbnail size. Now the image data in our object is that of the thumbnail. The parameters of width and height are passed with the appropriate variables with the size information.

```
23:        $image->Write("tn_$_");
24:    }
```

Line 23 writes the image data to disk using the *Write()* method. The filename will be "tn_" and whatever the name of the original is. So if the original filename is "gouda.jpg," the new thumbnail image will have the name "tn_gouda.jpg." Line 24 ends the *unless()* block.

```
25:     print qq(<A HREF="$_"><IMG SRC="./tn_$_" ALT="$_">
                </A><BR>$_<P>);
26: }
```

Line 25 prints HTML to the client. The HTML is a hyperlink to the original image with the thumbnail image being displayed as the hyperlinked element. Then after a linebreak the name of the original image is displayed. Line 26 ends the *foreach()* block. This all happens for each image file found in the directory that has the proper file extension.

```
27: print qq(</BODY></HTML>);
```

Line 27 ends the HTML code for the page. At this point, all the thumbnails that should have been created have been, and the final display is shown to the browser.

The preceding example showed you how to do a few things. First, you were introduced to the Image::Magick module and how it can be used to interact with the API for the Image Magick software. You also saw how to read the contents of a directory and, by using *grep()*, weed out the unwanted files. Creating physical[10] thumbnails of images was introduced, as well as using the optimization of comparing the last modified times of two related files. This type of application is a framework that can be expanded on to perform functions similar to that of the Apache::Album module. In fact, it can be combined with other techniques shown in examples all through this book to write an application that does exactly what Apache::Album does without needing mod_perl.

---

10. Physical as opposed to displaying image data directly to the browser without saving a file, as in the prior example.

15.5 Filtering Images with Image::Magick

In this section we continue to use the Image::Magick module to manipulate images. Something a little more fun will be covered, filtering. An image filter is a set of instructions that acts on an image to give it an effect of some sort. The instructions themselves are in the software—Image Magick, in this case—and all a developer needs to know is the name of the filter, such as swirl, emboss, and flip. It is most important that a developer read the documentation to see what filters the software offers and play around with them to see the types of effects they will give both alone and combined.

The example script we will walk through, named filter.cgi, will display a Web page listing various filters and the parameters those filters take. This is just a subset of the filters available so you can see how they can be used and have a sort of playground for testing what they do.

```
01: #!/usr/bin/perl -wT
02: # filter.cgi
03: use strict;
04: use CGI qw(:standard);
05: use Image::Magick;
```

Lines 1–5 begin the script as expected.

```
06: my %filters = (Charcoal => 'amount',
07:                OilPaint => 'radius',
08:                Spread => 'amount',
09:                Solarize => 'factor',
10:                Swirl => 'degrees',
11:                Implode => 'factor',
12:                Flip => undef,
13:                Emboss => undef
14:                );
```

Lines 6–14 initialize the %filters hash. This hash keys will hold the filters that will be available on the Web page created. The corresponding values will be the possible parameter that can be passed to the filter that tells the Image Magic software to what degree to use that filter. For example, the OilPaint filter takes a parameter called "radius" that defines the radius of the oil paintbrush used to filter the image. On the other hand, the Flip filter takes no parameters because it simply flips the image. If a filter takes no parameters, the value is "undef." Why it is "undef" will become apparent later in the script. This hash will assist in creating the Web page appropriately as well as properly call the filter routines.

```
15: my $filename = "kyla_smile.jpg";
16: (my $filtered = $filename) =~ s!(\.\w*$)!
                                ${filename}_filtered$1!i;
```

Line 15 defines the name of the file we will be using. Because this example is simply to help you see how to use filters, we are hard coding the name of the file here into $filename. Later, as an exercise, you can change the script to accept a filename in various ways that you have seen in this book. More on that at the end of this chapter. **Line 16** defines the $filtered variable. The name of the new file that will be created will be the name of $filename, without the extension, followed by "_filtered" and the file extension. Although line 15 defines a static variable, this line will work nicely when you modify the script to define $filename more dynamically.

```
17: if (!param('doit')) {
18:     print header,
19:     start_html("Filter Image");
20:     print h2(param('error')) if param('error');
21:     print h2("Choose Filter"),
22:     start_form(-action=>"filter.cgi");
```

Lines 17–22 start a conditional block. You will see that there is a hidden value in the form that is created named "doit." When this parameter exists, we know that the form was submitted and there is some filtering to be done. **Lines 18–22** use methods imported from the CGI.pm module to start the HTML and Web form. **Line 20** prints out an extra second heading if the input parameter "error" is passed. This will be explained later in the script, but in short, this parameter will exist if there was a programmer defined error anywhere in the script.

```
23:     for (sort keys %filters) {
24:         print qq($_ <INPUT TYPE="radio" NAME="filter"
                                VALUE="$_"> );
25:         defined($filters{$_})
26:         ? print qq($filters{$_} <INPUT TYPE="text"
                                NAME="$_" SIZE=3><P>)
27:         : print qq(<P>);
28:     }
```

Line 23 starts a block to iterate over the keys of the %filters hash. The first thing done in this loop is on **line 24** where a line of HTML is printed to create a radio button with the name of the filter as its value. **Lines 25–27** are a conditional broken up into three lines for clarity. The condition is to see if the %filters hash has a defined value. If there is a defined value, a text box is displayed for the user to enter the amount of the specific parameter for that filter. For example, when the OilPaint filter is being done, the text box will have the name "OilPaint." The label printed next to the text box will be the name of the parameter being asked for, such as "radius." If the value for the hash key is not defined, such as Flip would not be, a <P> tag alone is placed in that spot.

```
29:     print submit(-value=>"Alter Image", -name=>"doit"),
30:           end_form,
31:           end_html;
```

Lines 29, 30, and 31 finish off the Web form and HTML page. If the Web form has not been submitted, this would be the end of the display. You can see the result of this in Figure 15-3.

Figure 15-3   Form to choose a filter to manipulate an image

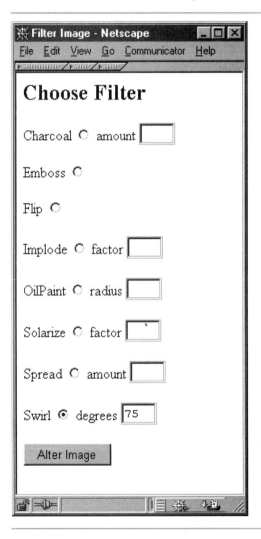

```
32: } else {
33:     my $filter = param('filter') ||
                    error("Please choose a filter");
34:     my $amount = param($filter);
```

Lines 32, 33, and 34 begin the other half of the conditional looking to see
if the script should be displaying a Web form or filtering an image. **Line 33**
is looking for the incoming "filer" form input. If it is being passed, the
$filter variable is set to its value. If it is not, it calls the *error()* subroutine
that will be shown later. You will notice that the *error()* method is passed a
string as an argument that will be used as the error message. **Line 34** sets
the $amount variable to whatever is being passed in the form parameter
that has the name that the filter does. Back in line 26 form input fields were
created when a filter was able to take a parameter, as OilPaint does. The
name of that form input field was that of the filter itself. If there is no value
passed in that input field, as there would not be for the Flip filter, $amount
will have no value.

```
35:     my $q = new Image::Magick;
```

Line 35 created a new Image::Magick object reference. This will be the
conduit to manipulating the image file.

```
36:     error("Couldn't read in image file") if
                                $q->Read($filename);
```

Line 36 will call the *error()* subroutine and pass it an error string if the *Image::Magick::Read()* method fails to read in the image data from $filename.

```
37:     defined($filters{$filter})
38:     ? $q->$filter($filters{$filter} => $amount)
39:     : $q->$filter();
```

Lines 37, 38, and 39 are really one line of code broken into three for clarity. If a filter accepts a parameter, we want to ensure that the filter is initialized accordingly. **Line 37** checks to see if the %filters hash value for the
chosen filter is defined. Recall that those that do not accept a parameter,
such as Flip, have a value of "undef." If it is defined, **line 38** calls the
method with the appropriate parameter. In Figure 15-3 the form has the filter Swirl chosen, with the "degrees" parameter set to 75. If that were submitted, line 38 would end up literally being the following.

```
$q->Swirl(degrees => 75)
```

If there is no defined parameter, then **line 39** calls the method with no parameters. At this point in the background, Image::Magick uses Image Magick to perform the actual data manipulation and saves the new image data in the $q object reference.

```
40:     $q->Write($filtered);
```

Line 40 writes out the new image data to a file, which is defined in $filtered. At this point, there is an actual image file, not just data stored in memory.

```
41:     print redirect($filtererd);
42: }
```

Line 41 redirects the browser to the new image. This is done using the *redirect()* method imported by CGI.pm. The image has been read, manipulated, a file was created with the new data, and the user is sent off to see the new file. **Line 42** closes the *if()* block.

```
43: sub error {
44:     my $error = CGI::escape(@_);
45:     print "Location: filter.cgi?error=$error\n\n";
46:     exit;
47: }
```

Lines 43–47 comprise the *error()* subroutine. This subroutine is called with a string value as an argument escaped string that is URI escaped using the *CGI::escape()* method on **line 44**. After being URI escaped, **line 45** redirects the browser back to this script with the parameter "error" and the URI escaped string as its value. When the script sees this parameter on line 20 the string will be displayed to the browser. **Line 46** makes sure that the script exits. Just because the browser has been sent elsewhere, it doesn't mean the script always stops, and in this case, we do not need the script to continue running when there has been an error. Finally, **line 47** ends the script. Figure 15-4 illustrates what the Swirl effect would have done if chosen with "degrees" set to 75.

Figure 15-4   **Effects of a Swirl filter**

15.6 Animated Images

In the last section you were shown how to use Image::Magick to access and filter images. In this section we will take this a step further and create an animated image. An animated image is essentially an image file that contains multiple images, also known as "scenes." There is an emerging image file format, Multiple-Image Network Graphics or MNG,[11] which is based on the PNG format that allows for multiple images and extended features that PNG doesn't support. The Image Magick software does support MNG images, but it isn't supported by the major browsers, it isn't a viable option for Web applications. The viable option to use is the widely supported GIF89a format. The following example script, animate.cgi, is a small script to demonstrate how to create an animated image. The example will take one image and read it in multiple times and running the Swirl filter while incrementing the degrees of the swirl each time. Much of this script will be familiar to you.

```
01: #!/usr/bin/perl -wT
02: use strict;
03: use CGI qw(:standard);
04: use Image::Magick;
```

Lines 1–4 are not new to you.

```
05: my $image = new Image::Magick;
```

Line 5 creates a new reference to an Image::Magick object.

```
06: my $i = 10;
```

Line 6 initializes the variable $i, which will be used within the coming *for()* block.

```
07: for (1..20) {
08:     $image->Read("kyla_smile.jpg");
09:     $image->Swirl(degrees => $i);
10:     $i += 10;
11: }
```

Lines 7–11 is a *for()* block where the image is read in and filtered. After **line 8** reads the image data in, **line 9** runs the filter with the "degrees" set to whatever the value of $i currently is. Each time the image is read in, a new

---

11. Pronounced "ming." See *http://www.libpng.org/pub/mng/*.

image is placed within the image file being created. **Line 10** increments the "degrees" of the filter by 10 each time there is an iteration of the loop. When this is complete, there will be data for an image file containing 20 images being stored within the Image::Magick object.

```
12: $image->Set(loop=>0);
13: $image->Write("kyla_ani.gif");
14: print redirect("kyla_ani.gif");
```

Line 12 sets the loop attribute for the image. The default value for this is 1, which will make the image loop through the scenes one time and freeze on the final scene image. By setting this parameter to 0 we create an image that will be in an infinite loop. **Lines 13 and 14** write the file to disk and redirect the browser to the new image. The result will be an image that continually swirls, which is unfortunately hard to show on the flat pages of paper.

As you likely noticed, multiple image files (although the same physical file in this example) can be read in without creating a new Image::Magick object each time. Earlier you learned that the *Read()* method can read in multiple files, which is very useful when creating animated images. For example, if you have multiple image files or scenes that together create a sequence, they can all be read in at once to create an animation. If you run the previous example, you will notice that the scenes play with no delay between them.

Let's assume you have multiple images wanting to be animated together with a delay between them. The following snippet of code can replace lines 6–11 of the animate.cgi script to read in multiple files to create an animation. The snippet also introduces the "delay" parameter that is what is used to have the scenes displayed with an interval.

```
$image->Read(qw{image_a.gif image_b.gif image_c.gif
            image_d.gif});
$image->Set(delay => 200, loop => 0);
```

Through this chapter you learned how to create thumbnails, filter images, create animated images, draw graphs, and manipulate images with text and figures. These are the basic tools that a developer can use to manipulate and create images. If more in-depth manipulations are desired, it is of course best to read the documentation for the modules that are available and experimenting.

15.7 Reader Exercises

- Alter the make_thumbnails.cgi script to walk down a directory tree and create thumbnails of all the images it finds.

- Modify the hits.cgi script to use another type of chart. A pie chart could be made to show the distribution of hits between the banner impressions or clicks.

- An interesting application could be made by modifying the filter.cgi script to accept a file that is uploaded by the browser, filters it, and returns the new image. In Chapter 11 you were shown how to return binary data to the browser in a way that the user can save the data to disk as a file. That technique can be used to send back the filtered image so users can filter an image on their disk using the application and save it.

15.8 Listings

Listing 15-2   **add_text.cgi script**

```
01: #!/usr/bin/perl -wT
02: use strict;
03: use GD;
04: no strict 'subs';
05: open (PNG,"kyla_smile.png") || die "$!";
06:    my $image = newFromPng GD::Image(PNG) || die "$!";
07: close PNG;
08: my $white = $image->colorAllocate(255,255,255);
09: my $black = $image->colorAllocate(0,0,0);
10: $image->arc(50,50,95,75,0,360,$black);
11: $image->fillToBorder(50,50,$black, $white);
12: $image->arc(60,95,25,25,0,360,$black);
13: $image->fillToBorder(60,95,$black, $white);
14: $image->arc(70,125,20,20,0,360,$black);
15: $image->fillToBorder(70,125,$black, $white);
16: $image->string(gdMediumBoldFont,10,45,"I Love Dad!",$black);
17: print "Content-type: image/png\n\n";
18: binmode STDOUT;
19: print $image->png;
```

Listing 15-3   **hits.cgi script**

```
01: #!/usr/bin/perl -wT
02: use strict;
03: use CGI qw(:standard);
04: use GD::Graph::bars;
05: use DBI;
06: my $dbname = 'book';
07: my $dbhost = 'localhost';
08: my @res;
```

```
09: my $dsn = "DBI:mysql:database=$dbname;host=$dbhost";
10: my $dbh=DBI->connect($dsn,"guest","cheese");
11: if (!defined($dbh)) {
12:    print header;
13:    print "\nerror: There is a problem connecting to the MySQL
                database:\n";
14:    print DBI->errmsg;
15:    print "-" x 25;
16:    exit;
17: }
18: my $sth = $dbh->prepare(qq{select IMAGE, CLICKS, IMPRESSIONS from
    image_tracker order by CLICKS desc limit 5});
19: $sth->execute;
20: while (my @results = $sth->fetchrow_array) {
21: push @res, @results;
22: }
23: $dbh->disconnect;
24: my @data = (
25:     [$res[0],$res[3],$res[6],$res[9],$res[12]],
26:     [$res[1],$res[4],$res[7],$res[10],$res[13]],
27:     [$res[2],$res[5],$res[8],$res[11],$res[14]],
28: );
29: my $my_graph = new GD::Graph::bars(640, 480);
30: $my_graph->set_legend("Clicks", "Impressions");
31: $my_graph->set(
32:    dclrs            => [ qw(lgreen lyellow) ],
33:    title            => "Top Banner Stats",
34:    x_label          => "Images",
35:    y_label          => "Count",
36:    long_ticks       => 1,
37:    x_ticks          => 0,
38:    x_label_position => '.5',    # centered x label
39:    y_label_position => '.5',    # centered y label
40:    bgclr            => 'white', # makes background transparent
41:    transparent      => 0,
42:    interlaced       => 1,        # show like venetian blind opens
43:    x_labels_vertical=> 1,        # display tick values vertically
44:    lg_cols          => 2,        # num legend columns
45:    bar_spacing      => 8,
46:    shadow_depth     => 4,
47:    shadowclr        => 'red',
48: );
49: my $format = $my_graph->export_format;
50: print header("image/$format");
51: binmode STDOUT;
52: print $my_graph->plot(\@data)->$format();
```

Listing 15-4   make_thumbnails.cgi script

```
01: #!/usr/bin/perl -wT
02: use strict;
03: use CGI qw(:standard);
04: use Image::Magick;
05: print header,
06:     start_html('Thumbnails'),
07:     h1('Thumbnail Images');
08: unless(opendir(IN,"./")) {
09:     print "Couldn't open directory ($!)";
10:     exit;
11: }
12: my @files = grep { !/^tn_/ and /\.jpe?g$/ } readdir(IN);
13: closedir(IN);
14: foreach (@files) {
15:     unless (-e "tn_$_" && ((stat("./tn_$_"))[9] >
                                 (stat($_))[9])) {
16:       my $image = new Image::Magick;
17:       print STDERR "Unable to Read() $_" if $image->Read($_);
18:       my ($o_width, $o_height) = $image->Get('width', 'height');
19:       my $tn_width =  $o_width * .25;
20:       my $ratio = $o_width / $o_height;
21:       my $tn_height = $tn_width / $ratio;
22:       $image->Sample(width => $tn_width, height => $tn_height);
23:       $image->Write("tn_$_");
24:     }
25:     print qq(<A HREF="$_"><IMG SRC="./tn_$_" ALT="$_">
                 </A><BR>$_<P>);
26: }
27: print qq(</BODY></HTML>);
```

Listing 15-5   filter.cgi script

```
01: #!/usr/bin/perl -wT
02: # filter.cgi
03: use strict;
04: use CGI qw(:standard);
05: use Image::Magick;
06: my %filters = (Charcoal => 'amount',
07:                OilPaint => 'radius',
08:                Spread => 'amount',
09:                Solarize => 'factor',
```

(continued)

```
10:                     Swirl => 'degrees',
11:                     Implode => 'factor',
12:                     Flip => undef,
13:                     Emboss => undef
14:             );
15: my $filename = "kyla_smile.jpg";
16: (my $filtered = $filename) =~ s!(\.\w*$)!${filename}_filtered$1!i;
17: if (!param('doit')) {
18:     print header,
19: start_html("Filter Image");
20:     print h2(param('error')) if param('error');
21:     print h2("Choose Filter"),
22: start_form(-action=>"filter.cgi");
23:     for (sort keys %filters) {
24:       print qq($_ <INPUT TYPE="radio" NAME="filter" VALUE="$_"> );
25:         defined($filters{$_})
26:         ? print qq($filters{$_} <INPUT TYPE="text" NAME="$_"
                        SIZE=3><P>)
27:         : print qq(<P>);
28:     }
29:   print submit(-value=>"Alter Image", -name=>"doit"),
30:           end_form,
31:           end_html;
32: } else {
33:     my $filter = param('filter') || error("Please choose a filter");
34:     my $amount = param($filter);
35:     my $q = new Image::Magick;
36:     error("Couldn't read in image file") if $q->Read($filename);
37:     defined($filters{$filter})
38:     ? $q->$filter($filters{$filter} => $amount)
39:     : $q->$filter();
40:     $q->Write($filtered);
41:     print redirect($filtererd);
42: }
43: sub error {
44:     my $error = CGI::escape(@_);
45:     print "Location: filter.cgi?error=$error\n\n";
46:     exit;
47: }
```

Listing 15-6   animage.cgi script

```
01: #!/usr/bin/perl -wT
02: use strict;
03: use CGI qw(:standard);
04: use Image::Magick;
05: my $image = new Image::Magick;
06: my $i = 10;
07: for (1..20) {
08:     $image->Read("kyla_smile.jpg");
09:     $image->Swirl(degrees => $i);
10:     $i += 10;
11: }
12: $image->Set(loop=>0);
13: $image->Write("kyla_ani.gif");
14: print redirect("kyla_ani.gif");
```

Chapter

RSS and XML

16.1 XML and RSS Overview

The Extensible Markup Language, commonly called XML, is a markup language for structured documents. A structured document is one that contains various elements, such as images and text, as well as an indication of what that element is. For example, a letter has elements such as address, body, and footer that all have different roles in the document. When there is some indicator on the letter as to what each part of each element does, then there is a structured document. Most documents do have structure, and XML can be used to define that structure in a usable, and standard, way. HTML documents are structured documents because they have elements and tags defining the role of that element.

HTML and XML are not the same, however. HTML has a known set of tags. XML, on the other hand, does not. XML isn't just a way to mark up documents; it is really a meta-language giving developers a way to describe markups. The developers of the XML documents and applications that use them define the tags for the document as well as the relationship between those tags. XML was created to allow developers to use their tags to create structured documents for the Web. Through this chapter you will learn some basics of an XML document and see how to use an XML variant, RSS, for the Web.

16.1.1 Structure of an XML Document

The look of an XML document is very close to that of HTML and should be easy to follow and understand. In Listing 16-1 you will see a simple XML document.

Listing 16-1   **Example XML document**

```
<?xml version="1.0"">
<Zappa>
<quote>Good night Cleveland, wherever you are!</quote>
<quote>Shoot low, they're riding Shetlands.</quote>
</Zappa>
```

Well, there is nothing too mystical looking in there. The first line declares that this is an XML document as well as the version of XML being used. This line is not obligatory, but it is a good practice to have it and it helps make the document well formed. Next a container is created. The name of the container is "Zappa". Inside of this container, there are two elements that are being tagged as "quote". Finally, the "Zappa" container is closed, containing two quote elements. The preceding example is a very simple one, and XML goes much deeper than what you see there, but it would take a book to show all the aspects (in fact, there are books that do). However, the preceding example shows enough to help you understand the coming examples and quickly get started using XML and its variants.

16.2 News Portals with RSS

A few short years ago, Netscape created what could be called the first Web portal. They developed the My News Network,[1] or MNN, which gave a facility for its users to get much of the news and search capabilities from their own starting page. Users can choose sites from which they would like to see news summaries and have them displayed. Netscape dubbed these summaries "channels," and that is now the common name. For Netscape channels, the backend server would periodically fetch structured XML documents from contributing sites and update the content of the channels. In order to ensure that all contributors' files were structured in the same way, Netscape developed the RDF Site Summary (RSS) format. This format uses XML and Resource Description Format (RDF)[2] to define a markup language for developers to use. The RSS format is not just for Netscape channels anymore. Using the XML::RSS module a programmer can use the same channel files to format data for the Web.

---

1. *http://my.netscape.com*
2. This is a format used to describe Web-based meta-data.

Before we jump into using XML::RSS, let's first cover the RSS format markup language. There is a finite set of tags to use with RSS. The main container for the document is the channel. Within this containter there are a few elements that can be used to define the content. Three main elements are title, link, and description. The channel container can also contain image, textinput, and other containers. Let's take a moment to break down an RSS document.

```
<?xml version="1.0" encoding="ISO-8859-1"?>
<!DOCTYPE rss PUBLIC "-//Netscape Communications//DTD RSS 0.91//EN"
          "http://my.netscape.com/publish/formats/rss-0.91.dtd">
<rss version="0.91">
```

This section is doing three declarations. The first is declaring that this is an XML document, as you saw in the previous section. The second declaration is the DOCTYPE for the document. The third is declaring that this is a RSS document, using version 0.91. Version 0.90 of RSS was introduced by Netscape in 1999, so this is all still very new. Now that we have the type of document we will be creating, the next step is to create it.

```
<channel>
```

This line opens the *channel* container. Everything up until this containter is closed will be a part of this container. The main container in all RSS documents is *channel*.

```
<title>My News</title>
<link>http://news.me.com</link>
<description>My news, for you!</description>
<language>en</language>
<copyright>Copyright 2000++, Me</copyright>
<pubDate>Sun May 21 15:43:45 2000</pubDate>
<lastBuildDate>Sun May 21 15:43:45 2000</lastBuildDate>
<managingEditor>me@me.com</managingEditor>
<webMaster>me@me.com</webMaster>
```

Here a list of elements is being defined. The three main ones, which are also required, are title, which is the title of the channel; link, which is the location of the Web site for this channel; and description, which is how to describe the channel. The remaining elements listed are optional for inclusion in the document but can provide useful information. We will not go into individual descriptions of them, since the name of each element does a good job of that on its own.

```
<image>
<title>My News</title>
<url>http://news.me.com/my_news.gif</url>
<link>http://news.me.com</link>
<width>119</width>
<height>30</height>
</image>
```

The preceding snippet shows the optional *image* container. This container will hold information about the image logo for the channel. Again, the simplicity of the RSS format makes each element name self-explanatory for what the element data is used for. The last line of the snippet closes the container.

```
<item>
<title>Man eats cheese, MPEG at 11.</title>
<link>http://news.me.com/news/story2.html</link>
</item>
```

The *item* container is extremely important, since it defines the content of the channel. This container is required, and there can be multiple *item* containers per channel. For example, if there were five news stories, there would be five *item* containers. There are two elements in an *item* container, and both are required. These elements define the title of the item as well as the link to the full story.

```
<textinput>
<title>Search My News</title>
<description>Search the Archives</description>
<name>text</name>
<link>http://news.me.com/search.cgi</link>
</textinput>
```

The "textinput" container will create a text box that people can use to search your site. This container is optional, since some sites may not have search capabilities. If the site does have search capabilities, then this is an excellent way to allow users to search the site from wherever the channel is displayed.

```
</channel>
</rss>
```

The document ends by closing the *channel* container and closing the RSS document. This is equivalent to closing an HTML document with

</HTML>. That's the entire RSS document. With this document, a Netscape channel can be created[3] and you can share it with others around the world who want to customize their Web pages and applications with your information. Now that you know the structure of an RSS document, we will show you how to use that file and then create your own using Perl.

16.2.1 A Home Page News Portal

Now that you have a general understanding what an RSS document is and how one in structured, it is time to see how a developer can use these files to create dynamic content and create a customized portal with them. The easiest way to use RSS formatted files in Perl is with the XML::RSS module, written by Jonathan Eisenzopf. This module allows a programmer to easily get the data that is inside an RSS formatted file in an object-oriented fashion. In this section we will walk through an application that fetches RSS files, displays the channels to a Web page, and allows a user to add channels to fetch and choose what channels are displayed on the Web page.

The first thing to know is where to get channel files to use! The xmlTree Web site[4] is attempting to categorize much of the XML content on the Web, and much of this content is RSS files. Using this Web site, you can search for the type of channel you wish you have and find the location of the RSS files[5] for those channels. Now that you know where to look for channel files, let's get on with the script.

We begin by creating a table that will hold information about the channels. We will be keeping information on three things: the URL of the RSS file, the name of the channel, and whether the channel is to be viewed on the Web page.

Listing 16-2   SQL to create the RDF table

```
CREATE TABLE rdf (
 URL varchar(250) NOT NULL,
 Name varchar(250) NOT NULL,
 Selected int(11)
);
```

To help you use this script as you read along, Listing 16-2 shows the insert statements of four channels. This will also give you an idea of what the data in the table looks like.

---

3. The RDF file needs to be registered with Netscape so they know where to fetch it.
4. *www.xmltree.com*
5. Many of these have an .rdf extension, although this is not required.

```
INSERT INTO rdf VALUES ('http://slashdot.org/slashdot.rdf',
                        'Slashdot',0);
INSERT INTO rdf VALUES ('http://www.news.perl.org/perl-news-
                        short.rdf','Perl News',1);
INSERT INTO rdf VALUES ('http://freshmeat.net/backend/fm.rdf',
                        'Freshmeat',1);
INSERT INTO rdf VALUES ('http://www.securityfocus.com/topnews-
                        rss.html','Security Focus',1);
```

The first thing that is needed is a way to get the RSS files locally so the XML::RSS module can parse it. To accomplish this, we create the script fetch, which can be run from the command line or via cron at regular intervals.

```
01: #!/usr/bin/perl -w
02: # fetch
03: use strict;
04: use File::Basename;
05: use DBI;
06: use LWP::Simple qw(mirror);
```

Lines 1–6 define the path to Perl and *use()* the needed modules. The *mirror()* method from LWP::Simple will be used to get the remote RSS files. When the file will be saved locally, they will be saved with the same name of the remote file. The *basename()* method from File::Basename will be used to easily get that information for us.

```
07: my $RDF_DIR = './rdf';
```

Line 7 initializes the $RDF_DIR variable. Its value will be used as the directory to store the retrieved RSS files.

```
08: my $dbh = DBI->connect("dbi:mysql:book", "user", "password");
09: my $sth = $dbh->prepare(qq{select URL from rdf});
10: $sth->execute or die $DBI::errstr;
```

Line 8 connects to the database. **Line 9** then prepares a query that selects all the URLs for the RSS files from the table. **Line 10** executes this statement or dies with the error from DBI.pm.

```
11: while (my $url = $sth->fetchrow) {
12:     my $name = basename($url);
13:     mirror($url, "./$RDF_DIR/$name");
14: }
```

Lines 11–14 loop through the results set from the database. The value returned and stored in $url will be a single URL. In **line 12** $url is passed to the *basename()* method, which will return the filename from the end of the URL. This value is stored in $name. **Line 13** does the real work. The *mirror()* method takes the URL as its first argument and in turn fetches the remote Web page. The second argument is the location of where the new file is to be saved. When this loop is done, all the available RSS files will be stored locally. This script would be most helpful if run in intervals to make sure the latest RSS files are local.

```
15: $dbh->disconnect;
```

Line 15 closes the database connect.

The next part of the application is to take the RSS files and make them useful. The index.cgi script, to be explained next, will create channel boxes on a Web page displaying the data from the RSS files.

```
01: #!/usr/bin/perl -wT
02: # index.cgi
03: use strict;
04: use CGI qw(:standard end_ul end_table);
05: use CGI::Carp qw(fatalsToBrowser);
06: use File::Basename;
07: use DBI;
08: use XML::RSS;
09: my $RDF_DIR = './rdf';
10: my $dbh = DBI->connect("dbi:mysql:book", 'user','password') or
                          print $DBI::errstr;
11: my $sth = $dbh->prepare(qq{select URL from rdf where
                          Selected = 1});
12: $sth->execute;
```

Lines 1–12 only introduce one new thing: using XML::RSS. This is the module that will be used to retrieve the wanted information from the RSS files in $RDF_DIR. We are also selecting all the URLs from the database where Selected is 1, which indicates that channel should be displayed on the Web page.

```
13: print header,
14:       start_html("My Home Page"),
15:       h2("My Favorite Sites");
16: print start_table({cellpadding=>0, cellspacing=>0, border=> 0,
                  width => '100%'}),
17:       td;
```

Lines 13–17 start off the HTML for the page. All the HTML is being printed out using methods from the CGI.pm module.

```
18: my $count = 1;
19: my @html = ('</TD><TD>', '</TD><TR><TD>');
```

Line 18 and 19 initialize two variables that will be used together as a sort of toggle. The channels will be displayed in two columns, and one way or another we have to know if a <TR> is to be printed to start a new row. Since every other column will have the <TR>, a simple little toggle can be used to switch between the two HTMLs.

```
20: while (my $url = basename($sth->fetchrow)) {
21:     my $rss = new XML::RSS;
```

Line 20 starts iterating through the results set, which will be URLs. As the results row is fetched, it is also put through the *basename()* method to get only the filename. For example, the URL *http://slasdhot.org/slashdot.rdf* will be reduced to "slashdot.rdf." That filename is then stored in $url. **Line 21** then creates a new XML::RSS object. The resulting $rss variable will be an object reference.

```
22:     eval {$rss->parsefile("$RDF_DIR/$url")};
23:     warn "$url will not parse $@" and next if $@;
```

Line 22 evaluates the *parsefile()* method. The *parsefile()* method takes the location of the RSS file on disk, opens it, and parses it. This is being wrapped in an *eval()* because if the RSS is broken, an exception may be thrown. By using *eval()*, the exception can be caught, and the script will continue. **Line 23** will print a warning to STDERR and move on to the next iteration of the loop if an exception is caught.

```
24: my $last_mod = scalar localtime((stat("$RDF_DIR/$url"))[9]);
```

Line 24 initializes $last_mod with the scalar value of the last modified time of the RSS file.

```
25:     print start_table({cellpadding=>0, cellspacing=>2,
                           border=> 5, width=>'75%'}),
26:     td({valign=>'CENTER', bgcolor => '#C0C0C0'});
```

Lines 25 and 26 begin the HTML table for the channel.

```
27:     $rss->{image}{url}
28:     ? print img({src=>$rss->{image}{url}})
29:     : print strong($rss->{channel}{title});
```

Lines 27, 28, and 29 are one line broken up for clarity. **Line 27** wants to see if there is a true value for $rss->{image}{url}. If there is, then the RSS file has an *image* container. If it is true, **line 28** then displays that image to the browser. If there is no *image* container, the title for the channel is displayed instead.

```
30: print ul;
```

Line 30 prints the <UL> tag. The items in the RSS file will be displayed as an unordered list.

```
31: for (@{$rss->{items}}) {
32:         print li(a({href=>$_->{link}}, $_->{title}));
33: }
```

Lines 31–33 iterate over the items in the channel container. $rss->{items} is a reference to an array and is being dereferences as such. **Line 32** prints out the item to the browser. The item is displayed as a hyperlink to the URL for the story. The text for the hyperlink is the items title. These values come from the link and title elements of the item container.

```
34: print end_ul;
```

Line 34 prints the </UL> tag.

```
35: if ($rss->{textinput}{link}) {
36:         print $rss->{textinput}{description},
                start_form(-method => 'GET',
37:                         -action => $rss->{textinput}{link}),
38:                 textfield(-name => $rss->{textinput}{name}),
39:                 end_form;
40: }
```

Lines 35–40 handle an occurrence of a textinput container. If **line 35** finds that the *link* element of the textinput container has a true value, the rest of the block prints the appropriate form.

```
41:     print qq(Last Updated $last_mod<BR>),
42:         end_table;
43:     $html[$count^=1];
44: }
```

Line 41 displays the last modified date that was retrieved in line 24. **Line 42** closes the table for the channel, but **line 43** does something fun. Remember lines 18 and 19 when we initialized @html and $count so they would act as a toggle? Line 43 is that toggle. We want to have two columns of channels being displayed, and by XORing the values of $count and 1, we can print the desired HTML to either end the table row with a <TR> tag or not. The higher the value to initialize $count with, the more columns you will have. Finally, **line 44** ends the *while()* loop.

```
45: print end_table,
46:        end_html;
```

Lines 45 and 46 end the script by printing the closing tags for the main table and the HTML. When this script is run, the Web page that is generated is similar to that shown in Figure 16-1.

Figure 16-1   Channels on a Web page

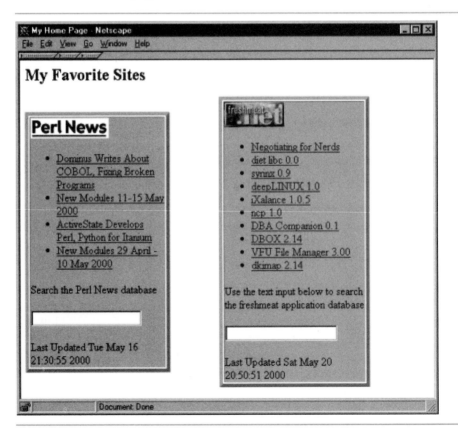

To this point, the application has a means to fetch updated RSS files and display the channel data to a Web page. However, the application still needs a way to add RSS files to the database, as well as choose which ones to display and which ones not to. To accomplish this, we will show the script admin.cgi.

```
01: #!/usr/bin/perl -wT
02: # admin.cgi
03: use strict;
04: use CGI qw(:standard);
05: use CGI::Carp qw(fatalsToBrowser);
06: use DBI;
07: my $dbh = DBI->connect("dbi:mysql:book", "user", "password");
08: param('Submit') ? add_new() : show_form();
09: $dbh->disconnect;
```

Lines 1–9 introduce nothing new. Line 8 is what is really important here. **Line 8** checks if there was a "Submit" parameter sent to the script. If there was, this means that the form to make changes was submitted and to call the *add_new()* subroutine. The *add_new()* subroutine will make the needed changes to the database, then reshow the form with the *show_form()* subroutine. If there was no "Submit" parameter sent to the script, the *show_form()* subroutine is immediately called. **Line 9** disconnects from the database.

```
10: sub show_form {
11:     my $sth = $dbh->prepare(qq{select * from rdf});
12:     $sth->execute;
13:     print header,
14:         start_html("My Home Page Options"),
15:         h2("Choose My Favorite Sites");
16:     print start_form(-method => 'POST', -action => 'admin.cgi');
```

Lines 9–16 begin the *show_form()* subroutine. This subroutine will do one thing: display the Web form to the browser. The form will consist of a list of all the channels in the database, each with a checkbox denoting whether it has been selected to be viewable on the main Web page. The page also will have a place to add a new channel by entering the channels' name, URL to the RSS file, and a checkbox to select if the channel should be shown on the main Web page. Figure 16-2 shows what the final form will look like. **Line 11** is the query that will select all the information from the database. This data will be used starting in **line 17** to display the channels. The other line of note is **line 16**, which begins the Web form with itself as the script to which the form will be submitted.

```
17:     while (my $data = $sth->fetchrow_hashref) {
18:         my $checked = $data->{Selected} ? "CHECKED" : "";
19:         print checkbox(-name => 'Selected',
20:                             -checked => $checked,
21:                             -value => $data->{Name},
22:                             -label => $data->{Name},
23:                         ),
24:                 p;
25:     }
```

Lines 17–25 are a loop that iterates over the data set returned from the SQL executed on line 12. The data returned is stored in the $data variable, which is a hash reference containing the data for the specific row being returned from the *fetchrow_hashref()* method. Each channel in the database has a Selected field, which denotes if the channel is to be displayed on the main Web page. This field will either contain a 0 or 1 to not display or display the channel. **Line 18** checks to see if the channel is selected or not to determine if the CHECKED attribute of the HTML checkbox input tag should be shown. If $data->{Selected} is a true value, the $checked variable is initialized as the string "CHECKED" and is an empty string if there is a false value. **Lines 19–23** display the checkbox for the channel. Passing parameters to the *checkbox()* method from CGI.pm, we can define the checkbox's name, which will be "Selected," whether or not the checkbox is to be displayed selected, as well as the value and label for the checkbox. The value and label parameters are both defined as the name of the channel, referred to as $data->{Name}. This continues for each of the channels in the database. **Line 25** closes the *while()* block we have been in.

```
26:     print h2("Add new channel") , p,
27:         "RDFs URL: ", textfield(-name => 'URL', -size => 50), p
28:         "Name of channel: ", textfield(-name => 'Name',
                                            -size => 50), p
29:         "Display on Home Page: ",
30:         checkbox(-name => 'new-Selected', -label => ''), p,
31:         submit(-name => 'Submit', -value => 'Make Changes'),
32:         end_form, end_html;
33: }
```

Lines 26–32 are a long *print()* to display three form elements that will allow a user to enter a new channel into the database. The first form element, aptly named "URL," is a text box (created with the *textfield()* method) that will be used to gather the URL of the RSS file. **Line 28** creates the second text box, "Name," which is where the user-defined name of the channel is entered. **Line 30** is a checkbox, named "new-Slected," where the user can select if the channel is to be displayed or not. You may have noticed that all the form elements except this one is the name of a field in the database. This is to make sure that when the form is submitted, this value doesn't want to get mixed in with the other checkboxes that were selected. The other selected checkboxes will be seen as an array when they are retrieved in the *show_form()* subroutine, and this value will be separate. **Line 31** prints the submit button for the form. A value is defined for the button so the value will have a true value when line 8 checks to see if this form is being submitted for an update or being called directly. **Line 32** ends the *print()* by ending the form and Web page.

```
34: sub add_new {
35:     my $qry_select = qq(update rdf set Selected = 1
                                where );
36:     my $qry_deselect = qq(update rdf set Selected = 0
                                where );
```

Line 34 begins the *add_new()* subroutine. **Lines 35 and 36** define two variables that are the beginnings of SQL UPDATE statements. When the data is parsed to see what channels were selected, there is no real way to know which ones are *not* selected. This means that after knowing the selected channels, two queries will be executed. One will update the Selected field of those selected to 1, and those that are not selected will have it set to 0. These queries will be built in lines 39 and 40.

```
37:     my @selected = param('Selected');
```

Line 37 builds the @selected array by getting all the parameters submitted with the name "Selected." The elements of the @selected array will be the names of the channels the user checked to be viewable from the form.

```
38:     $qry_select .= qq(Name = '$_' or ) for @selected;
39:     $qry_deselect .= qq(Name <> '$_' and ) for @selected;
```

Lines 38 and 39 build the update statements. Both scalars are concatenated as *for()* iterates through @selected.

```
40:     $qry_deselect =~ s! and $!!;
41:     $qry_select =~ s! or $!!;
```

Lines 40 and 41 clean up the queries being made. At the end of each string, there will be an extra "and" or "or" and they need to be removed before trying to execute them.

```
42:      my $sth = $dbh->prepare($qry_select);
43:      $sth->execute or print $DBI::errstr;
44:      $sth = $dbh->prepare($qry_deselect);
45:      $sth->execute or print $DBI::errstr;
```

Lines 42–45 *prepare()* and *execute()* the queries. When this is done, the database will match what the user wanted as far as what is Selected and what is not.

```
46:      if (param('URL') && param('Name')) {
47:              my $url = param('URL');
48:              my $name = param('Name');
49:              my $display = param('new-Selected') ? 1 : 0;
50:              $sth = $dbh->prepare(qq{insert into rdf (URL, NAME,
                     SELECTED) values ('$url', '$name', $display)});
51:              $sth->execute or print $DBI::errstr;
52:      }
53:      show_form;
54: }
```

Lines 46–54 complete the script. **Line 46** is checking to see if a URL and Name parameter have been passed to the script. Both are checked because we do not want to add a channel with no Name or no URL. If those parameters are true, the block continues and adds a record into the database, thereby creating a new channel. When this is all finished, the *show_form()* subroutine is called, and the form, with the updated information, is displayed to the screen.

Figure 16-2   Channel admin page

The three scripts explained in this section showed you how to create an RSS file as well as how to parse, read, and display them. The tools taught in this section can be used to provide, or receive other, information in Web applications. There are other features that can be added to this application, which will be suggested reader exercises at the end of this chapter. Using XML is growing in popularity and is an excellent tool for the programmer's toolbox. With the basic techniques taught in this chapter, you can already use Perl and XML to enhance Web applications.

16.3 Creating an RSS File

Now that you have seen how to use RSS files and are familiar with their structure, it is a good time to explain how a developer can create his or her own channel file. To make an RSS file useful in an application, it is necessary to have the essential element a channel needs—news to share with others—that is on the Web. For example's sake, we will assume that the information is kept in a text file. Of course, your information may be in a database or are HTML files in a special directory or some other type of data source.

The following example, make_rss, is not a CGI script. It is meant to be used as a command line script, which could be run from a schedule to automatically create the RSS file. This code, of course, could be run as a CGI, but unless your news changes by the minute, having it scheduled to run on intervals should suffice.

```
01: #!/usr/bin/perl -wT
02: # make_rss
03: use strict;
04: use XML::RSS;
```

Lines 1–4 define the path to Perl as well as pull in the strict pragma and XML::RSS module.

```
05: my $FILE = 'news.txt';
06: my $RDF_DIR = './rdf';
```

Lines 5 and 6 create two scalar variables we will be using later. **Line 5** initializes $FILE with the location of the text file that has the news information in it. This file, which we called news.txt, is a pipe delimited file with the URL for the news story to the left of the pipe and the description of the story on the right. On **line 6** the $RDF_DIR variable is created. This variable holds the location of the directory in which the RSS file is to be created.

```
07: my $rdf = new XML::RSS;
```

Line 7 creates a new XML::RSS object. The reference to that object is being stored in $rdf.

```
08: $rdf->channel(title => 'My News',
09:               link => 'http://news.me.com',
10:               language => 'en',
11:               description => 'My news, for you!',
12:               copyright => 'Copyright 2000++, Me',
```

```
13:                    pubDate => scalar localtime(time),
14:                    lastBuildDate => scalar localtime(time),
15:                    managingEditor => 'me@me.com',
16:                    webMaster => 'me@me.com'
17:                );
```

Lines 8–17 use the *channel()* method to define some of the main information about the channel itself and begin the "channel" container. Earlier in this chapter you were shown a complete RSS file, and you can see how each of these pairs is represented in the final document.

```
18: $rdf->image(title => 'My News',
19:              url => 'http://news.me.com/my_news.gif',
20:              link => 'http://news.me.com',
21:              height => 30,
22:              width => 119
23:            );
```

Lines 18–23 create the "image" container. This is optional, but if there is an icon available for the channel, this is how to add it.

```
24: open(FILE, $FILE) || die "Can't open $FILE ($!)";
25: while (<FILE>) {
26:    my ($url, $desc) = split /\|/;
27:    $rdf->add_item(title => $desc,
28:                        link => $url
29:                   );
30: }
```

Lines 24–30 get the data from the text file and use it to create the "item" containers. **Line 24** opens the file for reading or dies with an error. **Lines 25–30** are a *while()* loop that iterates over each line of the file. **Line 26** splits the input by the pipe (|) character and stores the values in the $url and $desc variables. **Lines 27 and 28** use the *add_item()* method to add an item into the "channel" container. As you saw in the RSS file example, title and link are the two elements in the "item" container. By simply creating named value pairs as arguments to *add_item()*, we can create a new container. When this loop is complete all of the items will be in the "channel" container.

```
31: $rdf->textinput(title => 'Search My News',
32:                  description => 'Search the Archives',
33:                  name => 'text',
34:                  link => 'http://news.me.com/search.cgi'
35:                );
```

Lines 31–35 use the *textinput()* method to create a "textinput" container. This is an optional container that will create a text box for people to use to search your site. The URL of the search script is the value of the "link" element, in which the name, title, and description of the link are the values of their corresponding key. At this point, the channel is created in the XML::RSS object.

```
36: $rdf->save("$RDF_DIR/my_news.rdf");
```

Line 36 ends the script by writing the file to disk using the *save()* method—and that easily a RSS file is created! This is the type of script that can be written and implemented in short time and needs little to no maintenance.

Now you are ready to take RSS full cycle from creating the data source, creating the RSS format file, and using that file for the Web.

16.4 Reader Exercises

- This application allows you to add and list channels. However, it doesn't have the functionality to delete them. Building on the admin.cgi script, add in delete functionality.

- Create your own channel. If your company has news items or you just want to link to your favorite sites, use the XML::RSS module to create your own RSS file. Then add that channel to your database and take a look.

- Use the application created in this chapter, along with other topics from this book so far, and make this a multi-user system.

16.5 Listings

Listing 16-3   **fetch script**

```
01: #!/usr/bin/perl -w
02: # fetch
03: use strict;
04: use File::Basename;
05: use DBI;
06: use LWP::Simple qw(mirror);
07: my $RDF_DIR = './rdf';
08: my $dbh = DBI->connect("dbi:mysql:book", "user", "password");
09: my $sth = $dbh->prepare(qq{select URL from rdf});
10: $sth->execute or die $DBI::errstr;
11: while (my $url = $sth->fetchrow) {
```

(continued)

```
12:     my $name = basename($url);
13:     mirror($url, "$RDF_DIR/$name");
14: }
15: $dbh->disconnect;
```

Listing 16-4   index.cgi script

```
01: #!/usr/bin/perl -wT
02: # index.cgi
03: use strict;
04: use CGI qw(:standard end_ul end_table);
05: use CGI::Carp qw(fatalsToBrowser);
06: use File::Basename;
07: use DBI;
08: use XML::RSS;
09: my $RDF_DIR = './rdf';
10: my $dbh = DBI->connect("dbi:mysql:book", 'user','password')
            or print $DBI::errstr;
11: my $sth = $dbh->prepare(qq{select URL from rdf where
            Selected = 1});
12: $sth->execute;
13: print header,
14:     start_html("My Home Page"),
15:     h2("My Favorite Sites");
16: print start_table({cellpadding=>0, cellspacing=>0, border=> 0,
                    width => '100%'}),
17:     td;
18: my $count = 1;
19: my @html = ('</TD><TD>', '</TD><TR><TD>');
20: while (my $url = basename($sth->fetchrow)) {
21:     my $rss = new XML::RSS;
22:     eval {$rss->parsefile("$RDF_DIR/$url")};
23:     warn "$url will not parse $@" and next if $@;
24:     my $last_mod = scalar localtime((stat("$RDF_DIR/$url"))[9]);
25:     print start_table({cellpadding=>0, cellspacing=>2,
                    border=> 5,    width=>'75%'}),
26:     td({valign=>'CENTER', bgcolor => '#COCOC0'});
27:     $rss->{image}{url}
28:     ? print img({src=>$rss->{image}{url}})
29:     : print strong($rss->{channel}{title});
30:     print ul;
31:     for (@{$rss->{items}}) {
32:         print li(a({href=>$_->{link}}, $_->{title}));
```

(continued)

```
33:     }
34:     print end_ul;
35:     if ($rss->{textinput}{link}) {
36:         print $rss->{textinput}{description},
                        start_form(-method => 'GET',
37:                             -action => $rss->{textinput}{link}),
38:             textfield(-name => $rss->{textinput}{name}),
39:             end_form;
40:     }
41:     print qq(Last Updated $last_mod<BR>),
42:         end_table;
43:     print $html[$count^=1];
44: }
45: print end_table,
46:     end_html;
```

Listing 16-5   admin.cgi script

```
01: #!/usr/bin/perl -w
02: # admin.cgi
03: use strict;
04: use CGI qw(:standard);
05: use CGI::Carp qw(fatalsToBrowser);
06: use DBI;
07: my $dbh = DBI->connect("dbi:mysql:book", "user", "password");
08: param('Submit') ? add_new() : show_form();
09: $dbh->disconnect;
10: sub show_form {
11: my $sth = $dbh->prepare(qq{select * from rdf});
12: $sth->execute;
13: print header,
14:         start_html("My Home Page Options"),
15:         h2("Choose My Favorite Sites");
16: print start_form(-method => 'POST', -action => 'admin.cgi');
17:   while (my $data = $sth->fetchrow_hashref) {
18:         my $checked = $data->{Selected} ? "CHECKED" : "";
19:         print checkbox(-name => 'Selected',
20:                                 -checked => $checked,
21:                                 -value => $data->{Name},
22:                                 -label => $data->{Name},
23:                             ),
24:                 p;
25:     }
```

(continued)

```
26:  print h2("Add new channel") , p,
27:              "RDFs URL: ", textfield(-name => 'URL', -size =>
                            50), p
28:              "Name of channel: ", textfield(-name => 'Name', -
                                        size => 50), p
29:              "Display on Home Page: ",
30:              checkbox(-name => 'new-Selected', -label => ''), p,
31:              submit(-name => 'Submit', -value => 'Make
                        Changes'),
32:              end_form, end_html;
33: }
34: sub add_new {
35:      my $qry_select = qq(update rdf set Selected = 1 where );
36:      my $qry_deselect = qq(update rdf set Selected = 0 where );
37:      my @selected = param('Selected');
38:      $qry_select .= qq(Name = '$_' or ) for @selected;
39:      $qry_deselect .= qq(Name <> '$_' and ) for @selected;
40:      $qry_deselect =~ s! and $!!;
41:      $qry_select =~ s! or $!!;
42:      my $sth = $dbh->prepare($qry_select);
43:      $sth->execute or print $DBI::errstr;
44:      $sth = $dbh->prepare($qry_deselect);
45:      $sth->execute or print $DBI::errstr;
46:      if (param('URL') && param('Name')) {
47:              my $url = param('URL');
48:              my $name = param('Name');
49:              my $display = param('new-Selected')  ? 1 : 0;
50:              $sth = $dbh->prepare(qq{insert into rdf (URL, NAME,
                        SELECTED) values ('$url', '$name', $display)});
51:              $sth->execute or print $DBI::errstr;
52:      }
53:      show_form;
54: }
```

Listing 16-6 **make_rss script**

```
01: #!/usr/bin/perl -wT
02: # make_rss
03: use strict;
04: use XML::RSS;
05: my $FILE = 'news.txt';
06: my $RDF_DIR = './rdf';
07: my $rdf = new XML::RSS;
```

(continued)

```
08: $rdf->channel(title => 'My News',
09:               link  => 'http://news.me.com',
10:               language => 'en',
11:               description => 'My news, for you!',
12:               copyright => 'Copyright 2000++, Me',
13:               pubDate => scalar localtime(time),
14:               lastBuildDate => scalar localtime(time),
15:               managingEditor => 'me@me.com',
16:               webMaster => 'me@me.com'
17:              );
18: $rdf->image(title => 'My News',
19:             url => 'http://news.me.com/my_news.gif',
20:             link => 'http://news.me.com',
21:             height => 30,
22:             width => 119
23:            );
24: open(FILE, $FILE) || die "Can't open $FILE ($!)";
25: while (<FILE>) {
26: my ($url, $desc) = split /\|/;
27: $rdf->add_item(title => $desc,
28:                link => $url
29:               );
30: }
31: $rdf->textinput(title => 'Search My News',
32:                 description => 'Search the Archives',
33:                 name => 'text',
34:                 link => 'http://news.me.com/search.cgi'
35:                );
36: $rdf->save("$RDF_DIR/my_news.rdf");
```

Appendix

Server Codes

100–199 **Provide confirmation that a request is being processed**

Code	Meaning	Explanation
100	Continue	The request was completed and the process may continue.
101	Switching Protocols	Request to switch protocols (like from HTTP to FTP) was accepted.

200–299 **Request was performed**

Code	Meaning	Explanation
200	OK	The transaction was successfully completed.
201	Created	A POST transaction was completed and new URL created.
202	Accepted	The request was accepted, but server is still processing.

203	Non Authoritative	The accepted information in the entity header is not from the original server but from a third party.
204	No Content	Request received but had no information to send back.
205	Reset Content	The server has fulfilled the request, and the user agent should reset the document view that caused the request to be sent.
206	Partial Information	The information returned might be in a form the client does not support.

300–399 Request not performed

Code	Meaning	Explanation
300	Multiple Choices	The requested address refers to more than one entity.
301	Moved Perm.	The data requested has been assigned a new URL.
302	Moved Temp.	The data requested has been assigned a new URL, and the redirection may be altered on occasion.
303	See Other	The redirection requires some other protocol than that specified in the initial request.
304	Not Modified	The client has sent a conditional GET request, but the document has not been modified since the date and time specified in the client's request.
305	Use Proxy	This tells the server the requested document must be accessed by using a proxy.

400–499 Request is incomplete

Code	Meaning	Explanation
400	Bad Request	The request used improper syntax.

401	Unauthorized	The request failed authentication conditions.
402	Payment Required	The request could only be satisfied if the client agreed to be charged for the transaction.
403	Forbidden	The request was forbidden. Authorization could not help. Usually, the object requested is protected by an entry in an ACL list associated with the directory or file.
404	Not Found	The server could not find the requested URL.
405	Method Not Allowed	The method you are using to access the file is not allowed.
406	Not Acceptable	The page you are requesting exists, but you cannot see it because your own system doesn't understand the format the page is configured for.
407	Proxy Authorization Needed	The request must be authorized before it can take place.
408	Time Out	The request timed out.
409	Conflict	Too many people wanted the same file at the same time. Server overload. Try again.
410	Gone	The page used to be there, but now it's gone.
411	Length Required	Your request is missing a Content-Length header.
412	Precondition Failed	The page you requested has some sort of precondition set up that your request did not pass.
413	Request Too Large	What you requested is just too big to process.
414	URI Too Large	The URL you entered is too long.
415	Unsupported Media Type	The page is an unsupported media type, like a proprietary file made specifically for a certain program.

500–599   **Internal server errors**

Code	Meaning	Explanation
500	Internal Error	The server encountered an unexpected condition that prevented it from fulfilling the request.
501	Not Implemented	The server does not support a facility required to fulfill the request.
502	Gateway Timeout	When the server accesses some other service, this indicates that the other service did not respond within the prescribed time.
503	Service Temporarily Overloaded	The service could not process the request due to a high number of requests.
504	Gateway Time Out	The gateway has timed out.
505	Version Not Supported	The HTTP protocol you are asking for is not supported.

Appendix

Environment Variables

This is a partial list of the most common environment variables. Check your Web server documentation for variables it may include or exclude. Chapter 4 has an example script that you can use to view all the environment variables provided by your Web server.

Variable	Explanation
AUTH_TYPE	The protocol used to authenticate the user. Only set if using some authentication, like Basic or Digest.
CONTENT_LENGTH	The length, in bytes, being passed through the input stream.
DOCUMENT_ROOT	The server path to the root directory of the Web documents tree.
GATEWAY_INTERFACE	The revision of the CGI specification that the Web server complies.
HTTP_REFERER	The URL from which someone comes to a page. If a visitor comes from a Bookmark or has typed in the URL by hand, this will be blank.

HTTP_USER_AGENT	The name and version of the client being used to view the page.
PATH_INFO	The extra path information as given by the client. This would be directory information passed after the script, for example, http://you.com/script.cgi/hello/world. The PATH_INFO would be /hello/world.
PATH_TRANSLATED	The server translation of PATH_INFO. This would be the full path to the DOCUMENT_ROOT followed by /hello/world. For example, /usr/local/httpd/htdocs/foo/bar.
QUERY_STRING	The query information passed by the calling URL. This is what follows the question mark after a script.
REMOTE_ADDR	The IP address of the client requesting the document.
REMOTE_HOST	The name of the host making the request. This is only done if reverse lookups are enabled for the server.
REMOTE_USER	The name of the user if the user is authenticated to access a protected script.
REQUEST_METHOD	The method used to make the request. Usually GET, POST, or HEAD.
SCRIPT_NAME	The virtual path to the script being executed.
SERVER_NAME	The name or IP address of the Web server.
SERVER_PORT	The port the Web server is listening to.
SERVER_PROTOCOL	The name and revision of the protocol the request, for example, HTTP/1.0.
SERVER_SOFTWARE	The name and version of the Web server software.

Appendix C

POSIX::strftime() Formats

SU—Single Unix Specification
TZ—Time Zone

Format	Explanation
%a	The abbreviated weekday name according to the current locale.
%A	The full weekday name according to the current locale.
%b	The abbreviated month name according to the current locale.
%B	The full month name according to the current locale.
%c	The preferred date and time representation for the current locale.
%C	The century number (year/100) as a two-digit integer. (SU)
%d	The day of the month as a decimal number (range 01 to 31).
%D	Equivalent to %m/%d/%y. (SU)
%e	Like %d, the day of the month as a decimal number, but a leading zero is replaced by a space. (SU)
%E	Modifier: use alternative format, see below. (SU)

%G	The ISO 8601 year with century as a decimal number. The four-digit-year corresponding to the ISO week number (see %V). This has the same format and value as %y, except that if the ISO week number belongs to the previous or next year, that year is used instead. (TZ)
%g	Like %G, but without century—that is, with a two-digit year (00–99). (TZ)
%h	Equivalent to %b. (SU)
%H	The hour as a decimal number using a 24-hour clock (range 00 to 23).
%I	The hour as a decimal number using a 12-hour clock (range 01 to 12).
%j	The day of the year as a decimal number (range 001 to 366)
%k	The hour (24-hour clock) as a decimal number (range 0 to 23); single digits are preceded by a blank. (See also %H.) (TZ)
%l	The hour (12-hour clock) as a decimal number (range 1 to 12); single digits are preceded by a blank. (See also %I.) (TZ)
%m	The month as a decimal number (range 01 to 12).
%M	The minute as a decimal number (range 00 to 59).
%n	A newline character. (SU)
%O	Modifier: use alternative format, see below. (SU)
%p	Either "AM" or "PM" according to the given time value, or the corresponding strings for the current locale. Noon is treated as "pm" and midnight as "am."
%P	Like %p but in lowercase: "am" or "pm" or a corresponding string for the current locale. (GNU)
%r	The time in a.m. or p.m. notation. In the POSIX locale this is equivalent to "%I:%M:%S %p." (SU)
%R	The time in 24-hour notation (%H:%M). (SU) For a version including the seconds, see %T below.
%s	The number of seconds since the Epoch—that is, since 1970-01-01 00:00:00 UTC. (TZ)

%S	The second as a decimal number (range 00 to 61).
%t	A tab character. (SU)
%T	The time in 24-hour notation (%H:%M:%S). (SU)
%u	The day of the week as a decimal, range 1 to 7, Monday being 1. See also %w. (SU)
%U	The week number of the current year as a decimal number, range 00 to 53, starting with the first Sunday as the first day of week 01. See also %V and %W.
%V	The ISO 8601:1988 week number of the current year as a decimal number, range 01 to 53, where week one is the first week that has at least four days in the current year, and with Monday as the first day of the week. See also %U and %W. (SU)
%w	The day of the week as a decimal, range 0 to 6, Sunday being 0. See also %u.
%W	The week number of the current year as a decimal number, range 00 to 53, starting with the first Monday as the first day of week 01.
%x	The preferred date representation for the current locale without the time.
%X	The preferred time representation for the current locale without the date.
%y	The year as a decimal number without a century (range 00 to 99).
%Y	The year as a decimal number including the century.
%z	The time-zone as hour offset from GMT. Required to emit RFC822-conformant dates (using "%a, %d %b %Y %H:%M:%S %z"). (GNU)
%Z	The time zone or name or abbreviation.
%+	The date and time in date(1) format. (TZ)
%%	A literal "%" character.

Appendix

General Public License

GNU GENERAL PUBLIC LICENSE

Version 2, June 1991
Copyright (C) 1989, 1991 Free Software Foundation, Inc.
59 Temple Place, Suite 330, Boston, MA 02111-1307 USA
Everyone is permitted to copy and distribute verbatim copies of this license document, but changing it is not allowed.

Preamble

The licenses for most software are designed to take away your freedom to share and change it. By contrast, the GNU General Public License is intended to guarantee your freedom to share and change free software—to make sure the software is free for all its users. This General Public License applies to most of the Free Software Foundation's software and to any other program whose authors commit to using it. (Some other Free Software Foundation software is covered by the GNU Library General Public License instead.) You can apply it to your programs, too. When we speak of free software, we are referring to freedom, not price. Our General Public Licenses are designed to make sure that you have the freedom to distribute copies of free software (and charge for this service if you wish), that you receive source code or can get it if you want it, that you can change the software or use pieces of it in new free programs; and that you know you can do these things.

To protect your rights, we need to make restrictions that forbid anyone to deny you these rights or to ask you to surrender the rights. These restrictions translate to certain responsibilities for you if you distribute copies of the software, or if you modify it.

For example, if you distribute copies of such a program, whether gratis or for a fee, you must give the recipients all the rights that you have. You must make sure that they, too, receive or can get the source code. And you must show them these terms so they know their rights.

We protect your rights with two steps: (1) copyright the software, and (2) offer you this license which gives you legal permission to copy, distribute and/or modify the software. Also, for each author's protection and ours, we want to make certain that everyone understands that there is no warranty for this free software. If the software is modified by someone else and passed on, we want its recipients to know that what they have is not the original, so that any problems introduced by others will not reflect on the original authors' reputations.

Finally, any free program is threatened constantly by software patents. We wish to avoid the danger that redistributors of a free program will individually obtain patent licenses, in effect making the program proprietary. To prevent this, we have made it clear that any patent must be licensed for everyone's free use or not licensed at all. The precise terms and conditions for copying, distribution and modification follow.

TERMS AND CONDITIONS FOR COPYING, DISTRIBUTION AND MODIFICATION

0. This License applies to any program or other work which contains a notice placed by the copyright holder saying it may be distributed under the terms of this General Public License. The "Program", below, refers to any such program or work, and a "work based on the Program" means either the Program or any derivative work under copyright law: that is to say, a work containing the Program or a portion of it, either verbatim or with modifications and/or translated into another language. (Hereinafter, translation is included without limitation in the term "modification".) Each licensee is addressed as "you". Activities other than copying, distribution and modification are not covered by this License; they are outside its scope. The act of running the Program is not restricted, and the output from the Program is covered only if its contents constitute a work based on the Program (independent of having been made by running the Program). Whether that is true depends on what the Program does.

1. You may copy and distribute verbatim copies of the Program's source code as you receive it, in any medium, provided that you conspicuously and appropriately publish on each copy an appropriate copyright notice and disclaimer of warranty; keep intact all the notices that refer to

this License and to the absence of any warranty; and give any other recipients of the Program a copy of this License along with the Program. You may charge a fee for the physical act of transferring a copy, and you may at your option offer warranty protection in exchange for a fee.

2. You may modify your copy or copies of the Program or any portion of it, thus forming a work based on the Program, and copy and distribute such modifications or work under the terms of Section 1 above, provided that you also meet all of these conditions:

   a) You must cause the modified files to carry prominent notices stating that you changed the files and the date of any change.

   b) You must cause any work that you distribute or publish, that in whole or in part contains or is derived from the Program or any part thereof, to be licensed as a whole at no charge to all third parties under the terms of this License.

   c) If the modified program normally reads commands interactively when run, you must cause it, when started running for such interactive use in the most ordinary way, to print or display an announcement including an appropriate copyright notice and a notice that there is no warranty (or else, saying that you provide a warranty) and that users may redistribute the program under these conditions, and telling the user how to view a copy of this License. (Exception: if the Program itself is interactive but does not normally print such an announcement, your work based on the Program is not required to print an announcement.)

These requirements apply to the modified work as a whole. If identifiable sections of that work are not derived from the Program, and can be reasonably considered independent and separate works in themselves, then this License, and its terms, do not apply to those sections when you distribute them as separate works. But when you distribute the same sections as part of a whole which is a work based on the Program, the distribution of the whole must be on the terms of this License, whose permissions for other licensees extend to the entire whole, and thus to each and every part regardless of who wrote it.

Thus, it is not the intent of this section to claim rights or contest your rights to work written entirely by you; rather, the intent is to exercise the right to control the distribution of derivative or collective works based on the Program. In addition, mere aggregation of another work not based on the Program with the Program (or with a work based on the Program) on a volume of a storage or distribution medium does not bring the other work under the scope of this License.

3. You may copy and distribute the Program (or a work based on it, under Section 2) in object code or executable form under the terms of Sections 1 and 2 above provided that you also do one of the following:

a) Accompany it with the complete corresponding machine-readable source code, which must be distributed under the terms of Sections 1 and 2 above on a medium customarily used for software interchange; or,

b) Accompany it with a written offer, valid for at least three years, to give any third party, for a charge no more than your cost of physically performing source distribution, a complete machine-readable copy of the corresponding source code, to be distributed under the terms of Sections 1 and 2 above on a medium customarily used for software interchange; or,

c) Accompany it with the information you received as to the offer to distribute corresponding source code. (This alternative is allowed only for noncommercial distribution and only if you received the program in object code or executable form with such an offer, in accord with Subsection b above.)

The source code for a work means the preferred form of the work for making modifications to it. For an executable work, complete source code means all the source code for all modules it contains, plus any associated interface definition files, plus the scripts used to control compilation and installation of the executable. However, as a special exception, the source code distributed need not include anything that is normally distributed (in either source or binary form) with the major components (compiler, kernel, and so on) of the operating system on which the executable runs, unless that component itself accompanies the executable. If distribution of executable or object code is made by offering access to copy from a designated place, then offering equivalent access to copy the source code from the same place counts as distribution of the source code, even though third parties are not compelled to copy the source along with the object code.

4. You may not copy, modify, sublicense, or distribute the Program except as expressly provided under this License. Any attempt otherwise to copy, modify, sublicense or distribute the Program is void, and will automatically terminate your rights under this License. However, parties who have received copies, or rights, from you under this License will not have their licenses terminated so long as such parties remain in full compliance.

5. You are not required to accept this License, since you have not signed it. However, nothing else grants you permission to modify or distribute the Program or its derivative works. These actions are prohibited by law if you do not accept this License. Therefore, by modifying or distributing the Program (or any work based on the Program), you indicate your acceptance of this License to do so, and all its terms and conditions for copying, distributing or modifying the Program or works based on it.

6. Each time you redistribute the Program (or any work based on the Program), the recipient automatically receives a license from the original licensor to copy, distribute or modify the Program subject to these terms and conditions. You may not impose any further restrictions on the recipients' exercise of the rights granted herein. You are not responsible for enforcing compliance by third parties to this License.

7. If, as a consequence of a court judgment or allegation of patent infringement or for any other reason (not limited to patent issues), conditions are imposed on you (whether by court order, agreement or otherwise) that contradict the conditions of this License, they do not excuse you from the conditions of this License. If you cannot distribute so as to satisfy simultaneously your obligations under this License and any other pertinent obligations, then as a consequence you may not distribute the Program at all. For example, if a patent license would not permit royalty-free redistribution of the Program by all those who receive copies directly or indirectly through you, then the only way you could satisfy both it and this License would be to refrain entirely from distribution of the Program. If any portion of this section is held invalid or unenforceable under any particular circumstance, the balance of the section is intended to apply and the section as a whole is intended to apply in other circumstances. It is not the purpose of this section to induce you to infringe any patents or other property right claims or to contest validity of any such claims; this section has the sole purpose of protecting the integrity of the free software distribution system, which is implemented by public license practices. Many people have made generous contributions to the wide range of software distributed through that system in reliance on consistent application of that system; it is up to the author/donor to decide if he or she is willing to distribute software through any other system and a licensee cannot impose that choice. This section is intended to make thoroughly clear what is believed to be a consequence of the rest of this License.

8. If the distribution and/or use of the Program is restricted in certain countries either by patents or by copyrighted interfaces, the original copyright holder who places the Program under this License may add an explicit geographical distribution limitation excluding those countries, so that distribution is permitted only in or among countries not thus excluded. In such case, this License incorporates the limitation as if written in the body of this License.

9. The Free Software Foundation may publish revised and/or new versions of the General Public License from time to time. Such new versions will be similar in spirit to the present version, but may differ in detail to address new problems or concerns. Each version is given a distinguishing version number. If the Program specifies a version number of this License which applies to it and "any later version", you have the option of following the terms and conditions either of that version or of any later

version published by the Free Software Foundation. If the Program does not specify a version number of this License, you may choose any version ever published by the Free Software Foundation.

10. If you wish to incorporate parts of the Program into other free programs whose distribution conditions are different, write to the author to ask for permission. For software which is copyrighted by the Free Software Foundation, write to the Free Software Foundation; we sometimes make exceptions for this. Our decision will be guided by the two goals of preserving the free status of all derivatives of our free software and of promoting the sharing and reuse of software generally.

NO WARRANTY

11. BECAUSE THE PROGRAM IS LICENSED FREE OF CHARGE, THERE IS NO WARRANTY FOR THE PROGRAM, TO THE EXTENT PERMITTED BY APPLICABLE LAW. EXCEPT WHEN OTHERWISE STATED IN WRITING THE COPYRIGHT HOLDERS AND/OR OTHER PARTIES PROVIDE THE PROGRAM "AS IS" WITHOUT WARRANTY OF ANY KIND, EITHER EXPRESSED OR IMPLIED, INCLUDING, BUT NOT LIMITED TO, THE IMPLIED WARRANTIES OF MERCHANTABILITY AND FITNESS FOR A PARTICULAR PURPOSE. THE ENTIRE RISK AS TO THE QUALITY AND PERFORMANCE OF THE PROGRAM IS WITH YOU. SHOULD THE PROGRAM PROVE DEFECTIVE, YOU ASSUME THE COST OF ALL NECESSARY SERVICING, REPAIR OR CORRECTION.

12. IN NO EVENT UNLESS REQUIRED BY APPLICABLE LAW OR AGREED TO IN WRITING WILL ANY COPYRIGHT HOLDER, OR ANY OTHER PARTY WHO MAY MODIFY AND/OR REDISTRIBUTE THE PROGRAM AS PERMITTED ABOVE, BE LIABLE TO YOU FOR DAMAGES, INCLUDING ANY GENERAL, SPECIAL, INCIDENTAL OR CONSEQUENTIAL DAMAGES ARISING OUT OF THE USE OR INABILITY TO USE THE PROGRAM (INCLUDING BUT NOT LIMITED TO LOSS OF DATA OR DATA BEING RENDERED INACCURATE OR LOSSES SUSTAINED BY YOU OR THIRD PARTIES OR A FAILURE OF THE PROGRAM TO OPERATE WITH ANY OTHER PROGRAMS), EVEN IF SUCH HOLDER OR OTHER PARTY HAS BEEN ADVISED OF THE POSSIBILITY OF SUCH DAMAGES.

END OF TERMS AND CONDITIONS

How to Apply These Terms to Your New Programs

If you develop a new program, and you want it to be of the greatest possible use to the public, the best way to achieve this is to make it free software which everyone can redistribute and change under these terms. To do so, attach the following notices to the program. It is safest to attach them to the start of each source file to most effectively convey the exclusion of warranty; and each file should have at least the "copyright" line and a pointer to where the full notice is found.
one line to give the program's name and an idea of what it does.
Copyright (C) yyyy name of author

This program is free software; you can redistribute it and/or modify it under the terms of the GNU General Public License as published by the Free Software Foundation; either version 2 of the License, or (at your option) any later version.

This program is distributed in the hope that it will be useful, but WITHOUT ANY WARRANTY; without even the implied warranty of MERCHANTABILITY or FITNESS FOR A PARTICULAR PURPOSE. See the GNU General Public License for more details.

You should have received a copy of the GNU General Public License along with this program; if not, write to the Free Software Foundation, Inc., 59 Temple Place, Suite 330, Boston, MA 02111-1307 USA. Also add information on how to contact you by electronic and paper mail. If the program is interactive, make it output a short notice like this when it starts in an interactive mode: Gnomovision version 69, Copyright (C) year name of author Gnomovision comes with ABSOLUTELY NO WARRANTY; for details type "show w." This is free software, and you are welcome to redistribute it under certain conditions; type "show c" for details.

The hypothetical commands "show w" and "show c" should show the appropriate parts of the General Public License. Of course, the commands you use may be called something other than "show w" and "show c"; they could even be mouse-clicks or menu items—whatever suits your program. You should also get your employer (if you work as a programmer) or your school, if any, to sign a "copyright disclaimer" for the program, if necessary. Here is a sample; alter the names:

Yoyodyne, Inc., hereby disclaims all copyright
interest in the program "Gnomovision"
(which makes passes at compilers) written by
James Hacker.
signature of Ty Coon, 1 April 1989
Ty Coon, President of Vice

This General Public License does not permit incorporating your program into proprietary programs. If your program is a subroutine library, you may consider it more useful to permit linking proprietary applications with the library. If this is what you want to do, use the GNU Library General Public License instead of this License.

Appendix E

Artistic License

The "Artistic License"

Preamble

The intent of this document is to state the conditions under which a Package may be copied, such that the Copyright Holder maintains some semblance of artistic control over the development of the package, while giving the users of the package the right to use and distribute the Package in a more-or-less customary fashion, plus the right to make reasonable modifications.

Definitions

"Package" refers to the collection of files distributed by the Copyright Holder, and derivatives of that collection of files created through textual modification.

"Standard Version" refers to such a Package if it has not been modified, or has been modified in accordance with the wishes of the Copyright Holder as specified below.

"Copyright Holder" is whoever is named in the copyright or copyrights for the package.

"You" is you, if you're thinking about copying or distributing this Package.

"Reasonable copying fee" is whatever you can justify on the basis of media cost, duplication charges, time of people involved, and so on. (You will not be required to justify it to the Copyright Holder, but only to the computing community at large as a market that must bear the fee.) "Freely Available" means that no fee is charged for the item itself, though there may be fees involved in handling the item. It also means that recipients of the item may redistribute it under the same conditions they received it.

1. You may make and give away verbatim copies of the source form of the Standard Version of this Package without restriction, provided that you duplicate all of the original copyright notices and associated disclaimers.

2. You may apply bug fixes, portability fixes and other modifications derived from the Public Domain or from the Copyright Holder. A Package modified in such a way shall still be considered the Standard Version.

3. You may otherwise modify your copy of this Package in any way, provided that you insert a prominent notice in each changed file stating how and when you changed that file, and provided that you do at least ONE of the following:
   a. place your modifications in the Public Domain or otherwise make them Freely Available, such as by posting said modifications to Usenet or an equivalent medium, or placing the modifications on a major archive site such as uunet.uu.net, or by allowing the Copyright Holder to include your modifications in the Standard Version of the Package.
   b. use the modified Package only within your corporation or organization.
   c. rename any non-standard executables so the names do not conflict with standard executables, which must also be provided, and provide a separate manual page for each non-standard executable that clearly documents how it differs from the Standard Version.
   d. make other distribution arrangements with the Copyright Holder.

4. You may distribute the programs of this Package in object code or executable form, provided that you do at least ONE of the following:
   a. distribute a Standard Version of the executables and library files, together with instructions (in the manual page or equivalent) on where to get the Standard Version.
   b. accompany the distribution with the machine-readable source of the Package with your modifications.
   c. give non-standard executables non-standard names, and clearly document the differences in manual pages (or equivalent), together with instructions on where to get the Standard Version.
   d. make other distribution arrangements with the Copyright Holder.

5. You may charge a reasonable copying fee for any distribution of this Package. You may charge any fee you choose for support of this Package. You may not charge a fee for this Package itself. However, you may distribute this Package in aggregate with other (possibly commercial) programs as part of a larger (possibly commercial) software distribution provided that you do not advertise this Package as a product of your own. You may embed this Package's interpreter within an executable of yours (by linking); this shall be construed as a mere form of aggregation, provided that the complete Standard Version of the interpreter is so embedded.

6. The scripts and library files supplied as input to or produced as output from the programs of this Package do not automatically fall under the copyright of this Package, but belong to whomever generated them, and may be sold commercially, and may be aggregated with this Package. If such scripts or library files are aggregated with this Package via the so-called "undump" or "unexec" methods of producing a binary executable image, then distribution of such an image shall neither be construed as a distribution of this Package nor shall it fall under the restrictions of Paragraphs 3 and 4, provided that you do not represent such an executable image as a Standard Version of this Package.

7. C subroutines (or comparably compiled subroutines in other languages) supplied by you and linked into this Package in order to emulate subroutines and variables of the language defined by this Package shall not be considered part of this Package, but are the equivalent of input as in Paragraph 6, provided these subroutines do not change the language in any way that would cause it to fail the regression tests for the language.

8. Aggregation of this Package with a commercial distribution is always permitted provided that the use of this Package is embedded; that is, when no overt attempt is made to make this Package's interfaces visible to the end user of the commercial distribution. Such use shall not be construed as a distribution of this Package.

9. The name of the Copyright Holder may not be used to endorse or promote products derived from this software without specific prior written permission.

10. THIS PACKAGE IS PROVIDED "AS IS" AND WITHOUT ANY EXPRESS OR IMPLIED WARRANTIES, INCLUDING, WITHOUT LIMITATION, THE IMPLIED WARRANTIES OF MERCHANTIBILITY AND FITNESS FOR A PARTICULAR PURPOSE.

The End

Appendix

Perl Documentation

These man pages are part of Perl 5.6. Some are not included in earlier versions on Perl.

Document	Explanation
perlapio	perl's IO abstraction interface
perlbot	Bag o' Object Tricks
perlcall	Perl calling conventions from C
perldata	Perl data types
perldebug	Perl debugging
perldelta	What's new for Perl 5.x
perldiag	Various Perl diagnostics
perldsc	Perl data structures cookbook
perlembed	How to embed Perl in your C programs
perlfaq	Frequently Asked Questions about Perl and the index of FAQs

perlfaq1	General questions about Perl
perlfaq2	Obtaining and learning about Perl
perlfaq3	Programming Tools
perlfaq4	Data manipulation
perlfaq5	Files and formats
perlfaq6	Regexps
perlfaq7	General Perl language issues
perlfaq8	System interaction
perlfaq9	Networking
perlform	Perl formats
perlfunc	Perl builtin functions
perlguts	Perl's internal functions
perlhist	History of Perl
perlipc	Perl interprocess communication
perlocale	Perl locale handling
perllol	Manipulating lists of lists in Perl
perlmod	Perl modules
perlmodinstall	Installing CPAN modules
perlmodlib	Constructing new Perl modules and fixing existing ones
perlobj	Perl objects
perlop	Perl operators and precedence
perlopentut	Tutorial on opening things with Perl
perlpod	Plain old documentation (POD)
perlport	Writing portable Perl
perlre	Perl regular expressions

perlref	Perl references and nested data structures
perlreftut	Mark's very short tutorial about references
perlrun	How to execute the Perl interpreter
perlsec	Perl security
perlstyle	Perl style guide
perlsub	Perl subroutines
perlsyn	Perl syntax
perlthrtut	Tutorial on threads in Perl
perltie	Using ties in Perl
perltoc	Perl documentation table of contents
perltoot	Tom's object oriented tutorial for Perl
perltraps	Perl traps for the unwary
perlvar	Perl's predefined variables
perlxs	XS language reference manual
perlxstut	Tutorial for XSUBs

Appendix

ASCII Codes

Decimal	Hexadecimal	ASCII	DESCRIPTION
0	00	NUL	CTRL/1
1	01	SOH	CTRL/A
2	02	STX	CTRL/B
3	03	ETX	CTRL/C
4	04	EOT	CTRL/D
5	05	ENQ	CTRL/E
6	06	ACK	CTRL/F
7	07	BEL	CTRL/G
8	08	BS	CTRL/H, BACKSPACE
9	09	HT	CTRL/I, TAB
10	0A	LF	CTRL/J, ENTER

11	0B	VT	CTRL/K
12	0C	FF	CTRL/L
13	0D	CR	CTRL/M, RETURN
14	0E	SO	CTRL/N
15	0F	SI	CTRL/O
16	10	DLE	CTRL/P
17	11	DC1	CTRL/Q
18	12	DC2	CTRL/R
19	13	DC3	CTRL/S
20	14	DC4	CTRL/T
21	15	NAK	CTRL/U
22	16	SYN	CTRL/V
23	17	ETB	CTRL/W
24	18	CAN	CTRL/X
25	19	EM	CTRL/Y
26	1A	SUB	CTRL/Z
27	1B	ESC	ESC, ESCAPE
28	1C	FS	CTRL<
29	1D	GS	CTRL/
30	1E	RS	CTRL/=
31	1F	US	CTRL/-
32	20	SP	SPACE
33	21	!	!
34	22	"	"
35	23	#	#

36	24	$	$
37	25	%	%
38	26	&	&
39	27	'	'
40	28	(	(
41	29	)	)
42	2A	*	*
43	2B	+	+
44	2C	,	,
45	2D	-	-
46	2E	.	.
47	2F	/	/
48	30	0	0
49	31	1	1
50	32	2	2
51	33	3	3
52	34	4	4
53	35	5	5
54	36	6	6
55	37	7	7
56	38	8	8
57	39	9	9
58	3A	:	:
59	3B	;	;
60	3C	<	<

61	3D	=	=
62	3E	>	>
63	3F	?	?
64	40	@	@
65	41	A	A
66	42	B	B
67	43	C	C
68	44	D	D
69	45	E	E
70	46	F	F
71	47	G	G
72	48	H	H
73	49	I	I
74	4A	J	J
75	4B	K	K
76	4C	L	L
77	4D	M	M
78	4E	N	N
79	4F	O	O
80	50	P	P
81	51	Q	Q
82	52	R	R
83	53	S	S
84	54	T	T
85	55	U	U

86	56	V	V
87	57	W	W
88	58	X	X
89	59	Y	Y
90	5A	Z	Z
91	5B	[	[
92	5C	\	\
93	5D	]	]
94	5E	^	^
95	5F	_	_
96	60	`	`
97	61	a	a
98	62	b	b
99	63	c	c
100	64	d	d
101	65	e	e
102	66	f	f
103	67	g	g
104	68	h	h
105	69	i	i
106	6A	j	j
107	6B	k	k
108	6C	l	l
109	6D	m	m
110	6E	n	n

111	6F	o	o
112	70	p	p
113	71	q	q
114	72	r	r
115	73	s	s
116	74	t	t
117	75	u	u
118	76	v	v
119	77	w	w
120	78	x	x
121	79	y	y
122	7A	z	z
123	7B	{	{
124	7C	|	|
125	7D	}	}
126	7E	~	~
127	7F	DEL	DELETE

Appendix

Special HTML Characters

These have little to do with Perl or CGI, but since HTML is generated with most CGI applications, this list could come in handy. This covers the ISO8859-1 character set.

Character	Numeric Code	Descriptive Code
"	&#34;	&quot;
&	&#38;	&amp;
<	&#60;	&lt;
>	&#62;	&gt;
¡	&#161;	&iexcl;
¢	&#162;	&cent;
£	&#163;	&pound;
¤	&#164;	&curren;

¥	&#165;	&yen;
¦	&#166;	&brvbar;
§	&#167;	&sect;
¨	&#168;	&uml;
©	&#169;	&copy;
ª	&#170;	&ordf;
«	&#171;	&laquo;
¬	&#172;	&not;
	&#173;	&shy;
®	&#174;	&reg;
¯	&#175;	&macr;
°	&#176;	&deg;
±	&#177;	&plusmn;
²	&#178;	&sup2;
³	&#179;	&sup3;
´	&#180;	&acute;
µ	&#181;	&micro;
¶	&#182;	&para;
·	&#183;	&middot;
¸	&#184;	&cedil;
¹	&#185;	&sup1;
º	&#186;	&ordm;
»	&#187;	&raquo;
¼	&#188;	&frac14;
½	&#189;	&frac12;

¾	&#190;	&frac34;
¿	&#191;	&iquest;
À	&#192;	&Agrave;
Á	&#193;	&Aacute;
Â	&#194;	&Acirc;
Ã	&#195;	&Atilde;
Ä	&#196;	&Auml;
Å	&#197;	&Aring;
Æ	&#198;	&AElig;
Ç	&#199;	&Ccedil;
È	&#200;	&Egrave;
É	&#201;	&Eacute;
Ê	&#202;	&Ecirc;
Ë	&#203;	&Euml;
Ì	&#204;	&Igrave;
Í	&#205;	&Iacute;
Î	&#206;	&Icirc;
Ï	&#207;	&Iuml;
Ð	&#208;	&ETH;
Ñ	&#209;	&Ntilde;
Ò	&#210;	&Ograve;
Ó	&#211;	&Oacute;
Ô	&#212;	&Ocirc;
Õ	&#213;	&Otilde;
Ö	&#214;	&Ouml;

×	&#215;	&times;
Ø	&#216;	&Oslash;
Ù	&#217;	&Ugrave;
Ú	&#218;	&Uacute;
Û	&#219;	&Ucirc;
Ü	&#220;	&Uuml;
Ý	&#221;	&Yacute;
þ	&#222;	&THORN;
ß	&#223;	&szlig;
à	&#224;	&agrave;
á	&#225;	&aacute;
â	&#226;	&acirc;
ã	&#227;	&atilde;
ä	&#228;	&auml;
å	&#229;	&aring;
æ	&#230;	&aelig;
ç	&#231;	&ccedil;
è	&#232;	&egrave;
é	&#233;	&eacute;
ê	&#234;	&ecirc;
ë	&#235;	&euml;
ì	&#236;	&igrave;
í	&#237;	&iacute;
î	&#238;	&icirc;
ï	&#239;	&iuml;

ð	ð	ð
ñ	ñ	ñ
ò	ò	ò
ó	ó	ó
ô	ô	ô
õ	õ	õ
ö	ö	ö
÷	÷	÷
ø	ø	ø
ù	ù	ù
ú	ú	ú
û	û	û
ü	ü	ü
ý	ý	ý
þ	þ	þ
ÿ	ÿ	ÿ

Resources

Recommended Reading

Effective Perl Programming by Joseph N. Hall. Addison-Wesley.
ISBN 0201419750 (1997)

Learning Perl (2nd Edition) by Randal Schwartz, et al. O'Reilly & Associates.
ISBN 1565922840 (1997)

Object Oriented Perl by Damian Conway. Manning Publications.
ISBN 1884777791 (1999)

Official Guide to Programming with CGI.pm by Lincoln Stein. John Wiley & Sons.
ISBN 0471247448 (1998)

Perl Cookbook by Tom Christiansen, et al. O'Reilly & Associates.
ISBN 1565922433 (1998)

The Perl Journal, a quarterly magazine dedicated to Perl. *http://www.tpj.com*

Programming Perl (3rd Edition) by Larry Wall, et al. O'Reilly & Associates.
ISBN 0596000278 (2000)

Web Security: A Step-by-Step Guide by Lincoln Stein. Addison-Wesley.
ISBN 0201634899 (1997)

Writing Apache Modules with Perl and C: The Apache API and mod_perl
by Lincoln Stein, et al. O'Reilly & Associates.
ISBN 156592567X (1999)

Web Sites

Perl Home Page
http://www.perl.com

Perl Paraphernalia
http://www.plover.com/~mjd/perl

PerlFaq
http://www.perlfaq.com

Perldoc.com
http://www.perldoc.com

PerlMonks
http://www.perlmonks.org

use Perl;
http://use.perl.org

Dr. Dobb's Journal (online)
http://www.ddj.com/topics/perl/

Randal Schwartz's Web Techniques Columns
http://www.stonehenge.com/merlyn/WebTechniques/

Apache Project
http://www.apache.org

ApacheWeek
http://www.apacheweek.com

Index

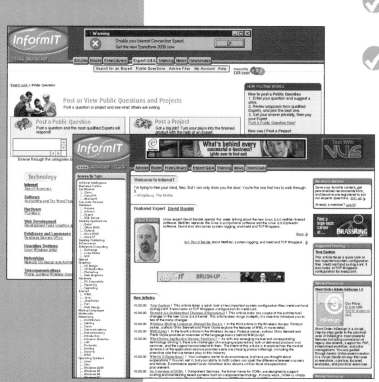